THE BLUE SALON AND
OTHER FOLLIES

THE BLUE SALON AND OTHER FOLLIES

A Jewish Boyhood in 1930s' Rural Germany

VERNON KATZ

To order additional copies of this book, contact:
Xlibris Corporation
1-888-795-4274
www.Xlibris.com
Orders@Xlibris.com
48422

CONTENTS

FAT SIEGFRIED AND HIS FRÄULEIN TÖCHTER

HEIR TO A BRUSH FACTORY

TROUBLE BREWING

NEW RELATIONS

FOLLY

BONDAGE AND DELIVERANCE

THE RETURN

APPENDICES

FAT SIEGFRIED
AND HIS
FRÄULEIN TÖCHTER

Chapter One

SIEGFRIED'S FAREWELL

December 1935

The neighbours are watching. Bulky Frau Dreier, Grandmother's tenant from across the road, pokes her big grey head between the curtains. The even bulkier Frau Profet watches from above Aunt Alma's. Elegant *Frau Doktor* Lux, scrawny and nervous, exits her door, pretending not to notice us. Pitzeritz, the grocer, a short shrivelled man, steps outside his shop with a customer and surveys us through tiny eyes. His daughter must be inside serving customers. Perhaps she is fishing salt herrings out of the big wooden vat. People are buying bread or pastries at Kordmöller's shop to take in the scene. I bet they are saying, "What a *Judenschule.*" Even before the Nazis, when I was very young, any disorderly gathering was called a "Jews' school."

The neighbours are watching the men in long overcoats and homburg hats as they huddle in groups outside our house in the Schülerstrasse. The men, our relatives and friends, keep jabbering. We boys have formed our own group. No one is getting into line for the procession.

The men are watching the watchers out of the corners of their eyes. They no longer feel at home in their hometown. Look at Father. Even Father—straight-backed, close-cropped, disciplined Father, who could pass for a Prussian officer on leave, who has said right from the beginning that the Nazis would soon come to their senses and realize that they needed the Jews—no longer looks straight out at the world.

Nor do I, aged eight and a half. I squint. A lot has changed since the first Nuremberg Laws were passed three months ago.

The horses' eyes bulge through black bandit masks. Black tassels dangle down their sides. Their steaming breath rises in the cold air. They are marking time with their hooves. These horses are not patient like our carthorse Hektor.

At last we are getting into line. I feel important as I walk directly behind the coffin with my cousins and my Uncle Walter. Father follows in the row behind us. I am in my good navy suit and overcoat, with the navy beret that Mother likes. Uncle Walter's dark grey jacket and overcoat are open despite the cold. He is very tall and wears his trousers very high. My eyes are in line with his stomach.

We have not gone far along the Schülerstrasse[1] when a lanky, red-haired lout standing behind some railings puts his thumb to his nose and shouts in a high-pitched voice, "I've seen some snouts in my time, but never anything like these!"

Cousin Walter, Uncle Walter's eldest son, says quietly, "That bastard's lucky he's protected by the fence. I'd like to knock him one on his muzzle. That would shut his big mouth. He'd remember me for a week or two." This is no vain boast. Walter has courage. He's not a coward like me.

We pass Urban's, the school sweet shop, grey and dreary but always stocked with liquorice sticks and caramels.

I look left to see what is on at our small cinema, although I miss the best films because I can't pass for a fourteen-year-old. A little further on, an S.S. man with stiff black breeches and jackboots climbs the steps to the Odeon pub and restaurant. The S.A. and S.S. are always in and out of there.

On the opposite side of the street stands the grand *Fachwerk* house of the Sprick family, a framework of black beams surrounding squares of white loam. The Spricks own a biscuit factory, and the old lady used to be Grandmother's friend. At the far end of the Schülerstrasse is the *Bürgermeisteramt*, where Ewald Beckmann's father presides.

Herr Beckmann is the mayor of our town of Schötmar in Lippe. It has some five thousand inhabitants and is one of the lesser jewels of our small but beautiful state of Lippe Detmold. Almost three years earlier

---

[1]   Perhaps already renamed Schlageterstrasse after the Nazi martyr.

the Nazis' success in the elections for the Lippe parliament played a crucial role in bringing Hitler to power. The *Führer* himself said that it was not possible to overestimate that success.

Our dark procession turns right, into the Begastrasse, past Potts, our largest store, and down the hill where Aunt Rosa lives, surrounded by stables and the smell of cow dung. Her husband Salomon is in the procession. Opposite their house, on our left, a man is reading a newspaper displayed in a glass box. I have seen copies of *Der Stürmer*. I had to laugh at the cartoons of fat Jewish *Plutokraten*. They resembled some people I know, Uncle Salomon, for instance, who is Jewish, and also Father's customer, Herr Birkholz, who is not. *Der Stürmer's* mastermind, the pug ugly Julius Streicher, looks like one of his own cartoons.

Cousin Helmut and I never dare stop by the glass box. When we walk down the Begastrasse to buy cigars for Uncle Julius, we always cross over to the other side.

I don't like marching along the streets with everyone staring at us. I wish we could get to the cemetery quickly. I turn around to look at Father and see the tiered steeple of St. Kilian's, the Protestant church that towers above the town. Behind Father, a sea of swaying homburgs. There are many doddery old men in the procession. Definitely not storm troopers marching with calm and steady step (*mit ruhig, festem Schritt*) as in the Horst Wessel song, which they sing at school.

The carriage wobbles as the horses drag it over the level crossing. The road passes over two rivers. Somewhere between the deep green Bega and the fast-flowing Werre, a horse lifts his tail and leaves a steaming yellow mound for us to avoid. Horses have no shame.

A few passersby snigger at us, but some older men doff their hats. "There goes fat Siegfried Silberbach," I hear one man say to another. I think all of Schötmar knows that a great character is taking his leave.

At last we reach the Oerlinghauser Strasse. The Jewish section of the cemetery is a small enclave. It is darker and denser than the Protestant and Catholic sections. There are no flowers, just bare trees, stone, and ivy. Father does not go near the grave. I ask him why.

"As a Cohen [a member of the priestly caste] I must not leave the pathway. You can, but only until you are Bar Mitzvah."

The coffin rattles as the men lift it from the carriage. There are no wreaths. The rabbi starts the prayers. Uncle Walter doesn't know any

Hebrew. He moves his lips, pretending he does. Father rattles off his prayers. There are tears, but not from me.

A fat little robin perches on the plank above the grave, not frightened by the chanting and the crowd.[2] "Even the birds want to say farewell," booms the rabbi. What a laugh. The redbreast stays with his big fat brother until the plank is removed and the coffin lowered into the ground. "May he rest in peace!" A blubbering Uncle Walter starts shovelling back the earth. There is a lot of noise as gravel hits the coffin. Fat Siegfried, my noisy grandfather, is taking his final leave.

---

[2]   Sixty-four years later, in 1999, my cousin Walter and I were cleaning and weeding our grandparents' grave. It was the first time we had been there together. As we were finishing our work, a robin flew in and took up residence on the grave. He hopped here and there, not minding us. Occasionally, he flew off to neighbouring graves, but always came back. This went on for several minutes. Perhaps, like his forebear, he was looking for worms, but still . . .

Chapter Two

THE MOURNERS

The visitors enter by the tall street door and climb the wide stone stairs where soft-leaved linden house plants (*Zimmerlinden*) stand guard like sentinels. They pass through the stained-glass doors and stream into the gloom. The tall mirror in the entrance hall has been covered by a white sheet. All the curtains are drawn. Candles flicker.

They come from far and wide, not just from Schötmar and its posh other half, Bad Salzuflen, the salt-spring spa. They come from Lemgo, Lage, Herford, Barntrup, and from Detmold, the capital of our small state.

"He was a good man," they murmur.

"He had a good *shem* [Hebrew for "name"]."

"His bark was worse than his bite."

"I have never seen a man who could judge a heifer the way he could."

"He was up in the middle of the night driving his cattle from the station."

"They don't make them like him anymore."

There were gentiles too, farmers and large landowners, old men who had been Grandfather's customers and suppliers, as well as a few neighbours. They came after dark, but they came. Grandfather did have a good *shem*, and that, says Mother, is the best thing a man can leave behind him.

The women of our family and Uncle Walter are sitting on low backless stools without a backrest, accepting the condolences. My mother, Aunt Grete, and the red-faced great aunts are wailing. Uncle Walter, the handsome giant, chokes back tears for the father who treated him so badly. Some local busybodies in long, old-fashioned dresses join in the family laments. As each new arrival sings Grandfather's praises, the wailing rises to new heights. The murmured prayers of the devout, led by Father, are drowned in the din.

Grandmother, sitting very erect even without the benefit of a backrest, is more composed. I think she is relieved that the long fight is over. Maybe she will come to miss her sparring partner. Her battles with Grandfather gave zest to her life.

Her grey hair is piled neatly on her head with the help of a series of rising combs. Her long pale face is a little longer and paler; her already hooded eyes are a little more hooded. She weeps but not enough to look ugly like some people I know.

"I was never beautiful," Mother often says. "My sister was, and still is, beautiful."

"You *are* beautiful, Mutti," I counter, "just as beautiful as Tante Grete, only different."

Today neither looks very dazzling. They both have red eyes and tear-stained faces. They make funny moaning sounds, all vowels. Always rivals for their father's love, they now compete as to who can make the most noise at his funeral.

I can understand Aunt Grete crying. She cries easily. But Mother—I have never before seen Mother cry. It gives me an awful feeling to see her cry. Crying is something I do when I fall and hurt my knees. Mother is always so in control of herself and everything around her. I don't know how many of those little lace-edged hankies she has used today.

Normally her long plaited hair is combed back, firmly twisted into a knot that is held in place by combs and needles. Today it straggles over her ears. The knot is loose. The combs have lost their grip. Aunt Grete's hair looks better because she sports a short *Bubenkopf* (literally "a boy's head"). Secretly, Mother envies her freedom. Father would never allow Mother to cut her hair, and I wouldn't like it either. I love her long dark brown hair, when she lets it down and combs it.

Today, everything is upside down. Mother never wears black. Dark blue, yes, a lot, but never black. She says it doesn't suit her, and she's right. Yet here she is in a baggy black summer dress. I don't know how she got hold of it. She looks awful. She's probably feeling cold too.

She goes to the kitchen and tries to speak to our cook, Erna, but she starts weeping again. I sidle up to her. She looks at me without seeing. That is the most unsettling thing of all. She pays no attention to *me*. And all this for a bad-tempered old man who was forever screaming the house down and, anyway, had been sick for years. When your mother, the bedrock of your life, on whom everything depends, starts behaving like a crazy woman, it makes you wonder.

Grief sends a shadow over everything. How could I imagine what Mother felt that day? Never again to see the beloved father who had played with her as a child, had bought her fine clothes as a young lady, had helped her when she married, had loved and admired her all her life. Thirty years later, almost to the day, when Mother died unexpectedly at the age of seventy-two, I was to experience the same wild grief.

I sneak into a corner near the kitchen door to watch and listen. I study the tower patterns on the tiles and jingle the marbles in my pocket. I could play with Helmut in the courtyard, but then I wouldn't know what I was missing. I could do without playing, or even without glazed apple cake, but I couldn't do without knowing what's going on. That's the awful thing about having to go to bed before everyone else. You miss what they are saying downstairs. But sometimes I slink onto the landing in my pyjamas and catch some of their conversation.

A black bundle waddles towards Grandmother's seat. That's Aunt Alma from across the road. It takes her some time to reach her destination. Aunt Alma carries a lot of weight. Her limp chins graze Grandmother's neat hairdo as she whispers her words of comfort. Grandfather's remarks about the meat and sausages she sells in her shop have been forgotten or forgiven.

A beam of light streaks across the slate grey tiles. Briefly, before a hand draws the curtains tight, it lights up a line of fresh wet boot prints. They lead straight from the glass entrance doors to Grandmother's seat. Aunt Alma has sinned. She has broken one of Mother's Ten Commandments: Thou shalt wipe thy feet on every mat thou encounterest, above all in wet weather.

Mother won't notice anything in her present state. When things return to normal, she will bless the tiles for taking the brunt of the slush and protecting her precious living room carpets.

Aunt Alma is followed by a slightly more up-to-date version of herself. Herta's chins threaten to outnumber her mother's. Her dresses usually display a lot of bosom, but today she wears a black dress buttoned to the neck. Mother and daughter have red flesh that reminds me of the meat they sell. Prickly black hairs set in brown spots inhabit their cheeks and chins, like odd clumps of trees scattered over fertile fields.

Herta, a very distant cousin, is pushing thirty, high time for her to get married. Mother is forever trying to find a husband for "poor Herta." So far, there have been no takers. Mother says, "There's no pot so crooked you can't find a lid for it." (*Es is kein Pott so schief es passt'n Deckel druf.*) She says it in dialect. It is one of Mother's favourite sayings, but Herta continues to disprove her point.

Aunt Alma and Herta make their way to the snacks arranged in the kitchen. Mother calls it a live-in kitchen (*Wohnküche*), an excuse for serving visitors there, especially in wet weather. It has white tiles that can be wiped at once after being soiled—and they are. Mother is not on duty today. She has other concerns. The cook does the honours with the mop. And then the tiles are polished, all the better to slip on.

I sneak in after our fat guests, not because I'm hungry but because it's fun to see them stuff themselves—a change from all the gloom. Herta is a guzzler, like me. She tries to stuff a whole doughnut (*Berliner*) into her mouth. Then she attacks the *petit fours*, and she rounds things off with a piece of *Topfkuchen*, a Madeira fruitcake stuffed with glazed cherries and sultanas. Herta will cost any husband dearly in food bills.

Herta never found a husband. Like so many Jews in our community, she was murdered. She was deported on March 30, 1942, her mother four months later, at the age of seventy-two. Herta was last heard of in the Warsaw ghetto; Aunt Alma was murdered near Minsk, far away from Lippe Detmold. They were harmless, hard-working women. May my levity be forgiven.

There is a hush. A tall frail elderly gentleman has entered the hall. His top hat adds height to height and dignity to dignity. He comes over to me and pats my head as if I were the chief mourner. I am a great favourite of Herr Rosenwald and a valued customer of the Rosenwald ladies who distribute sweets very generously. Father stops bobbing up and down and crosses the hall to greet the newcomer. Father does not interrupt his prayers for trifles. Herr Rosenwald is the doyen of the Jewish community in Schötmar. He *is* the Jewish community.[3]

At festivals, Herr Rosenwald, top hatted and frock coated, sits in his place of honour near the ark, surveying those who attend synagogue and, so Father says, making a mental note of those who do not. He must have stopped noting Grandfather's absence long ago.

Now Grandfather is getting his comeuppance. He cannot shout, "Stop this mumbo jumbo! Get out, Rosenwald! Get out, all you useless old women!" He lies helpless in his wooden box. His fight against the orthodox and their ways is over.

They wrapped him in the prayer shawl he did not wear when he was alive—the ultimate defeat.

"They need a good rasher of fatty bacon [*Speck*] inside them to make men of them," he used to say. In his younger days, he set a manly example. It did not endear him to those who kept the dietary laws. Grandfather was defiant.

"They think if they eat kosher and go to synagogue they can fool God and the rest of us—bunch of old hypocrites."

It was all part of a campaign against one particular old hypocrite "who never has her nose out of her prayer book." "Why can't she do something useful for a change?" Grandfather taunted. "Always mumbling over that infernal book."

That book—I still have the battle-scarred remains on my shelves—Grandmother's copy of the Jewish prayer book (*Israelitisches Gebetbuch*), Hebrew on the right side, German on the left, with a special section of "German Prayers for Private and Public Worship" at the back. It has a musty smell now. The leather is flaking, the binding crumbling—the last relic of the battle of cultures (*Kulturkampf*) that raged in my childhood home so long ago.

Then why is the guardian of our faith paying his respects to the *Speck*-eater's memory? Perhaps Grandmother's piety more than makes up

---

[3] The Schötmar synagogue actually appeared in my memory as an annex to the long narrow Rosenwald home and emporium (similar to a temple to Shri Hanuman appended to the house and place of business of a Delhi acquaintance) until, on a recent visit to Schötmar, I found it was in a different road altogether.

for Grandfather's lack of it. But I think there is more to it. Grandfather was big. You could not ignore him any more than you could ignore a steamroller. He may not be on his way to join the righteous in that enormous bosom of Abraham's, but he still commands respect. So here is Herr Rosenwald, bowing stiffly, assuring Grandmother that they will never see his like again.

I can see what Herr Rosenwald means when Uncle Julius comes in. He will never be able to step into the boots Grandfather has just vacated. Uncle Julius, or Jüller, as he is known in the family, is Grandfather's younger brother. He is smaller than Grandfather and has the Silberbach red hair. He has a blotchy face, and his red moustache droops. For once, he is without his cigar.

Grandfather did not rate his brother's talents highly, but I have heard Uncle Walter say to Mother, "Jüller may not be a genius but he's nobody's fool. He's not as stupid as Father makes him out to be."

Uncle Julius' small round eyes are vacant as he plonks himself next to Grandmother among the seated mourners. She is none too pleased. The aroma of *Schlemmerhappen* cigars from his clothes is mixed in with something less pleasant. Uncle Julius is losing control of his bowels.

Someone decides that the hall is no place for youngsters. We are banished to one of the staff rooms on the second floor,[4] well away from the action. It is a small room with a bed, a chair and a sideboard with a washing bowl and a jug of water. From up here, you can't hear a thing they are saying downstairs, even with the door open.

We are sitting on the bed when suddenly, without any warning, Helmut—my cousin, friend, and rival—lets out a piercing high-pitched yell. He continues yelling loudly proclaiming his grief. Does he want to be heard two floors down? Not to be outdone, I join in, but I can't match Helmut in volume or fervour. I dig my nails into my palms, but the tears won't flow. I try out Mother's vowel moans, but my heart isn't in it. I don't feel any grief, just discomfort at the madness that has suddenly overtaken my world. I want everything to return to normal.

Father says there is a soul, which he calls by the Hebrew word *ruach*. He says it is like breath though it doesn't breathe. Father says it goes on

---

[4] The American third floor.

after death, but he doesn't say how it manages to continue without a body and without breathing. I wonder if it can shout. What will Grandfather do if he can't shout at somebody? Shouting was his life.

Mother says all this business about the soul is outdated superstition. It doesn't belong to the modern age. "*Wer stirbt, stirbt sich,*" she says. She must have made up that sentence. It doesn't sound right, but I know what she means. When you're dead, you're dead, and no one bothers about you. I think I believe Father. You can't carry on like Grandfather and then just vanish forever.

Chapter Three

THE ROAST PIGEONS

Grandfather stretched himself like a well-fed lion and belched. He had just consumed what looked like a whole breast of veal—no vegetables, no bread, nothing to drink—just meat, potatoes and gravy. He looked at the mound of bones in front of him, then across the table at his three grandsons. His dark eyes smiled. The bones had been picked clean. Even the gristle was gone. Here was a fine example for the younger generation.

He wiped his mouth with a large linen napkin. It was too late. With each noisy intake of gravy-soaked meat, brown beads had formed in the thickets of his moustache, dangled there awhile and then, yielding to gravity, had landed on the grey hopsack waistcoat that tightly embraced the giant torso. The lapels of his black cotton jacket had also received their share at one time or another.

Not far away, along the avenues leading to the spa park, droplets of salt water trickled from thorny brushwood frames—Bad Salzuflen's famous Graduation Works (*Gradierwerke*). Grandfather had somehow managed to create his own graduation works version with droplets of food.

At home, Mother would have tucked his napkin into his collarless shirt, but Grandfather was not at home. We were visiting him at the Pension Adler, or some such name, in Bad Salzuflen—handsome Walter in long pants, sharp-faced little Helmut in grey shorts, and chubby moon-faced me in a sailor suit. Grandfather was *en plein pension* for a week, giving himself a treat and everyone else a rest. The Pension Adler had offered him a special price, a specially high price commensurate with his appetite. A small Jewish pension in a minor spa could not very well charge normal prices to guests who ate a breast of veal at one sitting, and still make a profit.

"I said to them, 'I don't mind paying a few marks extra, but I want to eat what I want to eat,'" Grandfather told us proudly. "I can't live on those piddly portions you give to your refined ladies who nibble at their food. I want a man-sized meal."

Judging by the evening's performance, a man-sized meal was what Grandfather got. At home in Schötmar, his rations were not nearly as generous or succulent. Like all of us, he had to suffer Erna's cooking. Grandfather was doing very well at the Pension Adler.

I was not doing so well. Grandfather had insisted we stay to dinner.

"Give them decent helpings," he commanded the long-robed proprietress who brooded over the dining table, surrounded by dark brocade curtains and mahogany furniture.

Breast of veal was not my favourite dish. I wasn't worried that I was eating a cow's baby. My parents had not brought me up to think that way. But the meat was covered with all kinds of inedibles, and once you got at it, the effort was hardly worthwhile. The taste was too bland. I never understood why Grandfather, Mother, and Uncle Walter raved about the horrid stuff.

I put my plate near the edge of the table, shovelled one piece on to the carpet, and kicked it into the dark. Helmut spotted my game and giggled. Mother would have been aghast.

Lions and gentlemen of advanced years tend to grow comatose after a heavy meaty meal. Not so Grandfather. As the giant digestive system began its work, he grew more lively and benign. When he had finished tackling the last bone, he looked up and saw me picking at my piece of breast, trying to free the meat from the skin, gristle, and mushy bits. He gave me a smile. Me! His least loved grandchild.

"Eat up, my boy," he sang in his kindest voice. "It will make a man of you."

If being a man meant becoming like Grandfather, I wanted none of manliness, but I gobbled up my food. No use drawing attention to oneself and spoiling the evening's good mood. As usual, Grandfather soon forgot all about me and Helmut, who did his best to be invisible.

Grandfather's attention was on his oldest and favourite grandson, the manly Walter. To him he could talk as man to man.

"You can't go by what Jüller says," he boomed. "He's a small-timer. Can't see beyond the end of his nose."

Grandfather gave a half whistle and dismissed his brother with a wave of his hands. "You listen to me. I'll advise you. I'll set you up. There is still good business to be done, even in these times. You have to keep more heifers and turn them over more quickly. For that, you need capital. Don't worry though; I'll be there to help."

Grandfather's eyes shone with a visionary light, like Mother's when she was laying plans. "You *must* use scouts. Don't worry what they cost; they're worth their weight in gold. They will find you good-looking heifers, bargains you would never hear about. The farmers just want to sell you the *Plautzen*, the scrawny old beasts."

I shuffled in my seat. Mother had taught me to look down on the cattle trade. Father had taught me to look up to poetry, opera, history, and French culture, on none of which Grandfather was an authority. I sat trapped as he rambled on about *Schwarzbunte Rinder, Rotbunte Rinder, Frieslaender,* and *Emmentaler,* about which cows gave the best milk and which the best meat, and what cuts of meat. Cows, cows, cows.

I never patted cows the way I did Hektor, our carthorse. Greve, our carter, washed and scrubbed Hektor, but no one ever seemed to wash cows. They smelt of dung and were often caked green with the stuff. And they had a nasty habit of swishing their dirty tails at me. Cows strayed far, far from Mother's standards of hygiene and cleanliness. Yet when I looked into their big sad shiny eyes, their blue gleam ringed with red, I knew that they were good animals. Perhaps it was the sheer size of their eyes. I had learned that big eyes meant a big heart.

"Beware of people with small eyes and sharp noses," Mother had said. She did not much care for upturned noses either.

"Before you buy an animal, always look at the veins near the udder," Grandfather advised Walter, and went on to detail the hallmarks of a *Plautze.*

"You're a *Plautze,*" I whispered to skinny Helmut. "And you're a fat pig," came the instant reply.

Walter, his round twinkly eyes alert, drank in Grandfather's words of wisdom. Nothing Grandfather said could have been new to him. He had helped his father in the cattle trade for years. But Grandfather was Grandfather. His words carried authority.

Walter went behind Grandfather's chair and put his hands round his neck. I could not understand how he liked Grandfather, though I was not surprised that Grandfather liked Walter. Everybody liked Walter.

Walter knew how to handle Grandfather. He was not afraid of him—as I was. He called him *Alter* (old man) as his father did, and Grandfather seemed to like it. I would never have dared to call him anything except *Opa*. Grandfather wanted desperately to be kept in touch, and Walter told him everything that went on—good or bad.

"Just listen to what happened to me at the market in Dortmund the other day." Walter smoothed back his quaff of wavy black hair, thinner and darker than mine. He always did that when he was excited.

"I bought three fine-looking heifers, but they pulled out three quite different ones from the stand. Talk about *Plautzen*. 'I did not buy these. I bought those three,' I said, pointing to my heifers.

"'What are you talking about?' said the auctioneer.

"Other people came along and said to him, 'We saw this young fellow bought those three heifers. We can witness to that.'

"They didn't take me for a Jew, but the auctioneer knew. There was a tremendous *kafuffle*. I won in the end, but we said, 'Forget it.' We didn't want trouble."

Grandfather, the fighter, approved. "You have to know when to join battle and when to retreat. Nowadays, when the odds are stacked against us, it's best to avoid trouble. I hope we shall see better days, but you never know. I have been urging Uncle Hermann [my father] to set up a business in France. He speaks French and it does no harm to have a second string to your fiddle."

He gave Walter a benevolent smile. "At least you stood up for your rights, my boy. It builds character."

Walter was not a boy to hide his light under a bushel. At school, he did what he could not do at the cattle market.

"When I came to Schötmar," he said proudly, "Günter Wallhausen and Egon Hamlet were regularly beaten up by the boys in their class. That soon stopped when I came on the scene. I gave the bullies a bloody nose."

Günter and Egon were Jewish boys, sons of neighbours. Their protector set his jaw and flexed his muscles as he told the story. I wished I could be brave like him.

As a Jew, Uncle Walter was no longer allowed to buy at markets, but young Walter had somehow managed to get his own *Legitimationskarte*, the licence to deal in cattle. Walter was a very persuasive fellow.

"Those beasts! There's nothing worse than taking away a man's living." Grandfather clenched his fists as they spoke of Uncle Walter's plight. "If only I were younger, I'd show them."

"You can't do that, *Alter*, they'd beat you to a pulp."

"I know it," said Grandfather bitterly. "I know it. It's just talk."

Fortunately, he did not live to see that there were worse things the "beasts" could do.

"But I'm proud of you, my boy," Grandfather told Walter. "My grandson is a proper cattle dealer now."

"And I am proud of you," said the other partner in this mutual admiration society. "You have a very high reputation. A man came up to me at Aurich market the other day. Guess what he asked me?"

Grandfather was not in a guessing mood.

Walter continued, "He asked me, 'Are you by any chance related to Siegfried Silberbach?' 'I'm his Grandson,' I replied. 'Your grandfather employed me at one time,' the man told me. 'I have never seen a man work so hard. He never stopped. Sometimes he did not see his bed for three or four nights in a row. When he came home late from his buying trips, instead of going to sleep he went off again on his travels to get business. He could not wait to sell the animals he had just bought. What a man!'"

Grandfather beamed at his grandson and admirer and proclaimed his philosophy, "From nothing, nothing will come." (*Von nichts, kommt nichts.*) "It's work, work, and again work." (*Arbeit, Arbeit, und nochmal Arbeit.*) "Of course you have to use your head, but it's no use just sitting on your behind and thinking. Roast pigeons won't fly into your mouth." (*Die gebratenen Tauben fliegen dir nicht ins Maul.*) "You have to go out there and get them. You make your plan and then you act on it."

Walter nodded his handsome head. I had heard all about *Arbeit* and *die gebratenen Tauben* before, but I perked up as Grandfather went on with his story.

"The man spoke the truth. When others slept, I was awake. I got used to being up at night. The cattle transports usually arrived at three or four in the morning. I had my wagons shunted onto the ramps. The cattle had travelled twenty-four hours from Friesland. They were very thirsty. It was harmful for them, especially when they were in calf. The quicker they were unloaded, the better. They needed water and rest."

The days were not that far off when Father and Uncle Walter would know what it was like to be thirsty in cattle trucks. In Grandfather's day, cattle trucks were still used only to transport cattle.

"Once the cattle were all out of the wagons, we drove them through the streets." Grandfather whacked the air with his stick. We had moved from the table, so the Adler china was not in danger. "The creatures had never seen the Begastrasse or the Schülerstrasse before. It was all unknown terrain. Some ran here, some there. I shouted to the boys, 'Watch it, watch it!' As you know, my voice is not very quiet at the best of times, and I was not popular with the neighbours."

Grandfather stood up on his shaky legs and mimicked the outraged citizenry, "Fat Siegfried forgot to say his prayers during the day," he moaned in dialect, "but he makes up for it in the middle of the night. Just listen to him shouting his head off at half past two when decent people are asleep."

Grandfather settled back in his chair. Another rare look of contentment stole over his red face as he remembered his days of glory, "While others were snoring, I was earning."

Chapter Four

THE MISALLIANCE

Local gossip had it that Grandfather was the natural son of a Count von der Schulenburg. His mother, Emilie, daughter of a wealthy landowner, was exceptionally beautiful.

"When she went shopping in Schötmar, people stopped to stare at her," Mother told me. Quite suddenly, this rich beautiful girl married a nondescript red-haired not-very-successful cattle dealer. It was widely rumoured that she needed a ring because she was carrying the count's child.

Grandfather's larger-than-life personality lent credence to the story. He outshone his more pedestrian siblings, and none of his descendants had the red hair that was always cropping up among the real Silberbachs.

Mother firmly believed this tale and vouched for it, as it was by our neighbour, Bertha Wallhausen. Frau Wallhausen's knowledge of the Schötmar of our day was so comprehensive that it seemed inconceivable that she should not be as well-informed about events that took place there long before her birth.

Mother was proud of her noble ancestry and attributed her interest in royal families to this heritage. In later years, I teased her, "Having a love-child for your father is nothing to be proud of, Mother." It made no difference. She felt she belonged to the elite.

Young Siegfried was a thrusting young cattle dealer (*Viehändler*) without great resources. He needed capital to expand. He also needed a wife. Grandmother would supply both needs.

Im Album von Frau Obermeyer
Hat er ihr Bild erschaut.

(In Frau Obermeyer's album
he glimpsed her picture.)

So runs my grandparents' wedding poem. It was a polite fiction. Grandfather Siegfried was no Tamino sighing over the portrait of Pamina/Bertha. The truth was more down-to-earth. He was short of ready cash; she had ready cash. Frau Obermeyer, Grandmother's cousin, knew he needed cash and she, a husband. Her parents, not wanting their daughter left on the shelf, sold her to the young boor from the country. Arranged marriages can turn out well. Not this one. Mother summed it up, "In our home we had everything except happiness."

Grandmother came from a comparatively cultured family of textile Jews who had moved from the ancient town of Hildesheim to Hehlen an der Weser. There were distant connections to the Warburg banking family of Hamburg. My great grandmother, Phillipine, received an annual stipend from the Warburg Foundation.

Bertha Bach was a conventional religious woman of narrow outlook, ready to put a damper on anything that smacked of imagination. Her suitor was a coarse brash and ambitious young man of large gestures with no interest in religion—Bertha's opposite.

"Oma should have married someone of her own background and age," said Mother. "She was seven years older than Opa. Never marry an older woman," Mother warned. "It will not work. Women age more quickly than men." Mother took the precaution of marrying an older man. Father was nine years her senior.

"My father was a man of vision whose style was continually cramped by a niggling small-minded wife. I love my mother but she was not the right wife for him.

"The fine house that we lived in would never have been built if my mother had had her way. 'We don't need such a house,' she argued. 'We are all right where we are. It's madness to spend that amount of money.' She fought my father at every step. He won that battle but he lost many others."

Mother and Uncle Walter both enjoyed telling the story of the Ribbentrop estate. Their versions differed slightly, but they agreed on the following: The von Ribbentrops were heavily in debt. Their family estate at Ehrsen was up for sale. Grandfather made an offer to buy it. When Grandmother heard of it, she threw a tantrum, "Your delusions of grandeur [*Grössenwahn*] will land us all in the poorhouse or in prison," she screamed. Grandfather took no notice and continued negotiations behind her back. As bad luck would have it, he was away on one of his business trips when a messenger came from Herr von Ribbentrop. Grandmother took the message. She was told that a higher offer had been received, but that Grandfather still had first choice. When Grandfather came home, Grandmother said nothing. Grandfather lost the estate.

Mother said, "He was really angry and yelled at her, but it was too late. As von Ribbentrop had not heard from my father, he accepted the other offer. If that deal had gone through, my father would still have been a wealthy man after the inflation."

In the years before World War I, Grandfather had become a very rich man. "He came home with bags of gold coins," Mother told me, "and his pockets stuffed full of gold also."

"Was the Kaiser's face on the coins?" I asked.

"I was not interested in the face on the coins, only in what they would buy," Mother replied.

"They will buy clothes for you. Go get yourself a fine dress made in Detmold," Grandfather said as I eyed the coins. "I want to see my *Fräulein Tochter* look even more beautiful than she is already." Grandfather's "Miss Daughter" did not wait to be asked twice.

In Grandfather's day, the cattle trade was largely in the hands of Jews, many of them rich—many, Silberbachs like himself. In his heyday, Grandfather outshone them all. Restless energy, single-mindedness, a good eye, and a good brain—these were the secrets of his success in Uncle Walter's view. "My father could be charming. He had the knack of making farmers feel that he paid the best prices and brewers[5] that he had the best cattle. And he paid promptly."

In Grandfather's room hung a wooden plaque with the following legend in ornate Gothic lettering:

Vertrau auf Gott, doch auch auf eigene Kraft
Gott segnet nur was Du Dir selbst geschafft

(Trust in God, but also in your own strength
God will bless only what you yourself have created)

Grandfather hardly ever mentioned God, but he certainly had faith in his own powers. Uncle Walter said, "When he wanted something he went after it. He saw no obstacles. There was no self-doubt."

Grandfather had a genius for making money, but he did not look after it. "He handed out money right, left and centre, especially to improvident relatives," said Uncle Walter. "It was as much pride as a sense of duty. 'I, the great Siegfried, will help you out.'"

"It would have been different if he had chosen a different wife," added Mother—a wife, she implied, who could have looked after his money the way she looked after my father's. "He did not keep his gold, so he lost heavily through the inflation. But at least he kept his land and his houses."

It was a little unfair to blame Grandmother for not foreseeing the great inflation, but then Mother always found excuses for her father. Take his way with the ladies. "It was his nature," Mother said of his escapades. "It was his von der Schulenburg blood. He could not help himself." She would not have been so lenient if Father had gone astray.

---

[5] When the heifers were about two years old, they were transported to our part of the world for calving and milk production. It was a halfway house between birth and death, an ideal place for middlemen like Grandfather. Once they had produced four or five calves, the elderly cattle were either sold locally or, more often, to the brewers of southern Germany, who fattened them up for slaughter with molasses and other waste products from their breweries. That was the final solution that awaited Grandfather's thirsty cattle.

On his travels, Grandfather had many opportunities to stray and seems to have taken full advantage of them. A photo of him happily driving a pony and cart in the company of a somewhat mature lady has found its way into the family album. That may or may not have been innocent. As each new liaison came to her ears, Grandmother grew more and more bitter and turned in upon herself. He was still at it during his last illness. He offered money to Alice, the Jewish girl who was looking after my grandparents, if she would sleep with him.

Religion provided another excuse for warfare. Not only was Grandmother's nose forever in that prayer book, she also kept the dietary laws. When Grandfather or anyone else used her cutlery to eat unclean food, she buried the sullied implements among the cabbages in the garden. Weeks later she dug them up.

She ran her kosher kitchen as an enclave of purity in a household of sin. It was her sanctuary. Grandfather was banned. I was allowed to go in occasionally and share her spartan meals. She did not believe in spoiling herself. The food was simple, but anything was better than the rubbish served up by Erna, our cook.

Grandfather, aware of his wife's sensitivities, once played a cruel trick on her. Uncle Walter told the story, "In the old days, we made our own sausages. Normally, we used only beef, but once my father said to me, 'Let's get old so-and-so to slaughter a pig for us.' So we mixed a good bit of fatty bacon [*Speck*] with the beef when we made the sausages. Then we offered them to Grandmother as kosher. She ate with relish. She even told us that they'd turned out exceptionally well. Then my father told her the truth. The poor woman was sick on the spot."

My grandparents' unhappy marriage produced five children. They lost their two oldest sons within a few weeks of each other at the first battle of the Somme. My mother felt that they never recovered from this double blow, "Such a terrible loss would have brought most couples closer together. My parents drifted further apart."

Mother was their third child and eldest daughter.

Chapter Five

MOTHER'S FINISHING SCHOOL

*"Aus der Jugendzeit, aus der Jugendzeit
Klingt ein Lied mir immer dar,
O, wie ist so fern, O, wie ist so weit
Was mein, was mein einst war."*

Mother sang in a soft sweet untrained voice that was a little hoarse. Her eyes were moist and far away. The melody was slow and beautiful and her singing touched my young heart, especially when she came to that trill on the first syllable of the second *Jugendzeit*. A song that the singer sang in her youth keeps haunting her, reminding her how far, how far away is that which once was hers. Mother sang on:

"Was die Schwalbe sang, was die Schwalbe sang . . ."

I do not remember what the swallow sang, but I remember the tales of Mother's youth (*Jugendzeit*). Her parents' quarrels may have cast a shadow, but they did not spoil it. She loved her young days and loved talking about them. It puzzled me how anyone young could be really happy. I lapped up her memories.

Even as a child, I was more interested in real life stories than in fairy tales. I hung around Mother while she was getting dressed or doing housework. Sometimes she would reminisce on our coffee and cake excursions. She never spoke about these things when Father was present. It was something between the two of us. I have pieced together

her story from my memories of those precious moments. And there are the photographs.

Four young ladies in light-coloured dresses and blouses, an older lady in a dark spotted dress, and two young men are standing in an open monoplane with toy wheels and butterfly wings. The propeller, a white disk, is fitted to a kind of radiator grill. The front part of the plane's body, a long rectangular box covered with bolts, looks like a coffin.

One of the young men is in a soldier's uniform; the other wears a dark suit with a wing collar and sports a strawhat. Both were soon to die. I know this because a small blackboard proclaims: *Erinnerung an die Senne, 1914*. The two young men were Mother's older brothers.

For the present, all is well. We are in Herr Metze's studio. The clever photographer has used two matching backcloths. The group appears suspended over a landscape of trees, fields, and houses, the lower part of their bodies hidden by the cloth nearest the camera. The young lady at the very back of the plane points below to we know not what, for it is hidden by the wing.

Arthur, the older brother, looks very earnest. His younger brother, Erwin, in uniform with a buttoned-up tunic and round, soft cap, half smiles. He holds a steering wheel that pops up from between the backcloths. Grandmother, between the brothers, sheepishly waves a handkerchief.

I don't know three of the other ladies, but I know the young lady in the spotless white blouse at the centre of the group. She is a beauty, full-faced, full-bosomed, with a curved mouth and beautiful dark almond eyes set in an enigmatic smile, and she is my mother. At first sight, she seems to be holding a parakeet, the white rods of whose cage form into a cone behind her luxuriant dark hair. The effect is of a bridal veil. Wrong. The parakeet is a large white handkerchief that she dangles and the white cone is probably meant to be the cockpit.

A larger blackboard set next to the other one proclaims, this time in florid *Süterlin* script, "at Uncle Siegfried's expense" (*Auf Onkel Siegfried's Kosten*). The ever-generous cattle dealer had financed this trip to the Senne, a heathland beauty spot not far from Bielefeld, as he had many others.

Another photograph of Mother enjoying a picnic with friends of both sexes seems to date from the same period. This time, Mother's sister is present, and Grandmother is again keeping an eye on things.

Until World War I shattered the idyll, Mother lived the carefree life of girls with her comfortable background. Her father refused her nothing that money could buy. One time he took his two daughters on a shopping spree to Berlin. Mother was sixteen, Grete, fourteen. They came back looking like *Parisiennes* with huge hats and frilly dresses far too grown-up for them. Grandmother was outraged.

"You must be crazy, Siegfried. You have dressed your daughters like streetwalkers. I will not let them wear such dresses." And she didn't.

Thereafter, Mother got her dresses in nearby Detmold, where fashions were a little more sober but still very smart (if the photographs are anything to go by).

Erwin, the second brother, who was a little slow of speech, sometimes complained:

"W-we have to w-work all day. The g-girls s-spend a lot of money w-while w-we are k-kept short." Grandfather was furious.

"Not another word. It is *my* money and *I* decide how to spend it. You ought to be proud of your sisters."

One has a certain sympathy with Erwin's point of view. The girls were forever going off to have their expensive dresses fitted so that their father could be still prouder of them. The workhorse in my mother's character still lay dormant. She seems to have done little useful work at the time, her sister even less. Arthur, the oldest brother, defended the girls.

"It is an honour to work for our sisters. What else is there to work for?"

Mother always felt surprised that Arthur was a member of her family. For her, he was the model of a perfect gentleman—polite, well dressed, and generous. I think she tried to mould me in his image. She respected him for not going into the cattle trade. He was apprenticed to a corn merchant in Detmold and was doing well when he was called up to the army and his life was cut short. Mother always mourned him.

Mother may have been well dressed, but she was not well educated. The combined efforts of my grandmother and the *Höhere Töchterschule* of Bad Salzuflen, the local high school for girls, had made little impact on her mind and she was, at the age of eighteen, a diamond in urgent need of polish.

Grandmother's main contribution was to bequeath to her daughters a fund of folk sayings, many with a somewhat pessimistic slant on life, which they in turn passed on to their children. My cousins and I have retrieved some twenty-eight of these gems from the recesses of our minds. One of the great favourites, "The nursery sets the standard for the whole of life" (*Die Kinderstube ist der Masstab zum ganzen Leben*), did not hold out much hope for Mother and her siblings.

As for the local high school for girls, it provided Mother with a few snatches of French and English, dreadfully pronounced, but so far as one could gather, with no knowledge whatsoever of history, geography, literature or, needless to say, the sciences. My father, who left school at fourteen, was far better informed. He and I would tease Mother about her ignorance, which she freely admitted. We tried to fill in the gaps in her knowledge, but she rarely remembered the lessons we taught her, and the next time Africa was mentioned on the radio, she would ask again, "Where is Africa?"

If Mother was not destined by nature to be a bluestocking, she could at least learn how to behave in polite society and be a credit to whatever man she managed to catch. Grandmother's cousin, Aunt Merry, scoured Jewish upper-middle-class Hamburg for a suitable family in which to place dear Emmy, and she struck gold. So it was that at age nineteen Mother found herself a member of the household of Hamburg's chief rabbi, Dr. Lerner. They lived in a large elegant mansion in the Hamburg suburb of Altona. It was to be her finishing school, where for two years she would learn how to be a lady.

Her status was that of *Haustochter*, a daughter of the house. She was treated as a member of the family. In exchange for the refinement to be won, she was expected to perform light duties such as sewing, laying the table, arranging flowers, pouring the tea, and running special errands for the lady of the house, while Grandfather paid a hefty sum of cattle dealer's cash for the privilege of having his daughter thus occupied. Her father wanted nothing but the best for his beloved *Fräulein Töchter*, and the best, she got.

The Chief Rabbi's wife (*Frau Oberrabbiner*), a small delicately built woman, seems to have been the very incarnation of elegance and good breeding. "She never ventured beyond her inner apartments except in a dress with a long train," said Mother, still awestruck after all those years. For twelve precious months, Mother sat at her feet, learning how to eat, how to dress, how to walk, how to receive guests and treat servants, how to look after her own person—her face, her hair, her hands, her feet, and above all, her nails.

She proved a willing and receptive pupil and revelled in the knowledge that the *Frau Oberrabbiner* was revealing to her. She was being initiated into mysteries unheard of in her rough cattle dealer's world. All her life, Mother tried to transcend the harsh milieu into which she was born. She wanted to get away from the smelly men and the rough language and enter a realm of ordered elegance and beauty where cow dung had no place. *Frau Doktor* Lerner proved the answer to her deepest needs.

There were two Lerner sons of around Mother's age, but it was the son-in-law who tried to flirt with her, and that while his wife was pregnant. When she came to Hamburg, Mother was a pretty red-cheeked country girl, who knew how to look after herself. There are some photos of her from about that time. The eyes are mild and the expression is sweet, but the chin is determined. Mother had no time for romance unless it was serious and likely to lead to the proper goal of all romance, a good marriage. So, when the son-in law tried his luck with, "Do you know that you are a pretty girl?" (*Wissen Sie auch das Sie ein schönes Mädchen sind?*), there was no coquettish denial.

"Yes, I know it perfectly well but that you should tell me so is not proper." (*Ja, das weiss ich genau, aber dass SIE es mir sagen gehört sich nicht.*) The poor man never tried his luck again.

Mother made friends with the Lerner sons, a platonic friendship that continued into later life, and meanwhile drank in the refinement that exuded from their mother.

The chief rabbinical household may have been strong on refinement, but it was weak on nourishment. Perhaps the two go together. All her life Mother enjoyed a healthy if not very discriminating appetite. She kept cheese rolls hidden in her room at one of the best Jewish hotels in Bournemouth, rather than revealing her inelegant hunger by asking for second helpings. No wonder that during the lean days in Hamburg-Altona, she looked forward with longing to the regular food parcels from home. Alas, they were but a drop in an ocean of scarcity, and in any case, the laws of polite behaviour demanded that they be shared with the family.

In gaining the rudiments of deportment, Mother was to lose a good deal of *avoirdupois*. When she went back to Schötmar for a holiday after a year away, the effects of the delicate Lerner meals on her plump charms were all too obvious. Her father, who liked his ladies well covered, was horrified by her ravished appearance and, deaf to all her pleas, absolutely forbade her to return to Hamburg for more refinement. Letters from Aunt Merry and from the *Frau Oberrabiner* herself, pleading that dear Emmy be allowed to go back for the final stages of her course in gracious living, failed to move him.

Frau Doktor Lerner was fond of Mother. What guru, moreover, wants to lose so eager a disciple? But Grandfather was firm, "I am not going to have my daughter looking like a consumptive and that's final. If I lose the year's payment I made in advance—no matter. My daughter is worth more to me than that."

So Mother went back to stuffing herself with bread, potatoes, meat, and sausage, the staple diet of her family, and soon her cheeks were rosy once more. But she never forgot the real lessons she learned from *Frau Doktor* Lerner and always remained grateful to her guru for exposing her to a new world. She even mentioned her stay with the Lerners in a half-page curriculum vitae, which she had to provide for the Nazi authorities when she applied to emigrate.

In my early years, I was to suffer a good deal from Mother's preoccupation with good manners, and I held the great *Frau Doktor* responsible. Mother tried hard to pass on to me the wisdom of the School of Hamburg, but I proved a lazy and inept pupil. Looking at my life as a whole, it seems that her lessons were not wholly lost, though I never did learn how to look after my nails properly.

If there was any conversation about religion or philosophy at the chief rabbi's table or in his drawing room, any spiritual depth to his household, it passed Mother by. She might just as well have been with the family of a banker. That may not have been the Lerners' fault.

Mother was not really curious about life's ultimate questions. She believed in God and turned to him in extremis and during her enforced leisure on the Day of Atonement each year, but religion did not play much part in her life. Her dream was of a secular paradise where everyone and everything was spotlessly clean, where persons of refinement passed on the elements of good manners and good taste to the young, where people lived in exquisite surroundings, eager to learn more about how to beautify their homes and gardens, and where she had the most beautiful home, admired by all. It was probably her own bent and not any lapse on the Lerners' part which brought her back from Hamburg with an interest in *Frau Doktor's* home and manners rather than *Herr Doktor's* God.

It must seem strange that Mother entrusted me with her confidences at so early an age. I realize now that she was only the first of a long line of people, mostly though not exclusively older women, who have confided their secrets to me. I seem to be a sympathetic listener. Notwithstanding St. James, there is not only a place for the doers of this world, but also for those who are listeners. They are the ones who write their memoirs.

Chapter Six

THE RAGSELLER

I was about seven or eight when Mother began to tell me about her courtship and marriage. With her parents' example before her, it may seem surprising that she decided to marry at all, but it never occurred to her to stay single. The Anglo-Saxon tradition of spinsterhood and good works was either unknown or not admired in the circles in which Mother moved. "No one ever married too late" was one of the many sayings Mother inherited from her mother—a triumph of hope over experience in Grandmother's case.

Mother wanted to marry, but she was choosy—no cattle dealer for her. She loved her father but could not bear his trade.

"I was tempted once," she told me. "He was rich, good-looking, had tolerable manners and a very nice house as well. His sister was a friend of mine and had set her heart on the match. But in the end, I could not go through with it." Mother could not face being involved for the rest of her life in the barbarities of the cattle trade, having her house invaded by coarse men using rough language, smelling of cow dung, and trampling the stuff all over her carpets.

Not long after her return from Hamburg, Mother met Walter Salomon. He was a dashing dark, handsome young man, and he was not a cattle dealer. Mother fell quite seriously in love. However, an engagement was forbidden because Salomon could not satisfy Grandfather about his prospects. I got the impression that on this point he could not satisfy Mother either. She does not seem to have put up much of a fight for her beloved. She was not a girl to let emotion rule her reason.

"Love goes when the *Rausch* is over." Mother did not specify what the *Rausch* was, and for some reason, I did not ask. The dictionary says "intoxication, passion." It was quite clear to Mother that in the long term, security and prosperity were the cement of marriage.

> *Kommt der Dalles in das Haus*
> *Fliegt die Liebe zum Fenster 'raus.*

This was a favourite saying. *Dalles* is a Yiddish word that means penury, bankruptcy. If that enters the house, love flies out of the window. I have a feeling that Mother had been more in love with Walter Salomon than she was with my father in the early days of their relationship, but Salomon was not a man of substance. That was his downfall.

When I was about nine, Walter Salomon came to see us. It was a business visit. He was some kind of representative. Mother, who had not met him since her youth, was red-cheeked with anticipation, and I too was excited, having heard all about the former heartthrob.

Salomon, who now had a family of his own, was received by my parents in their private office. I was presented to him and duly patted and complimented on being me. He was still handsome, a dark-complexioned man with fine Jewish features and lots of black hair. My father was bald by then and several years older than Salomon, but when the visit was over, Mother told me in one of our têtes-a-têtes that she had made the right choice. Her marriage was very happy, and Father was a much more successful businessman.

In the summer of 1913, Mother went for an excursion to a popular café overlooking Bielefeld, the largest town in the area. She was accompanied by two Schötmar friends, who were sisters. Some army men strolled in to see what they could find of interest. They found the three ladies and went over to talk and flirt a little. One of the men was my father, who was in the area on a retraining programme. He was immediately drawn to Mother. They were the only Jews present—and she was a very attractive young woman.

Mother did not have the fine bone structure of her mother and sister. Her beauty was of a different order. Her face was round, almost like a full moon. Her eyebrows sloped towards the bridge of her nose and that made her almond eyes seem even longer. And there was the enigmatic half smile that appears on all the photos of the period. The nose was broad and rounded, not conventionally well shaped, but it fitted its context. Even the determined chin had pleasing round contours. Her skin remained soft and smooth all her life.

Mother had long dark brown hair that was pinned up at the back and sides. It was rolled back from her left ear into a large bun, balancing the parting on the right, and she sported the sideburns popular at the time. She was above medium height and, although plump, had not yet put on the weight that was to broaden her beauty in early married life. There was nothing harsh or angular about this young woman. Everything was smooth and ample. Anyone with eyes to see would know that she would not turn into a shrew. And Father had sharp eyes.

He quickly recognized that outer charm was matched by inner good nature. Fortunately, it turned out to be an active good nature, not averse to work. It had to be, for Father abhorred lazy women. He wanted a helpmate, not an ornament. He was twenty-nine at the time, and it did not take him long to make up his mind that here was the girl he wanted to marry. Mother was not quite so overwhelmed, but she liked him well enough. When he asked if they could meet again, she agreed.

Soon he was asking very politely if he might exchange the formal *Sie* type of address for the familiar *Du*. Again Mother consented, and the next time they met, always chaperoned by Mother's friends, he asked if he could come to Schötmar to be presented to her parents. They had not known each other long, but Mother allowed herself to be persuaded.

She enjoyed the polite attentions he paid her. They reminded her of her beloved brother Arthur. He rushed to hold her chair as she sat down and again as she got up. He knew how to kiss hands. His manner of treating a lady was more Gallic than Germanic. Half his life had been spent in Alsace-Lorraine, and he had travelled widely in Eastern France. And then, Father had the born salesman's gift of speech. He knew how to turn a pretty compliment and tell a good story. He won Mother's sympathy with his account of early struggles and hardships and subsequent achievements.

"I was born in Laubach, in Oberhessen. My parents are poor but very honest and hard-working. I was only fourteen when I was sent to far off Moerchingen [Morhange] in Lothringen [Lorraine] to learn the textile business with a firm called Kuder. They had quite a large store. I missed my parents, especially my good mother, whom I love very much [that went down well with Mother]. There was not too much to eat. I stayed there five years and then moved to Strasburg, a beautiful old town with a wonderful cathedral. There I began to travel for a wholesaler, David Weil and Co. I did very well and my sales soon outstripped those of older, more experienced salesmen."

Father may not have used those exact words, but that was the gist of it. I had heard the same story many times. Even as a young man, Father did not hesitate to boast about his successes. One morning he found the following legend pinned outside his door by his fellow apprentice travellers:

Hermann Katz, Besitzer mehrerer Güter, Reisender der Firma David Weil and Co. (Hermann Katz, owner of several estates, traveller for Messrs. David Weil and Co.)

Father told this story against himself, and Uncle Moritz, his brother, confirmed it.

An early photograph shows Father on one of his sales trips to France. He is standing with a motley crowd in front of a flower-bedecked festival cart. In the background, on the right, is the very run-down one-story Hotel Terlinck, and on the left, the rather superior Villa Charles with ladies on its balcony. Between them is a little shop, La Ville de Venise—Specialitè Corailles et Ecailles (speciality coral and tortoiseshell). The period may be a little earlier, but the crowd could have stepped out of one of Pagnol's Marseilles films (the character in the strawhat could pass for Pagnol's Escartefigue). The men and boys have the same hats and suits as in the films, though the women wear the long dresses and huge picture hats of the period.

Father stands right in the centre of the group, and like Mother in the aeroplane, he attracts attention—dark, magnetic eyes, generous moustache above a winged collar and black bow tie. He wears a white straw boater with black band, carries an umbrella, and is enveloped by a dark double-breasted suit. The jacket is ill cut, too large and too long. He tried.

By the time he met Mother, Father had moved on. After two years in the army and some time working for a wholesaler in Saarlouis, he set up on his own. He chose the ancient town of Metz, capital of Lorraine, to establish himself as a textiles wholesaler. He was twenty-seven at the time. Soon he was able to call his young brother, Moritz, to be a partner, and his sister, Helene, to keep house. Moritz had started his career as a boy apprentice in a shoe shop, putting two left shoes into the boxes, but he proved a good businessman. Above all, Father made sure that his parents were well provided for.

In Metz, Father fell in love. It was serious. "She was by all accounts a very nice young lady, beautiful, with a good reputation, but she was not Jewish." Hedwig Bing, Father's cousin, told me this.

"Her name was Emmy, like your mother's."

She continued, "When your grandmother heard about it, she wrote to your father, begging him to break off the engagement. 'Nothing good will come of it,' she wrote. 'You may be happy at first, but the reckoning will come later. The differences will show. You should marry a Jewish girl with whom you can share everything.'"

Mother filled in the rest of the story:

"Vati loved and respected his mother, but he could not let Emmy go. Yes, her name was Emmy, like mine. Perhaps that is why he took such an interest in me. His mother wrote again. By this time she was not well enough to travel, so she sent a friend to Metz as an emissary, imploring Vati not to go through with the marriage. Vati listened to his mother in the end.

"He has often told me, 'If it were not for my mother, I would not have found happiness with you.'

"So you see," continued Mother, never one to let a chance to moralize slip by, "it is good to do what your mother tells you. No one in the world means better by you than your mother."

I wonder what became of the other Emmy. I never heard Father speak of her. But he did speak a lot about Metz. Father loved it like no other city. It had only been German since 1871, and the French influence was still very strong. It was in Metz that Father acquired his love for all things French—the language, the culture, the cooking, and French opera. He spoke perfect French, made friends with professional people and artists, and got some kind of education in the humanities. The photos of the period show that he had left the Hotel Terlinck and La Ville de Venise well behind him.

During their early meetings, Mother saw her suitor only in uniform, but even then he managed to look impressive. Appearances were important to Mother, and Father had learned all about appearances. Although not an officer, he had the gall to wear the stiff white collar of an officer and was sometimes mistaken for one. The sepia photos show him with large clear stern eyes and a bushy, neatly upturned moustache, managing to look remarkably like his emperor, every inch a military man. It may have been a pose, but he carried it off. In every photo he holds a cigar between the second and third fingers of his right hand. The stiff white collar shows above the buttoned-up tunic.

Hedwig Bing said, "My father greatly admired your father and his brother because they were both exceptionally smart and good-looking. They are like staff officers."

When I was a boy, Father still looked like a staff officer. The thick brown wavy hair, which I inherited (for a while), had gone; the Kaiser Wilhelm moustache had been trimmed down to Adolf Hitler size, but the grey-brown eyes were still clear and direct and the back was straight as ever. "Chest out, stomach in," he often commanded me. Until late in life, he retained a military bearing that made him seem much taller than he was. I was astonished to find later that he was an inch or two shorter than I am. The giants of the nursery have a way of dwindling down to size, but for me, Father always walked tall.

At the time that Mother met him, he was at his best, a handsome young man with an air of maturity, who seemed capable of handling anything. The upper lip is curved, the lower sensual. The nose, long and thin, appears slightly curved only in profile. And he made the most of his looks. In a studio photograph taken in Metz, he is wearing a stiff-winged collar under a smart summer overcoat with velvet trimmings. He carried a walking stick and a bowler.

Perhaps Father was wearing this outfit when he knocked on the door of Schülerstrasse 17. Mother herself opened the door. It was the first time she had seen him in civilian clothes. She was impressed, her father less so. He knew an adventurer when he saw one. When talk of marriage came up and Father finally asked for Emmy's hand, Grandfather exploded. He was not going to let his cherished daughter waste herself on this ragseller (*Lappenfritze*). His smart appearance and ready tongue cut no ice with him. They only made him more certain that here was an unscrupulous upstart out to steal a rich man's daughter.

Grandfather was a better judge of cattle than of men. He entirely misjudged the suitor, as he did his other children's partners.

Father was not averse to marrying into a wealthy family, but that was not his main concern. He was perceptive enough to see that Mother, with her sweet disposition and her steadiness, would make him a jewel of a wife, and he was determined to have her.

This time Grandfather met his match. He had to deal with a far wilier customer than Walter Salomon, a man, moreover, of great persistence and willpower. The deepest levels of another person's being, perhaps even of his own, may have been closed to him, but Father had the astute extrovert's insight into character and motive. Grandmother proved no problem. She automatically said yea when her husband said nay. When Father told her how important religion was in his parents' house, he had her in his pocket.

The old man was the obstacle, and Father realized that in order to deal with him, he first had to get my mother fully committed to the marriage. A very level-headed young lady, she had no intention of marrying into penury. If her father could persuade her that this would be her fate if she married the *Lappenfritze*, then good-bye to the *Lappenfritze*. She liked my father, but I think she could have lived without him.

Father played his cards right. In order to convince her that he would be able to keep her in the style to which she was accustomed, he sent Mother large sums of money for safekeeping. They were not even engaged, but he could see that he was running no risk with her. The move had the advantage of impressing both father and daughter, and also of safeguarding his hard-earned wealth, which was vulnerable in Lorraine.

Mother did not want the money, and Grandfather did not want the money; they found it a responsibility and an embarrassment. But Father kept sending more and more until they had in their keeping some thirty thousand marks, a considerable sum in those days, comprising most of Father's wealth. He insisted that it was only for safekeeping; no obligation was involved.

These transactions set a pattern, which, except for a blip in the very early years, continued throughout my parent's marriage. In old age, Father rarely carried more than ten shillings in his wallet. When Mother pressed him to take more, he refused. "I don't need it. It's safer with you." Mother was always in charge of the money, and although she spent generously on her homes, she looked after it well.

Father was interested in making money, not for its own sake but to please her. When he was in his sixties, a commission agent in Britain, he phoned her every night from Manchester, Cardiff, Glasgow, or wherever he might be. He would say, "Today I sold so many dozen, and this is what my commission comes to." He had worked it all out in his little book, so that he could make her happy. In the days of rationing during and after the World War II, he brought home chicken, eggs, sugar, cheese, and other rarities—a male bird bringing back tidbits for his mate. It was his greatest joy to see his wife happy and be the agent of her happiness.

Grandfather recognized from the monies received that his daughter's suitor was indeed a man of substance. His resistance was already beginning to crumble when Father delivered his coup de grâce. He invited Grandfather to Metz and showed him his home, his business, introduced him to his sister, and opened up the books. Grandfather came home very impressed by the Metz establishment. He generously admitted that he had done the *Lappenfritze* wrong and gave his consent to an engagement. But he stipulated that the wedding should not take place until the war was over. He had just lost two sons, and he did not want a war widow on his hands.

He need not have worried. Father saw to it that he had a quiet war. He loved all things French too much for his heart to be in the fight. He worked in supplies, and unlike his younger brother who was wounded in Russia and was left with a limp, he saw little action. When the war ended, he came to Schötmar to claim his prize.

Chapter Seven

A WEDDING HAS BEEN ARRANGED

There was one person in the Silberbach household who looked on Mother's progress towards matrimony with a heavy heart and with a bit of a jealous eye. That was her only sister Grete. Mother may have been attractive, but Grete was beautiful. She had inherited Grandmother's finely chiselled features but without the hooded eyes, long nose, and thin lips. Mother's full-moon face was spread out, a gentler version of Grandfather's. Grete's features were more concentrated and sharply edged, her eyes rounder, with more sparkle.

She retained her good looks in old age. When she was eighty and living in Los Angeles, I took her to a Hollywood studio where the Merv Griffin television chat show was being recorded. I introduced her to my friends there and was complimented all around on my beautiful aunt.

"I am the first to admit that my sister was prettier than I was," Mother said. "She always had a lot of men swarming around her because she took anything that came along. They were men who just wanted a flirtation. Men whose intentions were serious found her too superficial and kept away."

Mother portrayed herself as choosier than her flighty sister. "I had fewer admirers. I looked for quality, not quantity. I was not so pretty and I was not so frivolous. I was only interested in men who were looking for a companion for life." The portrait of Mother was probably correct. Mother was a serious woman.

In many ways, the sisters were as different as the parents they resembled, and relations between them were never smooth; each coveted what the other had. Grete told her daughters that Mother was proud and full of her own importance, explaining, "I called her 'the proud one' [*Die Stolze*]. It was always 'I, Emmy Silberbach'" (*Ich, Emmy Silberbach*). Grete conceded that Mother had good teeth. "They were like pearls."

According to Mother, Grete was fidgety as well as flighty. Perhaps the two go together. "We called her '*Zappel* [fidget]. She couldn't sit still for a moment, always on the move, always on the lookout for something."

Both girls adored their father and he them. "*Mein Fräulein Tochter*" (This is my Miss Daughter), he proudly announced when one of them was introduced. But Grete believed, perhaps correctly, that Grandfather preferred his elder daughter and gave her extra advantages. She was always watching for any slight, determined not to lag behind her sister, though lag behind she invariably did. Mother was after all, to use Jane Austen's language, Miss Silberbach, her sister merely Miss Grete Silberbach.

When Mother had a dress fitted in Detmold, Grete laid siege to her father until he consented to have her fitted as well. She got her dress, but not from such a good dressmaker. When Mother came back from Hamburg as a fine lady, Grete could not wait to be "finished" too. She was sent to a spa in the Harz Mountains to a family not nearly as grand as were the Lerners. But when my father came on the scene, Grete really became envious.

Father did not just send money. He showered Mother with gifts, the finest of which was a very beautiful diamond engagement ring. Grete gave Grandfather no peace until he had bought her a diamond ring. "The ring was not as fine as mine," said Mother, "but then, she was not engaged."

That was an omission that Grete wanted to be made good without delay. Although two years younger than Mother, Grete could not afford to sit back and twiddle her thumbs while her elder sister was racing ahead in the most important of all stakes. It was high time that she too got her head under a wedding canopy.

"Alas, for all her beauty, Grete had no offers. There were plenty of admirers but no suitors," was Mother's version.

According to Grete's daughter, Gisela, there was one serious contender. He was the Dutchman, Alex Zeckel, son of Grandmother's cousin, Henriette. He visited Grete at her finishing spa, but Mother maintained that he never got around to asking the only question that mattered. Gisela says that he did, but that Grandfather vetoed the match because Alex was not a man of substance.

They say in German, "*Er hatte nichts hinter sich.*" (He had nothing behind him.) "That was not the right expression in Alex's case," quipped Gisela. "It was what he had behind him that attracted my mother. Unfortunately, that was his principal asset." According to Gisela, her mother never forgave Grandfather for not allowing the match and making her marry someone she did not want.

Mother's account was very different. She told me that Grete was in such a hurry to catch up that she pestered Grandfather until he had found her a husband. A match was arranged with Paul Silberbach from Cologne, a distant cousin. Whether or not Grandfather made the match, everyone agreed that it had his immediate and unqualified approval. Grandfather being Grandfather, his approval did not bode well for the marriage. My father he had reluctantly accepted; Paul he welcomed with open arms.

Fresh from the big city, the prospective in-laws arrived in Yokeltown "covered from head to foot in expensive furs," as Mother put it, "with case upon case of expensive leather luggage." At the station they actually hired a motor carriage to take themselves and the luggage mountain to the Silberbach residence. The neighbours' eyes popped. They had seen nothing like it. And Grandfather congratulated himself on his choice.

Unhappily it was all a blind. The visitors' debts were piled as high as their luggage. They showed Grandfather a list of their properties, omitting to mention one minor point: they were all heavily mortgaged. Grandfather learned the facts painfully as he had to dig deeper and deeper into his pocket.

That was Mother's version of events. Gisela's is again somewhat different. She agrees that in Cologne her mother was considered a good match—she had a large dowry. But she insists that at that time, Paul's father and her paternal grandfather, Hugo, was well off, owning butcher shops in prime locations.

Grandfather gave Grete a wedding commensurate with her catch. Now it was Mother's turn to be jealous. She was already a little envious because her sister was able to keep the beloved name of Silberbach, while she herself laboured under burden of being Frau Katz, a name she detested. Father had told her with pride that all the Katzs were *Kohanim*, priests, direct descendants in the male line of Aaron, brother of Moses, the first high priest. Since her views on religion were closer to her father's than to her mother's, that did not make a great impression.

Now Mother had to witness her sister being married very grandly at one of the best hotels in Bad Salzuflen, while she had had a very quiet wedding at a Schötmar hostelry of little distinction, with only a few guests being invited. The food at Mother's wedding had been good and plentiful in the way of the Silberbachs: soup with egg dumplings, fish with salt potatoes and Hollandaise sauce, breast of veal (of course) with young peas and asparagus, young chicken with roast potatoes and various mixed salads, ice, compotes, dessert, coffee. But the unnamed soup, fish, and dessert on the menu shows that the venue was not first class.

The ostensible reasons for Mother's quiet send-off in June 1919 were the deaths of her brothers just a few years earlier and of my father's mother's death in January 1918. The real reason, Mother suspected, was Father's modest background. Fortune hunter or knight errant, he had come into Mother's life from nowhere. Paul was part of the known world, the son of a Cologne grandee, raised on marble floors. There were people at his wedding who had to be impressed.

Knowing Grandfather, I am sure he enjoyed flaunting his wealth at Paul's father, Hugo, with his marble-topped butchers' shops and his suburban villa in Marienburg, Cologne. Hugo had to be impressed. But what satisfaction was there in making an impression on an obscure little shopkeeper from a place no one had ever heard of?

My paternal grandfather, Joseph, was not among the more successful of Aaron's descendants. Laubach, a tiny town in the Oberhessen backwoods, was too small to support his textile business.[6] Joseph himself

---

6 Recent research has shown that he sold not only clothes and textiles but also shoes and hats and that he was an *Ellerwarenkrämer*, as well as a butcher and cattle dealer. Anything to support his family. See Stefan Wiesekopsieker, *Die Bürsten-und Besenfabrik "Hermann Katz and Co.,"* in *Jahrbuch Bad Salzuflen, 1998,* (Verlag für Regionalgeschichte, Bielefeld 1997), p.155-6.

did not help matters. "His heart was not in his work," Hedwig Bing told me. "He preferred religious study to standing behind the counter." The family had to struggle, even with Father's subsidies, witness a letter from Grandmother Henriette to Uncle Moritz from about that time, in which the price of apples merited several sentences.

Grandfather Joseph was small, thin, pale, and shy. His rather threadbare clothes seemed to hang on him. Hugo by contrast was tall, smartly dressed, sported a cane, and had a face even redder than Grandfather Siegfried's. He had a bit of a paunch, a large wart on his face, and a friendly chuckle (he was the Goldenberg to Joseph's Shmuile in the picture that Mussorgsky depicted in his music). The fur coat had dwindled to a fur collar when I knew him, but mortgages or no mortgages, Hugo still had an aura of prosperity and was still often seen at the smartest cafes in Cologne. He wore spats, like Father. They called Hugo a *boulevardier*.

That Opa Joseph was a good and honest man did not enter into Opa Siegfried's calculations. He was too preoccupied with externals. The Cologne crowd had to be impressed. Grete had to be given the grander wedding because hers was the better catch.

It did not turn out that way. In the end, it was Mother who got the better bargain.

The post-nuptial rescue operation launched by Grandfather to put Paul's finances in order was the first of several.[7] Mother said that more than once Aunt Grete came home to Schötmar in tears, asking for help. Grandfather never refused her, but his finances were not unlimited. The great inflation had hit him hard. If only he had kept those bags of gold.

Paul owned a share in a factory that made glue from albumen. Soon after the Nazis came to power, his gentile partners, with Nazi support, sent him packing with only a token sum in compensation. He was forced back into butchering.

From his father and mentor in matters of business, Paul had inherited a rather grand butchers' shop in one of Cologne's best shopping streets.

---

[7]   Years later when I spoke to Gisela, she commented that her parents had plenty of money until the Nazis came to power.

I was awed by its high ceilings and the big white marble slabs, stained momentarily with the blood of victims, but quickly wiped clean by assistants. Because everything was so white and clean, the rituals of the butchers' trade, for which I did not care at all, seemed less gruesome than in the grubbier butchers' shops of Schötmar. Fortunately, I never saw my uncle and aunt cut up the meat. They left that—and much else—to their helpers.

A year or two before Grandfather's death, the shop failed and Paul went bankrupt. Grandfather made his way to Cologne for the creditors' meeting. Uncle Walter, who accompanied him, told the story with relish.

"As soon as they saw Siegfried, the hungry claimants swarmed around him like wasps in a honey pot."

"You'll all be paid, every one of you, to the last pfennig," the old man roared in his forceful fashion, waving one of his sticks.

"I knew better. I kept a book of all the claims and I knew the state of my father's finances. When the claims reached one hundred thousand marks, I told him, 'Old man, your finances are not that strong anymore. You can't pay them everything.'"

"He yelled at me, 'My word is my word,' but he did not know what he was promising. He was a man of the old school. He believed that debts had to be paid. He had to come down from his high horse, and it hurt. He had to tell them, 'I'll give you 50 percent if you'll forget the rest.' They forgot the rest. A bird in the hand . . . And so more of the old man's resources went down the drain."

There were different schools of thought about the bankruptcy. A charitable interpretation of events—one to which Grandmother at any rate did not fully subscribe—held that Paul had been careless.

Uncle Walter, who investigated the matter on Grandfather's behalf, explained that, while Paul himself bought the carcasses at the abattoir, he failed to make sure that all his purchases reached the cold store below the shop. He entrusted the collection of the meat to his employees, and they had other ideas about its proper destination.

"For every three carcasses they collected," said Uncle Walter, "two went to Paul's shop and one to clients of their own. They divided the profits among themselves. The suppliers knew all about it and got their cut."

It was this constant shortfall, so the theory went, that accounted for Paul's difficulties. Once these had become apparent, members of the family took turns checking the incoming meat and standing guard over it. Cousin Walter was one of them and caught a chill from the cold store for his pains. But, by the time these precautions were taken, it was too late to save the firm.

Grandmother, clearly not one of Paul's admirers, commented that he would have been better off attending to his cold store than attending to his lady friends. I do not know if there was any connection in Paul's case between financial failure and success in love, as Grandmother implied. In any event, Paul was not a faithful husband.

Grandmother enjoyed circulating this rather far-fetched story. "He was caught red-handed one night clambering down the drainpipe of his own house on his way to see some woman, while his wife was in her ninth month." There were snorts all around from the black-, brown-, and grey-clad crones to whom Grandmother was regaling this tale of horror.

"And after all Siegfried has done for him," said one of the crones. "It's bad blood," Grandmother sniffed. It was her standard explanation for all disreputable behaviour. "His father was the same."

Whenever the drainpipe story came up, as it did quite often, I wondered why Paul did not use the front door, but I never dared ask. Perhaps he climbed up rather than down.[8]

In the early years of the marriage, Grete was tempted more than once to leave Paul and return to her parents. This phase seems to have passed with the birth of Gisela, their first child. Grete decided to stick with her errant spouse. She helped him loyally in his shop and later in his shirt business in Chicago's Merchandise Mart. There was clearly more to Grete than her sister was willing to see. When, in his sixties, Paul developed Parkinson's disease, Grete, often worn out, nursed him

---

[8]   Gisela commented on the drainpipe story: "My father was a womanizer and he did not go to much trouble to hide it. He certainly never did, and never would have, climbed a drainpipe to get in or out of our house. My mother knew about his womanizing and was unhappy about it, but respectable people at that time did not divorce; it just wasn't done."

through his long decline. By then, she was the boss and sometimes gave him a hard time.

Gisela believes that her father went after other women because her mother made him feel small. Throughout her married life, she blamed Paul for not being another Siegfried. Her father was her ideal. True that he too was no model of marital fidelity, but he was a strong man, a generous man, a man on a large scale, a winner. Paul bore no comparison to him.

Like her own mother, Grete had married the wrong man, but unlike her mother, she did not proclaim the fact from the rooftops. She had decided that she would abide by her all-too-hurried choice. At home in Cologne, smartly dressed, cool and smiling, she led a busy social life. No one would have guessed that anything was wrong. Mother commented unkindly, "My sister has missed her vocation. She should have been on the stage."

When Grete came home to Schötmar, the facade sometimes cracked. Once she arrived alone, red-eyed, crying. I put my arms round my favourite aunt. "Why are you crying, Aunt Grete?" I asked. "You don't have to cry when I am here to comfort you."

She looked at me with beautiful strange unseeing eyes and said bravely, "I am not crying, sweetheart, I'm laughing."

Siegfried

From left to right: an unidentified woman, Erwin, Emmy, Bertha,
Arthur, and two unidentified women

From left to right: Grete, Hugo, Emmy, two unidentified women,
Bertha, an unidentified man, and an unidentified woman

Emmy

From left to right: Emmy and Grete standing and Bertha sitting

From left to right: Emmy, Grete, Arthur, Walter, and Erwin—
the five children of Siegfried and Bertha

Hermann, on a sales trip in France, is in the middle of the picture
wearing a white straw boater, bow tie and dark suit.

Hermann in Metz

Hermann in his World War I army uniform

Grete soon before she was married

Alex Zeckel, who courted Grete

Hugo

Billa

From left to right: Paul, Emmy, and Grete

Grete with Gisela and Ingelore

HEIR TO A BRUSH FACTORY

Chapter Eight

WILLIAM AND MARY

Mother may have fared better than her sister, but the early years of her marriage were not exactly an ocean of bliss.

So far as I know, Father was a faithful husband. "If ever I catch you with another woman, I will tear you from limb to limb," said Mother, smiling a secure smile. Father grinned sheepishly. "You are the only one for me," he crooned.

Not that he lacked opportunities. When I was small, he was away from home for most of the week, sometimes for several weeks at a time, selling his factory's production. Karl Weinhorst, his chauffeur and friend, had a reputation as a womanizer. Frau Weinhorst appeared in Schötmar from time to time to investigate her husband's indiscretions. But I think Father loved his Emmy too much to follow his chauffeur's example. My parents' difficulties lay elsewhere.

"The first four years were the hardest," said Mother. "We had to get used to each other. I came from a home where we did not have to deny ourselves." Mother did not say that Father came from a poor background. She said he "originated from limited circumstances."

"He had to work very hard to establish himself. He spent freely enough when he was courting me, but once we were married he started counting the pennies. I was used to spending. He wanted to know what I had spent. I thought him mean. But he soon learned to trust my judgement.

"The other problem was more difficult. You know how temperamental Vati is. I was not used to being shouted at. Even my father, a great shouter, rarely raised his voice to me. But Vati lost his temper over the smallest things." Again Mother was generous and blamed it on Father's early struggles.

I can see them now in their later years. Mother has tidied up Father's office, and he can't find the odd sheets on which he made his notes. His face goes red; the veins on his temples stand out; the eyes bulge. "Blast and thunder, where did you put my papers? I have to prepare my plans. I can't be out of the room for a moment without you interfering. It has to stop."

Mother says nothing. Nose in the air, she finds the papers, turns her back, and walks out. Ten minutes later, he is after her again. "Why do you look so stern, dear Emmy? What have I done? I am only trying to do my best for all of us. I need those papers for my customers." He strokes her cheek. She turns her head away. "You look so beautiful today." He smiles sheepishly. "Have you got everything you need for the house?"

She ignores him at first, but after a suitable period has passed, she smiles and he is forgiven—unless strangers were present when he lost his temper. Then it might take days before he is reinstated. And when she does consent to speak to him, it is to give him a lecture:

"You have demeaned your wife before strangers. That is not proper. You do not know what is due to a wife. How can one forget oneself like this? You lack education." She goes on, "It all comes down to the nursery" (*Kinderstube*), conveniently forgetting that hers was not one to boast about. He listens contritely, and having had her say, she relents.

There were genuine differences of temperament. Father had exposed nerve endings and was easily roused, but he calmed down just as quickly after the storm. And he did not bear grudges. Mother hardly ever lost her temper, but she was easily hurt and tended to nurse her grievances. I was like her. The few times Father beat me—always in anger—he seemed genuinely surprised when I would not speak to him.

Then there was Father's habit of advertising, and sometimes exaggerating, his achievements. This had amused his fellow apprentices at David Weil and Co., but Mother was less amused. It was a habit she had to get used to, though not without trying hard to change him. She was still trying when I came on the scene. "Don't brag," she would lecture him. "People are jealous. Make yourself smaller than you are, not bigger."

Experience had convinced Mother, as it has me, that envy is the most common, perhaps even the deadliest, of the seven deadlies. It persists long after lust, gluttony, and even pride have disappeared. But Mother's advice had little effect. No sooner had she admonished him when some new rodomontade came to her ears, like this one, via a customer's wife.

"Your husband has told me that you have just bought a Beau Decca Radiogram [the *non plus ultra* of the post-war years] for 350 pounds. How nice that you can afford it."

Or Father might give himself away while reporting some conversation he had had with a customer, for he told Mother everything. "Hermann, you have been boasting again," she would say, wagging her finger as he smiled guiltily. For him, it was a way of being friendly. He liked telling people about his affairs, with a little ornamentation here and there. He never boasted to people who were poor, quite the contrary.

Every good salesman knows how to exaggerate, how to sell himself and his products. Mother never understood that Father's little boasts were inseparable from his brilliance as a salesman. She blamed his deprived background for the habit. In the end, she had to learn to live with it, since no amount of lecturing could cure him. To this day, a gullible old Indian customer of his believes me to be a veritable Croesus. "His father has left him a fortune," he tells interested parties, and nothing will persuade him otherwise. Father was a good salesman.

It may not have been wise of him to boast, but Father had good reason to be proud of his achievements. He built up three careers from scratch— first in Alsace-Lorraine, then in Schötmar and, finally, in England when he was nearing sixty. He was a good son, brother, husband, and father, and more than fulfilled his family responsibilities—not a bad record.

After World War I, Father suffered for being a German, as he was later to suffer more cruelly for being a Jew. There was no future for him in Metz as a German after World War I, and he lost all his possessions there. As soon as the war ended, he came to Mother's hometown. He brought no furniture, but he brought his dog, a St. Bernard. Mother did not care for animals, especially around the house. They were harbingers of dirt and disorder.

She accepted the St. Bernard as one of the burdens of married life, as she did Father's habit of asking old army cronies and their wives to come and stay. They were not the refined people she had hoped to entertain; she did not care for some of their language. In time, she managed to weed out most of them.

Father was less liberal than Mother with the intimate details of his life, but the early years of marriage cannot have been easy for him either. Here was a man, thirty-five years of age, set in his ways, who had lost his home, his business, his possessions. Here was a man steeped in French culture, who had landed in Schötmar, a place thick with *têtes carrèes*. After basking for a while in the splendours of bilingual Metz, he was back where he started—in a backwater.

Schötmar, as I knew it, was a town of some five thousand souls, a little larger than Father's native Laubach, a little more industrialized, the grubby sister of Bad Salzuflen, the smart spa, some half an hour's walk away. Laubach had its *Marktplatz*, Schötmar its *Rathausplatz*; Laubach had its counts Solms zu Laubach, Schötmar its barons von Stietenkron, each with a *Schloss* (castle), each with its *Schlosspark*. Both my parents hailed from small towns, but Father had transcended his background as Mother had not done. She retained her small-town vision.

Father had married into a family without culture. They did not read books, did not play or listen to serious music, had no interest in literature, no intellectual curiosity—none of the qualities or interests for which German Jewry was famous. The house was full of cattle dealers. The men talked cattle prices, the women engaged in tittle-tattle. Father had little in common with these people, but he adapted.

Father was a great adapter. He had a knack of moving across cultural, social, and personal divides. He spoke and acted as the occasion demanded. He was everybody's friend.

Everybody included hotel maids, porters, and waiters. When they were on holiday, Mother, her glass-eyed silver fox dangling over a smart blue costume, liked to play the fine lady, gracious but distant. It was no use. Father joked, passed the time of day with every maid he encountered. Mother looked daggers, but she could not change his ways.

When he was working in London and I was helping him, he frequented a little teashop in Middlesex Street, just opposite Liverpool Street Station. It was run by a Welsh couple. Somehow, they understood his broken English and he their Welsh lilt. Soon he was on the best of terms with them. Had he not lived in Cardiff himself and was he not therefore an honorary Welshman? Yes, they had a lot in common.

One of the teashop regulars was a tall gaunt dustman with a purple face and a goitre so awful it put me off my cheese roll. The thing hung there, where his Adam's apple should have been, like a fat red sausage. I could not bear to look at it. The dustman became Father's best friend in the place. As soon as one of them entered the café, he headed for the other's table. They talked of garbage collection and the sins of the government towards those who collected it; they talked of the traffic and of the difficulties of making a living. I once mentioned the goitre to Father. He shut me up. "He is a human being." (*Er ist ein Mensch.*)

The moment he got on a London bus, Father sought human contact. He eyed the charlady opposite. She was on her way to work. "Vee vorkink people," he told her conspiratorially, moving nearer, "vee haff to look after ourselfs." This was a favourite opening gambit. The cleaner would agree wholeheartedly and pour out her troubles. If she noticed Father's grey overcoat from Simpsons in Piccadilly, his smart grey homburg from Locks, the St. James' Street hatters, or the grey spats, she gave no sign of it. Father put up no barriers.

Once they had sorted out the world between them, Father's new friend would try to draw me into the conversation. "Is that your son?" she would ask, giving me a friendly smile. I sat there tongue-tied, squirming. I was an intellectual, after all. I had no idea what to say to the woman. When we got off the bus, I got a lecture:

"Don't sit there like a dummy! Talk! This is training for life. One must declare one's solidarity." This was a communist slogan Father had picked up and made his own.

It was not all pretence. He genuinely loved human beings in all their variety, not very deeply perhaps, but with an amused tolerance and interest. He never looked down on anyone. True, he did not greatly care for the work-shy, but even here humour broke through. When he saw the great British public standing around and gawking at the workers on building sites after the war, he nudged me, eyes twinkling. "Look how they sweat just watching other people work."

Father's ability to take people and situations as he found them stood him in good stead when he came to settle in Schötmar. To Grandfather, he talked business, to Grandmother religion. He might complain to

Mother in private, but I never heard a cross word pass between him and that difficult pair. He did not get involved in disputes, and he did not take sides. He never mastered the intricacies of the cattle trade—who but an insider would—but once cornered, he was a good listener, and he kept his eyes open. He could produce perfect imitations of the local grotesques.

Even Grandfather agreed that Father could not be expected to go into the cattle trade. But what was to be done with the *ex-Lappenfritze*, who had arrived on his doorstep to marry his daughter?

"You won't make a go of textiles in Schötmar, any more than your father did in Laubach," he told Father. "There are no sheep for wool. This is cow country. And we don't grow cotton here. But we grow wood. The Teutoburger Forest is full of it. How about a brush factory? I'll help you to get started." And he did. He sent Father to a brush factory to get his hands dirty and learn the trade, and meanwhile looked for a place to start the factory.

On 19 March 1919, three months before their marriage, my parents started their factory in rented rooms. Grandfather offered them his home as their home. Mother would have been delighted, but Father would not hear of it. So they began their marriage, like their factory, in rented rooms. It was a comedown for both of them. For the first years of their marriage, they lived above Hansmeyer's shop, which I remember for its toys. It was a few doors away from my grandparents' house.

Very early in their life together, my parents began a division of labour that was to benefit both their business and their marriage. Father, inspired salesman, kept the factory rolling with orders; Mother's job was to make sure that the goods would go out according to specifications. He, the stranger who had come from afar, went off once more on his sales campaigns, glad to get away from the small, backward town that was Schötmar—and perhaps from his parents-in-law; she, the local girl, held the fort. I see her now, as she moved from department to department, organizing, advising, supervising, directing, coaxing, and mollifying.

On weekends they came together, exchanged news, planned ahead, happy in each other's company. Both were strong characters, and I never had the feeling that one of them was the boss. Like William and Mary, they exercised joint sovereignty over their domain. Father, like William of Orange, was the stranger who had come to his wife's kingdom. Mother was not queen consort but queen sovereign. They were equal partners, a fact recognized by the German government after the war, when it awarded them equal pensions.

Grandfather saw that the seeds he had planted had not fallen on stony pavements, as he felt they had in Cologne. He decided to give my parents the meadows behind his house to build a factory there, with space for a plentiful supply of logs. He was getting old, he said, and no longer wanted to keep so many cows. There was one condition: his beloved daughter and her mate were to share his house. No doubt, this was also a means whereby he could escape from his wife's company. In the spring of 1924, my parents began to build their factory and surrendered their independent life.

A year later, tragedy struck. After a difficult birth, my sister Margot briefly saw the light of day. She was born with a cranial malformation and died after nine days. Her death left a deep impression on Mother. She shrank from Aunt Alma's other daughter, who was handicapped, and from any other such children that crossed her path. She called them "unfortunate children" (*unglückliche Kinder*) and always expressed great sympathy for the parents.

Mother and I stood in front of the little tilted stone in the shady grove that served as the Jewish cemetery. She wiped away a tear with one of her tiny, lace-edged handkerchiefs. "I know it was better this way," she sighed. "Our lives would have been ruined."

She squeezed my hand and then tidied up the warring factions of my thick brown hair. No occasion was too sacred to tidy me up when I was looking *ungepflegt*—one of Mother's favourite words—"ungroomed" is perhaps the closest English equivalent. "We did not know if we would ever have another child, but God heard our prayers and sent you to us."

Chapter Nine

CONCEIVED IN PARIS

I like to think that I was conceived in Paris on my parents' honeymoon. I cannot claim to be the product of their first raptures, since the honeymoon took place seven years after the wedding. There had been no time for such frivolities while they were nursing their new factory.

Margot's birth had been difficult and had left its mark on Mother. Father insisted that she needed a holiday, but it was not until the autumn of 1926 that he was able to take her to Paris. They went by train, second class, and stayed in a good hotel. They called it their honeymoon.

The bride had never been out of Germany before. The groom still spoke perfect French and proved a good guide.

"We went up the Eiffel Tower and Vati showed me the landmarks, even though he suffers from vertigo. Paris is so well laid out."

Mother was even more impressed by the palaces and the undreamt-of elegance of their interiors.

"Vati took me to Versailles. Such taste. Such perfect proportions. How I would love to have such rooms. I wanted to run my hands along the sideboards but the attendants wouldn't let me."

Mother sighed with longing for the exquisite furniture that could have graced her drawing room. She had only one criticism. "I could have done with less gold. I know it is a palace, but the gold is overdone."

Mother kept the vision of French elegance in her heart. When she came to furnish her Blue Salon, she confessed that she was looking for velvet curtains in the same shade of blue as Marie Antoinette's.

The elegance of the *Parisiennes* also left its mark. Mother spent much time in shops and department stores, investigating how she could take a little Parisian *Schick* back to Schötmar.

It needed patience to shop with Mother, and Father was not a patient man. As she pondered over the various choices, he told her to stay where she was and wandered off. Mother was thrown back on the knowledge of French she had acquired at her alma mater. And how did the alumna of Bad Salzuflen's *Höhere Töchterschule* acquit herself in Europe's most elegant tongue? On a quest for an easy-to-wash blouse, *Waschbluse* in German, Mother went up to an assistant and confronted her with the following demand:

"Madame, donnez-moi s'il vous plait une blouse pour la vache?"

"Mais Madame," said the astonished saleswoman, not knowing whether to laugh or to call for a doctor. She and Mother went in search of *Monsieur*, who was able to explain his wife's puzzling tastes.

I could never get enough of the cow blouse story. Father told it with a straight face. Only his eyes twinkled. Then he made me practice.

"Le boeuf, der Ochs,
La vache, die Kuh,
Fermez la porte, die Tür mach zu."

Mother's smile was very faint indeed. Humour was not her strong point. That is why Father and I so enjoyed teasing her.

It is just possible that I was conceived on cow blouse night—in laughter, at least on Father's side. The Paris dates fit. I was born on 11 July 1927, at the Catholic Hospital in Herford, and delivered, like my sister, by Caesarean section. My birth too was a difficult one. Mother's gynaecologist, Dr. Wolters—"such beautiful manners, he really admired me"—strongly advised against more children. I had to carry my parents' hopes for the future alone. The long-awaited son and heir of parents no longer young—Father was forty-three, Mother almost thirty-four—I enjoyed the privileges and suffered the drawbacks of being an only child.

I was duly circumcised and given my Jewish name: Joseph ben Naphtali, ha Cohen—Joseph, son of Naphtali, the priest. At least I think that was it. When it came to Bar Mitzvah time, Father thought that I had been named after his father, but he was not sure, which shows how often my Jewish name was used.

His mother did not suckle the young priest. Her advisory panel of old women told her that breast-feeding was bad for the figure and not particularly good for the baby either. So, I was farmed out to a wet nurse, and weaned early. Thereafter, I endured the cold embraces of a succession of nurses. Perhaps they were not all cold. But nothing can replace the warmth of one's own mother. Mother herself had second thoughts.

"If only I could have stayed at home to raise you myself," she told me when I was in my teens. "But we were working for your future, building up the factory. Well, it's too late now, and you have grown up a good boy just the same."

Perhaps, but a very insecure one.

In my very first very vague memory, I am climbing up something brown and wet and slippery. True to my nature, I slip and scratch my knees. Tears mingle with blood. The squat nurse picks me up and comforts me, as well she might. A moment of inattention is no excuse, as Miss Prism later found to her cost.

There were no mystic moments in the rose garden. I never felt one with the universe. On the contrary, I was forever banging my knees against it.

"That boy never looks where he is going," commented Grandfather, not one of my admirers. "I don't know where it will end."

That early brush with the universe was by the fountain in the front garden. Four thin streams issued from curved sprouts that spun round and round. Some of the water trickled onto the mossy stones that backed up the basin and made them very slippery. Hence, my fall.

I loved this part of the garden. I toddled along the grass between the fountain and a small box tree, taking care on the way to step with my dirty bootees onto a small white pedestal, which also held a flower pot. Or I might lean against the box tree and contemplate the peeling stucco garden wall that grew old men's faces, dogs or horses—the images changed with my moods and the seasons.

Opposite, a profusion of violet clematis and copper-coloured leaves almost hid the garden side of the house. For reasons best known to them, Grandfather and his architect had endowed this sunny side of the house with several false windows.

At the far end of the lawn, separating the front garden from the long vegetable garden that ran along side the factory, there was a grotto, made from the brownish mossy stones like those near the fountain. Spiders spun their webs across the stones without fear of interruption. In the house, their spinning never got very far. However high the ceiling, Mother had a brush with a handle long enough to reach the offenders and destroy their work, and them too, if possible.

I liked to lie there in a hammock strung between the grotto and the tall lime tree, watching the spiders, smelling the sweet blossoms above me, and swaying gently. This is one of the few really happy moments I recall from early childhood. All the others are painful, like the fall by the fountain.

During my babyhood, my mother had a committee of grannies who subscribed to the diabolical theory that it was good to let children cry. It would teach them to behave themselves and build character. So I was left to scream until I grew tired of screaming.

Mother had a deep respect for older women. Our houses were always swarming with them. When she was forty, they were about sixty. When she was sixty, she surrounded herself with eighty-year-olds.

At the back of our house, separated from it by a paved yard, was the *Bürohaus*, our office building. Only the ground floor was used as offices. The upper floor had bedrooms that served as an overflow when we had guests. Sometimes I had to sleep there, alone, in one of those bare white rooms. My nursemaid had a room there, but she had other duties too and helped with the cleaning. If Mother had been there to hear me, her instincts might have brought her to my aid, but she was in the factory and the staff followed instructions. It seems incredible now that caring parents—and they were caring—could have left me alone in the office building when the house was full of guests.

While sleeping there, I had the one childhood dream that I still remember—less dream than nightmare. I saw the perimeter of our property, where the timber yard bordered the railway line, surrounded by a wall of fire. Out of the fire there rose fearful, fiery, orange and black demons, hundreds of them, small but deadly, baring their teeth, licking their tongues. I was trapped. I knew I could not get past them. They blocked every exit. I woke up, screaming. A prophetic dream?

I was scared of noises, scared of Grandfather, scared of men with beards, and scared of animals, especially dogs. It started with one particular dog. Father's huge St. Bernard was still around when I was a baby. The ancient beast appointed itself my protector from strangers. Apparently, I was the love of its life, but I mistook its intentions. It frightened the life out of me, as it pestered me with noisy, slobbering, unwanted affection. I remember crying as a huge, four-legged presence licked me with a giant tongue. Perhaps it thought that crying was my form of barking.

In extreme old age, the old retainer signed his own death warrant by killing our neighbour's chicken. He had to be destroyed, much to Father's grief and Mother's relief. We never had another dog, nor did we have a cat, a budgie, or even a goldfish. Some frogs croaked by the fountain at times, but they were transitory migrants, too slippery for friendship. My early companions were all humans.

There was teddy, but he was almost human, an alter ego. One sepia edged studio photo shows the two-year-old with his woebegone stuffed-animal companion, fatty with well-brushed hair, all smart in frill-fronted blouson shirt and outsize velvet pants with shiny mother-of-pearl buttons, standing on that photographer's standby, the fur rug, while teddy sits disconsolately at his well-shod feet. This photo was followed about a year later by a three-year-old with a Mona Lisa smile, arrayed in a brown velvet two-piece, sitting with teddy on the inevitable fur rug. Teddy is by now an even limper specimen. His long arms hang down his sides like an ape's. The photos could not do justice to his jaundice-yellow skin.

On my fourth birthday, a day full of promise, Grandmother gave me a gorgeous canary yellow cart, with tomato-red wheels and handle. I inaugurate a brand new smock in honour of the day, a lilac affair with a band of darker braid around what in a less pudgy specimen would have been a waist. The braid is embroidered with a ferment of fishes. One eyed, they stare at me, and I stare back as I admire my new outfit and myself in it.

Decked out in this finery, I take the cart to the courtyard between our residence and the *Bürohaus*. The cart is made entirely of wood—nuts, cogs, bolts, and all. Not a single piece of metal with which a small boy could do himself damage. But the makers have not reckoned on one small boy. The handle indicates that the cart is meant to be pulled, perhaps with a teddy inside. I soon grow tired of this and decide to have a go at sitting in it myself. I roll up and down the courtyard, using my hands for locomotion when necessary.

The yard is paved with large rectangular stones. They are flat and even, but with gaps between them and these prove my undoing. The cart is clumsily put together—Grandmother does not believe in throwing away money—and I am no featherweight. The loose contraption, laden with a pudgy, clumsy four-year-old, just cannot take the repeated encounters with the gaps. It comes completely apart, tomato-red wheels scattering in every direction.

In a cart without a large handle I might have landed on my bottom, protected from the stones by the seat of the cart. But the handle gets stuck in one of the gaps and I fall forward on my face. Blood streams from my nose and from my ever-sensitive knees. I am not one to nurse my wounds quietly and cut my losses. Soon it is clear to all who have good ears to hear, and even to those who are hard of hearing, that a young person has sustained damage to property and, in the process, suffered grievous bodily harm, and all that on his birthday. My new cart is a write-off, my new smock is in shreds, and so are my knees. No wonder I remember that day so very clearly

We often took walks in and around the beautiful *Kurpark* in Bad Salzuflen, where photographers lay in wait to snap the spa guests. They still do. Most of the early nonstudio family photos were taken by these paparazzi. In the earliest photo, I am about two years old, dressed in a long white blouse that almost covers my short pants but cannot hide my robin-like paunch. I am guarded by four females. Walking on either side are my two older cousins from Cologne, the dark Gisela and the blonde Ingelore. Making up the rear are our respective nursemaids, theirs short and dark, mine, Else, is tall and blonde with the face and figure of a film star.

My beloved Else must have been about sixteen when she first came to us, and she was to stay more than five years, until those twin disasters, her marriage and the Nuremberg Laws, took her away from me. Until then, we were inseparable.

Also pictured in Bad Salzuflen is a slimmer four-year-old standing in front of two mountains, his mother and the enormous Frau Birkholz, who keeps turning up in family photos like a big, bad penny. She was the wife of an important customer and came from eastern Germany—Potsdam, I think. She must have thought the long journey worthwhile since she made it so often.

A child is supposed to have a leg-eye view of the world, but I remember faces. Frau Birkholz's was purplish red and fell in layer upon layer of fat. She had dark button eyes, a small nose and black ringlets that made her face look even bigger. Like most of the older women I knew, she had lots of wart-like protuberances.

In another photo from that period, a very dapper little boy in short-sleeve white shirt, smart navy pants and white shoes and socks is holding the hand of a mother looking larger than ever in her *crepe de chine*, navy and white check two-piece. Mother's face and body were all of a piece, unlike the layered Frau Birkholz. She was more big than fat. In this photo, her expression is mild but her hair style is very severe with her long hair pulled back tightly into a knot.

The next photo is a distinct change—I have become a lanky six-year-old and I wear a sensible shirt and sensible short pants, with sensible brown shoes and striped socks. It is a sunny day in the country. This time I am among men. The group could have passed for Chicago gangsters on an outing. Father is in a double-breasted grey suit with white pocket handkerchief, grey homburg and spats; Karl, the chauffeur has a similar outfit, *sans* the homburg and the spats. Herr Koschni from Düsseldorf, the only one of Father's army cronies to have survived Mother's purges, is dressed more sensibly in a short-sleeve shirt, his beer-gut chafing at the constraint of grey flannels. He was a square-headed friendly man who sometimes played games with me. His loud voice went with the rest of him.

The real gem of these early photographs is a half-length studio portrait of a bare-chested four-year-old with large ears, fleshy nose, well-formed mouth, benevolent almond eyes of considerable beauty and just the suggestion of a double chin. A dark kiss curl falls over his forehead, almost down to the right eyebrow—a fashion copied by the *Führer*. This photo formed the model for a half-length portrait in oils that Mother commissioned for her new salon. It was later acquired by the S.S. together with other chattels of greater value.

Chapter Ten

BORN INTO A FACTORY

"*Das eine Wort: Ich muss!*" Mother lingered over the double *ss* as she shoved and kicked aside the mountainous featherbed under which she was roasting. She emerged, yawning but determined, in sky-blue winceyette pyjamas patterned with delicate royal blue forget-me-nots. It was 5:25 a.m. precisely.

"Really, Mutti. How can you say 'the single word: I must'? Can't you see that 'I must' is two words?"

In summer I often got up before Mother. I was fresh and newly numerate, and ready for an argument. Mother did not oblige. She was not given to logic chopping, especially so early in the morning. She must have known in her gut that a personal pronoun is married to its verb—whom God has joined.

Ignoring my remarks, she trotted out another old favourite to reinforce her resolve to be done with the warm embrace of that featherbed.

"*Die Pflicht, sie ruft, und ich muss folgen!*"

"*Ich muss*" again—beloved tenet of duty-loving Germans. "Duty calls and I must follow!"

What actually called was an alarm clock—large, round, loud. and with Roman numerals—to be replaced in later years by a sleek green leather travelling model with Arabic numerals and a softer sound. The clock was calling on behalf of the slumbering brush factory, waiting to be reborn into activity.

Father snored peacefully on. His call would come at 2:45 a.m. on Monday. He would be ready to leave for Hamburg or Cologne at 3:30 a.m. sharp, driven by Karl, his chauffeur and friend. He had to be the first salesman to see the wholesale or department store buyers as they reopened at 8:00 a.m. precisely.

It was rare for Father to be at home during the week. He was on the road, returning in triumph on Friday afternoon with a full order book. Meanwhile, Mother used her considerable diplomatic and organizational skills to run the factory. I believe she was the only woman in the area, certainly the only Jewish woman, to run a large business, and she ran it very successfully. The factory employed more than eighty people.

By 6:30 a.m., Mother had completed her ablutions, her knee bends and arm exercises, eaten a perfunctory breakfast of coffee and rolls, and inspected the house. I followed her about like a puppy. I had to make the most of the time when she was at home.

"Look at the dust on this sideboard. It's not just the legs. They don't even dust the top. If I've told them once, I've told them a hundred times."

Mother's eyes turned heavenward, while I expressed the disgust expected of me. With vigorous swipes of the duster, she removed the offensive particles. Her reprimands to the guilty though were always very mild. No wonder the staff never left.

Mother was dressed in her factory overall, dark blue brushed cotton with white spots. She wore a matching head scarf tied at the back under her bun. It protected her hair from the sawdust. There was a small pencil behind her right ear. She never entered the factory without that pencil. It was the only outward sign of her authority, since she dressed exactly like the other women workers. Her shoes had seen better days. The bunions had pressed too long against the leather, and it was starting to show its grey inner parts. A strap ran across the broad expanse of brown stocking.

"Oh, how I envy women with small narrow feet," Mother sighed. "They can wear such elegant shoes." In her younger days, Mother had tried to squeeze her feet into elegance, hence the bunions.

By 6:40 a.m., Mother was at the back of the factory, closely followed by her offspring. The butchers, hefty men with bullet heads, were waiting with their carthorses or vans. They came to collect the previous day's sawdust and wood chippings, which they needed for their floors and their *Räucherkammern*, the rooms in which they smoked their delicious hams and sausages.

As they loaded the sacks, I pumped them for information. "*Guten Morgen, Herr Kutschera*," I addressed a tall, fine-looking specimen of German butcherhood. "*Haben Sie heute schöne Frankfurter?*"

Yes, Herr Kutschera had good frankfurters. I would try to persuade Else to take me to Bad Salzuflen, where Herr Kutschera had his shop—with Mother's permission, of course.

By 7:00 a.m., Mother had met her expenses for the day. "While Anna Hamlet is still dreaming in her bed, I have earned more than she gets from her husband for a week's housekeeping." Anna Hamlet was Mother's friend, a thin pale woman who had married beneath her into the cattle dealer's family across the road. She came from the Hanover area, where they spoke the most correct German, and her careful accent was widely imitated.

Mother rarely boasted, but she was speaking to Father. She always felt that she had to convince him that she was doing her bit, for if there was one kind of person Father detested more than a lazy man, it was a lazy woman.

"They sit at home and cultivate their behinds!" (*Die sitzen zu Hause und pflegen sich den Hintern!*) It was enough to make a man see red. Father actually turned red, and his eyes blazed whenever he came across a flagrant example of idle womanhood, especially if it was fur coated, bejewelled, and had painted its fingernails.

Mother made sure she was blameless. She put in a twelve-hour day; she was first in the factory and last out. She *was* the factory. After the butchers had left, she went into consultation with Drexhage, the factory manager, a rather ugly red-haired man in charge of the technical side of the plant. He knew the ins and outs of every machine and was always addressed as *Meister* (Master).

When she had finished with Meister Drexhage, Mother hurried to the empty office to open the post and filter out letters not meant for other eyes. While she was reading, I tinkered with Fräulein Nagel's typewriter.

Mother called me over to her desk. "Hurry up or you'll be late for Kindergarten," she said as she bent down to kiss me. She was a big woman, but she kept in shape with those exercises. They made her puff a bit, but she did them every morning "with iron diligence" (*mit eisernem Fleiss*)—another German favourite.

She handed me an envelope. "On your way, take this to Frau Profet."

Fat sickly Frau Profet lived above Aunt Alma. Her son, Hans, later to turn Nazi, worked for us. I knew what Father did not know, that Mother used some of her sawdust petty cash to help employees or their dependants. It made her a popular employer. For her, it was duty (*Pflicht*).

As soon as I was back from Kindergarten, I ran to find Mother, heavy with the weight of the news I had to impart. It was sometimes difficult to find her.

"*Wo ist meine Mutti, Fräulein Kaiser?*" Fräulein Kaiser, the office supremo, brown, dumpy, tight-corseted, bent down as far as she could without splitting. Her voice said, "Your Mutti is not here. Go and look for her in the factory." Her grimace said, "How dare the brat come here at all hours and disturb my office routine."

I knew what she was thinking, but I did not care. What could she do to me? I was under the protection of a higher power. My mother ran Fräulein Kaiser as she ran everything else in my universe. Still, I was always glad to see the back of the nasty brown creature.

"*Wo is meine Mutti, August?*" A door led directly from the office building to the *Expedition*, the dispatch department, a long narrow room with a loading bay. August Beckmann was its overlord. He was tall with a yellow complexion and a face not unlike Benjamin Britten's. His dark curly hair, cut short, rose like a mop at the sides. I suspected him of being a rival stamp collector.

I could never prise enough stamps out of him, and we received plenty. Some came from as far away as India, Persia, and China. It was all to do with the raw materials for our brushes. Those magic names: *Piassava*, Madagascar, China, even *Rosshaar* (horsehair), and Delbanco, Meyer and Co., our raw material suppliers.

"Your mother was here ten minutes ago," said August. "I think she may have gone to the broom finishing room." I could read the Kaiser like an open book. August's expression gave nothing away, though I suspected he did not like stamp-collecting busybodies.

I left August to his packing cases and went to the room that housed the *Automat*, a machine so big it needed a room to itself. The bundles of fibre stacked against the factory wall were brought here to be cut down to size. Coarse brown *Piassava*, used for street brooms, was emerging neatly cut from the monster's cavernous interior on a conveyor belt. It reminded me of fairground cars coming out of a tunnel from darkness into light. My mission was to find Mother, but there were plenty of distractions on the way.

"Don't go too near, or you'll get hurt," warned the operator. Grown-ups were forever trying to shield me from the machines. Even though I was a timid little soul, machines never frightened me. I had grown up with them and knew their dangers. If my mother was the factory, the factory was also my mother. It surrounded my life like fluid in the amnion. I was practically born into it.

A pungent acidic smell announced the paint room, where brushes and brooms were sprayed. Our more highly finished products, like clothes brushes, hairbrushes, and hump-backed nail brushes of white China fibre, were dunked in great vats of lacquer. I loved the smell of lacquer and could not pass the vats without watching the ever-different patterns of streaky gold and red.

A steel contraption held the brushes on trays. The wooden backs were shaped so that the fibre side sloped gently upwards from the edges. The trays were lowered to just the right degree for the lacquer to cover the wood to where the first row of China fibre or pigs' *Borste* began. It was a skilled operation.

Even after sixty years, the lacquer on our old clothes brushes still shines; the fibres are still regular and strong. The base of the clothes brush is smooth and rounded, slightly concave, which makes for easier handling. The side of the base is indented and very smoothly polished, a perfect fit for the thumb on one side and four fingers on the other. The fibres are regularly spaced and fan outwards. This makes for more efficient brushing. You hold the brush at a slight angle, and dirt and dust, those enemies of the German soul, capitulate immediately. And the glaze! The glaze on our lacquer brushes (*Glanzbürsten*) was the glory of Hermann Katz and Co. It was renowned throughout Germany as German workmanship at its best. We gave value for money. No wonder our order books were always full.

A little further towards the back of the factory, on the right hand side, there was a room where several women worked at a long table, putting the final touches on the horsehair brooms. The brooms were cheap and ugly, strictly functional, not meant to please. The horsehair was rust coloured, the backs were bright scarlet, and the finish was crude—very different from the clothes brushes. August had thought that Mother might be there.

I walked carefully up the three steps to the room, poked my head around the opening, covered my eyes with my fingers, and peeked through the gaps. If I did not see my mother, I would grimace, stand there awhile, then bolt down the steps and run off as fast as my legs would carry me.

I was not afraid of machines, but I was afraid of one woman in that room. She worked near the window. She did not move her face and carried on with her work, but she had seen me. Her eyes seemed to follow me everywhere. Other female eyes softened, faces broadened into smiles, when they saw the little dumpling cavorting round the factory. "He has such a sweet smile," they said, "such soft rosy skin, and look at that wavy dark hair. He's good enough to eat." This woman just stared ahead with piercing black eyes and not a flicker of a smile. She was big and swarthy with straight jet black hair, her skin a shade darker than that of the fair-skinned beauties around her. She did not gossip like the other women. In fact, I never saw her speak to anyone.

I had never heard of the *malocchio*, the evil eye. This was Schötmar, not Naples. But as an avid follower of the Brothers Grimm, I knew all about witches. I shared my suspicions with some of the factory girls. One of them burst out laughing and said, "That one has just eloped with a sixty-sevener." (*Die ist gerade mit einem siebensechziger durchgebrannt.*) After that, they always laughed when I came into the room. But the scary woman did not laugh.

At that time, my head was full of the battles led by great German warriors like Frederick the Great (*Der alte Fritz*), von Moltke, and so on. So I understood the "sixty-seven" to refer, not to the man's age, but to the campaign in which he had fought. I did not calculate that anyone who had fought in 1867—if it was indeed a fighting year—would have been well into his eighties, though, as Mother would have said, "Age is no protection against folly." (*Alter schützt vor Torheit nicht.*)

It did not surprise me that a witch would do something as awful as eloping. I had not the vaguest notion what eloping was, but the German equivalent, *durchbrennen* literally, "burning through" gave me a very good idea of how witches passed their time.

After these revelations, I took even more precautions as I peeped at her, just in case she burned me with her glance. One day I was doing my peep-and-run routine, and as I turned around, I almost ran into Mother. Her eyebrows rose, "Whatever are you doing?" she asked.

I took her arm. "We can't talk here. I have something secret to tell you." When we were out of earshot, I disclosed to my astonished parent that she harboured a witch in her factory.

Mother firmly shook her head. "I have never heard such nonsense. There are no witches. They don't exist. It's bad enough that Else and Erna teach you to sing pop songs [*Schlager*]. Now the girls at the factory put this nonsense into your head. I want no more of it. That woman is highly respectable and a good worker."

Mother did not punish. Her way was to admonish and exact promises. "Now, I want you to promise not to harass this lady and never to talk such nonsense again."

I promised and I always kept my promises to Mother, but as the song goes:

"*Die Gedanken sind frei.
Wer kann sie erraten?
Sie ziehen vorbei
Wie nächtliche Schatten.
Kein Mensch kann sie wissen,
Kein Jäger erschiessen.
Es bleibe dabei,
Die Gedanken sind frei.*"

(Thoughts are free.
Who can guess them?
They pass by like
the shadows of the night.
No man can know them,
no hunter shoot them.

And so let it be,
Thoughts are free.)

I still thought she was a witch and avoided her as I would a raging fire. I never knew why the woman left. One day she was gone. The girls did not know, and I did not dare ask Mother. My behaviour and the girls' laughter must have hurt. I feel sorry now that I may have caused her pain, all perhaps because she had an eye defect. Or did I see what others could not?

Years later, in London, I discovered that Mother harboured a similar fear and dislike of a neighbour to whom she had never spoken. She too was dark-eyed and swarthy. As Mother would say, "The apple doesn't fall far from the tree." (*Der Apfel fällt nicht weit vom Birnbaum.*)

"*Gustel, wo ist meine Mutti?*" I was in the room of the *Stanzmaschinen*. It was here that China met the Teutoburger Forest—rows of machines bound small bundles of China fibres or bristles with wire and noisily stamped them into the wood with drills. In this room, I was among my greatest admirers. I treated it like my own private Forest of Brindaban, a little Lord Krishna surrounded by devotees. In place of milkmaids, I had factory girls. They petted me, laughed with me, and told me tall stories.

Gustel Kampmann, a girl in her early twenties, was my number-one fan, and her devotion was returned. Open-faced, straightforward, uncomplicated, she was the kind of person I have always liked—my opposite in every way. She was tallish, dark blonde, and beautiful, which helped. She patted me on my cheek, "Your mother was here ten minutes ago. My guess is that she is down at the sawmill."

Gustel wore high-heeled shoes with a strap across, like Mother's, but she had smaller feet. Her three-quarter-length dress showed under her light overalls. Perhaps she was going out after work. I would look for Mother, but not yet.

"Gustel, will you let me help you?" She looked around to see if the coast was clear. She was the only one who actually let me operate her machine, under supervision, of course. She placed her hands over mine, so that nothing could go wrong. I was in heaven. I loved Gustel, and I loved the machine. The bundles of fibre met the wood with movements so quick and sharp that the wood could not resist. Then I remembered that this was merely a staging post. My true quest was for Mother.

Gustel's machine was fully engineered. No skill was required of her. Everything had been set up beforehand. In the next room, the largest in the factory and even noisier than Gustel's, were the men who operated the turning lathes. They were the factory's real artists. Once the machines had given the wood a rough shape, these men worked the brushbacks with graceful movements, their only tool a chisel. As the wood spun round on the lathe, they sculpted it into pleasing regular shapes. I liked to stroke the finished brushbacks. They were smooth, rounded, and uniform. And the men never even used a gauge! I would remember these artists some years later, when I was twelve years old.

I am sitting at the feet of the formidable Mr. Urban Hook, woodworking teacher and sadist. He wields the longest cane I have ever seen, to control and improve the skills of the Buckinghamshire village woodworking class, of which I am unfortunately a member. From his raised desk, only half bothering to look up from his prayer book, Mr. Hook metes out long distance retribution on the clumsy and the idle. "Pe'er Shaw, you are a bloomin' nuisance," he booms, as his cane bears down on the unfortunate Shaw's knuckles.

The bookshelf, on which I am labouring, is monstrously askew, and as the instrument of torture finds my unskilful hands, I see the steady fingers of our workmen, shaping a hand brush with a handle from a single piece of wood. The wood turns round and round, the chisel moves very little. Slowly the handle begins to look like a handle, now broader, now narrower, faultlessly shaped to provide a perfect grip.

The brushback room was the last one in the factory. I went out to the platform where the wood was brought in and ran down the steps into the timber yard. There was only one other place where Mother could be. A young fellow was unloading the trolley that plied between the woodwork room and the sawmill. It was stacked high with blocks cut down to brushback size. On its way back to the sawmill, it would be empty. I asked the young man if I could hitch a ride. He nodded his taciturn head. The trolley ran on a thin rail and was operated by manpower, a steel rope for pulling, two hands for pushing. Only one hand was needed to push me as I stood in front, like a captain on his bridge, surveying the ocean of timber around me.

The sawmill was a low-slung building not far from the boundary of our property, the railway line where the demons of my dream had cavorted. It was a year older than I was, a landmark of progress for my parents' firm. Unlike the factory, it was dark and gloomy with few windows. There was a smell of dank wood, and the air was thick with sawdust.

We had no cranes. Men levered the tree trunks onto a conveyor belt by means of long wooden poles with metal hooks attached. The trunks moved inexorably towards the ravenous saws, their teeth huge and curved like those of wild animals. They sliced the wood horizontally into the thicknesses needed for brush and broom backs. I feared those killer saws. They were different from machines. Father, who was infatuated with the ancient Phoenicians, had told me how Moloch swallowed his victims.

No use asking anyone near the saws about Mother. You could not hear yourself speak. Then I suddenly spotted her by the smaller unit that sawed the planks into blocks. I ran and hid my face in her overall. A fine layer of sawdust gently scratched my face.

Chapter Eleven

WEEKEND FATHER

Visiting customers often complimented my parents on the layout of their factory. It was a good layout. The brushbacks prepared at the rear of the factory met the fibres prepared at the front in the stamping machine room. The issue of this marriage of wood and fibre then moved forward to be lacquered and finished, and finally dispatched from the point nearest to the road.

"But where," the visitors asked the proud owners, or Meister Drexhage, if he was doing the honours that day, "where are the shaving brushes and the toothbrushes and the paint brushes made?"

There was a standard answer to that question, and it was a white lie.

"We have them made to specification in a smaller factory some distance away. We have no facilities for celluloid production here."

The truth was that we bought them from factories as far afield as Nuremberg and the Black Forest. We put on a good markup, even though we were acting only as wholesalers. Our badger shaving brushes were an expensive and high quality item. I knew because I tried them on my cheeks as a boy. They were wonderfully soft. And until a few years ago, I was still using one of them for shaving.

Father had no difficulty in passing them off as our own. He was a brilliant, and creative, salesman who was very popular with his customers. I only saw him at work in England, when he was no longer selling brushes, but the technique must have been the same, whatever he was selling: subtle compliments, especially to women buyers, casual dropping of the names of competitors who already enjoyed the advantage of buying from him, a joke or two, a sample for the wife, or for the household, and the sample order.

"Just take a dozen and try them out. You won't regret it. You'll be ordering a hundred dozen the following week. And if you don't like the sample dozen, just send them back. But I guarantee you won't find a better product. Any complaints, or, more likely, repeat orders, come back to me. I'll look after you."

It was not just sales talk. He had convinced himself first. And he liked and respected his customers. I was astounded to find him bowing to the telephone when they were on the other end of the line.

Father was rarely at home during the week. Sometimes, when he visited southern or eastern Germany, or exhibited at the Leipzig and Cologne fairs, he stayed away several weeks at a time.

From early Friday afternoon, I was on the lookout for the Green Nash and in later years, the dark blue Minerva. As soon as I spotted the car, I ran to the entrance of the Bürohaus, where they would stop and Karl would unload the cases, full of samples.

I put my arms around Father's neck, and he kissed me on the mouth. His small moustache rubbed against my face, and his stubble tickled. He must have shaved very early in the morning.

"I will call Mutti," I said, running to the factory with my familiar cry: "*Wo ist meine Mutti.*"

When I had found her, we ran to the office building. Mother took out the key to the *Privatkontor*, the private office, from her large bundle. I followed them in. Father took out the orders he had brought back. It was a kind of ceremony. Out came the sheets from the side pockets, the breast pocket, the lower inside pocket, the waistcoat pockets, the back trouser pocket, sometimes even from the small pocket in which he kept his watch and eyebrow brush.

There was a look of triumph on his face, and there was joy, as he basked in Mother's approval. She took the pencil from her right ear and made a note of the most urgent orders. Then she told Father about her successes and also of troubles with production. It was in the private office that I first heard the comparison between the busy sawdust seller and the recumbent housewife from across the road.

When there was a gap in the mutual flow of news, I squeezed in my questions:

"Vati, show me what you have brought home for me."

Mother looked shocked. "A polite boy does not ask such questions. He waits for his presents."

"But it's Vati. I can ask him."

"Not even Vati. The same rule applies for everybody. One waits."

"Tonight, when we've got more time, I'll show you, and you'll be surprised," said Father, smiling.

"Vati," I asked, when there was another gap, "did you see any *Wildschweine* this time?" Ever since Father had told me that driving one night through the Teutoburger Forest, he had seen a wild boar crossing the road, these animals had occupied my imagination.

"You'll have to wait till Sunday," he said, with a twinkle in his eye.

This time Mother ignored my remarks. Animals did not enter her consciousness, except as harbingers of dirt and disorder. Visitors' dogs, with their unwashed paws and surplus body hair, were on a par with cattle dealers' cow-dung-coated boots. After Father's St. Bernard had signed his own death warrant, no resident pet ever disturbed our routine again.

"Vati, how many robber baron castles did you see?" It was my third and last question, and again I was told to wait. My parents had more important matters to discuss. I did not mind. I took a keen interest in the factory. And I knew my time would come.

There were various parcels, some with nice wrapping paper, next to Father's samples. I had kept my eye on them, making sure they were taken to the house. Father never came home empty-handed. Even before the evening meal, I began unwrapping them. I yelped with delight as I uncovered the toys he had bought at a discount from his department store customers. I ran to kiss a beaming Father. Once he even brought home a small train set.

I liked toys, but things to eat were more important. There were chocolates, dried figs, bananas, dates, all things not readily available in Schötmar. One day he came home from Hamburg with a large slightly prickly brownish oval object with a top like a cactus. After our Friday evening meal, Mother cut it into slices, one piece for each one of us. After sampling my first juicy yellow morsel, I was hooked. I loved the smell and the look of it as well as its taste. When Father set out on another journey, I reminded him not to forget to bring home a pineapple.

The Friday evening meal was the most formal of the week. If he came home early, Father got Karl to drive him to the synagogue. He walked back because one was not supposed to drive on the Sabbath, his prayer book wrapped in paper. Before the meal, Father kissed Mother. Then he laid his hands on my head and blessed me in Hebrew. I wish he had said it in German. Then I could have understood it. After that, still with his hands on my head, he whispered in German, "*Gott lasse Dich werden wie Ephraim und Manasseh.*"

I sometimes wondered what was so special about Ephraim and Manasseh, for Father to ask God to make me like them. He had told me they were Joseph's sons. It was much later, in England, where I read the Bible, Old Testament and New, from cover to cover three times, that I learned the origin of this blessing. On his deathbed, the boys' grandfather, Jacob, had blessed Ephraim and Manasseh and instituted the blessing for future generations. Jewish girls have an even harder task. They are meant to become like Sarah, Rebecca, Leah, and Rachel.

Father broke off small pieces from the French loaf—his favourite—which we had on weekends as a special treat. He put some salt on each of the pieces and handed them out, first to Grandfather, then to Mother and me, each time repeating the ancient blessing over the bread and then over the wine.

He said these blessings very quietly and quickly, almost as if apologizing for them. He was usually the only religious person present, unless Moppi, professional *schnorrer* (scrounger) to the Jewish community, was invited, or had invited himself. Father took the commandments about hospitality seriously. Moppi was a godsend, a convenient object on which to exercise charity without too much trouble or expense. He was the archetypal *nebbish*, useless and ineffectual. Jewish communities often boasted at least one such *nebbish* and kept him going with handouts. Moppi was a little man, with reddish hair, none too clean, and no favourite of Mother's.

Women took no part in the proceedings. No hands went up in maternal blessing over lighted candles. Grandmother would not eat with us, even to welcome the Sabbath on Friday night. She did not trust the meat dishes, quite apart from the crockery and cutlery. Mother considered all ritual as hocus-pocus. In England, towards the end of Father's life, she started lighting candles on Friday night, carefully mouthing the blessing Father had taught her. Maybe she had grown more reconciled to her religion; maybe she wanted to make use of a pair of George III candlesticks she had acquired.

Father's palate was more refined than Mother's, but his demands were modest. The one thing on which he insisted was a good Friday evening soup, and wise man that he was, he liked Mother to prepare it. She did so, whenever she could. It was usually a beef soup with celery, leeks and carrots, and free-floating bits of beef which had become separated from the mother piece. Father liked his meat overcooked.

When the season was right, Mother made a *Frühlingssuppe*, a clear "spring soup" with fresh peas, lots of parsley and *Eierschwämmchen*, little egg sponges.

The soups were not up to the standard set by the legendary Mère Didier during Father's apprenticeship days in far-off Morhange. I was sometimes regaled with mouth-watering stories of her onion soups and other delights. But Father enjoyed whatever Mother made, and so did I. Anything was better than our Erna's cooking. If only Mother had invested as much energy in cooking as she did in cleaning.

After the meal, Father spent some time on his prayers, using a pocket prayer book that he had covered in brown paper, less for protection than to hide its nature from prying eyes. He was shy about his religion.

It was not all habit. Sometimes, as he said his prayers, he had that absorbed look that I also noticed when he listened to music that he loved. I think his belief in God was deep and genuine.

Father often found himself co-opted as *Vorbeter* (prayer leader) in the synagogue. Rabbis are learned men, not priests, and any male member of the community can lead the service. Father was a popular *Vorbeter* because he rattled off the prayers at a crackling pace, leaving people time to get on with more important business.

Sabbath morning Father had a lot of praying to do, but Sunday morning he was relaxed. It was the best time of the week. As soon as I was awake, I went to my parents' bedroom. There was that reassuring smell of stale urine. Father was home. Try as she might, Mother had not been able to wean him from the chamber pot. She had trained me always to use the lavatory, but it seemed that Father was too old to be housetrained. It did not bother him that he lived in the Middle Ages. He pulled up his white nightshirt and, chamber pot in hand, released a steady stream of golden liquid. Sometimes, when Mother was not around, I added my thinner, lighter coloured stream. We stacked the pot away in the commode by the side of Father's bed. Mother had a pot too in the commode on her side, but hers was always empty.

It was not to last. One day, soon after the new apartments had been opened, the chamber pots disappeared, never to re-emerge. Father's nightshirts vanished at the same time, and the last of the Old Believers, newly pyjamaed, had, *faute de mieux*, to enter the twentieth century and use the lavatory like the rest of us.

But back in the good old days, when I was small, the smell of urine still welcomed me on Sunday mornings. Mother was already rummaging about the house. Father was still in bed. He lay there on his side, a bald moustachioed innocent, pretending to be asleep. I knew he was pretending because he wasn't snoring. I crept into bed beside him. The next moment I was giggling helplessly. Father had turned around suddenly and was tickling me. He knew my most sensitive spots. If he got me in the armpits, I was helpless.

Then we got down to poetry and opera. "*Da draussen am Wall von Sevilla,*" he croaked. "*Wohnet mein Freund Lilas Pastia. Dort tanze ich den Seguidilla und trink Manzanilla. Bei meinem Freunde Lilas Pastia.*" In between the joys and sorrows of Carmen and Mignon and Martha, there were some fairly dirty ditties with which I could shock Mother later on and make Else and Erna laugh. I knew they were dirty from the reaction of my listeners, even when I could not catch the full meaning. Why, for instance, did the huntsman from Kurpfalz smear his behind with butter? Such a waste.

Other material was more on my level. "There was the old aunt, who was a wicked Frau; she neither washed nor combed herself, and was an old . . ." At this point, Father sang "tra la la" while I, to my own great amusement, supplied the missing *Sau* (sow).

When we were done with dirty rhymes, music, and poetry, I could get my most important questions answered.

"Vati, you were going to tell me about the wild boars." Vati obliged.

"Last Sunday night we were driving through the Teutoburger Forest, where the forest is very dense. It was pitch dark. Suddenly, there was this enormous boar in the middle of the road, caught in our headlights. It was the biggest boar I had ever seen."

I put my head under the featherbed and snuggled up to Father. I felt deliciously safe.

"His body was covered with black bristle."

"Like yours, Vati," I said.

"*Spitzbub* [rascal]. We could have made several clothes brushes out of him. You could see the ink skin under the bristle. He stood there with his huge snout, head down, hump up, snorting loudly, ready to charge. Karl knew what to do. He put his foot on the accelerator and made a fearful noise. The beast fled."

I knew Father was making it up. It did not matter. He gave me what I wanted to hear. It *could* have happened. There were wild boars in the Teutoburger Forest. The first time Father told me about seeing one, he really did. But I wanted him to produce a wild boar practically every week.

"Were you frightened, Vati?"

"Not for myself or Karl, only for the car. He might have charged. They weigh hundreds of pounds, you know. The Nash is a good car, but faced with several hundredweight of boar, it could have done a lot of damage."

"Could a boar kill a man, Vati?"

"No doubt about it. But they are getting rare these days, retreating deeper and deeper into the forest. Don't worry. You won't find one in Schötmar."

I wasn't worried. I was after vicarious thrills. Father obliged by making these shy animals into car attackers and man killers.

When the subject of wild boars had been milked dry, I turned to my other great interest, robber baron castles, but Father changed the subject.

"Now tell me something, *Spitzbub*, what did they teach you this week at school? Did you learn any poems?" Father's eyes laughed, but not his muscles.

"Only stupid drawings and silly games and rhymes, no proper poems." I wished Father had been our teacher in place of those two tall boring old Fräuleins. Then we might have learned some *real* poems. Real poems were Schiller's *Die Glocke* and *Die Bürgschaft*, and Heine's Donna Clara, with its great punch line, where the anti-Semitic woman finds out her beloved is a Jew. All these poems had a moral, but *Der*

Abt von St. Gallen was funny too. It was about this stately abbot, whose shepherd, sad to say, was smarter than he was.

> *"Es war 'mal ein Abt, ein gar stattlicher Herr,*
> *Doch schade, sein Schäfer war klüger als er."*

The bad-tempered emperor presented the abbot with three riddles. If he failed to solve them by a certain time, he would lose his living and perhaps his life. The abbot had a lot to lose.

> *"Wie Sonne glänzt sein feistes Gesicht,*
> *Drei Männer umspannen den Schmerbauch nicht."*

(His fat face shone like the sun,
three men could not span his stomach.)

These were my favourite lines. In the end, the abbot is saved by his humble shepherd who solves the riddles for him.

I asked Father to tell me again about his grandfather driving the sheep to Paris, but he wanted his breakfast. "We'll talk about it later. Now let me get ready."

Sunday breakfast was special. We were all together and there were rolls, French bread, and *Prinzkäse*, the nearest we could get to Camembert in our backwater. And Father had a large omelette. Erna's omelettes were always overdone, but any omelette in any form was a treat, one of which I was rarely considered worthy in my own right. I glanced sideways at Father's plate.

"Are you squinting again?" (*Schielst Du schon wieder?*) he said with his dry smile, and proceeded to cut me a slice of omelette. I tucked it carefully into the roll I was saving for my final treat, after I had finished the *Prinzkäse*.

"So, it's not enough. You are squinting again, *Monsieur le gourmand.*" Another piece of omelette came my way. The roll grew higher until yellow exceeded brown. At one time I had so stuffed myself that when I came to the precious roll, I could barely finish a quarter of it.

There was another side to Father, his red side. The heavy featherbeds (*plumeaux*) under which we sweated had been deprived of their white covers and given a beating. I was to suffer a like fate. For a little fatty, I was quite nimble, clambering over these billowy mounds of red to what I thought was safety, but Father was behind me, beating the air, lashing about before he had even cornered me. Once he had me, I got the beating of my life. I held up a feather mountain as a shield. He snatched it away. I used my hands to avert his blows but could not avert them. Face, arms, legs, seat, he beat anything he could lay his hands on. His face and my body were as red as the featherbeds.

Mother, alerted by my cries, rushed in. "Hermann, Hermann," she cried, "how could you?" She tried to come between us and nearly got hit herself. In the end, she was able to save me from further blows. Father calmed down as quickly as he had blown up, but I nursed my wrongs. There were three or four other beatings, surprisingly few, considering Father's temper. They were always handed out in anger—none of this "it hurts me more than it hurts you" business. This was red rage.

The beatings never really turned me against Father. It was only in adolescence that real conflict arose as the difference in our characters became more apparent. During childhood I saw so little of Father that every moment of the weekend was precious. The stories, poetry, opera, and history created a bond between us. We were almost fellow conspirators because Mother did not know what we were talking about, and we could tease her about her ignorance.

On Sunday afternoon, we often walked to Bad Salzuflen, sometimes with friends. When we returned, Father and Karl packed up the car with samples. By 7:30, Father was in bed. At 3:00 on Monday morning, he was up. About 3:30, he and Karl set off. By 8:00, Father was seeing his first department store buyer in Hamburg or Frankfurt.

Chapter Twelve

A FORAY INTO ORTHODOXY

Else and I ran hand-in-hand to the *Schlosspark*, the castle grounds. We found a bench by some roses and celebrated our freedom by digging into the contraband sandwiches that had been languishing in Else's luggage.

We bit into the thick rye bread and savoured the juicy interior layer. Here was real food.

By this time, the fat was oozing out of the *Mettwurst*. Some found its way onto my beige jumper.

"Do you think anyone will notice, Else?"

Else shook her blonde head.

"We'll get it off with hot water."

"And do you think our breaths will smell of *Mettwurst*?"

Else was used to reassuring her anxious charge.

"Of course not, and I have some apples to eat afterwards."

I remembered those jumbo sandwiches once I had been introduced to the English tea ceremony, with its dainty crustless apologies for a sandwich. You could stuff three of those into your mouth when no one was looking, and hardly notice the difference.

Well satisfied with my *Mettwurst*, I pulled Else along towards the castle. This castle was not my ideal, since it was in fairly good repair and not situated on a crag. But it was a proper castle with round towers, turrets, and a moat, not like the symmetrical little palace of the Stietenkrons back in Schötmar. I was hoping that Count Solms zu Laubach would be out there inspecting his domain, but I never caught sight of him. I overheard my relatives telling my parents that when the Nazis tried to arrest an employee, a social democrat, the count took out a shotgun to defend him. That was in the early days. Later on, like so many others, he had to conform.[9]

We were on our annual pilgrimage to Laubach, Father's birthplace. We went every year for the High Holidays to visit Grandfather Joseph and Father's sister, Aunt Helene, and her husband, Josef Strauss. They were very orthodox in that they kept the Sabbath very strictly, had a kosher household, and did a lot of praying. While they did not dress up in those black eighteenth-century costumes of Polish noblemen that you see on the streets of Stamford Hill or Golders Green, they would not have approved of *Mettwurst* sandwiches.

When we visited our relatives in Cologne, we usually went by train, but Laubach was what Mother called *ein Nest* (a hamlet, a hole), though her own Schötmar was not much better. A car was essential.

The green Nash was roomy and shaped rather like a London taxi, but with a longer bonnet. Sometime in the midthirties, the Nash was replaced by a lower-slung dark blue Minerva. It was of Belgian make. Henry Ford drove one. It was said to be his favourite car. The Nash had been large; the Minerva was enormous. Father said he needed a larger car to house all his samples. On this occasion, we were the samples.

Father sat in front with his friend Karl. Mother and Else spread themselves on the backseat, which could seat four with ease. I sat on one of the folding seats facing them, so that I could talk to Father through the open glass partition. Karl was quite a ladies' man and sometimes I heard the two of them laughing about adventures I only half understood. Mother and Else were safely out of earshot.

We travelled more or less due south. At first the country was rather flat, no use to me at all. Like Catherine Morland, the heroine of *Northanger Abbey*, I was besotted with Gothic ruins. And a good ruin needs to stand on a hill. Father told me stories about robber barons and their castles when I crept into his bed on Sunday mornings. All safe and snug in bed, I could let my imagination run riot.

---

[9]   During the war, Father met the count's brother when both men were interned for a while as "enemy aliens" on the Isle of Man.

I had a clear picture in my mind of what occurred. Bands of ruthless horsemen, armour shining in the sunlight, ride on white horses swift as the wind over the drawbridge of the castle. They swoop down on the caravan in the valley below. The wealthy merchants transporting their spices and cloth of gold from one walled city to another are lucky to get away with their lives and their underwear. The robber barons escape with the loot and return roaring with laughter to their aeries.

As we got into hilly country on the fringes of the Weserbergland, I began to pester Father to produce a robber baron fortress (*Raubritterburg*).

"It won't be long now," he said, trying to soothe me. "Soon we'll be in Warburg and then you keep your eyes open."

"Vati, Vati, I see it," I cried. High on an outcrop near the lovely old town of Warburg was as authentic a ruin as you could wish to find. I pointed to the massive crumbling tower on high.

"I am sure they used that as a lookout," I informed Father. "From there they could see everything that went on in the valley."

"Heinrich der Löwe [Henry the Lion] lived there," Father told me.

I don't think Father really knew if the place had been used to rob merchants. That did not worry me. No matter if, as in Marburg, St. Elizabeth herself had lived there, a castle on a hill belonged to robber barons. I belonged to the merchant class, but my heart was with the robbers who lived in high places.

I might have felt less sympathy for them a few years later when I had learned what it was like to be at the receiving end of a brigand's attentions. One Hermann Göring used such foolproof means to despoil the likes of us that the knights of old would have been very envious.

We turned southeast and made a detour to Kassel. Kassel housed Julius Strauss. He was tall, his face was puce, shot through with purple veins, and he wore spats. Mother said he was an apron chaser (*Schürzenjäger*). I knew that meant that he went after women, as Karl did. That aspect of his activities did not greatly bother my parents, but when they found out that Uncle Julius had cheated Uncle Josef, his own nephew and Father's brother-in-law, we stopped making the detour. Uncle Julius was now beyond the pale. He was nothing but a swindler (*Hochstapler*). I was sorry, because I liked Kassel and the Löwenburg (the Lion's Castle), which looked old but wasn't.

After driving south through lovely river valleys—the Fulda, the Eder, and finally, the Lahn—we came to the castle at Marburg, a massive building towering above the river and the old town. Marburg was a landmark. It was magically beautiful, and it marked the last lap of our journey.

Soon we were in Giessen, home of father's brother, Uncle Moritz, and his wife, Aunt Erna. Uncle Moritz looked like Father, but with sharper features and a limp, the result of a war wound on the Russian front. He was a very restless man—twitchy. His sharp nose turned here and there, like a bird's. Aunt Erna seemed calmer, though she wasn't really. She was a handsome woman with prominent dark eyes and very short hair, something unusual in the circles in which I moved. It proclaimed her a modern woman, according to Mother.

Erna's sister, Ilse, had married a Schötmar cattle dealer, Bruno Eichmann. Erna had come to live with them for a while. My parents had invited Moritz and made the match. They were not thanked for their pains.

Uncle Moritz had stayed in textiles. Since the marriage was childless, Erna was able to help full-time in the business. It wasn't easy for her, she told Mother. Uncle Moritz, like Father, had a fiery temper, and there was not that love between him and Erna which, in my parents' case, bridged the differences of temperament.

"They live parallel lives" (*Die leben nebeneinander*), was Mother's verdict. Even I could feel that there was little human warmth in that well-arranged apartment.

After Erna was widowed, my mother met her by chance in Switzerland. While they went on a shopping expedition together, Erna told Mother about a rendezvous she and Moritz once planned in downtown New York, but they could not find each other.

"That was the happiest day of my life," Erna had said.

Mother could not get over that.

"Her own husband! It was the happiest day of her life when she failed to find her own husband!"

As we moved deeper into Upper Hesse (Oberhessen), things became very curious. Piles of wood stacked in front of the houses, and even mounds of manure. How unhygienic! They must be very dirty, these Hessians. Chickens running all over the place. Bearded old men with huge curved pipes and funny conical hats sitting on benches by the wood and the manure, as if they had nothing to do. We, North Germans—Mother, Else, and I—felt very superior.

We passed through Lich and reached another sleepy townlet with mounds of manure to rival the best of them. It was Laubach. The huge car made its way to the market square, tightly packed with houses, and halted outside number three Marktplatz, where it was parked among the horsecarts.

On a wooden bench in front of the tall narrow house—no wood, no manure—there sat, good Hesian that he was, my favourite grandfather, lost in thought. When he spotted us, he jumped up and shook his head as if in disbelief. Tears trickled down his cheeks. Aunt Helene told us later that he had been sitting there for the last three hours, waiting. At first he had eyes only for me, his one and only grandchild.

"*Ai, yai, yai, yai, yai, da ist ja mein lieber Junge,*" he sang.

Every year he greeted his "dear boy" with the same words, the same number of *yai's*. He ruffled my hair, stroked my cheeks, and then turned his attention to the rest of the party.

This grandfather was very different from his opposite number in Schötmar. Grandfather Siegfried was big and fat, bulbous nosed, noisy, rough, bad tempered, and, as far as I was concerned, totally unlovable. Grandfather Joseph was small and thin, with a long narrow nose, soft-spoken, gentle, kind, and very lovable. I freely expressed my preference, especially in Laubach where it was safe to do so.

"I think you are much nicer than my Schötmar Opa," I announced loudly for all to hear. He bent down to kiss me. He had high cheekbones, long thin lips, and large ears that stood away like my own. His eyebrows and their sockets were very curved, the eyes almost almond shaped. Looking at his photos now, I see something of the Chinese sage.

Years later, Fred (formerly Fritz) Freudenthal, Uncle Josef's apprentice, told me that Grandfather Joseph had a fiery temper, like my father. I never saw any sign of it, but then Father too mellowed in old age.

"You must love both your Opas," Grandfather said in his soft voice. "Your Opa Siegfried is your mother's father, just as I am your father's father. We must love those who are near and dear to us and then we can learn to love everybody."

I was not convinced, but I liked the way he spoke, the way his eyes twinkled. Grandfather Siegfried would have snorted a command.

Grandfather took his watch from the pocket of his long black waistcoat. It was either Friday afternoon or the day before *Rosh Hashanah* (the Jewish New Year), and he was in his Sabbath best, black coat, striped trousers, and an old-fashioned winged collar.

"Soon it will be time to go to synagogue," he said. We did not use the Yiddish word *shul*, common in England.

We went into the old gabled house where Father was born. Downstairs was Uncle Josef's little textile shop and his mail order depot. There was nothing in the shop window.

I was not interested in brown paper parcels. I was looking for something much more exciting—a small door that was never opened. It marked the end of an underground passage that led straight to the castle. In case of danger, Count Solms zu Laubach and his family would be able to escape via number three Marktplatz. My imagination was working overtime.

"Can't you just see it, Fritz?" I confided to the apprentice who was helping us with the luggage.

"The castle is under siege. The count's enemies are about to cross the moat. He gets his family together and they all escape through here."

"It's not the count who is in danger," said Fritz. "It's us, and I doubt if that passage can save us." It was 1934 or 1935, and I knew what Fritz meant, but I still wanted to talk about the "bad old days." I prattled on about sieges, when Mother called me to order. She would not have minded being late, but our hosts were Orthodox. There was not much time.

We climbed the wooden stairs, very different from those at home. These stairs were narrow, rickety and steep, with little sideways room. In Schötmar, it was all potted plants and polish. These stairs had never seen a coat of polish and were so dark that no plants, had there been room for them, could have flourished.

The first-floor living room was also dark, with a sofa covered in faded red velvet, and a tall brown sideboard. There was a lot of pewterware—ceremonial dishes used for various festivals.

We were welcomed by Father's sister, Aunt Helene. She was in her Sabbath best, an almost ankle-length black dress in a flower pattern and a cape falling over her shoulders. It reappeared every year.

Mother looked overdressed by comparison, with her smart costume, lace blouse and a pendant of yellow diamonds round her neck.

Aunt Helene was no Aunt Grete. I felt the downy hair on her cheek as she kissed me, but there were no large gestures or fancy speeches. In the soft accents of Hesse, she welcomed us and asked about the journey.

My aunt did not look at all Jewish. Her fair hair, turning grey, was parted in the middle and tightly bound in a knot. Her eyes were round and greyish in colour, eyes that were sad, truthful, and good. "Behold an Israelite in whom there is no guile." Mother said she was a saint, but, in my view, not a happy saint. She hardly ever smiled. There was little to smile about.

Life was hard for Aunt Helene. She was not well off, as we were. Mother said she had married badly. Uncle Josef was fat, flabby and given to depression. I did not know what depression was, but I knew a *schlemiel*[10] when I saw one, and according to my parents, Uncle Josef was a *schlemiel* of the first order. Anyone could pull the wool over his eyes and many did. He was a harmless man, but nothing he touched flourished. He looked very unprepossessing with those bulging eyes and fat lips. I was expected to kiss him and did not relish the prospect.

Aunt Helene signalled to Mother that Else should do the rest of the unpacking. It was almost time for a Jew to cease from labour. Aunt Helene had done the cooking and laid the table. She lit the candles while such work was still permitted and raised her hands over the flames and the pewter. Then she put her hands over her eyes. They were still closed when she removed them.

On Friday evenings and on those special days when the New Year started on a Friday evening, she beckoned in the Sabbath three times with a "come hither" gesture. Father said that when a festival fell on the Sabbath, the day was doubly holy.

A dumpy grey-haired woman came in to switch on the electric lights and the stove. I tried to help her because I liked to know what people did, but she stopped me.

"No, no. Frau Strauss wouldn't like it. She wouldn't like it at all. She is very particular about these things."

---

10 A *schlemiel* is an awkward clumsy person, a foolish or unlucky person.

This woman was the *shabbes goyeh*, the non-Jewish woman who did the work that Jews were not allowed to do on Sabbaths and festivals. Even to switch on the light was considered "work" and therefore forbidden. The woman, a neighbour and friend, was paid for her services, although no money was exchanged on the Sabbath.

"It's all so absurd," Mother commented in the privacy of her bedroom. "It belongs to the Middle Ages."

In this age of automatic timers, the *shabbes goyeh* has gone out of fashion. There has also been a change of sentiment. It is now felt that a Jew should not expect others to do what he is not prepared to do himself.

We all trooped off to the synagogue, all except Mother, who stayed with Else. In our hands were packets wrapped in newspaper. These hid our prayer books and the embroidered velvet bags in ruby red or royal blue that closed with two press studs. They contained the men's prayer shawls. No use exposing holy objects to public gaze and us to ridicule. One or two passersby doffed their hats, but most just stared.

"Those Jews," I could hear them saying, or thought I could hear them saying, when we were out of earshot. "I wonder what those bloodsuckers are up to?" I sometimes thought that Uncle Josef with his thick lips looked like a bloodsucker, but he was a very innocent man. Others sucked his blood.

I was too tired to take in much of the service. I needed my dinner.

As we climbed the narrow stairs, a welcoming smell of chicken came from the kitchen. I wanted to get going, but Grandfather chanted another longish prayer, as if we had not prayed enough. Then he said *Kiddush*, the blessing over the wine, and we all went to wash our hands. At home, only Father washed his hands before eating. For some reason this rule was not included in Mother's set of commandments. She made me wash my hands only when they were dirty. For Father, it was a religious duty rather than a cleansing exercise. He merely moistened his fingers—he called it *netzen*.

Grandfather said a blessing over the bread, putting a pinch of salt on each chunk. I could see where Father had learned to break bread. Then Grandfather said another blessing, gave us all a piece of apple, which he dipped in honey, and asked God to grant us a happy and prosperous

New Year. Only then did Aunt Helene help us to the chicken soup with dumplings that had been steaming in the tureen.

The boiled chicken was delicious. In those days, chicken still tasted of chicken. It was served with a horseradish sauce so pungent that it went up my nose and made me sneeze. Chicken was a special treat. This one had come by courtesy of Mother's subsidies. She often sent money without Father's knowledge.

I asked for breast, my favourite kind of meat, barring goose. For dessert, there was *Apfelshalet*, another great favourite. This was a mound-shaped pie, stuffed to capacity with apples and sultanas, seasoned with cinnamon, and baked in the oven.

Now and then I was allowed to sip a little sweet red wine from Father's glass. My head felt funny, in a pleasant sort of way. Grandfather could go on as long as he liked, thanking God for his mercies, and he did. Occasionally his singsong stopped, so the others could join in the refrain. Mother looked sheepish. This was foreign territory for her. I did my best. My Hebrew was not very fluent, but I liked the tunes the Laubachers used. My favourite was their version of David's Psalm 144, sung at the conclusion of the Sabbath.

"Blessed be the Lord, my rock." (*L' dovid boruch adaunoi zuri.*)

Well-brought-up boy that I was, I thanked Aunt Helene for the meal. No prompting from Mother was needed. The splendid meal did the prompting. Aunt Helene put her hands on my head like a blessing. She looked at me with those sad benevolent eyes and said, "You are the only child in our family. All our hopes rest in you. I know you will not disappoint us." I did not really know what she was talking about, but a shiver went through me.

Aunt Helene brought out some old photos of Grandmother, looking very severe, with stern eyes above a velvet choker, blonde hair also stretched very tightly into a bun. No trace of what one might think of as Jewish features. Her influence was still very strong, fifteen or so years after her death. During the meal, there were constant references to what "Mother did." She had been very observant and brought up her children to follow her example.

"What a beautiful service," Mother had commented as she fingered the gold rim of her plate during dinner, wistfully eyeing the distant reminder of Great-grandfather Wolf Siesel's prosperity.

"It's still from Mother's dowry," replied Aunt Helene. "We have a similar *fleischdik* service for *Pesach* [Passover]."

In kosher households, dairy (*milchidik*) and meat (*fleischdik*) are kept apart, eaten from different dishes at different meals, a rule extrapolated from the biblical commandment: "Thou shalt not cook a kid in its mother's milk." So, four sets of dishes are kept, two that are used only during Passover and two for the rest of the year.

Mother had given me instructions not to say anything about our loose eating habits at home.

"What if they ask me?" I objected.

"Then you have to tell the truth," said Mother. "But don't volunteer information the way you often do to make yourself important."

No one asked. I think they knew.

Next morning I was up early so that I could walk to synagogue with Grandfather. I took his bony hand. He shuffled in soft shoes; I skipped in brown bootees, but we held on to each other.

This grandfather was more my scale than Grandfather Siegfried. He posed no threat. He was all kindness. I loved him as much as a spoiled and selfish only child can love anyone. His eyes began to twinkle the way Father's did as he was about to tell one of his jokes, only what Grandfather was about to say was not in the least funny.

"Tell me about the synagogue in Schötmar," he asked.

I prattled on about it being in the Aechternstrasse, which was behind the Lange Strasse—about it being bigger than the Laubach synagogue, but not all that much. Herr Rosenwald was the *panes*, the head of the synagogue committee. *Lehrer* (teacher) Rülf sometimes came from Bad Salzuflen to give us Hebrew lessons, and so on.

"And do you go to synagogue every *shabbes* [Sabbath]?"

I had not been programmed to cope with this question, and others like it. I had to admit that I did not, nor did Father. By the end of the High Holidays, I must have given Grandfather quite a comprehensive picture of our less-than-perfect Jewish observance at home. However, he refrained from commenting.

The Laubach Jews were much more orthodox than those of Schötmar. I think that even on weekdays they managed a *minion*, the quorum of ten males required for a service.

There were about fifteen Jewish families in the region. The Heinemanns ranked on top, followed by the Wallensteins.

"Show them what a nice *Diener* [bow] you can make," Mother instructed me, as we met the crème de la crème after the service. My relatives were among the poorest of local Jews, but Father's success and his rich wife gave them extra status.

The small synagogue was packed. Every able-bodied Jew and quite a few decrepit ones went to the High Holiday services, and there were also some visitors like us.

All about me, the silky rustle of prayer shawls were in motion, as their owners, each in their own way, made their obeisance to the unseen. Not being wholly absorbed in my devotions, I watched the scene as best I could through the gaps between the men around me. Most men were rocking back and forth, interspersing these quick jerky movements with deep bows. Some nodded all the time. One man swayed so far sideways that I feared he would keel over. Each man carried on at his own pace, in his own manner.

Every time I went to synagogue, I wondered why they gabbled their prayers so. If I hurried my prayers with Else, I was told off. Later I found out the principle: if the posts are set close together, no pig can get through the fence. In other words, if you gabble without a pause, no sinful thoughts can enter the prayer stream. It was of course impossible to pray in unison at that speed, but even for the refrains, each man chose his entry in a confused counterpoint. How different, I thought, when we sang the hymn "Great God, We Praise Thee" (*Grosser Gott wir loben Dich*) at the Küsterschule, the little Protestant school almost next door to our house.

I could see now why the teacher spoke of a *Judenschule*, a Jews' school, if during lessons everyone spoke at the same time.

Later on, I remembered the High Holidays when I went to Church of England services. There it was as if the congregation behaved as one man or, more accurately, as one woman, since soaring female voices brooked no opposition. They all sang in synchrony, repeated their creeds and made their responses in unison, whereas in an orthodox synagogue, each member of the House of Israel seemed to pursue his own negotiations with the Lord.

The women in their upstairs ghettoes, faintly heard and only partially seen, played a very secondary role.

Perhaps it is less a question of Jew and Christian and more one of east and west. I believe Eastern Christians come closer to the Jewish pattern.

Father was unusually discreet in his dealings with his superior in heaven. He prayed softly and rocked modestly, as if he did not want to call attention to himself from God or man. But his fellow congregants were determined to heap honours on the local boy made good.

"Naphtali ben Joseph Hacohen."

Amid the babble, I recognized Father's Hebrew name. Naphtali, son of Joseph, the priest, got up and walked slowly to the podium, where the reader had unrolled the first scroll of the Torah. With his right hand, Father took the fringes of his prayer shawl and put them on the scroll at the place the reader indicated with a silver pointer, the *yad*. Then Father put the fringes to his mouth and lightly kissed them. It all happened in a second. After that father pronounced the first of the blessings:

"Blessed art Thou, O Lord, our God, King of the Universe, who hast chosen us from all nations, and hast given us the Law. Blessed art Thou, O Lord, the giver of the Law."

All in Hebrew, of course.

"Did you notice I was called up first,[11] *Muttchen*?" he asked Mother later. He called her "little Mother" when he felt very affectionate.

"Of course I did, Hermann. It was only your due." She added as an afterthought, "How much money did you pledge?" Mother was a practical woman.

Did Mother really notice? I have my doubts. When I went upstairs to see her, sitting there in her aura of 4711 and Mousson Crème, her face looked unusually vacant. Mother on the ladies' balcony was like a busy railway engine shunted into a siding. Enforced inactivity did not bring out the best in her. Once she had scrutinized the other women's appearance, she lost interest. What boredom one had to endure to please one's husband and in-laws! Occasionally she turned the pages of her

---

[11]   Father belonged to the priestly caste; otherwise, he could not have been called up first, however important he might have been.

prayer book and moved her lips. She looked only at the right side, the translation. Any dealings Mother had with God, and she did believe in some kind of deity despite her doubts about its wisdom and powers, were conducted in German.

Father was given other honours during the holidays. He was called on to carry one of the Torah scrolls in procession, or he was given the scroll to hold while someone else put it back into its swaddling clothes. It was heavy, and his thin arms trembled a little. When it was Father's turn to close up the Torah and place it in its embroidered velvet cover, I was thankful that I was not on the podium. Normally I liked doing jobs with grown-ups, but not this time. Like Mother, I did not enjoy taking part in rituals. They seemed unnatural and made me feel uncomfortable. And what if I did something wrong?

After Father wound the bandages tightly round the two halves of the scroll, he put on the velvet cover. Father had to fit the wooden frames on which the scroll was wound into the two holes at the top of the cover, so that it could slip down and envelop the parchment. Then he hung the silver shield over the cover and the silver pointer over the shield. Two silver finials, called *rimonim-pomegranates*, were then put on the frames. They were hung with little tinkling bells. Father placed the crown on the Torah, and it was ready to be put back in its coffer to rest. I was reminded of this scene in India years later when I saw the Brahmins dress and ornament their deities.

The service went on and on. By this time, I was almost as torpid as Mother. Too much human breath and too little air.

"When will we have the *shofar*?" I asked Father, desperate for some action. The *shofar* is a curved ram's horn that is blown only on the holiest days, the New Year and the Day of Atonement.

The reader intoned strange meaningless words, and the horn echoed his ululations: a long uninterrupted sound, then shorter bursts, then something like a shudder, then long sounds again. It seemed that God was calling us as was his wont, spelling out his commands faster and faster and ending with another roll call.

I knew from Father that God was not like other people. He could not be seen, he could not be touched, but he spoke a great deal. For instance, he first told Abraham to sacrifice his son, Isaac, and then allowed him to sacrifice a ram instead. "That's why we blow a ram's horn."

Being both squeamish and logically minded, I asked why God could not have reprieved the ram as well.

"We can't question God's word," said Father. "That is what happened at that time."

I was not convinced. I don't think Father was either. I could sense uncertainty behind adult assurance the way children can. Father was squeamish like me. When he ate meat, he wanted it cooked so well that it lost all traces of its origins; the slightest hint of red and he would send it back. It was the same with fish. In orthodox households, fish are served with their eyes gouged out. Father had his fish decapitated. He did not want the empty sockets staring at him. He abhorred animal sacrifice, but felt that he had to defend scriptural authority.

Not long after the blowing of the *shofar*, Grandfather and some others got up and walked towards the ark. Father took my hand and walked in the opposite direction towards the door. Grandfather turned back and, with a look of impatience, beckoned Father to join him. Father shook his head and went out, dragging me with him.

While Father was alive, I never witnessed the scene that was about to take place in the synagogue. In the order of the service, it is called the Blessing of the Priests. The *Cohanim*[12] face the congregation, spread out their prayer shawls, put them over their heads, and raise their hands to bless the people. They use the same beautiful words with which Father blessed me on Friday nights.

"The Lord bless thee and keep thee. The Lord make his face to shine upon thee and be gracious unto thee. The Lord lift up his face unto thee and give thee peace."

Father felt that I was entitled to his blessings, but he could not bring himself to bless the congregation. "I am not worthy," he told Grandfather, when the latter remonstrated with him. "I am not a good Jew. I cannot go out there and bless the others." And he never did, not in Schötmar, not in Cologne, not in Oxford, not in London. Since it was not proper for him to be blessed by his peers, he took the air while fat cheaters showered their blessings without compunction.

---

[12]   The *Cohanim*, or priests, are the direct descendants of Aaron, brother of Moses, the first high priest. Rabbis are not necessarily priests—they are learned men.

Theologically, Father may have been in error. The capacity to give out blessings depends on lineage, on blood, not on conduct. But Father's heart was in the right place.

In an ideal world, Father would have closed the factory on the Sabbath. In the real world, one had to face competition, make profits and support the family. In an ideal world, Father would have gone to synagogue every Saturday. In the real world, that was the only time he could dictate letters to Fräulein Nagel and give instructions about the particular needs of his customers, whom he worshipped. Early on Monday morning he would be off again.

Father did hold to certain taboos. He did not ride in a car on the Sabbath. Even as an old man, he would walk rather than accept my offer to drive him to the synagogue. But he did not insist on kosher food at home. He did not want to give Mother all the bother with the four sets of dishes, and so on. "And how can I have kosher food when I am always travelling?" he asked his imaginary prosecutor.

I suspect, having seen him eat egg and bacon in a Glasgow hotel, that he strayed further from kosher than was strictly necessary. "Dear God," I can hear him say to his Superior in heaven, "there is nothing else that is nourishing on the menu."

Father had given up using phylacteries, laying *tefillin* as the practice is called—the little black boxes containing God's word, tethered to the forehead and left arm with leather straps. He no longer even had the equipment. He still wore his fringed prayer vest when he raced through his morning prayers, but where was the time for elaborate rituals?

Father felt guilty before God. And this guilt insinuated itself into many religious teachings that he gave me. They did not carry real conviction. Father was too scrupulous. He could not call on me to keep commandments that he himself was not prepared to keep, or even those that he was so prepared. I sometimes feel that I would have liked to possess the rocklike conviction of those who are firmly rooted in a tradition, but I understood Father because I understand guilt.

The yawning gaps in my religious education were cruelly exposed as I walked back with Grandfather from the synagogue one day.

"Come, make your old Opa happy," he said. "Recite the *Shema* for me 'when thou walkest by the way.'" This was a quotation from the prayer itself, one of the holiest in Judaism, and most commonly recited. It exhorts man to speak of God's commandments while sitting, walking, lying down, and rising up. I knew the German version, but Hebrew was another matter.

"*Shema Yis'ro'el Adaunai Elauheinu Adaunai Echod,*" I intoned, using the old Ashkenazi pronunciation. "Hear O Israel, the Lord our God the Lord is One." That much I knew. I went on for another few lines, then faltered, went rigid, and stopped. Grandfather's eyebrows rose in surprise. He helped me on, word by word. I responded to certain cues, recited a few words, then stopped again. For once I felt uncomfortable with Grandfather, happy to reach the house.

"Hermann, it is not right. The boy doesn't even know his *Shema,*" Grandfather said over lunch. Father hung his head.

"I send him to Hebrew school."

"And thou shalt teach them diligently unto thy children," quoted Grandfather. They said no more.

Grandfather had touched on a sore point. If Father had sat me on his knee and taught me Hebrew prayers and psalms in place of the poems of Schiller and Heine, I might feel more at home at an orthodox service today. Father left Hebrew to Hebrew school.

Hebrew and I never had a love affair. I learned by heart quickly, but not Hebrew. I felt much more at ease kneeling by my bed with Else, repeating those maudlin children's prayers, where I ask God to let his eyes be above my bed. I was puzzled that Mother and Else's German God had eyes while Father's Hebrew God did not. It was useless talking to women about it. They were no good at theology. I meant to bring up the subject with Father, but I don't think I ever did.

The prohibitions imposed by Orthodoxy were strange and a little irksome. It was the difference between our broad and light staircase at home and those dark steep stairs at number three Marktplatz. I was happy to escape with Else to the *Schlosspark.*

There were walks with the family too, usually after lunch on Sabbaths and festivals. I could not understand why it was proper for Aunt Helene to bring us our lunch but improper for her to light the oven and heat it. These were mysteries beyond comprehension. Our bellies filled with cold chicken, we walked in the hills around the town but not too far. There was another rule about that. I remember Aunt Helene saying that you must not walk more than half an hour's distance from your home. Anything longer would be exertion. It conflicted with God's wish that we rest from our labours.

Father and Aunt Helene set a brisk pace. I sometimes had to run to keep up with them. Father wore his thick double-breasted suit and grey homburg hat, Aunt Helene was in her black flowered dress, its cape fluttering in the wind. The dress was quite thin, georgette perhaps, and when I fell behind, I could see the straps of two inner garments—one white, one black—showing through faintly at the shoulder. Perhaps she did not have a thicker dress suitable for festivals. I do not remember seeing her in an overcoat.

Mother and Uncle Josef made up the rear—he puffing and licking his lips, she breathing heavily, bosom heaving. Their conversation was not animated. They had little in common except bulk and a tendency to baulk at the slightest acclivity. The rest of the party had to wait for them to catch up. Later in life, Mother took to morning exercises which she did "with iron diligence."

When time permitted, we stayed in Laubach ten days after the New Year to celebrate *Yom Kippur,* the Day of Atonement. On that solemn day, there was not even a cold lunch. I did my bit of atoning by going without breakfast and felt very holy. No one expected me to fast all day, so after doing my morning stint in the synagogue, I went off with Else and Karl to eat somewhere. No one was allowed to eat in the house. Mother, pleading indisposition, skipped the services and kept out of sight. Considering her very healthy appetite, the only way she was able to fast was by staying in bed all day.

Father agreed that it was easier to fast if you stayed in one place. The place he chose was the synagogue. "You breathe the same air and you forget about food."

I could not say I agreed with him. During the morning, while all around me were asking God to forgive their sins, I was guiltily fantasizing about the goodies with which I would reward myself for having missed breakfast. It had quite slipped my mind that this was the day on which my fate would be sealed. Some days earlier, in his efforts to educate us about the holiest days of the year, Father had read out to Mother and me—more for her benefit than for mine—a terrifying tenth-century prayer attributed to Rabbi Amnon of Mainz:

On the First Day of the Year it is inscribed, and on the Fast
Day of Atonement, it is sealed and determined, how many
shall pass away, and how many shall be born; who shall live
and who shall die, whose appointed time is finished and
whose is not; who is to perish by fire, who by water, who by
the sword, and who by wild beasts; who by hunger or thirst;
who by earthquake or who by the plague; who by strangling
or who by lapidation [stoning]; who shall be at rest and
who shall be wandering; who shall remain tranquil and who
be disturbed; who shall reap enjoyment and who shall be
painfully afflicted; who shall get rich, and who become poor;
who shall be cast down, and who exalted.

But Penitence, Prayer, and Charity
Avert the evil decree.[13]

This warning is delivered both on the New Year and on the Day
of Atonement. In the intervening days, Father meant us to ponder
and repent before it was too late. His reading did not have the desired
effect on either of us. I was awed by the repetition of the alternatives,
the certainty, the terrible power of God. It was like listening to a spell.
But I didn't feel that any of it applied to me.

Mother was not even awed. When Father had finished, she shook
her head.

"Do you really believe all that, Hermann? Killed by wild beasts? We
are living in the twentieth century. You can see it is outdated. It does
not apply to the modern world. I don't believe it."

Perhaps she should have. I need not labour the point about the
wild beasts lying in wait for us, far more dangerous than lions and
leopards, who would devour many who heard that prayer in the Laubach
synagogue.

Father smiled benignly. "You have made your own accord with the
good Lord." It was his standard response when Mother cast doubt on
his beliefs. He put his skinny arms around her ample waist.

---

13   Service for the New Year. The Complete Festival Prayers, Vol. One, London,
     Shapiro, Valentine and Co. 1943. ET. Rev. D.A. de Sola, p. 192.

"God knows you are a good woman in spite of your words."

Religious arguments always led to demonstrations of affection. Father had his own argument from design, which Mother had no difficulty in toppling by pointing to the injustices of the world, and the Nazis saw to it that her arguments grew more cogent by the day. Still, she always let Father have the last word. These arguments were not things that mattered. They would not keep clothes clean or cash flowing. I wonder too how deeply Father cared, since argument always ended in embrace. Perhaps the marriage worked better because their belief systems were so different.

The penitence that was to avert the evil decree began at sunset after a substantial meal that would have to last all diners except me until the following night. Carrying our newspaper packets, we walked to the synagogue, Mother included, for the evening service, known as *Kol Nidre*—all vows—after the opening prayer asking God to absolve those present from all vows they may make and not be able to keep from this Day of Atonement to the next. For this, the most solemn prayer of the most solemn day of the year, the congregation was hushed and still. Three times the reader slowly chanted the beautiful mournful modal melody. As he retailed the different kinds of promises we might rashly make to God and absolved us in advance from each, his voice grew more intense and high pitched. I thought that at any time he might burst into tears. No chatter, no private murmurings. You could hear a pin drop. And when the congregation made its response, it was almost in unison. I clutched Father's hand.

Nothing that followed could match this moment. The next day was very long. The synagogue was in continuous session. I was present much of the time. It made Father and Grandfather happy. Their bright smiles as I entered the synagogue made me feel warm and wanted. Other people smiled too. In Laubach I had the reputation, richly deserved, of a well-brought-up boy. "*Ein gut erzogener Junge*," they said. My bows were exemplary, my remarks polite. I did not let on how bored I was.

In later years, I was able to appreciate the beauty and fascination of the Day of Atonement service with its detailed description of the different orders of angels and their functions, and above all, its account of my ancestor, the high priest's doings on the great day, when he entered the Holy of Holies.

"And when the priests and the people who stood in the court heard the glorious and awful *name*, pronounced out of the mouth of the high priest, in holiness and purity, they knelt."

This passage occurs three times in the Order of the Service of the High Priest, and each time the congregation, young and old, gets on its knees, as did its fathers in the days of old. I cannot recall seeing this in Laubach, but my astonishment was great when I met it in England. Jews don't kneel, but this was an act, not of intercession but of commemoration.

"We remember what the high priest did in the Temple," Father told me in England. And you know we are descended from high priests. We go back even further than the Count Solms zu Laubach."

Father often told me that it was forbidden to pronounce God's real name, though he never told me why. This was such an article of faith that it never occurred to me to ask the reason. Nowadays it is for me the most fascinating question of all. Was this name the ancient Jews' *mahamantra*, repeated in the silence of the heart, repeating which they could "be still and know that I am God"? If only Father were here to discuss this with me!

In the old Laubach days, I was more interested in Jonah and the whale. The whole book of Jonah is read on Yom Kippur afternoon. Father passed his forefinger along the German translation for my benefit. Every now and then, he glanced sideways to see if I was following. He need not have worried. I identified with Jonah. I felt the sailors picking on me and throwing me into the sea, where I found refuge in the whale's capacious belly. What puzzled me was the gourd protecting Jonah from the sun, which "came up in a night and perished in a night." I knew how long it took for anything to grow in our garden. How could a plant come up that quickly and how could a mere worm destroy something big enough to give shelter to a man?

"Plants grow much more quickly in hot climates," Father assured me. "It's the sun that makes them grow. And the worms there are much bigger than ours."

I was not sophisticated enough to question this impromptu piece of scriptural exegesis. In any case, I wanted to believe in Jonah's adventures.

After Jonah's story, the propitiatory prayers went on and on. My tummy was rumbling.

"Is it time to go home soon, Vati?" I pleaded.

Father replied that *Nilah* will soon be here. *Nilah* is the concluding prayer on the great day, and we used to say "*Nilah* will soon be here" when something was coming to an end.

For the last time that long day, the men beat their breasts.

"We have trespassed, we have acted treacherously, we have robbed, we have spoken slander . . . ," and on and on. They accused themselves of every sin under the sun and for each putative transgression pounded their chests. Most of them went about their task with vigour, almost with glee, but Father, holding his fist very near to his chest, moved it only very slightly. When it came to religion, his was an almost aristocratic reticence. He did not go in for show. He himself can have committed only a few of all those sins, but the prayer says "we," not "I." Someone in the House of Israel may have been guilty of them.

At the end of *Nilah*, the conclusion of the conclusion, the *shofar* was sounded. It seemed like a warning. "Be good until the following year, or else . . ." But the prospect of food soon blotted out all thoughts of sin and repentance. I skipped along the road pulling Grandfather with me, happy it was all over.

For supper we had challah, the very soft white braided loaf, glazed with white of egg. With it came pickled herrings and boiled eggs.

"An ideal meal for *Anbeissen*" (the breaking of the fast), Mother commented as she filled her plate with fish and onion rings. "Nothing stimulates the appetite like herring."

I didn't think Mother's appetite needed much stimulation, but her favourite fish was an extra bonus, after the many hours of abstinence. Mother could face heartburn and much else for a herring.

During our stay in Laubach, the question came up as to what to do about Else and Karl, the gentiles in our midst, during the evenings. Fritz, the apprentice, was deputized to look after them. Karl wanted to drink and Fritz took them to a *Wirtshaus*, the German version of a pub. Karl could drink anyone under the table and poor Fritz came home singing and swaying. He was told off by Aunt Helene. That he had been asked to look after the *goyim* (gentiles) was no excuse for behaving like one.

Fritz was in far deeper trouble a year or two later. When we met in America later, Fritz, now Fred, told me that some enemy had accused him of laughing during a solemn moment of heil hitlering and had brought two false witnesses to prove his point. A good friend of Fritz, a smith by trade, had heard at the Town Hall that Fritz was about to be arrested. When he got word of this, Fritz fled to Giessen, the capital of the region. There he plucked up courage and went of his own accord to Gestapo headquarters, explaining that the accusation was false. The case against him came up later, but the Gestapo did not pursue it. They agreed that it was a case of personal enmity. His courage probably saved his life.

Fritz was a very impulsive young man. He was in trouble again later, fighting with an S.S. man. He tried to kill the man but could not find the throttle. Somehow, he escaped and got to America.

Grandfather also escaped. He died in March 1936, not long after Grandfather Siegfried. I did not accompany Father to the funeral.

My last memory of Grandfather is of him standing in front of the house in the *Marktplatz* in his striped trousers and long black jacket, tears again trickling down his cheeks as he waved us off.

Aunt Helene and Uncle Josef were less fortunate than Grandfather. The wild beasts caught up with them. They were deported in 1941 or 1942 and murdered in Poland.

Later on, my parents and Uncle Moritz often asked themselves if they could have done more to rescue their relatives. Like many in their position, they suffered from survivors' guilt. But what could they have done? Moritz and Erna were working as valet and maid in New York. My parents only got out by the skin of their teeth.

I don't think any of us were better people than Aunt Helene and Uncle Josef. Why then did we survive?

Sometimes I still see Aunt Helene's good grey eyes that shone out on the world so long ago, and I ask myself the question many have asked: If there is a moral universe, how could such a person meet such an end? I hope against hope that she and others like her have paid off some old and heavy *karmic* debt. I want the law of *karma* and rebirth to save the moral universe for me. It is either that or blind chance. I cannot accept a God who plays moral dice.

"The Lord giveth and the Lord taketh away." I cannot bless the name of such a Lord unless I understand his reasons. Perhaps that is the Jew in me.

In 1978, I visited some of the holy places in the Holy Land. In the Moslem shrines, especially the Dome of the Rock, there was a feeling of great power. In the Churches of the Holy Sepulchre and the Nativity, I experienced a very tender feeling in the heart. And contrary to all expectations, when I visited the Western Wall, the so-called Wailing Wall, I was overcome by a feeling of great sweetness and joy, almost elation. This also happened at the Tomb of Rachel and in the holy city of Safed, home of the Kabbalah.

Whenever I block out the great tragedy and just let my awareness rest on Laubach and the High Holidays, I get a touch of that feeling of sweetness and joy. There were the long services and unaccustomed rules, but something must have got through to me of the happiness that comes from living by old and treasured values, values that point beyond our narrow needs and desires to a larger transcendental goal.

It was a very different world from the more self-indulgent, hedonistic values that prevailed in Schötmar and Cologne. All my life, I have been a battleground for these different values. Laubach and Schötmar—Father and Mother have always battled for supremacy in me.

Chapter Thirteen

THE FAT *KRAKEELER*

In the Schötmar world, we lived with my grandparents in the house that Grandfather had built in spite of his wife's opposition. I saw more of them than I did of my parents, and I did not like what I saw. By then, Opa and Oma no longer spoke directly to each other. From their headquarters on either side of the hall, they abused each other in the third person. Grandfather did most of the abusing.

"What has the old crow done with my sticks? [*Das alte Luder, Das alte Luder?*],"[14] he bellowed, eyes blazing, cheeks inflamed.

Grandmother had not been near his sticks. She gave him and his possessions a wide berth. Fortunately, she had a knack for cutting herself off from his tantrums. Otherwise, she could not have survived. "Let him do or not do what he will." (*Er soll tu'n und lassen was er will.*) Then she set her mouth, shut her door, and waited for the next onslaught. He knew how to goad her, and occasionally, when she had had her fill, she let fly. I do not remember what she said but I do remember a very angry face.

Mother was the only one who could intervene. "Calm down, Father. It's not good for your health to get excited." She patted him, guided him to his red armchair, and chatted to him about other things. To Grandmother, she said, "He doesn't mean it. He's a sick man."

---

[14]   *Luder* is a very derogatory word that is usually applied to women. The dictionary defines it as a carrion or damned wretch.

Grandfather called for Fritz Schmidtpott, the office boy, to take him to the Wevelsburg, the local hostelry, glaring at Grandmother's shut door as he went out.

"My grandfather is nothing but a fat *Krakeeler*," I confided to Frau Birkholz, forgetting that the lady's girth exceeded Grandfather's and that I was no silhouette myself. "Fat" was less a description than a term of abuse, like "old." Father called me a *Krakeeler*, a loudmouth, a brawler, but affectionately, with a twinkle in his eye. I had no such affection for Grandfather. My feelings were reciprocated. He was the one adult in my circle who failed to respond to my charms.

I was forever tripping over things and then moaning while nursing my raw knees. Everyone else was sympathetic. Not Grandfather.

"Can't you see where you are going, you stupid boy?" He snorted. "And don't howl. Be a man."

Grandfather looked on me as a mollycoddled milksop. The birthday poems I recited in honeyed tones, masterminded by Mother, left him cold. Behind the facade of good manners, he saw an anxious, insecure child.

"You spoil that boy, Emmy," he told Mother. "He'll never grow up to be strong and self-reliant. The day will come when he will have to fend for himself, and then what will happen?" And looking at my outfit, he added, "Velvet pants! I ask you?"

I preferred Grandmother. "She never shouts at me," I told my confidante, Frau Birkholz. "She gives me presents and lets me collect her rents. But Grandfather yells at her all day."

Frau Birkholz must have been well aware of this. You could not stay long in our house—and Frau Birkholz stayed for weeks—without hearing his performances. Mine was a voice in the wilderness. His children, Mother especially, took Grandfather's side. His other grandchildren loved him.

By one of those little ironies of fate, I was the grandchild who most resembled Grandfather. "Oh, Mrs. Katz, what a lovely plump little boy. Isn't he just the spitting image of your father?"

Apparently, people had thus drooled over me in my pram. They continued these compliments when I was old enough to understand and resent them. Why like *her* father, why not like *my* father? Likening me to Grandfather was meant to be the highest accolade they could bestow on me.

It still happens. "Doesn't he look just like our grandfather?" said cousin Gisela, pointing to me at a recent family meeting. "He even has the same hands, the same tapered fingers." The others agreed that the likeness was remarkable. And when my childhood friend, Ursula Eichmann, visited me from Florida the day before my sixtieth birthday, she vouchsafed, "You know, you look just like your grandfather, only you're not fat."

My look-alike was a huge broadly built man, fat-powerful rather than fat-flabby. He had big bones and hefty shoulders. As I brought him his slippers or picked up his sticks, he towered over me like a mountain.

Mother said, "When he enters a room, the walls tremble." (*Wenn er ins Zimmer kommt, dann wackeln die Wände.*) But she was not referring to his bulk. He had a commanding presence that instilled respect and fear in equal parts.

The photographs show him as only just over medium height, but he looked much taller. The deep-set, fierce eyes said, "Whatever you can throw at me, I will throw back with interest." His face was broad with a heavy chin. A high forehead was adorned with a large cyst and crowned by a shiny baldpate. The fat rather bulbous nose did not look out of place on that large face. His hands were surprisingly delicate. Even in his decline, there were traces of his mother's fabled good looks. He treated the world with an assurance that seemed to confirm Frau Wallhausen's account of his origins.

Grandfather's legs were his weakest part. They were too short and feeble for the bulk they were expected to carry. When he stood up, they almost formed a circle. They were bandy legs (*O Beine*). Even when he had his sticks, he sometimes stumbled and fell. When I helped him up, he barked at me for my pains.

"Not like this, you stupid oaf! Take my arm here, under the elbow!"

He was very heavy, but I finally managed to get him upright. He stood there on his shaky legs and scowled. I thought I should defend myself.

"It's your felt slippers, Opa. They make you slide."

"I'll make you slide on your behind if you're not careful. You have no muscles, boy. Too much reading. You don't know how to move."

He was probably right. I was clumsy. But even had I been agile and athletic, he would have found some reason to bark. He was quite aware that he was getting weaker all the time, and this did nothing to lengthen a habitually short temper. As he grew weaker, more helpless, a thicker air of restless menace hung around him.

Grandfather suffered from diabetes, gout, and muscular dystrophy. All that meat and those helpings of goose dripping can't have helped. He fought hard for his life, in his angry way. It took stomach cancer to destroy him. The last days of this proud man were spent in a wheelchair with built-in toilet facilities.

His voice was the one organ not affected by the ravages of sickness and age. While he still had some use of his legs, Grandfather would make periodic forays to the factory, which was within easy walking distance of the house. Even when I played in the surrounding streets, I could hear him hectoring the workmen.

I rushed as fast as my legs could carry me to my bosom friend, Anneliese Saure, a little girl of my age.

"Quick, Anneliese!" I panted, "Let's go to your kitchen. My grandfather is on the warpath again."

Anneliese lived in a cul-de-sac that ran parallel with the factory, separated from our grounds by a wire fence. Anneliese's grandmother, Frau Poppe, who made excellent *Pickert* (the local potato cake), occupied the ground floor, while Anneliese and her parents lived on the first floor. The factory windows were kept open because of the sawdust, and we had a clear view of its largest rooms from Anneliese's kitchen. We watched Grandfather's antics as he hobbled about the factory—yelling. We mimicked him. I made my legs into an *O* and brandished Frau Saure's broom at Anneliese. She stood in for the workmen.

"You want to be paid for doing nothing? I'll show you how to make more brushes in less time." Then it was Anneliese's turn to berate me. Afterwards, we danced about, laughing and hugging each other.

Grandfather did not like to see me in the factory. If he spotted me there, he yelled, "Get out of here, you rascal. You are only here to cause trouble." To Mother, he said, "Why do you give your boy free run of the factory? He's disturbing the concentration of the workers. You are the one to lose out, if he disrupts production." Mother kept her peace, but did not forbid me the factory.

One day, I was helping Gustel Kampmann operate her stamping machine. She had just placed her hands over mine to direct them, when we heard Grandfather's roar. I scampered to the back of the machine while Gustel stood in front of me, working away. Grandfather hobbled past us, his face purple. He positioned himself by the door that led to the next room where the brushbacks were shaped, in order to keep an eye on both rooms as the same time. His voice roared above the noisy machines:

"Trees take time to grow. Don't waste wood. You don't have to pay for it. I'll show you how to make more brushes in less time."

He used one stick to support himself, the other to brandish at the men in the brushback room. He never waved his stick at the women in Gustel's room, nor inflicted actual bodily harm, but he gave a frightening performance. My game with Anneliese was nothing like the real thing.

Perhaps Grandfather's schemes were brilliant, but no one any longer took notice of them. The workers smirked. He was just a voice. Mother was the real power in the factory, and she did not shout. Fortunately, the Nazis had not yet fully established their influence over the workforce, or we would have been in real trouble. When Grandfather had gone, we all laughed, and I did one of my imitations.

I am glad Grandfather never saw me laughing with the workers as he tried, cramped, and crippled to help my parents improve their factory's productivity. My parents were none too pleased with his excursions. When Mother told him that he should not exert himself, that he needed rest, he shouted at her too.

"It's his illness," Mother explained. "He can't do what he used to do. He has our best interests at heart. He is such a good man."

For once, I did not believe her. I was too young to recognize the tragedy of this powerful and successful man, who saw his strength slipping away. I knew him at the end of his busy, useful life. He still wanted to play a part in what he had helped to create. He had cofounded the factory, had helped to run it in its early days, had provided the land on which it was built, and had sent Father to be trained in the brush trade. Without him, there would have been no "Hermann Katz and Co."

He kept his wits to the end and continued to be consulted on all matters of importance. He had more foresight than my parents when he urged my father to open a new branch in France. His visits to the factory may even have been therapeutic, giving him a sense of purpose and achievement.

In 1934, the authorities made us install a ventilation system. They claimed that the sawdust and wood chippings were damaging the workers' health. Under the new system, the chippings were sucked directly from the machines and transferred by tube to the *Spänebunker* at the back of the factory.

The *Spänebunker* soon attracted a steady flow of customers. Practically every household in the neighbourhood sent emissaries, mostly children, to collect wood chippings. There was an adjoining unit that housed branches still left on the logs when they were delivered, as well as blocks of wood with knots that, if used, would leave holes in the brushbacks, and finally sawn-off ends.

When I was very small, Grandfather had stomped and roared all around the factory. As he became less mobile, he stayed in the brushback room where he was among men. In his final year, he retreated from the brushback room to the new bunker, meting out helpings of shavings and firewood to the neighbours' children. In that voice, which had not deteriorated like the rest of him, he boomed out directions. The youngsters obeyed while within the reach of his sticks, but once at a safe distance, they sniggered and made faces. The *Spänebunker* was Grandfather's last stand before the chair with the built-in toilet took over.

Chapter Fourteen

TENANTS, PIGS, AND *PLUMPSKLOOS*

I felt no animosity towards Grandmother after the debacle on my fourth birthday. I blamed the cart, not its giver. My relations with Grandmother remained excellent, and not long after my fifth birthday, they were put on a commercial footing. I became her rent collector.

Grandmother owned an old half-timbered house, almost opposite the factory gates, at the end of the inaptly named Neue Strasse. This street must have been new once, but when I was small, it was full of ancient half-timbered houses. Grandmother's was one of its lesser jewels. I had to negotiate a dozen or so dangerous-looking steps to reach the doddery front door. This opened onto the grand entrance hall, a corridor with a wooden floor, grey with dirt and age. More danger awaited a wobbly-kneed small boy in the form of hollows and bulges, and gaps in the planks.

The first time I called, my legs almost gave way for quite a different reason. I opened the door, and an unearthly voice chuckled, "*Kukurukoo! Kukurukoo!*" It was some time before I noticed a cage in the semidarkness. I had never heard or seen a laughing dove, for that was what greeted me. I was always shy with animals. Mother kept the brute creation at a distance. I looked at the creature and it at me. It was tiny, much smaller than the pigeons kept by some of my friends. It had a speckled band around its neck, rather like Grandmother's neckband. We were to become good friends. It spread out its wings for me, showing off some brilliant blue feathers. I tried to return its greeting, which was rather like a cuckoo's.

Two families inhabited this rickety mansion, as well as some beasts that occupied the lower quarters and used a side entrance. I soon learned that I would have less trouble earning my commission on the left-hand side of the corridor than on the right. I needed that commission. My parents kept me short, well aware that whatever they handed out would end up in the baker's till.

Grandmother paid a flat rate of ten pfennigs per successful collection. She did not believe in overpaying those who served her, but I was quite content. She gave me my first chance at earning some money. She fumbled about in her purse for some time before she brought out the yellow coin. She did not find it easy to part with money, even to a beloved grandson. Still, she always paid up. I gave her a peck on the cheek and ran to the baker Kordmöller, next door. Ten pfennigs would buy either a piece of glazed apple cake or a piece of *Bienenstich*, a light sandwich tart with custard cream filling and, on top, a hard crust of flaked almonds glued together with honey—the "bees' sting." *Sahnehöernchen* (horn-shaped cream pastries) cost more. I had to save up for those.

I knocked on the left-hand door. A large grey-haired woman with a good-natured face appeared.

"My grandmother presents her compliments, Frau Dreier, and says, would you please give me the rent?"

Frau Dreier felt for a purse secreted somewhere about her ample person and carefully counted out the coins on the kitchen table. It was always Frau Dreier who paid. Herr Dreier was not to be trusted with money. He blew it on drink. August Dreier was a red-nosed, twinkle-eyed gnome of a man who danced his way from one pub to the next—one of those little men with little say at home, who find their form among cronies. He had learned to assert his manhood where his wife could not cramp his style.

Herr Dreier belonged to the *Schützen*, the famous sharpshooters of Lippe. His finest moment came on their festival day, the *Schützenfest*. The procession was led by Karl Höner, the local carter and one of our neighbours. He acted as herald and rode proudly on a large horse. Not far behind marched August Dreier, leading a mule. He was dressed in white

trousers and a dark green jacket, a wooden rifle slung over his shoulder
and a large feather in his hat. He looked like one of Snow White's dwarfs,
swaying a little as he led the animal, which carried a bag with medical
supplies. Herr Dreier was in charge of first aid, his status as regimental
doctor (*Stabsarzt*) indicated by a Red Cross armband. It was well-known
that the medicine bag contained a plentiful supply of *Wacholder* liqueur.
In a croaking voice, Herr Dreier sang with the rest of them:

> "*Vor Zeiten zogen die Lippischen Schützen*
> *Nach Frankreich hinaus, um das Vaterland zu schützen.*
> *Und zum tro-de-ri-de-ra, und zum tro-de-ri-de-ra,*
> *Und zum tro-de-ri-de-ra, ja die Lipper die sind da.*"

That's how I remember the song, which tells of the sharpshooters
of Lippe setting out for France in order to protect the Fatherland—the
usual thing.

Frau Dreier's face lost some of its good nature when Herr Dreier came
home from his binges. Still, she must have been a good housekeeper, for
she nearly always paid on time.

The Dreiers never harmed anyone. They were duly rewarded by
a gang of boys of which I was, I am ashamed to say, an occasional
member. We displayed our knowledge of forbidden words under their
windows; we knocked on their door and ran away. One New Year's
Eve, we threw *Knallerbsen* at their windows. These little pealike balls,
which exploded on contact, were much prized in the circles in which I
moved. Herr Dreier's little head, topped by a white nightcap, face red
with fury or the effects of drink, popped out of the window. "Get out,
you rascals, or I'll shoot the lot of you," he shouted. Frau Dreier added
some imprecations of her own.

If the old couple knew that I was one of their tormentors, they
never let me feel it. Rather, they treated me with all the respect due an
emissary of Grandmother.

I had a very different reception when I knocked on the right-hand
door. It was opened by a small woman surrounded by a brood of
children.

"My Grandmother presents her compliments—"

"Sorry, we haven't got it," she interrupted. "My husband has not been paid for his work. People don't seem to realize that we too have to live. And there are the children."

"But you didn't pay me last time, Frau Schlicht," I replied, annoyed that the woman was depriving me of my cake.

"I'll look to see if I have anything to give you on account," she said, leaving me to cool my heels in the corridor. The rent was minimal, but Frau Schlicht usually found some excuse for not paying.

Herr Schlicht was the local piano tuner. In the cultural centre that was Schötmar, this was not a full-time occupation. He was also an expert on radios and did repairs. At some stage, a plaque appeared outside the front door announcing, "*Telefunken-Niederlage, Varta Akkumulator.*"

Herr Schlicht further supplemented his income by playing at local festivals, family gatherings, pubs, and dance halls. Although he walked with a stoop, dragging a game leg, he was very popular with the ladies. It appears that very late one night, Frau Schlicht, a determined woman, appeared at the place where he was playing—I think it was the Wevelsburg—and caught her husband with a floosie on his knee. He was dragged home in disgrace. At least, that was the story. In Schötmar, everyone knew everyone else's business.

The lighter side of Herr Schlicht's character failed to manifest itself in his relations with me. In the end, Grandmother had more or less given up on the rent and took payment in kind. Herr Schlicht was to teach me piano. We walked up a further rickety flight of stairs to his studio, the stooped and lame followed by the clumsy and feeble kneed.

A lesson with Herr Schlicht was not a life-enhancing experience. He failed to communicate anything of the beauty and mystery of music. True, I was no young Mendelssohn. While blessed with an agile brain, control over my limbs was minimal. It was not just my legs. My father said that I was born with two left hands. When I came to play the piano, I knew he was right. I press-ganged my fingers into the correct positions, but I could not change chords quickly enough. And my left hand knew not what my right was doing, or if it did, it kept the knowledge strictly to itself.

Herr Schlicht was no help at all. He taught me no tricks to ease my awkwardness or to make my fingers more nimble. All he did was complain about my stupidity. I think we got to Czerny, but never played any real music. It was all grind and almost put-me-off instrumental music. Fortunately, it only took a concert by the London Philharmonic under Sir Adrian Boult to undo the damage. They played Rossini's William Tell Overture and Beethoven's Second Symphony—I was hooked.

A third family lived in the house, below stairs. It was not normally seen, but it was heard and—smelled. While waiting in the corridor for Frau Schlicht to come up with some cash, I knelt on the rough floor and peered through the gaps into a world of dark shapes and subterranean grunts, careful to hold my nose. It was no use. The smell of pig is very potent.

Altogether, Grandmother's house was not a good place for a boy nurtured on 4711 Eau de Cologne and Mousson Creme and saddled with a very sensitive nose. There was the time when my rent collecting was interrupted by squeals from the backyard. They sounded almost human. Then the nauseating sweet smell of freshly slaughtered pig assailed my nostrils. It brought tears to my eyes and made me feel like vomiting. I scampered down the stairs into the street, my mission for Grandmother unaccomplished.

Freshly slaughtered pig is the worst of all possible scenarios for a sensitive nose, but the house in the Neue Strasse held other hazards. There was the *Plumpskloo* in the garden, sending out its fumes. A *Plumpskloo* was an outside loo with the simplest of wooden thrones, erected over a very deep hole that went "plump" every time you did your business. When, after many days, enough mess had been accumulated, you emptied it with a *Jauchefüllle*, a special bucket hooked to a long wooden pole, and spread it round the garden, or emptied it straight into the manure pit.

We were spoiled at home with our water closets, where evil smells did not linger too long, but some of our neighbours still had *Plumpskloos*. These were always situated next to the stable to keep the squatters warm.

Grandmother's house also had a manure pit in the garden. If you added the perfumes from the lower quarters, the *Plumpskloo* and the occasional slaughter, you knew that you had earned your ten pfennigs.

There are still half-timbered houses, beautifully renovated, in the Neue Strasse. Grandmother's is not among them. A British bomb, meant for the railway line, chose instead to make its way into the middle of the Dreier/Schlicht manure pit. The house went up in stink and smoke. The gods had done their homework.

Chapter Fifteen

ALMIGHTY SAUSAGE

No one who has lived in Germany can remain unaware of the central role played by the sausage in national life. It was thus when I grew up, and judging by a recent visit to Germany, not that much has changed. The forty-seven varieties still beckon from butchers' windows, and now from supermarket shelves. The posters still show slim girls in folksy costumes (*Tracht*) and fat men in *Lederhosen* doing their bit by the national dish. There are still sausage stands at many street corners. True, they now eat pizza and pasta and the hamburger vies with the frankfurter, but German stomachs still process a lot of sausage meat.

When I was young, I did my share. As far as sausage eating was concerned, I was German to the core. Now that I no longer eat meat, I shudder at what I ingested. I have stopped yearning for meat sausages. I could not bring myself to eat them now. But I still relish the pleasure they gave me. I fry my grey, soya-filled bangers until they develop a brown crust, but it's not the same. It's definitely not the same.

The local fair, *Kirmes*, was a big event in a small town. The open spaces in town were crammed with all the attractions of a country fair. But as far as I was concerned, the rocking horses, the pedal cars, and the shooting booths with their prizes, could wait. I made straight for the white-painted sausage stand, where *Bratwurst* sizzled on charcoal grills. The smell was intoxicating.

"Could I have that one please?" I asked the man in the striped apron, pointing to the longest, brownest specimen on the grill. The man put it on a rectangular paper plate. It lay there, deliciously curled up, together with a roll and a generous helping of mustard. But not for long. The sausage was too hot to handle, so I started by biting off the tail, which hung over the edge of the plate, and then demolished the rest. The skin, hardened by the grilling, yielded its treasure of juicy, highly spiced, coarsely minced pork. Here was the greatest good this earth could offer.

I counted the days from one fair to the next. There were long chunks of time between *Kirmes*, the *Schützenfest* and the feast of St. Kilian, to whom the local church was dedicated. But I found other avenues.

"Mutti, can I come with you to Bielefeld to help you choose the curtains at Alsbergs?" I wheedled deceitfully. Or, I might offer to help her choose Father's shirts at Hettlage's, or select one of those wide-brimmed navy strawhats Mother bought from the lady whose smile never left her face. I could not very well offer to help choose Mother's corsets, although many of Mother's visits were dedicated to corset choice or alteration. In any case, the corset shop was off limits after I had experimented with various models to see which would make the best concertina, while Mother and the *corsetière* were in the changing room. The *corsetière*, a slim woman who did not have the figure for the job, claimed that I had loosened the elastic of one of her fortresses, but because Mother was such a good customer, she was prepared to overlook the matter.

"Such a nice woman, so decent of her" (*Solch 'ne nette Frau, so anständig*), said Mother, and found herself more firmly bound than ever to this particular prison warden.

I could see Mother was pleased when I offered to accompany her on her shopping trips. It meant I preferred her company to that of my playmates, though she knew me well enough to realize that my motives were not unmixed. No one *volunteered* to shop with Mother. She smiled a conspiratorial smile.

"We'll have coffee and cakes after we've finished shopping." Coffee and cakes are all very well, I thought, but I can get those even in Schötmar, if I'm lucky. I was aiming for something higher.

"Mutti, can we stop? There's a man grilling sausages. I know Karl would like one too." When Father was home, Karl took us in the car. At some stage in her career, no one knew when or how, Mother had acquired a driving licence. There were dark rumours of bribery and corruption. Karl had strict instructions from Father to never, under any circumstances, hand over the car keys to her. Behind the steering wheel, Mother became a dangerous woman—she could not steer.

"I think it's true what they say," Karl joked once, when she had had a go, under supervision. "She must have bribed the tester." Now Karl smiled and said that he did not want a sausage. Mother wrinkled her nose. "I don't know how you can eat those things. Even the smell of them gives me nausea."

Mother saw my sagging face. She found it hard to refuse me anything. "You can have one later, near the *Kaiserhof*. You can wash your hands there and rinse your mouth; otherwise I can't have you in the car. And be careful not to get your suit dirty."

I had a sausage later. It was so good that I had wanted another, but Mother said one was enough, especially in addition to the coffee and *Sahnehörnchen* (those horn-shaped cream pastries). I could see that she was firm and did not argue. Even with one *Bratwürstchen*, the visit had been worthwhile.

At home, I lived on a staple diet of *Mettwurst*, which is a member of the salami family, but whereas salami proper, the bright red variety, contains beef as well as pork, *Mettwurst* is pure pork. It is pink, coarse and very fatty. In warm weather, the fat oozes out and leaves an aftertaste.

Mettwurst was in plentiful supply. Friends, neighbours, and workers made their own and brought them as gifts or thank-you offerings in return for wood shavings. Grandfather and I were the only family members who ate them. At least we had that in common. The staff heartily ate the rest.

"*Wenn's Mettwürste regnet und Bratwürste schneit*," goes the song. When times were good, it rained *Mettwürste* in our house, but alas, it did not snow *Bratwürste*. I liked the rain, but I had much rather it snowed. The song shows how deeply the sausage is embedded in the German psyche. In the illustrations of *Schlaraffenland*, the never-never land of pure sloth, where desires are fulfilled by mere wish, the trees are hung with goodies—and many of the goodies are sausages.

The Jews, good Germans that they were, had their own versions of the national dish. "German citizens of the Jewish persuasion," as they called themselves—*Deutsche Staatsbürger Jüdischen Glaubens*—ate German sausages of the kosher variety. Kosher salami was a darker red than the ordinary variety, since it was all blood-drained beef. It looked very uninviting and tasted the way it looked. Kosher frankfurters looked all right, but they were not bouncy, juicy and spongy like the real thing, and they did not taste of pork. For me, sausage without pork was like Hamlet without the ghost. I felt sorry for Mother and Grandmother. Why did they deprive themselves of the best things in life? I ate *Mettwurst* with the staff. I also ate *Aufschnitt* (cold cuts).

Every pork butcher in Schötmar, whether his shelves were wooden or marble topped, displayed a wide selection of boiled and cured meats and bloated Bologna-type sausages. There were also loaves of sausage meat with scattered bits of pink pork—a cornucopia of goodies. You took your pick. The slices fell in folds from the machine, the butcher wrapped the medley in greaseproof paper, and you had your *Aufschnitt*. While Mother and Grandmother were eating their kosher imitations, I asked if I could buy some *Aufschnitt*, ostensibly for Else and Erna. Mother could not refuse, especially when she was enjoying what she liked.

"Go, if you must," she said wearily. "I know who the real customer is. I shall never understand how you can bring yourself to eat that stuff. Can't you see how dirty pigs are?" Mother made a face but handed over the money. Her objections were not religious. She had a physical disgust of pork, absorbed from her mother.

There was a kind of hierarchy in our household, as far as the dietary laws were concerned. At its apex stood Grandmother with her kosher kitchen and her habit of burying contaminated knives in the garden. Next in line, quite some way behind, came Mother who would not eat pork but who was easy about everything else, prawns included.

One would have thought that my religious father would have come before Mother, but while he avoided pork products at home, he was less rigid about such things on his travels. He told himself that he had to work hard and had to nourish himself properly. As mentioned earlier, I saw him eat bacon in a Glasgow hotel with evident relish.

Father was not unlike the hero of one of his favourite jokes, the rabbi who saw some delicious looking Parma ham at a neighbouring table in a restaurant. "Give me some of that smoked salmon," he told the waitress, pointing at the ham. "That's not smoked salmon, that's ham," said the waitress, wedded to literal truth. "Did I ask you what it was?" came the swift reply.

A long way behind Father, on the kosher-keeping chart came Grandfather and me. I cared as little as Grandfather whether something was beef or pork; it was one of the few things we had in common. All I knew was that pork sausage tasted better.

The best place for *Aufschnitt* was the butcher Bröker in the Begastrasse, next to Kaisers, where we bought our coffee. On the way there, many tasty meat loaves and sausages passed before my mind's eye. My choice was made. It only remained to tell the butcher. But as I approached the Bröker premises, everything changed. I hated butchers' shops. I tried not to see the carcasses hanging by the wall—two legs on hooks, two dangling below. I tried not to breathe the smell of blood and decaying flesh. I concentrated all my attention on the *Aufschnitt* counter. Though gluttony battled with disgust, gluttony won.

"Give me one slice of this, please, two slices of that . . ." Somehow I managed to focus on my tasty selections and not think about their origins—the carcasses on the hooks, the stinking remains of what was once alive and snorted. Deep down I think I knew that it was wrong to kill and eat animals. It took more than forty years for the message to sink in.

I first learned about death in the cellar. Ours was a *Wohnkeller*, a cellar fit to be lived in (just like the *Wohküche*, the live-in kitchen), though no one lived in ours except the occasional mouse, which did not stand much of a chance with cheese traps all over the place. The cellar was laid out like the ground floor with rooms around a central hall. One room held preserves; in another, there was a mountain of potatoes. Then there was the room that housed the central heating and a great stash of coke. We also had a cellar bathroom where the workers heated their metal lunch baskets in the hot water. There were cupboards in the central hall. Amidst the cupboards stood a very large kitchen table of light-coloured wood.

One day—I must have been about four—I went down to the cellar, for what reason I do not recall. I forgot to switch on the light by the cellar door and, walking down the stairs, deep in thought, switched it on downstairs. I shrank back. There, splayed on that light kitchen table, was a huge carcass—two legs at the top, two at the bottom, and a trunk in between. The animal had been skinned and was a dark wine red, with cream-coloured areas of fat. I screamed and ran back up to the ground floor. "Else, Oma, come quickly. There's a most awful thing in the cellar." It took them a long time to calm me down.

"It's only a goat [*Ziegenbock*]," said Grandfather, appearing on the scene. "Don't be such a baby! Your boy has no backbone," he explained to Mother later. "It's all because you spoil him so."

How the goat got there and who killed it, was not explained, and I was too shocked to ask. I knew that Frau Wortmann, who lived by her Christian principles in the Neue Strasse and gave away goats' milk to the needy, passed on her tough old veterans to our neighbours, the Wallhausens, for slaughter. The Wallhausens had a small house and shop diagonally across the street from us, and butchered in a small way. Their name was synonymous with *Ziegenfleisch*, the despised goats' meat, which people like us never touched.

Perhaps it was the dark cellar. I must have seen carcasses before, but only after the goat did I start to notice them. I ran past butchers' shops, averting my eyes and holding my nose, until I became a customer at Bröker's, overcoming my nausea for the sake of a greater good.

Death was never far away. Grandmother's tenants were not the only ones who killed pigs. In neighbouring gardens all around us, there were bodies spread-eagled on sloping wooden boards. They were strung up with a couple of hooks and the board was placed against a tree. There was a porker right next door. When his time had come, I heard his squeals and ran for cover. I told my cousin Helmut. He was very knowledgeable in these matters and determined to share his knowledge with me.

"A butcher comes. He stuns and kills the pig." Helmut mimes with both hands. Helmut's right hand draws a knife in the air and pulls out the guts. "They collect the blood for *Blutwurst*."[15]

---

[15] Helmut explained: "They pour boiling water over it. Then they cut it open and take out the insides. An inspector comes to make sure the animal does not have a disease, and then they can do with it what they like. They cut it up. The ham part is pickled in those wooden vats that look like hollowed tree trunks. Then the ham is sent to the butchers to be smoked. The meat and the fat are also sent to the butchers, who use them for making sausages, mostly *Mettwurst*. The pigs' ribs are pickled and then used for an *Eintopfgericht*, a 'one-pot meal' [usually some kind of stew much recommended to the German people by the Nazis to help the economy]."

I started to cough. Tears of nausea ran down my face, to Helmut's great delight. "What an old sissy you are," he said condescendingly.

I had a particular aversion to blood sausage, a German version of black pudding. I could never get myself to buy it for my *Aufschnitt*, even though Else and Erna liked it. The idea of eating blood!

"I can't stand the smell when all the blood runs out," I said, justifying my squeamishness.

Helmut looked at me sharply. "It's only a pig. Don't pretend. I know you like ham. I've seen you eating it at our house. You like *Mettwurst*, don't you?" I had to admit I did. "Then stop pretending that you don't like pigs being killed."

"I know, Helmut. I'm thinking of the ham before it is smoked. I can't stand meat when it's raw. It's the blood. I won't eat underdone meat. My father won't either. And steak tartare makes me sick."

"You *are* a sissy," said Helmut.

Helmut was right, of course. His strictures apply to all those who don't like the killing, but enjoy its results, leaving the dirty work to others. Our back-garden killings were a gruesome thing, but perhaps it is better to kill what you eat than to buy it in the supermarket, wrapped in cellophane. At least our neighbours were in close contact with their victims. They took responsibility for what they ate. Better somehow than abattoirs, where the animals line up to meet their doom, hearing the cries and smelling the blood of their fellows. Some think that the abattoir paved the way for the holocaust.

The Jewish cattle dealers must have slaughtered some of their old veterans as well. Grandfather certainly did in the old days, but fortunately, I never saw their doings. I only remember the pigs and how I failed to make the connection between the smell of their blood and the mouth-watering aroma of freshly grilled sausages.

Chapter Sixteen

THE *SCHLAGER* SINGERS

I loved Mother very much, but for a time, I loved Else Holländer more. We grew up together, since she came to us when she was only sixteen or seventeen. She was a farmer's daughter from a hamlet in the area. Her job was to look after me—*Kindermädchen* was the term used—and also help around the house. I don't think she had any qualifications beyond elementary school, certainly nothing like an English nanny or governess.

Else was under strict instructions to teach me *Höflichkeit*—politeness. *Höflich* (polite) was Mother's favourite word—although *sauber* (clean) ran a close second. *Höflich* derives from *Hof,* meaning "court." In other words, Mother demanded courtly behaviour. Opening doors for ladies, letting them walk on the right of you, picking things up for grown-ups, especially ladies, bowing in the German way, not speaking until you are spoken to. This last was the most difficult. Else did not know that much about Mother's kind of *Höflichkeit* when she first came to us, but she learned quickly. Mother educated us both together.

Else was tall, slim, and blonde. She was the most beautiful person in my world and she was kind to me, more like an older sister than an authority figure. If there were ever any cross words between us, I don't remember them. We both had to conform to Mother's wishes, but we did that together too. We worked as a team. Mother educated both of us. We sang together, prayed together, and recited together

I have forgotten the sound of Else's voice, but I remember her songs. She was always singing *Schlager*, the latest hit songs. I knew they were shocking because they shocked Mother, though I was not sure exactly why. As soon as Mother came home from the factory, I greeted her with my latest acquisition:

> "*Wenn die Elisabeth*
> *Nicht so schöne Beine hätt,*
> *Hätt sie mehr Freud*
> *An ihrem langen Kleid.*"

In English the song goes: "My friend Elisabeth, out of temper, out of breath." The version Else sang was all about Elisabeth's legs. If she did not have such pretty legs, she would enjoy her long dress more.

Mother looked pained. "Else, you must not teach him those *Schlager*." Mother addressed Else by her first name, but with the formal *Sie*.

"I did not teach him," said Else, looking very pretty and innocent. "I don't know where he picks them up."

The first statement was true, the second false. She did not teach me; I taught myself. I had only to hear such simple tunes and lyrics once or twice, and I remembered them. Else knew very well, though, from whom I picked them up. We often sang them together. While this discussion was going on, I piped up once more:

> "*Wenn sie auch Beine hat,*
> *Tadellos und kerzengrad . . .*"

Again, something about Elisabeth's faultless straight-as-a-candle legs.

"Stop it," said Mother, but she was smiling now. I saw her gold teeth sparkle. Encouraged by her softer attitude, I continued:

> "*Das kann man wohl verstehen*
> *Beim Gehen, beim Drehen . . .*"

It was perfectly understandable that Elisabeth should want to show her nice legs as she walked and turned.

Else too had pretty legs. Everybody said so. Egon Hamlet said so, as did Fritz Schmidtpott, who was older and more of an authority.

I learned lots of *Schlager* from Else. She sang softly and with ease, as she did the dusting Mother that was so keen on, never forcing her clear light voice. That voice was never more beautiful than when she sang sad ballads. These were more mysterious than the *Schlager* and left a deeper impression:

> "*Maria sass weinend im Garten,*
> *Im Grasse lag schlummernd ihr Kind.*
> *Mit ihren gold-blonden Locken*
> *Spielt säuselnd der Abendwind . . .*"

Thus, if my memory serves me well, begins one of the most beautiful of her songs. Mary sits disconsolately in the garden, her slumbering child in her arms. The evening wind blows softly through her red-brown locks.

For some reason, I thought that this song referred to the Virgin Mary, a great favourite of mine, because there were so many beautiful songs about her. Only much later did I realize that the whole point of the ballad was that this particular Mary had lost her virginity.

> "*Es kam ein Reiter geritten,*
> *Ein Reiter wohl hoch zu Ross.*
> *Er kniete Maria zu Füssen,*
> *'Maria vergib mir doch.'*
> *'Dir ist schon längst vergeben,*
> *Dir Reiter wohl hoch zu Ross.*
> *Für Dich lass ich mein Leben,*
> *Für Dich geh' ich in den Tod.*"

A man of noble bearing comes riding on his horse; he kneels at Mary's feet and asks for her forgiveness. She replies, "I forgave you long ago, proud rider. I will give my life for you and will go to my death for you."

That's the version Else sang. In another, which I came across in a book not long ago, Maria is about to drown herself and her child in the lake, but when the child opens its eyes and laughs, she decides that they should live. Again, the father is forgiven.[16]

The haunting tune of this ballad, and its air of mystery, still affects me. I never sang it to Mother. It was too private, too sacred. Also, it might not have annoyed her, so what was the point?

I don't know why I became fond of the Virgin Mary. Else did not speak about her. Like most people around me, she was Protestant. She was not devout and never tried to convert me, but she instilled Christian attitudes in me.

Before I went to sleep, I knelt by my bed, sometimes joined by Else and crooned the mawkish prayer she taught me. It had a sort of tune to it. Father would have been shocked. It was a most un-Jewish thing to kneel, but Mother liked the humility it conveyed. She also liked the meekness of the sentiments expressed. If she came late to kiss me good night, I put in a repeat performance.

Nothing about Jesus Christ in the prayer, but the sentiments are Christian. "I am tired, take my rest, and shut my little eyes. Father, watch over my bed. If I have done wrong today, overlook it, dear God. Dear Father, have patience and forgive my offence."

I was much admired as a child, probably more as the scion of prominent brush manufacturers and as Fat Siegfried's resident grandson, than for my own qualities. But I had one undisputed talent. I was exceptionally quick at learning by heart. Mother had discovered my facility early and did her best to nurture and exhibit it. My talent and I were put on show for visitors, at family gatherings and, above all, on birthdays. There was no relative or family friend too sick or senile to escape my birthday recitations. Great Aunt Pauline, Uncle Julius' wife, must have been practically on her deathbed when I recited for her. I just remember her grey dress and her grey face. I was three when she died.

Mother chose the appropriate poems to recite from a little beige book. The lyrics were so glutinous that it's a wonder the pages did not stick together. I remember the poems Father taught me; I remember the hit songs of the day; I even remember the Nazi songs. But those poems

---

[16] See *Sabinchen war ein Frauenzimmer*, ed. Walter Hansen, Artemis and Winkler, 1996, p. 56.

that Mother chose were so fatuous, so without substance, that there was nothing for my memory to grab onto.

"Else, you sit with him and see that he makes no mistakes," Mother enjoined. It was not a hard task, given my facility.

"I bet I can learn more quickly than you, Else," I dared her. At first she took up the challenge. I beat her hands down. She soon recognized my superior talent, but we still learned together. Even before I was literate, Else just had to read the poem out loud a few times and I could repeat it.

Sometimes Mother's duties prevented her from attending my recitals. But she was not to be robbed of the joy of my performance. On the morning of the great day, Else and I appeared before her. It was a full dress rehearsal. At least she could enjoy that. I was in the outfit I would wear later that day: off-white linen suit with white shoes and socks in summer, velvet or sailor suit in winter. Mother checked the words in the little beige book. Sometimes she made suggestions.

"A little more slowly . . . a little more emphasis on 'dear Aunt Rosalie.'" But she never caught me making mistakes or forgetting my lines. During the actual performance later that day, I often raced through my lines. I thought more about the birthday cake to come than about the old dear whose birth I was lauding. No one seemed to care that I was in a hurry. The reports filtered through to Mother: "He spoke so well, such good German. He never faltered." Mother glowed and I basked in her approval. Else too came in for her share of praise.

Only on Mother's Day was Mother not involved in the preparation. Else and I did it all. I still have a Mother's Day card that I gave Mother, with Else writing the greetings in my name on the back in a florid Gothic script. The card has a coloured photo of a blonde young mother with a permanent wave bending forward to receive tulips from a small blond boy in rose red short pants and a fancy white shirt with rose red buttons and trimmings. I was obviously not the only boy dressed by his mother in this sissyish way. Below the photo, there is a poem of cloying sentimentality that is untranslatable.

> "*Mutter! Du meine Sonne*
> *Du einzig Glück, meine Wonne*
> *Fühle die heiligen Triebe*

Höre den Wunsch voller Liebe:
Möge ein gütiges Walten
Dich Deinem Kind erhalten,
Mütterlein! Segen und Frieden
Sei Dir noch lange beschieden."

Else was with me as I read the poem, and presented some flowers like the little boy in the picture. Mother hugged me, put her arm on Else's shoulders, and we both basked in Mother's approval. The birthday poems were part of Mother's campaign to teach me *Höflichkeit*.

Else accompanied us on most of our outings and longer journeys, yet I can only find two photographs in which she appears. In the Bad Salzuflen photo, with the two cousins and the two nursemaids, she is wearing a white patterned sleeveless dress with a low neckline and a dropped waistline, highlighting her slim waist. My cousins' nursemaid, short and swarthy, in a dark dress, makes Else shine all the more.

The other photograph was taken about three years later, when I was five. Else has made progress. She is leaning against a wall and wearing a clinging ankle-length dress of black crepe draped diagonally about her shapely figure. Her pretty legs, like those of Elisabeth of the *Schlager*, are hidden from view. I am sitting on the wall between her and another woman, who wears a shorter belted black dress with a pleated skirt and a white collar. Once again, Else makes her companion look frumpish; she is so elegant and beautiful. I am sure that Mother helped with her wardrobe, both with finance and advice. Mother was her *Frau Doktor Lerner*.[17]

This photograph was taken at the famous Rolandsbogen of song and legend, a historic beauty spot overlooking the Rhine. We were visiting Father's chief sales representative, Herr Dresbach, who lived with his family in Königswinter. We took a steamer across the Rhine to the Bad Godesberg side. It was my first river trip. I did not know where to rest

---

[17]   Else's daughter, Hildegard Schreiber, recently sent me a photograph in which Else and her husband are walking in a park. Else is pushing her first child in a pram. She is dressed exactly as Mother dressed when pushing my pram, with the same belt and same buttons in front of her white dress.

my eyes, on the strange shape of the Drachenfels, the Dragon's Rock, towering above Königswinter, which we were leaving behind, or on the beautiful spa and Roland's Arch on the other side, or on the mighty Rhine with its powerful current, so unlike our local rivulets.

"Look, Else, look." I kept on tugging at her sleeve, in the hope that she would share my enthusiasm, but she was more interested in talking to a young man in our party.

I went over to Father, who was well read on Charlemagne's circle and had told me something about the Knight Roland. I was excited about actually seeing the arch. Father pointed to a building on an island.

"That place can tell a story. The young lady whom Roland was to marry heard that he had died in The Crusades. She was so grief stricken that she entered the nunnery on that island. Nuns have to vow, to make a solemn promise, that they will never marry. The day after she had taken her vows, however, Roland returned, safe and sound. Now he was forbidden to marry his betrothed or even visit her. So Roland became a hermit, in his castle high up on the hill, where he could look down on her every day of his life. All that remains of the castle now is the Rolandsbogen, which we are going to see."

When we got to the other side of the Rhine, Else and I raced ahead, accompanied by a female relative of the Dresbachs, the other woman in the photo, and the young man. It was quite a climb. The view was spectacular. I was sitting where Roland had sat, looking down on his beloved.

I did not like it at all when Else started going out with August Beckmann from the brush factory's dispatch department. I was unhappy not to be the sole centre of Else's attention, and I did not greatly care for August. It was bad enough that he was a rival stamp collector; now he was also a rival for Else's favour. Also, you never knew what he was thinking. He gave nothing away. I liked people who wore their faces on their sleeves, like August's brother, Fritz, who also worked for us.

You would never have thought that they were brothers. Fritz, the fixer, was blond, with a handsome open face, and was shorter than August. He could turn his hand to anything. When there was an electrical fault in the house, when the central heating went out, and when a machine broke down, Fritz was called to fix it. Sometimes Fritz took me on his motorbike to the Beckmanns' old farmhouse, where sausages hung in the old farm hall, the *Diele*, as if it were *Schlaraffenland* (that magic land of wish fulfilment). Frau Beckmann always made me mouth-watering sandwiches and gave me a *Mettwurst* to take home.

Why doesn't Else go out with Fritz? I thought. I wouldn't mind that so much. But Else was not stupid. She knew that August was more ambitious and had better prospects.[18]

"I am going to Bielefeld with August on Sunday." Else was all smiles. "What shall I wear? Shall I wear my white flowered dress?"

"Yes, you look nice in that, Else," I replied unenthusiastically

Else and August went out practically every Sunday. I dreaded the day when she would leave us. I did not know then that she would have to leave us in any event, August or no August.

Recently, Else's daughter sent me the wedding photograph of Else and August. The bride looked so beautiful. A little girl and I are the only children in the photo. I am in my best velvet, with Peter Pan collar blouse. I look miserable, sadder than in any other childhood photo.

There was another *Schlager* singer in our house. When I was very small, Mother had hired a scrawny young woman, all bones, to cook for us. She did not look like a cook, and she was no cook. Anyone might have had the misfortune to hire Erna, but only an employer profoundly uninterested in good food would have failed to fire her within the month. Sadly, my mother was such an employer. Year after year, she allowed Erna to bore us with a monotonous diet of sugary vegetables, soggy potatoes, and insipid meat. Grandfather was fed large chunks of meat, the rest of us, small pieces. You could tell it was meat from its appearance and texture, but it had no taste. Erna must have been clean, or she would not have lasted. As it was, it took the Nuremberg Laws to terminate her tenure in our kitchen.

I can imagine her now, hunched witchlike over the long kitchen range, brewing her tasteless potions. Occasionally a red-haired rogue strayed into one of the pots and was promptly fished out with a tasting spoon.

---

[18]   He also had a longer life. Else's daughter told me that Fritz was killed in Belgium in the war in 1942. Her parents had a happy marriage and were able to celebrate their golden wedding.

"*Wenn am Sonntag Abend die Dorfmusik spielt,*
Hei diedel deidel diedel dum dum," she warbled. Her singing voice
was better than her grainy-speaking voice.

"*Jedes kleine Mädel die Liebe gleich fühlt,*
Hei diedel deidel diedel dum dum."

As the village band plays on a Sunday evening, says the song, every
young girl feels she is in love. I think Erna would have liked to be in
love.

"*Und der lange Jochen spinnt wieder durch den Saal,*
Denn die Katerina will immer noch mal."

It was all right for Katerina. There was no tall Jochen spinning Erna
through the village dance hall. She was older and uglier than Else and
had no steady beau. Where Else was tall and straight, Erna was on the
short side, and her back was slightly hunched. Else's blonde hair was
held in a bun, like Mother's, though later she had a more wavy hairstyle;
Erna had reddish hair that expanded outwards in a profusion of curls.
The two women looked very different, but they often sang in unison
as they went about their mission of keeping Mother's house clean and
free from dust.

Erna also had her own special *Schlager*, which tended to be more
risqué than Else's. They had the advantage of shocking Mother more.
When I really wanted to annoy Mother, I came out with something
like:

"*Ich habe die Männer am Schnürchen*
Und zieh mit Berlin noch daran,
Sie zappeln wie kleine Figürchen,
Mann zieh, Mann zippel zappel Mann.
Ein feuriges Lied durch die Adern mir brennt,
Kein Mann meinem Blick wiedersteht.
Wie Lippen so süss als von Honig der Wein,
An den der sich daran d'ran hängt . . ."

I cannot vouch for the accuracy of all the words, but the tune, like all the *Schlager* tunes I learned, is as fresh as ever. The gist of the woman's song is that she has men on a string and can pull, even with all of Berlin hanging on to the string as well, and can see them wriggle like little figures. A fiery song is burning through her veins; no man can resist her gaze; her lips are sweet as honey wine for the man who hangs on them. It was wishful thinking, as far as Erna was concerned.

Mother felt that the only place for a boy who sang such songs was an *Internat*. This is not an internment camp, but a boarding school. The barbarous custom of sending young children away from home had not really caught on in Germany, and an *Internat* was a place to be dreaded. As I got older and naughtier, the word came up more and more.

Erna always kept a mop with a long handle at the ready to wipe off any overspills on her range. The polished surface must never be marred. Every so often, she allowed the flames to go out, cleared the dead coal from the interior, and then got to work on the top until it shone a dark silver. By the time she had finished, you could see your face in it. She even polished the range chimney. Would that she had lavished equal care on the food!

While she was busy replenishing the furnace with coal from the tall metal scuttle, I crept up from behind and peered into the pots, hoping against hope. Erna did not like snoopers and told me to go away.

"Erna, can't you make some *Rindsrouladen* the way Mother makes them?" I pleaded, as I smelled another unappetizing meat dish in the making. *Rindsrouladen* were pieces of prime beef, cut fairly thin and further flattened with a wooden hammer. They are coated with mustard and filled with gherkins and pieces of fat to make the meat very soft. Then they are rolled up, bound together with white thread, and put into the oven. At least, that was how Mother made them—more or less—on her all too rare excursions into Erna's domain.

Mother could cook quite well, when she set her mind to it. In England, where she was the cook and, at first, the breadwinner as well, she gradually lost her touch. Unlike cleaning, cooking did not really interest her. "It takes so long to prepare and is so quickly eaten," she complained.

Erna was not interested in my suggestions. "Your mother makes what she makes and I make what I make," she rasped. And that was that. When she was in a good mood, she might consent to make me something less complicated, like my favourite creamed spinach with fried eggs, but as often as not, she burned the onions in the sauce.

Erna's meals were a daily trial. I especially detested her sweet vegetables, of which red cabbage was the most disgusting. She prepared it with apples, vinegar, and as much sugar as it would absorb. To most vegetables, especially to those naturally sweet, she added sugar—lots of it. She gave us sweetened carrots and beetroot and would have given us sweetened parsnips, had they been grown in our part of the world. I liked sweetness in cakes and puddings, where it belonged. Sweet vegetables went against the natural order of things.

Erna was particularly fond of kohlrabi, a turnip-shaped vegetable that looks like pale green wood and tastes like it, too. In England it was, until recently, used mainly as cattle feed. After chewing what was chewable, you spat out the rest, politely, on your fork. Erna, who was more or less given *carte blanche* to compose her menus, served it in a thin pale sauce—twice weekly. When there was meat, the sauce mixed with the gravy to produce a watery light brown fluid.

The grown-ups around me realized early on that they had a *Feinschmecker* on their hands, a lad with a discriminating appetite. Father called me "Monsieur le Gourmand." I insisted, once I knew the difference, that I was a gourmet, not a gourmand. It was one of Else's tasks to make this gastronome ingest what Erna had cooked up.

"I can't eat it, Else," I cried, burying my head in her lap. "It's too awful."

Else gave me lots of sympathy but no alternative nourishment. That would have been more than her job was worth. My parents were not overly strict. Mother moralized a lot, but in practice, she gave me a good deal of latitude. However, where food was concerned, there was one unbreakable rule: Eat what is on your plate—or at least most of it. Mother had read that this was good for a child's character; and always with her child's best interests at heart; she followed the book's instructions. Father concurred. He did not like waste.

When I was little, I fought against these dictates, but it was useless. If I did not eat everything, I was given the same food for supper. This happened very rarely. Else's methods usually worked.

"One spoon for Grandmother, one for Grandfather," and so on, via Great Aunt Pauline to Aunt Grete in distant Cologne. Mother was left to the last. One could not refuse to eat for Mother. As I got older, Mother became less strict. Character had been formed.

Kohlrabi does not come my way these days. I am still served red cabbage and like it as little as I did as a child. I fight wildly against spiced vegetables as I once fought sugary ones. But what I am given, I eat. One who ate Erna's food can eat anything. Character had indeed been formed.

Chapter Seventeen

STATE VISIT (FROM THE BIG CITY)

Every summer, and sometimes two or three times a year, my Cologne cousins paid us a state visit. They were accompanied by their *Kinderfräulein,*[19] or by their mother, or by both, and by at least one empty suitcase. When their father came as well, Grandmother took precautions.

Grandfather hobbled from his soiled armchair to his lookout by the window, grumbling that trains were always late. This was an hour before the *Kölner* (those from Cologne) were due to arrive. He could hardly wait to have the females of his tribe under one roof. The visit would be costly, but no matter.

"Are their rooms ready, Emmy?" he shouted. "They will be here soon." He loved both his daughters, but Mother was now the everyday garden sparrow, Grete the rarer bird of passage. And Grete had born him his only granddaughters. He was as proud of his granddaughters as he had been of his daughters when they were Gisela's and Ingelore's age.

Grandmother, for her part, was well able to contain her joy, especially when Uncle Paul was also expected. A day before the guests were to arrive, she called me to her room. She looked grim. The drawers of the tallboy had been pulled out and the family silver and other valuables assembled on the table.

---

[19]   A somewhat superior nursemaid. Else's status was merely that of *Kindermädchen.*

"I want you to help me close those drawers," she said. "They will be very heavy and you have to push hard." She wagged her finger. "Not a word about this to anyone."

"I won't tell, Oma," I assured her. "You know I can keep secrets." Grandmother did not look wholly convinced, but then, she was not a very trusting person.

She wrapped the silver cutlery, saltcellars, cake-shovels, sugar tongs, and butter dishes in newspaper, mumbling that one couldn't be too careful, that she had learned to be wise before the event. "My own son-in-law," she kept saying, shaking her head, "my own son-in-law."

I was well informed; I knew what she was talking about. She had told Mother that on a previous visit Paul had rifled some of her silver.

Grandmother pulled up her long grey skirt and got on her knees. I handed her the cutlery, the silver plates with the dancing shepherds and shepherdesses, the silver filigree spice box that you were supposed to sniff as the Sabbath ended. She even packed away the better crystal vases. Uncle Paul would have had a job to put those under his jacket. Together we pushed back the heavy drawers.

"So long as he is here, you keep an eye on my room when I'm in the kitchen," she told me. "I've had better locks put in," she told me, "though much use that will be. He can unpick any lock, and he doesn't take much time doing it." I wondered how she knew and why she bothered.

Grandmother did not leave much to chance. She hardly left her room while Paul was in the house. Old people are prone to suspicion, and Grandmother was much more prone than most. Her "case" against Paul had no basis in fact. Also, Uncle Paul was something of a prankster and could well have played a joke at Grandmother's expense.[20] It would have taken more than a few pieces of silver to bolster his allegedly uncertain finances. But it seems that family silver losses were discovered shortly after one of his visits, and so Grandmother, on the basis of suspicion alone, blamed Paul.

Mother certainly believed in Paul's guilt, since she took similar precautions when many years later Grete and Paul visited us from America.

---

[20]   Years later when I spoke to Gisela about this story, she commented that the thought that her father would steal silver was ridiculous.

I was not worried about the family silver. I wanted some excitement in my life and the *Kölner* could be relied upon to bring it.

"Karl, Karl, we have to go," I cried. "Plenty of time," replied the phlegmatic chauffeur. "It only takes five minutes to get to the station, and the train won't be in for another half hour—if it's on time."

"But we might get stuck behind Hektor and Greve." Together carthorse and carter were responsible for getting our brushes to the station. There were always great mounds of corrugated cardboard cartons and fewer wooden chests. Karl smiled. "We can pass them quite easily. Remember we are driving a Nash." It was no use. I pestered him and pulled his arm until he decided that waiting at the station was less trouble.

The train pulled in at last. Gisela emerged and ran towards me, teeth out front. Her chubby, good-natured face with the sparkling brown eyes breathed affection. She hugged me and pinched my cheeks, a trick she had learned from her parents—great cheek-pinchers. Gisela was five years older than I was and mothered her little cousin. Ingelore followed, blonde pigtails flying. She was only two years older than me and less demonstrative, the pretty face giving little away. Then the round head of Uncle Paul bent down as he lowered the suitcases, grey eyes alert. He held out his hand to help Aunt Grete and the *Kinderfräulein*.

The moment Aunt Grete stepped down, my world changed. I ran towards her and fell round her neck. She kissed me on the lips with great force, hugged me, pinched my cheeks, and told me how wonderful I was. I took her hand, and we walked towards the car. I don't know if the rest of the family were in front of us or behind; I had eyes only for her. She looked so smart in her black travelling costume. I was proud.

"I came all the way from Cologne just to see this tasty morsel [*Leckerbissen*]," she cooed, and kissed me again.

Aunt Grete was heavily built, like Mother, but slimmer and not quite so tall. Her round sparkling eyes were brown with a bluish hue. They never quite seemed to reach you, only a private world of their own. One eye looked straight at you; the other took in a fraction of Schötmar as well. It was not a squint but a slight imperfection in a beautiful woman that hinted at darker currents flowing beneath the sea of honey. I did not take much notice and just let the honey flow over me.

The days that followed were a love feast.

"You are my favourite nephew [*Lieblingsneffe*] and I love you." The words rang out for all to hear. "Kiss me!" I did as I was told.

"I love you so much I could eat you." Pinch of right cheek. "How I envy your mother! She is so lucky. I only wish I had a boy like you." Pinch of left cheek. "Yes, I will steal you, pack you in my suitcase and take you back to Cologne with me."

My cousins looked with some disdain on the love affair between their mother and their cousin. They did not fully share their mother's opinion of my mother's good fortune. On one occasion, when Aunt Grete was threatening once again to pack me in that suitcase and take me back to Cologne with her, she asked her daughters, "Wouldn't you like to have such a sweet little brother at home?" The girls looked at each other and said not a word, but the silence screamed, "What! A soppy overprotected little bread pudding like him! That's all we need to make our lives complete."

I do not mean to say that my cousins were not fond of me. They were. But from an early age, they showed a pained awareness of the shortcomings in my character and upbringing, which the fuss their mother made of me could only exacerbate. Moreover, when it came to intelligence and knowledge of the world, I was just not in their league, and they patronized me accordingly.

Aunt Grete may not have been all that serious and the empty suitcase was to serve other ends, but her love for me was genuine. My cousins complained that even back in Cologne she raved about me—what a good boy I was, how polite, how lovable, what a model child. Perhaps Aunt Grete had wanted a boy. Did she think that her sister had once again won out: a good husband, a successful business—and a son?

Whatever the reason for my aunt's affection, I was delighted that I was actually worth stealing. To a child, always a little uncertain of its place in the world, her endearments were a welcome balm. I lapped them up as a poor man his gruel. True, the endearments flowed more freely than the presents, but no matter. She gave me what I craved for most, a sense of my own worth.

"And I love you too, Aunt Grete. I love you more than all my other aunts put together. You are definitely my favourite aunt [*Lieblingstante*]."

This was a weighty statement. Aunt Grete had only five nephews, two of whom she had never even seen at that time. My aunts were legion. Still, I had given the matter some thought and meant what I said. Among the three score or so women I called aunt, Mother's sister had no rival. She was *prima zia assoluta*.

I followed her like a dog. "A lot of use you are," Grandmother sniffed. I had forgotten all about my role as guardian of her treasures. "You can't rely on anyone in this house." I felt that Grandmother couldn't have had an aunt like Aunt Grete or she would have understood.

Mother was *un po' pesante*, as the Italians say. Her manner was a little heavy. It reflected her weight. Aunt Grete was an airier version of Mother. She spoke in superlatives; and her exaggerated compliments bathed me in light. Ayurveda, the ancient Indian system of natural medicine, prescribes a blissful cure where a continuous stream of warm oil flows over you as you are gently massaged. Aunt Grete's endearments worked like that. It was warm oil, honey and light.

Mother was not at all displeased by the attentions Aunt Grete paid me. On the contrary, they reinforced the bond between the sisters. Human relationships are hardly ever simple. When they met, the sisters had embraced with great tenderness. But already there were second thoughts.

"How smart you look," said Mother, eyeing Grete's well-cut travelling costume after the sisters had embraced. "I like the basket weave, and the lapels are so unusual. Where did you buy it?"

"Oh, I got it in the sale at Tietz," Grete replied. Mother's eyes showed that she did not believe her. "She has time to go and look at all the shops because she never does any housework. She has Billa to slave for her." Billa was Grete's mother-in-law.

I overheard Mother's comments, made in the bedroom to Father. I did not have similar access to Aunt Grete's secret thoughts, but even I, besotted as I was with my aunt, sensed the undercurrent of tension as the visit progressed. Their love for me and sisterly affection pulled one way, ancient rivalries pulled powerfully in the other direction. The sisters did not actually quarrel; it was an armed truce with each party on its guard. I knew that look of Mother's—the shorter focus of the eyes, the red blotches on the cheeks, the furrowed forehead.

The fate of the cutlery did not come into it. Mother's real fear was that Grete, presumably goaded by Paul, would put pressure on Grandfather to hand over yet more cash. Grete may have been afraid that

Mother would try to dissuade Grandfather from helping her. Mother never did; she just made barbed comments to Father. "My sister belongs to the tribe of takers. [*Meine Schwester ist vom Stamme Nimm.*] She will put on an act for my father's benefit."

I took it all in, but it made not a jot of difference to my love for Aunt Grete.

I was heartbroken when the time came for Aunt Grete to go back to Cologne, but I shed no tears over her consort. It was not just the bad things that I had heard about him. I was uncomfortable with the boom of his voice, and there was something about those eyes. They were never still. His sister, Aunt Hede, had a similar look.

Uncle Paul taught me to play chess. He found it a thankless task. "You are a dunce," he rasped. "What do you have in your head? Wood shavings from your factory?" The tone was dismissive, the look, contemptuous. "The rules for moving a knight are so simple. Two squares straight, one to the side, or one straight, two to the side. Even a four-year-old could understand it."

My uncle had the quick-witted man's impatience with those of slower wit, while I had the instinctive distrust of the slow for those of nimbler wit. It was unfair of fate to have married my favourite aunt to my least favourite uncle.

Their supposed mission to fleece Grandfather presumably accomplished, the Cologne pair returned to the big city, leaving their offspring and the *Kinderfräulein* behind. The girls would not go back empty-handed.

"I can see my young ladies need new outfits," he chortled, as they wound themselves around Grandfather and kissed his stubbly cheeks. He loved to see his womenfolk look smart; Grandmother always excepted.

"He always started with new shoes," Gisela remembers. "I only want the best for my granddaughters," he told the assistant at Tiemann's shoe store in Bad Salzuflen; and the best they got—strap-over shoes, just like those of the *Kinderfräulein*.

Next came the dresses and with them, accessories, belts, caps, even little handbags. As happened with his daughters long ago, the styles he chose were often too grown-up. Aunt Grete, although happy to receive donations, sometimes protested, but Grandfather usually got his way.

A proud smile stole over his red ravaged face as the girls paraded before him in their new finery.

"Now I can bear to look at you," he told them, and addressing his daughter, he added, "Cologne is not the only place where they have smart clothes." He turned to the assistant, usually a full-bosomed woman of mature years. "Fräulein, please pack up the old clothes. My granddaughters will wear their new outfits." With Mother adding her own gifts, the formerly empty suitcase was full to bursting by the time they left.

As they grew older and more ladylike, my cousins also became more snooty. They made it plain that in lending their presence to our negligible township, they were lowering their standards. "What a village [*Dorf*] to be marooned in," they sighed.

"It's not a *Dorf*," replied their mother, defending her birthplace. "It's a town [*Stadt*]." Technically, Aunt Grete was correct, but the girls continued to speak of the *Dorf*. It was all a facade. They loved the country, loved every minute of their stay. Schötmar for them was *Schlaraffenland* (the magic land where all their wishes would be fulfilled).

One day, when Grandfather asked Gisela what she wanted, she said she wanted a bicycle. Grandfather bought her one. Uncle Paul was none too pleased because of the Cologne traffic, but she was allowed to ride it if the *Kinderfräulein* accompanied her. Schötmar was indeed *Schlaraffenland*.

Even so, as young ladies used to the sophistication of one of Germany's oldest, largest, and most cultured cities, they owed it to themselves to look on our town and its inhabitants *de haut en bas*, and to wear a permanent air of boredom. No one in such a place was worthy of their attention—certainly not the village boys (*Dorfjungen*). Egon Hamlet, the scrawny cattle dealer's boy from across the road had the misfortune to fall for the charms of the beautiful Ingelore. She was tall and slim now, with striking deep-set green eyes, a finely chiselled nose and those long blonde pigtails.

Egon made the mistake of asking me where "Lieselotte Lore" was to be found. He was never allowed to forget that he had forgotten Ingelore's name. Whenever he showed himself, peering shyly from a distance at the object of his adoration, Gisela and I sang in unison, "Egon Hamlet, Lieselotte Lore. Egon Hamlet, Lieselotte Lore." As for

"Lieselotte Lore," she paid more attention to Hektor the horse than she did to her admirer.

Ingelore loved horses. She got around old Greve. He could not refuse such a pretty girl's request for a ride on Hektor. He gave her beets to feed the old chestnut and let her stroke his mane. When they had made friends, he lifted her up onto the horse and led her up and down the factory driveway. "Look how tall I am!" she cried, as they passed the office building. "I can see into the upstairs windows."

Egon stood watching forlornly in front of the Hamlet's house, opposite the driveway. Ingelore did not consider him worthy of even a glance.

Ingelore had several admirers. Gisela, the older sister, was not troubled by the same degree of local interest. The country boys responded to physical charm, and there Gisela did not score so highly. She was a dumpling like me—plump, rather swarthy, with teeth that were forever in braces. She tried to compensate for her physical shortcomings by peppering her conversation with long words and discoursing on philosophy and science, but there was no response from the boys.

Gisela told me recently that she did have a kissing tryst in our garden grotto with a handsome blond in his early twenties who worked in our dispatch department. From the description that she gave me, I think it was Fritz Beckmann. She may not have attracted the boys, but she clearly did something for the men.

Gisela was the first member of her family to visit us after the war. I went to meet her at Victoria Station. I recognized only the glowing dark eyes; the rest of her had undergone a miraculous transformation. From the train stepped a slim, lithe young woman, still not conventionally pretty, but attractive and very smart.

We had been prepared for a change when her first husband, a U.S. Army radiologist stationed in England during the war, had shown us photographs of a beautiful young woman who, he claimed, was his wife. However, he was a camera buff and admitted to using quite a few lights. Mother, who loved Gisela, could not resist observing that it might have been a case of art taking over where nature had failed. (*Wo die Natur versagt, da hilft die Kunst.*) But when she stepped off the train, we knew that nature had not failed Gisela.

Mother and Gisela had a special relationship, less effusive than Aunt Grete's and mine, but perhaps deeper. It could be that Gisela was the daughter Mother had lost.

"Gisela has heart," Mother used to say, even when her niece was a child. Coming from Mother, this was high praise. Mother also found Gisela *sportlich*, a quality Mother much admired. The way Mother used the word, it had nothing to do with being good at sports, more something to do with being a good sport, and everything to do with being straightforward, acting and dressing without frills. Mother admired this quality in women, not in men, or she would have dressed me differently.

Gisela too felt close to my mother, perhaps closer than to her own. Aunt Emmy could not by any stretch of the imagination be called an intellectual, but Gisela admired her solid virtues, her devotion to work, her love of home, and her big heart. Seeing Gisela in her home in Chicago, I saw Mother dusting the sideboard, cleaning the door handles, tidying up.

Ingelore got on even less well with her mother than did Gisela. She turned to her father rather than her aunt. But even there, things were not always smooth. When she was sent to school in England, one of her first acts of independence was to cut off the blonde pigtails her father adored and send them to him in Chicago. He did not write to her for six months.

Chapter Eighteen

TO THE BIG CITY

"The Romans built a fortress here two thousand years ago, when they were fighting the ancient Germanic tribes." Father was enlightening Mother and me, as we sat comfortably in our plush second-class carriage. It was a nice change after the wooden benches in third class, which we used for shorter journeys. Those left marks on your behind.

"They called the fortress 'Colonia Claudia Ara Agrippina' after the empress who was born there. Her own son, Nero, murdered her. You have heard of Nero. He was the emperor who burned Rome."

Father was very good on names and historical facts of little importance. I lapped them up. Before I could count to ten, I knew that Pippin the Small was Charlemagne's father and that Frederick the Great's father kept a regiment of giant grenadiers.

"The French call the city 'Cologne.'" Father said in the still faultless French he liked to display. "You know Mutti uses eau de cologne. That's French for . . . ?"

"*Kölnisch Wasser*," I replied, quickly. "Mutti calls it '*otte Kolonje*.'" My eyes met Father's. We both looked at Mother and smiled. "Mutti has her own version of the French language, as of much else," said Father.

Mother laughed sheepishly. She never minded being teased about things of no importance to her.

Father's lesson was not over yet. "There were Jews in Köln, even in Roman times. Who says we are newcomers to Germany? We have as much right to live here as anyone else."

There were no other people in the carriage.

I had my nose glued to the window as the train crossed the mighty Rhine. "Look, Vati! It's even wider than the Weser at Minden. I wouldn't like to be in that current."

"There is the *Dom, der Kölner Dom*." Father's voice was solemn, as he pointed to the twin spires that towered above all the other church spires in view. "That cathedral took over six hundred years to build."

I wondered if it was worth it. I did not like the look of the dark pile. I was searching for Roman temples with endless columns. Father was in his element.

> *"Im Rhein, im heiligen Strome,*
> *Da spiegelt sich in den Well'n*
> *Mit seinem grossen Dome*
> *Das grosse, heilige Köln."*

"That poem in praise of the Rhine, the cathedral and the city was written by Heinrich Heine, one of our greatest German poets and, as you know, a Jew."

I had never been to a really big city before. The station, practically opposite that horrible dark cathedral, looked like an elegant hotel. I was counting the endless platforms when Aunt Grete appeared and smothered me with kisses and compliments.

Uncle Paul showed us some of the sights on the way to their house. But I wanted him to produce some Roman temples. Alas, there were none. I had to make do with some of the old walls and a massive medieval gate. We drove along the Ringstrasse, the broad boulevard that encircles Cologne. In no time, I had learned by heart the names of its different sections.

We reached the posh suburb of Marienburg and turned into a small road with large villas. We stopped outside one of them. It had an ornate wrought iron gate and spiked red fence. There were small trees and shrubs in front of the villa. Our house in Schötmar was right on the pavement; we had no gates or fences, but no one had ever broken in.

There was something peculiar to me about the *Kölner's* villa. Our house in Schötmar was symmetrical, with the balcony railing in the middle and the same number of windows on either side. Here, nothing seemed in its proper place. The left side of the house was topped by an elaborately rounded gable, rather like those I was to see in Holland a year or two later. There was a small rounded window under the gable. Below it were large square windows and a defiantly square balcony. Below that was a square window bay.

We went in, and we gaped. We passed through a mosaic marble foyer to a rust-coloured marble entrance hall with an elegantly curved banister. The marble was highly polished and slippery. Upstairs, a marble bathroom awaited us. This was not what I had expected, considering all that talk at home about the *Kölner's* shaky finances.

Mother eyed the marble and the Persian rugs, and said nothing. Before we went upstairs to our bedrooms, she examined the sliding doors that separated the reception rooms and paid special attention to the smoking room—gloomy with dark oak furniture, a large round table, and dark red velvet curtains. We did not have a smoking room in Schötmar—yet. She had opened the door of the bookcase and rummaged about in there. Mother was not interested in the books; she wanted to pick up ideas for improvements at home. I could read her like a book.

As usual, Mother's real thoughts surfaced when we were *entre nous.*

"I realize that the house was built by Uncle Hugo in better times, Hermann, but they have managed to make quite a lot of improvements since I was here last. They live above their means."

After Uncle Hugo's death, Aunt Grete and her family, who had lived on the first floor, took over the ground floor as well. My uncle and aunt had the large master bedroom and fine balcony on the first floor—while Oma Billa, Uncle Paul's mother, just had a smallish room on the ground floor. My cousins, their *Kinderfräulein* and the maid occupied the top floor.

Like Mother, Aunt Grete valued her paid help. One of her favourite sayings was, "The maid is the home's happiness." (*Das Mädchen ist die Glückseligkeit des Hauses.*)

Father could not wait to show me the wonders of the wretched *Dom.* No one else volunteered to come along. He persuaded Mother, but she soon lost interest and went shopping. There was nothing at the *Dom* that would give her ideas about how to improve her home.

The place looked even more ominous than it had from the train. The twin spires loomed above us, menacing and dark, with an even darker emptiness between them. They were towering and overpowering. In those days, when skyscrapers had not yet reached Europe, their 157 metres (515 feet) was high. I felt no more at ease when we went inside. Why was the place so dark and cold? It was enough to give you the creeps.

I understood everything when Father told me that the cathedral had been built to house bones. The bones of the three Magi had been presented to the citizens of Cologne by a generous Barbarossa—Father's hero and mine—who had looted them from Milan. The cathedral had been erected over the remains. It was a grisly giant cemetery.

Gothic cathedral architecture certainly had no charms for a down-to-earth child like me—all those soaring arches aspiring heavenward, all those gables, pinnacles, finials, and flying buttresses drawing the attention away from earth. My feet were firmly planted in the world of cakes and sausages. This cathedral had no light and no warmth. It left me cold, stone cold. Father was always talking about the Strasburg Cathedral. I wondered if it was as awful.

We were in the largest church in Germany, the first Catholic church I had ever visited. I was shocked by all the statues and images, Christ on the cross, the omnipresent Virgin Mary cradling her son as a baby and as a corpse, and then all those saints. Among them, St. Ursula in blue brocaded dress and gold cloak dominated the scene. There was the famous *Dombild* that shows her together with many women—just a representative number of her eleven thousand virgins.

I had learned my Ten Commandments. I may have been a little vague about adultery, but I knew all about graven images. I tackled Father on the subject. He was always tolerant of other faiths, but had to agree that when it came to images, Christians, and especially Catholics, had strayed. He admired Islam for not straying similarly. It was so obvious that God, being invisible, could not be pictured, while the others in this image shop should not be pictured.

There was some relief from the gloom in the stained-glass windows. I loved colour. I kept staring at those rich red, blue, green, and gold panes that somehow grew into a story. Father explained those from the Old Testament.

The next day was much better. Aunt Grete, well aware of her favourite nephew's favourite occupation, took all the children out for coffee and cakes. Father had gone to visit customers. Mother stayed at home with Oma Billa for *Hausfrau* talk.

The Café Eigel[21] was near the Hohe Strasse, one of Cologne's best shopping streets. I had never seen such shops, not even in Bielefeld. I was mightily impressed. Those girls really had something to be snooty about. We went to browse in Kaufhaus Tietz, a department store. I was told that it was not even in the top price bracket, but it looked like a palace to me. There were columns and Greek friezes on the walls. The jewellery and other precious wares were kept in large glass cases. The café was also very grand and the *Sahnehörnchen* (horn-shaped cream pastries) were exceptional. Aunt Grete and cream cakes too—I was in heaven.

I do not recall the time of year, but it couldn't have been summer because the girls were dressed in navy overcoats trimmed with grey Persian lamb and matching hats. Grandfather would have been surprised, and he might have been less generous. The girls looked extremely smart.

Alas, beneath the finery all was not well. As I was savouring my *Sahnehörnchen*, I noticed that the girls kept scratching themselves between their legs.

"Why do we have to wear those things?" Gisela moaned.

"Oma wants to keep you warm," replied Aunt Grete, pouring oil on very troubled waters.

"But we are not cold, Mother. It's not a cold day."

"Oma knows best," soothed Aunt Grete.

Gisela's face dropped, and she scratched herself again.

I thought "those things" referred to their overcoats, but when we children were alone, all was revealed.

"Oma knits these woollen knickers for us. She knits all the time. The knickers have to be navy blue, same colour as our overcoats, so that our undercarriage won't show too much."

Their fashionable overcoats were ultra short, and Oma Billa's handiwork stuck out from under them. They looked rather like the bloomers once worn by women tennis players.

---

21   This was in the days before the famous Café Silberbach, opened by one of our relatives, when Jews were no longer welcome in "Aryan" cafés.

"I know what you mean," said I, with a mixture of sympathy and self-pity. "My mother makes me wear heavy black velvet pants even in summer for special occasions. They are so tight, they hurt where it hurts, and they are hot and make me sweat. I can't do anything about it. Mother says they look nice and that's most important."

"But our knickers itch like hell, and they stink," said Gisela, not to be outdone. She pulled up her coat fully to reveal Oma Billa's version of the hair-pant. And she was right about the smell. Apparently, the knickers were not changed too often. There were lighter patches where the dark blue had been discoloured by urine. If ever there was a case of Mother's *oben hui, unten pful*,[22] this was it.

"Mother knows we are right," said Gisela, "but she can't do a thing. Oma is the boss." Ingelore nodded her agreement, but without enthusiasm. I noticed that she had not complained much. She was her grandmother's favourite.

The formidable Oma Billa held the Marienburg household in a grip of iron, very much as she herself was held in place by a heavy steel brace. A motor accident, years back, had broken her spine. Like many people who have chronic problems with their bodies, she was tough and lived to a ripe old age with all her faculties intact. She was a small woman, bent double and shrivelled and, like most old women of my acquaintance, well supplied with warts. Oma Billa's frizzy iron-grey hair was held in a bun. Bushy eyebrows overhung her small eyes like thorny twigs over a narrow window. The eyes reminded me of her son's, but they had more of a twinkle.

Oma Billa was a workhorse. I woke up very early one morning and went down to the kitchen to eat something. There she was, a hunched black form, on her knees, with bucket and brush, scrubbing the floor.

"The week before Passover she has the house under two metres of water," Gisela told me. "We have to move with Mother to a hotel during that time."

No wonder my own mother admired Billa. Mother started dusting at six in the morning; Oma Billa, encased in leather-padded brace,

---

22   The saying points to the contrast between the elegant outerwear on top (*oben*) and the dirty underwear below (*unten*).

was *in situ*, scrubbing the floors, soon after five. She started with the kitchen and then tackled the hall marble. She had scrubbed the kitchen table so often and so thoroughly with her hard brush that some of the wood had come off. I sometimes wondered what there was left for the *Glückseligkeit des Hauses* to do. Mother did not envy Grete her husband; she envied her his mother.

"If only I had a woman like Billa to supervise the running of the household while I am busy in the factory," Mother sighed when we were home, remembering perhaps that her own mother's interests stopped at the door of her kosher kitchen. "If Billa came here, she would not have to be a slave, the way she is in Cologne. She would not have to do anything; only to see that everything was in order."

Mother's admiration for Billa was genuine, but she could not resist taking a dig at her sister. "While Grete has a good time, her poor mother-in-law has to slave away at home."

While Grete could work very hard, as she did in their posh butcher shop during Paul's butcher period, she did like to go shopping, visit friends, and entertain her *Hausfreunde*, mostly middle-aged bachelors with artistic leanings. They were happy to be around a beautiful woman. I remember her receiving one such in a beautiful pastel silk georgette dress with pleats.

She and Paul could go to carnival and Purim[23] balls, secure in the knowledge that Billa was guarding the home. Once, in answer to Ingelore's pleas, Aunt Grete dressed up for us in a Turkish style harem blouse and pantaloons, the outfit she had worn for the carnival. Try as I might, I could not imagine Mother dressing like this. Fortunately, my parents had gone home by that time, or Mother would have made some comments.

In return for her slavery, if indeed slavery it actually was, Oma Billa demanded obedience. I was to hear endless complaints about her autocratic behaviour, especially from Gisela. "You are lucky to live with Oma Bertha. She does not poke her nose into everything like Oma Billa."

I agreed that Oma Bertha was an unexceptionable woman, though she might have been more generous in rewarding a grandson who put himself out to collect her rents.

---

[23]   A Jewish festival.

"At least she does not stop you eating the fruit out of your own garden." There was bitterness in Gisela's voice.

"Of course she doesn't," I replied. "I help myself whenever I want to." Our strawberries were protected by nets, our fruit trees by a scarecrow, but these were directed against a different kind of predator. Oma Bertha hardly ever went near the garden, except to bury knives that had been contaminated by unspeakable things like pork sausages.

"Well, this Oma is different," Gisela sighed, and regaled me with the story of Oma Billa and the orchard. I had already heard about the smelly knickers and the water-driven exodus at Passover time. There seemed to be no end to Oma Billa's misdemeanours.

The orchard was in a corner lot adjoining the garden, but separated from it by a high wooden fence. It was a paradise, complete with gazebo and, more to the point, the most luscious cherries, strawberries, apples, plums, gooseberries, and even peaches. But it was a forbidden paradise. The door to it was locked and Oma Billa held the key. She would let no one enter, not even her daughter-in-law. She said that she needed all the fruit for preserves. In their cellar, there were enormous shelves filled with bottles of once fresh fruit. If they wanted their fruit in season, Aunt Grete and her daughters had to climb over the fence and help themselves. This they regularly did when Oma Billa was out of the way.

I could not help thinking that a great deal of clambering went on in that household, with the tale of Uncle Paul making his way up and down drainpipes to visit his lady friends and his wife and daughters scaling orchard fences. It made our life in Schötmar seem very dull.

I never joined Gisela in Billa-baiting. I judged people mainly by the way they treated me. Oma Billa, while not particularly affectionate or liberal with sweetmeats, treated me kindly. There was never a harsh word. That may have been because I was my mother's son. The two women were very close. I would watch them in the conservatory, Billa explaining to Mother how she kept the plants looking so fresh and lush. The view from the windows was somewhat spoiled by the wire netting of the chicken coop at the back of the garden. Aunt Grete once complained about it so near to the villa.

"But it's such a saving and we have fresh eggs," said Billa, while Mother added, "See, Grete, how your mother-in-law has your interests at heart."

When a chicken's time had come, Billa made short work of it. She quickly twisted its neck. Then she ran with the headless chicken to the cellar, where she plucked it and prepared it for the pot. It was enough—almost—to take away one's appetite.

Mother loved the spacious conservatory at the back of the house with its rare plants and flowers, its large oval table and wicker chairs. All her life, Mother dreamed about having a conservatory. Her sister had one; her brother was to acquire one in London; only Mother never achieved her *Wintergarten.* But she did manage to get Oma Billa for a while.

After much persuading, the old lady came to Schötmar for a month's visit, bringing the girls with her. Mother, true to her promise, would not let her do any household chores. But Oma Billa was not a woman to idle away her time. She spent it rug making. She worked, appropriately enough as it turned out, in the smoking room, carefully matching the colours of her rug to those of the brocade curtain that separated the room from Mother's Blue Salon. I got to know that rug well, since I was to spend much time in the smoking room reading, after I was banned from school. It lay there in its glory, turquoise blue and rust, admired by all who were allowed to enter.

Mother urged Billa to stay longer, but our household was too well run to engage her interest. She felt that she was not needed in Schötmar and kept worrying about how her family would cope without her. There may have been a grain of truth to Mother's picture of the work-shy daughter-in-law, always out on the town, dressed in her finery, and the poor mother-in-law slaving away at home. But Billa enjoyed working and enjoyed playing the martyr. At dinner, she insisted on being served last. When there was not enough of one dish to go around, it was she who went without. Gisela said that Oma Billa adored her daughter-in-law and was quite happy to spoil her.

When the time came for Grete and Paul to make a fresh start in America, they suggested that Billa might like to live with her daughter, Hedwig, who was already well established in England. Billa would not hear of it. She begged to be allowed to come to Chicago with Grete and Paul. She would not mind roughing it. She was used to work. And so it was that in Chicago, she breathed her last, nearing ninety. Almost to the end, she wrote to Mother in her long spindly Gothic hand, the letters keeling over at some forty-five degrees. Mother wrote back, telling Billa about the latest improvements to her home, and she made Father and me add a few lines. It was a genuine friendship between two women for whom work was a religion and a beautiful clean home its temple.

Most people have some secret weakness or vice. The more respectable they are, the more secret it has to be. On my first visit to Cologne, I discovered Oma Billa's. One day, as we were passing the old martinet's room, Ingelore put a finger over her mouth and tugged at my sleeve. She looked through the keyhole and motioned me to follow her example. I could hardly believe my eyes. There was the shrivelled little woman sitting in an armchair, sending up clouds of smoke. She was taking a well-earned rest, puffing at a pipe. In the circles in which I moved, the rare woman who smoked a cigarette drew unfavourable comment—but a pipe!

"When someone surprises her," Ingelore told me, "she just stuffs the burning pipe into her pocket."

Now I knew why the big pockets of her long black overalls often had holes in them.

Everyone was aware of Oma Billa's weakness, but for forty years, the family kept up the pretence of ignorance. The time came, in Chicago, when she could no longer go out to buy the tobacco herself. Gisela says that they would all have been delighted to bring her supplies, but no one dared broach the subject. In desperation, Billa took to shredding her son's cigar butts, with predictable results. She coughed and coughed and the place reeked. Had she lived in the age of women's liberation, all that pretence, and the suffering it doubtless entailed, would have been unnecessary.

My cousins and I grew closer because they could complain to me about Billa and we could laugh together, and I would not tell. Gisela was especially gifted in telling Billa stories.

Gisela belonged to a Jewish youth organization called *Schwarzes Fähnlein* that promoted the outdoor life. That suited Gisela's *sportlich* instincts. Ingelore refused to join the junior version of this outfit, the *Pimpfen*. One New Year's Eve, after a long vigorous hike, Gisela came back to the house with a gaggle of girls, dressed in their white blouses and blue skirts. It was well after midnight. They were having snacks in the kitchen when Oma Billa, disturbed by the noise, rushed in from her downstairs room, in her voluminous white nightgown. Oma Billa was ready to confront burglars. The girls, seeing this bent apparition in the dark kitchen, thought they were confronting a witch or a ghost. There was panic on both sides, until Billa got the picture and started bawling out Gisela, mortifying her in front of her friends.

Gisela and Ingelore were not above mortifying their little cousin. They must have got very tired of their mother forever singing my praises and comparing their behaviour unfavourably with mine.

"What a wonderful nephew I have. He always pulls out a chair for his aunt. He never eats before the grown-ups have started. He always says 'please' and 'thank you.' He never shouts or loses his temper. [She did not say 'he never sulks.'] And he doesn't slide down the banisters like some people I know. If only you two were more like him. How I wish I could have him here with me all the time," and so on.

Most of the time, they took this in their stride. After all, I was little, and I was a boy—no real competition. But sometimes they took it out on me. One day they appeared with a huge tin of Nivea cream. "Let's rub him all over," Gisela threatened, "the way his mother does. Every day she rubs him with Nivea from head to foot." She took my face in her hands and cooed, "Don't you miss being rubbed with Nivea cream?"

"No, I don't," I shouted and added, "No, she doesn't. She doesn't have time to rub me every day. She's far too busy in the factory. Only about once a week."

"And you comb her hair too," they jeered.

"No, I don't," I cried. "And if you come near me, I'll pull your hair, Gisela, and I'll pull out your pigtails, Ingelore. And I'll bite the both of you."

They didn't put me to the test, but they continued to tease me, making threatening faces and imitating my country accent. Ingelore crooned:

> "Wenn Du wüsstest, wenn Du wüsstest, mein Kind
> Wie gefährlich, aber ehrlich, doch die Rheinländer sind.
> Sie sind voll Übermut
> 'D'rum sei auf Deiner Hut,
> Sonst ist's im Handumdreh'n
> Um Dich, mein Kind, gescheh'n."

The song warns of the dangers of getting too close to Rhinelanders, who are dangerous but honest. At the drop of a hat, your fate could be sealed. I realize now that the child to whom the song is addressed was somewhat older than my eight or so years, and female to boot.

When Uncle Paul's sister, Hedwig Stern, came for a visit with her family, her younger son, Werner, was rude to his mother. I do not recall what he said, but it was evidently something quite outside the range of my experience of mother/son relationships. I exclaimed, "He says that to his own mother!" (*Das sagt er zu seiner eigenen Mutter!*) My cousins never let me forget that. They mocked in chorus, attempting to imitate my look of astonished disbelief and my country accent.

The visit of the Stern family was memorable. It was a lazy pleasant Sunday afternoon when the telephone rang.

"We are on our way." I could hear the booming voice from where I was sitting. It was Alfred Stern, Paul's brother-in-law, calling from his home in nearby Elberfeld.

"Not a 'Can we come? Is it convenient?'" commented Aunt Grete. "Just an accomplished fact. They might have given a little more notice. But that's their way." She accepted the inevitable.

Not so her daughters. They ripped open a shoe carton and liberated a piece of cardboard on which Gisela wrote in large letters: *SEUCHENGEFAHR!* (*DANGER! EPIDEMIC!*). Ingelore pinned the notice to the front door. Then Gisela got to work on me, and this time I let her. She laid me out on the chaise longue and rubbed my cheeks so furiously that I half imagined I had fallen victim to some dread unnameable disease. I looked red and felt feverish.

The Sterns came, they saw, they laughed and they stayed. It was my first contact with the people who were to help save my parents' lives and later start my father on a new career. Alfred was a dark tubby little man with a very red face, cruel eyes and a snarl; his wife Hedwig, also on the stout side, had Paul's enigmatic eyes. They had two sons: Hans, dark-haired and already running to fat; and the younger, Werner, blond, handsome, and rude to his mother. Finally, there was Oma Stern, a harmless, fussy little lady with delicate features who could never get herself together.

"Hedwig and I are going back to Elberfeld tonight," announced Alfred. "We are leaving mother and the boys with you."

The announcement was met with stunned silence. The Stern boys were not popular. They were not considered part of the family the way that I was. I do not recall why their parents parked them and their grandmother in Cologne. We could all have done without this invasion, but they were family and we were helpless. There was nothing left but to turn to the muse:

> "*Des Sonntag Nachmittag's, Oh Schreck!*
> *War die ganze Freude weg.*
> *Familie Stern kam an, was nun.*
> *Wie sollt man sie aus dem Hause tu'n?*
> *'SEUCHENGEFAHR!' ein schönes Schild,*
> *Familie Stern, die wurde wild.*
> *Aber sie blieben trotzdem da,*
> *Da wurde die ganze Bescherung wahr.*"

> (That Sunday afternoon, O horror!
> All joy disappeared.
> The Stern family arrived.
> How to get rid of them?
> DANGER! EPIDEMIC! A lovely poster,
> The Sterns went wild.
> But they stayed just the same,
> And the whole mess came to pass.)

And so it went on for twenty-nine couplets. I counted them and remember the number. The chief rhymesmith was Ingelore, but I contributed generously. Our verses were governed less by the facts than by the requirements of rhyme. But the verses that touched on Oma Stern were dead accurate.

> "*Nun wollten wir 'ne Schiffahrt machen.*
> *Die Sternsche sucht ihre Siebensachen.*"

> (Now we wanted to take a boat ride.
> The Stern woman looks for all her belongings.)

We were all looking forward to that boat ride on the Rhine. Oma Stern was the obstacle. Etiquette demanded that, as a visitor, she be included in the party. Now, Oma Stern was as indolent as Oma Billa was spry—and she was an expert and obstreperous procrastinator. Her strategy was to agree, but delay. Yes, she would love to come, but she was not feeling well today. Yes, she was looking forward to the boat ride, but she had tired herself out the day before.

One day, we were almost ready to go when, at the last moment, some article indispensable for travel, went missing. No, she could not possibly go without it. Oma Stern was never to be seen without a large leather shopping bag that contained essential belongings. She turned this bag inside out, very slowly, as was her wont. Then she went to work on her chest of drawers. By the time the missing bric-a-brac was found, we had missed the boat. In the end, she ran out of excuses, and we managed to get her on the river.

I was wildly excited as we embarked on the shiny white steamer. The Rhine made our little Bega seem like a brook and cut even the terrifying Werre down to size. We saw many barges, most of them carrying coal. They were pulled by tiny tugs. A tug sometimes had three or four barges in tow, just like a railway engine. I waved to the men on the barges, and they waved back. They wore pullovers and red kerchiefs.

From the moment we got out on the river, I was on the lookout for ruined castles perched on the tops of crags. At first, I was disappointed. There was only a wide green valley with the hills forming a faint line in the distance. Once we passed Bonn, the action began. One after another, the rugged hills of the *Siebengebirge* came into view, and then, what I had been waiting for. The *Drachenfels* (Dragon's Rock) was wild and craggy, the sort of place no self-respecting dragon could resist, and it was topped by a ruined castle.

Someone on the boat had been up there, seen the actual cave where Siegfried slew the monster and, in the gentle manner of his people, bathed in its blood in order to become invincible. The blood keeps on flowing—the *Drachenblut* is a local vintage.

I was hoping for the Lorelei Rock, for I knew the song and wanted to display my good memory, but the boat turned back before we reached that part of the river.

I got to know Father Rhine even more intimately when we went bathing in Cologne, near the *Siedbrücke*, a swimming pool actually in the river, a kind of houseboat with the floor resting on pontoons. You reached it by way of a pontoon bridge. Metal barriers, set about five centimetres apart, kept out some of the dead rats and river rubbish. It also reduced the force of the current, but it was still powerful, far beyond anything in my experience. I was swept down the pool, thoroughly frightened. The water was a filthy brown, with the occasional stick and debris floating by. Not like the sanitized bathing places that I was used to.

The girls laughed at my moans and patted their timid little cousin. They showed me how to let myself be carried down the current, get out of the water, walk back along the gangplank, and repeat the procedure. Only a few sturdy young men battled against the tide.

When I returned to the Rhineland recently, I was a little disappointed. The landscape was harsher and less inviting than I had remembered it. And after London, New York, and São Paolo, Cologne was not the great city it had seemed then. Also, it had been, to my taste, horribly rebuilt. After the Mississippi and the Ganges, the Rhine was just another big river.

Yet the Rhine must have made a deep impression on me. I don't dream about the cathedral or the house in Marienburg, but I still dream occasionally about the Rhine. The dream is always the same: I stand on one of the Rhine bridges. The bridge is either very low or the water level very high, because the strong current almost touches the bridge. It is about to carry the bridge away, and me with it, when I wake up.

Chapter Nineteen

THE EXILE

"Catania, Palermo, Vicenza, Viterbo, Venezia, Firenze, La Spezia, Livorno."

Father continued to snore, so I tried again, louder. "Catania, Palermo, Vicenza . . ." He opened one eye, "You have forgotten Livorno."

"No, I haven't, Vati. I said it, but you were snoring."

"I never snore," said Father, yawning. "I just breathe loudly. So, let's hear it again."

"Catania, Palermo . . ."

"You should add Roma, Napoli, but always finish with Livorno."

"Vati, do you want to hear my list of poets or emperors?"

"Later," said Father, "let me have my breakfast first."

I loved to catalogue and display my good memory. Father had taught me the names of many Italian cities. For him, all the romance languages spelled romance, but he relished the sound of Italian above all others. He had to make do with place names, since his knowledge of the language was confined to one word, *avanti*. On his only visit to Italy, he put his meagre vocabulary to lavish, if superfluous, use. As if Milanese taxi drivers had to be told to get a move on.

Father also loved poetry, history, and opera, which meant that I could rattle off the names of German poets from Klopstock to Hölderlin; of German emperors from Charlemagne until I got lost among the interminable Habsburgs; of Father's favourite operas, mainly French, which included rarities like Auber's Muette de Portici and Halévy's La

Juive, as well as Father's much-loved Carmen and Ambroise Thomas' Mignon. Father had met someone in Metz who had seen Thomas at a performance of his opera there. "What did he look like?" I asked Father. "A man with a beard," was Father's laconic reply.

Although I was happy to display my knowledge for Father and to share it with the ignorant, my real joy lay in exercising my powers of memory. The "what a clever boy you are!" was just a bonus.

There was one performance I enjoyed giving above all others. It covered a field on which I was an unquestioned authority: my relatives. I made them into a catalogue just like all the others, but they were my own in a way that Mignon and Livorno were not. In my mind's eye, I could see Great Aunt Mella crying over the infidelities of Great Uncle Hermann, and Great Aunt Emilie, who did not seem to like water, cleaning a dirty cup with her forefinger.

Hearing my catalogue of relatives was a price visitors like Frau Birkholz had to pay for the hospitality they enjoyed. Given the slightest encouragement, the floodgates would open:

"Aunt Katinka, Aunt Rosalie, Aunt Henriette, Aunt Emilie, Aunt Pauline, Aunt Mella . . ." The great aunts were like one of those hors d'oeuvres that are bigger than the main course. Grandmother Henriette had many sisters, and I threw in Grandmother Bertha's numerous cousins for good measure. The list always began with Aunt Katinka, even though I had never set eyes on this relative. "Katinka" sounded so grand and strange.

When I came to the main course, the names got shorter and the numbers fewer, but now I fattened the narrative with extra detail:

"I have another grandfather, Joseph. He lives with my father's sister, Aunt Helene and her husband, Uncle Josef. Yes, he has the same name but it's spelled differently and he's big and fat, whereas my grandfather Joseph is small and thin. They live in Laubach, which is in Oberhessen, and we visit them every year for the High Holidays. On the way there, we visit Father's brother, Uncle Moritz and Aunt Erna. They live in Giessen, which is a big town and cleaner than Laubach, where pigs and chicken run all over the place.

"On my mother's side, there is my favourite aunt, Grete, and her husband, Uncle Paul. They live in Cologne, which everybody knows."

And, turning to the dessert: "They have two children, my cousins Gisela and Ingelore. Gisela is five years older than me, Ingelore two years."

"I also have another uncle, Walter. He is my mother's brother. His wife is called Minna. They have three children, my cousins Gertrud, Walter, and Helmut." And until I was seven years old, I would add this loaded postscript: "I have never met any of them. They live in Lage."

The business visitors felt it their duty to listen to the babblings of the precocious child.

"Where is Lage?" they asked. "It must be far away."

I then dropped my bombshell and waited for their looks of surprise and curiosity. I was never disappointed.

"Lage is the next town from here. It's about nine kilometres away."

"Then why have you never visited this uncle and his family?"

"Because Grandfather won't let me."

"Why won't he let you see them?"

"Because of Aunt Minna."

Emmy, my mother, was the oldest of my grandparents' surviving children. Grete was two years younger. Three years after her came Walter, the after-thought. Uncle Walter was very tall and handsome. He looked more characteristically Jewish than the rest of the family. He was not unintelligent, but he was useless at book learning. He never finished his studies. Excused from military service because his brothers had died for the Fatherland, he received his education in the rough and tumble of the cattle trade.

His sisters, themselves no great credit to the German school system, teased him about his ignorance. In particular, they persecuted him with a song from a popular operetta—the *Gypsy Baron*, I think. Mother taught it to me like this:

> "*Sein idealer Lebenszweck*
> *War Borsten, Vieh und Schweinespeck,*
> *Denn schon von Kindesbeinen*
> *Beschäftigt er sich mit den Schweinen.*
> *Das Schreiben und das Lesen*
> *Sind nie sein Fall gewesen.*"

(His ideal in life consisted of bristle, beasts, and pigs' bacon. From childhood on, he busied himself with pigs. Reading and writing were never his strong points.)

Walter vigorously defended himself, using the arguments his brother Erwin had used before him, "I have to work in muck to keep you in fine clothes, so that you can give yourselves airs. You are useless, both of you girls."

In his late teens, this callow youth fell in love with Minna Steinheim, a widow, who was quite a few years older than Walter. She had kept house for a cattle dealer, many years her senior, and had later married him. He had left her with a son, a house, and a business. Walter had met her through the cattle trade. She asked for his advice, and the rest is history.

When Grandfather heard that his son wanted to marry the widow, his fury knew no bounds. He issued an edict:

"If he marries this woman, he will never cross my threshold again." (*Wenn er diese Frau heiratet, darf er mir nie wieder über die Schwelle treten.*)

My mother, too, was angry. I heard that she called on Minna, asking her to release her brother. When Minna refused, Mother threatened her with an umbrella—my mother, whom I never saw lay hands on anyone! The story may be apocryphal.

It was all to no avail. The couple were married and promptly excommunicated by Grandfather. Grandmother begged for mercy for her son. This made her husband only more determined. The whole family was forbidden to have anything to do with the guilty pair—no visits, no letters, no communication of any kind. The edict was later extended to the three children of the marriage.

Grandmother disobeyed. Chaperoned by her sister-in-law, Great Aunt Pauline, she went secretly to Lage, bearing gifts. These visits not only satisfied the demands of natural affection; they also allowed Grandmother to indulge in a delicious defiance of her husband. Even Grandmother never dared tell me about these excursions, though I remember some vague whisperings about the matter. I heard the details later from my cousins. No one else dared to go to Lage.

Grandfather did not want his son to marry a widow, moreover one with a child from her previous marriage. "Soiled goods," he said. There was also the little matter of choosing an older woman with means, so uncomfortably reminiscent of Grandfather's own youth—"old enough to be his mother."

That he should have objected to the marriage was perhaps natural. That he should have continued his ban for so long was stubborn and mean, especially since Minna proved to be a very good wife and mother. Fortunately, Walter had no need of his father's help and carried on his predecessor's cattle business in Lage.

Grandfather almost broke his own ban once. Years later, Cousin Walter, my Uncle Walter's son, told the story:

"I was with my mother at the Lage train station. We were expecting Albert's [Minna's son from her first marriage] aunt. She had come from America and landed in Hamburg. The train from Hamburg was late. Another train pulled in. Through the barrier comes this big man, hobbling on two sticks. He can only just put one foot in front of the other. He stands right in front of me and my mother and looks down at me and smiles.

"He had already hobbled away in the direction of the toilet when my mother realized who he was. 'Do you know whom you have just seen?' she asked me. 'That was your grandfather.' He must have recognized my mother because he had never seen me. He knew straightaway that I was his grandson.

"When we got home, my mother told my father what had happened. He said, 'I know where he'll be. He has to visit Borsdorf in the Paulinenstrasse. I'll go there and wait for him.'"

My cousin continued, "My father went to Borsdorf and waited. He stood at the back because he did not want to be seen. When he came home, he said, 'The old man has not changed, except for the sticks. He looks exactly the same.'"

On that occasion, Grandfather almost allowed the demands of natural affection to overcome his stubbornness. But still he would not give in. Great events of state compelled him eventually to change his mind.

Nurse and Vernon

Teddy and Vernon

Vernon on a fur rug

From left to right: Ingelore, Else, Vernon, Gisela, and
the *Kölners' Kinderfräulein* in Bad Salzuflen

From left to right: Frau Birkholz, Vernon, and Emmy

Vernon and Mother

From left to right: Hermann, Vernon, Karl (our chauffeur), and
Herr Koschni from Düsseldorf, one of Father's army cronies

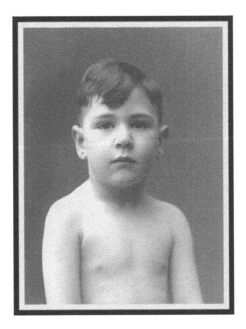

Barechested Vernon; this photo was the basis for a
painted portrait that hung in the Blue Salon

The back of the brush factory

Father's ancestral house in Laubach

Henriette and Joseph

From left to right: Hermann, an unidentified man, and Helene in Metz

From left to right: Moritz, an unidentified man, Joseph, Helene, and Josef

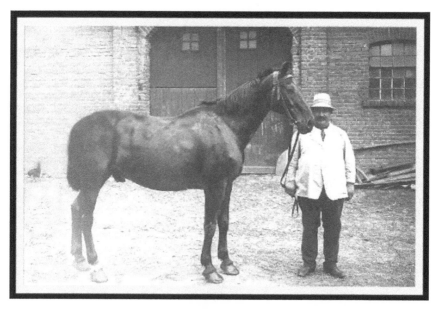

Siegfried

From left to right: Bertha and Siegfried

From left to right: Frau Birkholz, Emmy, and Hermann

From left to right: An unidentified woman,
Vernon, and Else at the Rhine

Else's wedding to August; Vernon is in the chair on the right

Gisela

From left to right: Gisela and Ingelore

Ingelore

Gisela soon after she was married

TROUBLE
BREWING

Chapter Twenty

THE CROOKED CROSS

It all began innocently enough. We were taking our Sunday afternoon stroll to Bad Salzuflen, my parents and I, accompanied by my parents' friends, the Mohrs. He was the director of the Lippische Landestheater in Detmold, our "state" theatre. She came from Schötmar and was a good friend of Mother's. We walked in the hazy winter sunshine along the Allee, the broad tree lined avenue that at that time connected Schötmar to its posh neighbour, Bad Salzuflen. I walked, and occasionally skipped, between my parents, holding their hands. The road running beside the Allee began to slope steeply down towards the spa town, but the walking path had not yet begun its descent. As the houses spread out below us, I noticed the flags.

"Why are the flags out today?" I asked the grown-ups around me. It was Herr Mohr who replied:

"A new chancellor [*Reichskanzler*] has been installed." No name, no details. Nothing more was said. I was five and a half years old and not politically inclined, so I asked no further. But, as we walked towards the old Gothic Town Hall, I noticed that far outnumbering our national flag with its familiar black, gold, and red stripes were flags and huge banners, blood red, with a crooked black cross, all arms and legs, dancing in the middle of a white circle. There was no wind; the flags hung still.[24]

---

[24] Anyone familiar with ancient Indian symbolic diagrams known as "yantras," might have foretold that the Nazis would come to a bad end. They had appropriated the sacred symbol of good fortune, so dear to Ganapati, the elephant-headed remover of obstacles and bringer of blessings, and turned it to their own ignoble ends.

That fateful Sunday afternoon when the flags failed to flutter I was witnessing the beginning of the *Machtergreifung*, the Nazi seizure of power. I am amazed now that I was not more aware of the cross with hooks (*Hakenkreuz*) earlier on. Its votaries had descended on us in force with their banners and their uniforms, marching, singing, agitating, holding hundreds of meetings, and stirring up the good citizens of Lippe. I was living in the midst of the biggest propaganda effort Germany had ever seen, and it was focused on our little state of Lippe. While I was dreaming about the next gift that Father would bring me from Hamburg, the fate of Germany and the world was being decided right under my five-and-a-half-year-old nose.

Had I been older, I could have attended the giant gathering (*Riesenversammlung*), addressed by Dr. Göbbels in Bad Salzuflen, where I had noticed the flags. That was on January 4, 1932. On January 14, 1933, I could have heard the *Führer* himself in our twin town of Bad Salzuflen, half an hour's walk from my home. I could have witnessed that moment, captured in a famous photograph of the meeting, where Göring put his hand under his belt, presumably to make more room in his breeches for his giant stomach. It would be impressive to report now that I was there.

While the Nazis were preparing to take over my country, I was perfecting my *Süterlin*, the traditional German script, using a broad nib. In my leisure hours, I was dreaming of the heroes of German history. At that time, I was going through my Frederick the Great phase.

The swastika (from the Sanskrit: *su-asti* or *svasti*—well-being) is auspicious because its limbs, which face the four directions of the outside world, are connected with their own central point, which represents the transcendental Self, identified with universal Being.

The Nazis, who were in the deepest sense Nastikas (Sanskrit: "it is not" people), those who deny universal Being, stole the garments of the Astikas (Sanskrit: "it is" people), those who uphold Being. They were also, in the deepest sense, non-Aryans. In Sanskrit literature, "arya" stands for all that is noble and honourable; the Nazis brought shame and dishonour, not just on their own country, but on the whole of humankind, for they, more than any other group before or since, exposed the depths to which our human nature can sink.

I had a friend named Werner Böthel, who lived a few houses down the Schülerstrasse with his mother, presumed widowed, and his grandmother. I remember him as thin with spindly legs, carrot red hair and a face full of freckles. Like many weak boys, he had a strong imagination. His mind was peopled by German heroes—Hermann, Prince of the Cheruschi, Charlemagne, Roland, Frederick Barbarossa, and, above all, by another Frederick, the great King of Prussia.

Werner was older than I and, I felt, wiser. His den was full of books, some of which he had actually read. He found me a willing pupil. As we lay on the floor of the den, he read to me, in his thin creaky voice, the exploits of Frederick. Together we refought the great battles of Leuthen, Liegnitz, Rossbach, and Torgau. Frederick the Great was also a great favourite of Father's, but he was an amateur in Frederick studies, compared to Werner. Werner shot questions at me to make sure I had imbibed his teachings in all their detail.

"Where were the *Cuirassiers* at Rossbach and Leuthen?"

"In the first line, Werner."

"What uniform did the *Jäger* wear?"

"Light green coats with red round collars and cuffs, and light green waistcoats."

Werner gave me a crooked smile. "They must have worn breeches."

"Yes, yellow leather."

Parading outside, in the Schülerstrasse, were marchers with breeches of a deeper hue. I did not give them a thought.

"Was there any difference between the uniforms of the foot soldiers [*Jäger zu Fuss*] and the cavalry [*Jäger zu Pferd*]?"

"I don't know, Werner."

"The foot *Jäger* corps wore a waist belt with a brown leather cartridge pouch on the waist."

We skipped over the fact that the foot *Jäger* corps were wiped out by the Cossacks. In fact, we skipped over all of Frederick's reverses—Kolin, Hochkirch, Kunersdorf. We ascribed them to the machinations of his enemies.

How we hated them, especially those arch villainesses—the Empress Maria Theresa and the Marquise de Pompadour. We did not realize what strange bedfellows they made, the royal mistress and the strait-laced empress with sixteen legitimate children to her credit, eventually.

Frederick sent out a forged letter purporting to be from the empress to the marquise, in which she called her *ma cousine*. The old boy had a sense of humour.

"*Fridericus Rex, unser König, unser Herr.*" Werner and I often sang this song, and really felt that Frederick was our lord and king—*der alte* Fritz (old Fritz) hunched on his horse, his head half hidden by an enormous cocked hat. In the picture on Werner's wall, the only ornament on his shabby uniform was a big star, probably the order of the Black Eagle. In the song, the king berates the empress for allying herself with the French and turning the Holy Roman Empire against him.

> "*Die Kaiserin hat sich mit den Franzosen alliert.*
> *Und das römische Reich gegen mich revoltier . . .*"

The woman's real crime, of course, was her stubborn refusal to let Frederick gobble up more and more of Northern Europe. In the end, she had to yield part of Silesia, but got part of Poland in exchange. It is said that she wept. "She weeps, but she takes" (*Sie weint, aber sie nimmt*), commented Frederick, sharp as ever.

The irony of it all! Here was I, conjuring up enemies long dead while my real enemies were gathering all around me, waiting to destroy me and my kind. I remember Grandfather's words as he thumped the table in the upstairs living room. I didn't take much notice at the time. Grandfather was always thumping the table.

"These upstarts will never win here. The Lipper are not that stupid." (*Diese Herrkoemmlinge werden nie hier gewinnen. So dumm sind die Lipper nicht.*) But stupid the Lipper were, fatally stupid. Only much later did I learn about their crucial role in Hitler's rise to power.

The Munich satirical weekly, *Simplicissimus*, summed it all up in a cartoon. It showed Hitler replacing Hermann (the German hero who defeated the Roman legions with a small force) on his plinth in the nearby Teutoburger Forest. The caption read:

"Away with Hermann. It is Adolf who should be in the Teutoburger Forest. With a mere six thousand Lippe-Detmolders he succeeded in defeating a nation of sixty million!" (*Fort mit Hermann! In den Teutoburger Wald gehört Adolf! Ihm gelang es, mit nur 6,000 Lippe-Detmoldern ein Sechzigmillionen Volk zu schlagen!*) Written in jest, but sadly true.

When the Lipper lost their princes in 1918, they clung to their privileges. They had a very strong sense of identity. After all, they had been ruled by the same family for a staggering eight hundred years, almost as long as the Conqueror's descendants had ruled England. When the Weimar Republic was formed, Lippe-Detmold became one of its constituent states. It was a Freistaat, a free state within the Republic, a state of 165,000 people theoretically on a par with Prussia and its thirty-eight million or Bavaria and its seven million. It had its own three-man government, the *Landrat*, and its own parliament, the *Landtag*. It even had its own territorial church, the Lippische Landeskirche, a sort of Church of England in miniature. It also had its own state theatre, Herr Mohr's Lippische Landestheater, and its state newspaper, the *Lippische Landeszeitung*. It was the *Landtag* that mattered.

The Nazis had suffered a setback in the November 1932 general election. If they were to be invited to join the government, they needed, above all, to remove the impression that their support was on the wane. It so happened that the Lippe-Detmold *Landtag* elections were scheduled for January 15, 1933. The Nazis decided to make the most of this historical accident. Their big guns descended on our cabbage patch, headed by the man who was to give house painting a bad name. They combed the towns and villages of the little state, haranguing the yokelry. Between the beginning of the year and the grand finale in Bad Salzuflen on January 14, the day before the election, Hitler himself spoke in sixteen towns and villages.

The effort paid off. The Nazis became the largest party in the *Landtag*, with 40 percent of the votes and nine seats. That they sent their followers to register in Lippe must have helped, but even without that they would probably have triumphed. Göbbels breathed a sigh of relief. "Overnight the party's situation has altered fundamentally. We are right on course again."[25]

The whole affair was on the scale of a council election in a county town. The Nazis actually increased their votes by only six thousand—therefore the *Simplicissimus* caption—but the indefatigable Göbbels blew this up into what he called *Signal Lippe*, an enormous

---

[25] *Lippe im Dritten Reich*, VolkerWehrmann, Detmold 1987, p.78.

propaganda campaign to show that the Nazis were winning the hearts and minds of the people.

"The decision of the citizens of Lippe," Göbbels wrote in his paper, "Der Angriff" (Attack), on January 20, "is not a local affair. It corresponds to the sentiments prevailing throughout the country. Again the masses of the people are on the move—in our direction."[26]

The group around the aged President Hindenburg was impressed. Years later, Hitler remembered: "After the electoral victory in Lippe—a success whose importance it is impossible to overestimate—the advisers of the Old Gentleman [Hindenburg] approached me once more."[27]

I have been told that Hitler had used his stay in Lippe to get a *Regierungsrat* (government counsellor) to make him a German citizen. He was just in time. Two weeks after the Lippe election, he was Chancellor of Germany.

And it all passed me by, this election that gave such a crucial and unhappy turn to world history and to my family. I have a vague recollection of a pedal cart with a wooden frame around it, on which names and slogans were posted—a primitive version of the election van. This must have been sometime before March 5, 1933, the last multiparty election. I took little notice. However, there was a sense of foreboding in the air. Adult conversation was becoming more agitated. I did not know what they were talking about. I was there to pick up local gossip. But I remembered names—Hindenburg, Schleicher, von Papen. One or another of these was always going to do great things for us, save us from some undefined menace.

Of course, I knew all about Hindenburg. Had not Werner Böthel and I fought the battle of Tannenburg together? The president's picture hung in our school. A hulk of a man with a walrus moustache, close cropped, iron-grey hair and the archetypal German square head (*tête carrée*). He seemed very impressive in his field marshal's greatcoat, the square head crowned by a spiked helmet that looked as if it could run straight through you. My parents spoke of him with great respect. They

---

26   Ibid, p.78.
27   Hitler's Table Talk, May 1942.

were not to know that the hallowed hulk was a hollow shell, a perfect incarnation of the republic over which it presided.

One morning Mother caught me, head down, body bent forward, knees raised, tiptoeing after Else. Her eyes widened. "What on earth are you playing at?" she asked.

"I am the creeper" (*Ich bin der Schleicher*), I replied. Lucky for me that I wasn't, for Schleicher came to a very bad end.

Schleicher was an unforgettable name. The word conjured up someone sneaky, who slinks about in bedroom slippers, listening at keyholes. In my innocence, I had stumbled upon a real coincidence of name and form. General Kurt von Schleicher was a sneaky fellow, a behind-the-scenes man who got his way by scheming and intrigue while doing his best to avoid political responsibility. He had been Hindenburg's aide after the war. He made and broke one chancellor after another. The last man he made and unmade was Franz von Papen, a minor but very well-connected aristocrat. Schleicher then had to assume the chancellorship himself, only to be toppled in turn by the enraged von Papen.

There the game came to an abrupt end. Von Papen, after a secret meeting with Hitler, having noted in his diary that the Lippe elections "showed surprisingly high gains for the Nazis,"[28] persuaded the aged president to accept the despised "corporal" as chancellor. This was to be a necessary, but short-term, measure, with the able von Papen on hand to pull the strings and control the little upstart. Little Red Riding Hood stood a better chance with the wolf.

Von Papen's name stuck in my memory because it sounded so grand—patriarchal and papal at the same time. My parents always referred to him as von Papen, whereas Hindenburg and Schleicher, although equally entitled to the noble "von," remained plain Hindenburg and Schleicher.

Schleicher, the kingmaker, was murdered with his wife by the S.S. during the Röhm purge on the night of June 29-30, 1934. Hindenburg died on August 2 of the same year, honoured by a funeral oration from the *Führer* himself. Von Papen was the great survivor. He did make

---

[28]   Diary, Frankel, p.105, also Franz von Papen, *Memoirs*, Deutsch, 1952.

one brave speech before the Röhm purge, but thereafter served Hitler in various capacities. As ambassador to Austria, again overestimating his own sagacity, he helped to do for Austria what he had done for Germany. Acquitted of war crimes, he died in his bed in 1969 at the ripe age of ninety.

There must have been other political names mentioned in that smoke-filled upstairs sitting room, as Father and an assortment of Silberbachs puffed at their cigars and prognosticated on the future of the nation. I do not remember them. Perhaps the Nazis' names made no impact because they were so ordinary. If, on that fateful afternoon walk, Herr Mohr had told me the new chancellor's name, it would have meant nothing. This happy state of affairs could not long continue. The days of my political innocence were over.

Chapter Twenty-One

THE FIRST *HEIL HITLERS*

Herr Sasse, pudgy and short-sighted, sat at his tall desk and polished his glasses, the better to observe what we were made of.

"Stand up straight! Heels together!" Our schoolteacher brayed.

The boy with braces over his checkered shirt who stood before him tried to obey. He was short and stooped shoulders.

Herr Sasse eyed the boy closely. "Now, let me see what you are made of."

The boy raised his right arm, clicked his heels and shouted, "*Heil Hitler!*" The accent was on the "hit," the "ler" was clipped.

"That's what I like to hear," said Herr Sasse, smirking. "Next!"

The boy went back to his desk and another came up, and then another, boys and then girls. One by one, he made us practise the sacred salute in front of him. I say "us," but I cannot for the life of me recall if I was considered worthy of being included in this exercise. I doubt it.

More and more people we knew suddenly appeared in uniform. A pork butcher on the make, a carpenter in search of trade, a cigar shop owner who could do with more customers, factory bosses, master bakers, motor mechanics, all busy advancing their prospects. Men, who in saner countries might have been tending their gardens or joining an amateur dramatic society, were strutting about in polished brown jackboots, trying to ape their absurd *Führer*. They were not always marching with tranquil steady step, but there was that delicious feeling of "I am on top now." The whole thing seems ludicrous in retrospect, but it was not funny then. I soon learned to fear those uniforms.

Up and down the Schülerstrasse they marched in their ridiculous fecal-coloured uniforms, and their absurd high caps, rather like those of French *gendarmes*, only floppier. Their paunches and potbellies were pressed into, but still protruding from, their puffy breeches. A leather strap running diagonally over the right shoulder and clipped to the left side of the breeches assisted a wide leather belt in its noble work of keeping up National Socialist morale.[29]

The wide swastika band worn on the left arm showed up the imperfections of their marching technique. The swings were all over the place. But these were early days. As time went on, the marching improved and the jackboots came in handy for kicking opponents. One day Herr Sasse strode into the classroom in the hated uniform. He did not kick me, but I felt as if he had.

The S.S., smarter and mostly younger, in their black outfit with skull and crossbones, were less prominent but more menacing. They had a cell almost next door to us, and I grew afraid of them.

A few months earlier we had still been singing "*Stolz weht die Fahne schwarz weiss rot*," a paean to the tricolour flag of the merchant navy. That song too had threatened the enemies who hated the flag, but they were left unspecified.

The *Horst Wessel Lied* was now the staple musical fare of marchers and the school system. It was a marching song written to celebrate a dead hero, which soon became a second national anthem. Horst Wessel was a Nazi leader and a pimp, who was shot during a clash with the Communists.

It was many years before I realized what *Dierotfron-tundreaktion* meant. I sang the words, but my political vocabulary did not include "red front" and "reaction." I thought the whole thing was one long word.

However, other parts of the *Horst Wessel Lied*, which we sang in class, soon became painfully clear, especially that bit about the S.A. marching "with quiet steady step."

At first, I sang the *Horst Wessel Lied* along with the others at school, and raised my hand in the Hitler salute. It was no longer "Good morning,

---

[29]   If the strap was meant to be an Aryan symbol, they again got it wrong. Indian Brahmins wear their sacred thread over the left shoulder across to the right.

teacher" (*Guten Morgen, Herr Lehrer*). When Herr Sasse strode into class, he raised his right hand at an angle of about 110 degrees and shouted, "*Heil Hitler! Heil Hitler!*" the class roared back, hands raised at the same angle, the girls screaming as loudly as the boys did. Herr Sasse had trained his class well. It was soon made clear that privileges such as yelling the sacred name and belting out the sacred songs were not for the likes of me. More and more I was made to realize who I was.

Forlornly we stood, Susi Eichmann and I, the only Jews in the class, arms hanging down our sides, silent—she, skinny, with long, black pigtails and a sad little nun's face, shy and self-contained; me, tubby, cherubic, so friendly by nature, but soon destined to be friendless and alone.

The change was very gradual. The children did not immediately turn against me. We had grown up in the same town, and I was one of them. If they objected to me, it was more because, courtesy of Mother, I was better dressed. There were the Goeke twins—blond, close cropped, sons of a council worker on the make—who suggested more than once that I go home to Palestine, but most of my fellow pupils still accepted me. They were nothing like the bastards who persecuted me when I went to high school in Bad Salzuflen in 1936.

We often sang together in the playground, songs like "*Petersilien Suppenkraut*" and "*Schötmar is' 'ne schöne Stadt.*" The former song names a boy and a girl and links them romantically. In each verse, the names change. The song about Schötmar being a beautiful town has something about the teacher being big and fat and snatching the pupils' sandwiches. The fat bit certainly applied to Herr Sasse. His was another Nazi paunch at war with its S.A. encasement. When not in uniform, he favoured double-breasted suits to hide his paunch. He was a Nazi by conviction, not convenience, who, during the war, became mayor of Schötmar.[30]

He was surprisingly kind to me, perhaps because he admired my intelligence. Fortunately perhaps, I was not the cleverest child in the

---

[30] Towards the end of World War II, Sasse saved Schötmar from needless destruction by enabling the American troops to advance through the town, contrary to the demands of the die-hard Nazis.

class. Herr Sasse regularly gave us oral exams. Often it was expertise at *Wettrechnen*, competitive arithmetic, which mainly meant multiplication; sometimes it was history or geography. He lined us up along the walls of the classroom in order of merit, next to where we hung our coats. I was usually number two or three, alternating with a square-jawed, good-sort girl named Ursula Küster, the daughter of a local manufacturer.

Invariably number one was Lotte Frass, a tiny friendly girl with long narrow eyes, the obligatory pigtails hanging over a neat checkered dress. Quietly but firmly, she gave the right answers. She was teased because her name means "grub," but the class soon took her omniscience as a law of nature.

I was somewhat jealous of Lotte. Her mother had given her a knitted scarf and matching hat, blue with red and white stripes. She was very proud of these new accessories. Out of pique at her superior brainpower, I snatched her hat and strutted about the class, wearing it. She ran to teacher (*Lehrer*) Sasse and complained bitterly.

"He has stolen my new hat and put it on his big fat head. It's much too big for me now." Herr Sasse took no action. He was much more concerned with the quality of our work. When it was shoddy, he showed no mercy. He was particularly hard on a small boy with a short wide face crowned by a fringe. This Siepmann—I think that was his name—was not blessed with great intelligence. He could not spell and was not good at essays. More than once, Herr Sasse hauled him over his desk, face down, with his seat over the inkwell, and laid into him with a cane.

Herr Sasse valued fine penmanship. He made us practise with our steel-nibbed pens, first the Gothic type *Süterlin* script and later *latainische Ausgangsschrift*, a simplified Latin script with less rounded letters.

Considering his Nazi convictions, he treated me well. However, he insisted I come to school on Saturdays. My father would have preferred to keep me at home. My Jewishness also presented problems when he gave us an essay on Christmas presents. We did not much celebrate this festival at home, and I had to invent.

It was outside school that the new dispensation first really hit me. I was a popular child, less for my innate charms than because I controlled access to what was by far the best hide-and-seek playground in Schötmar. Our timber yard was crammed with logs. Often they were stacked crosswise, so that one could hide in the hollow areas in the middle. If you did not give yourself away by coughing or loud breathing, your pursuer might have to climb twenty or more stacks before finding you. There were also the large sheds in which the sliced wood was stored. These too had plenty of good hiding places. The whole yard was full of unexpected recesses. Sometimes you could even shout your whereabouts and still not be found.

I presided over this Shangri La. I decided who could enter and who should cool his heels outside the gates. It was up to me whom I invited in to play. As the first months and years of the thousand-year Third Reich wore on, I found that I was no longer so popular. In the end, I found myself presiding over a timber yard empty of children. I was like a millionaire who finds that no one wants to be invited on his luxury yacht any longer. My old friends began to stay away: Dieter Lux, the doctor's son; Robert Kordmöller, the baker's brat; Werner Böthel, the bookworm; and many others. They were not, for the most part, actively hostile; they just preferred not to be seen with the likes of me.

At some point, Werner Böthel, not a great hide-and-seeker, completely disappeared from my world. So did Anneliese Saure. Whether it was because they distanced themselves or because Werner and his mother moved from Schötmar, I do not recall. I was thrown more and more into the company of adults. Everything was discussed in front of me. By the time I was eight, I was a little old man.

It is difficult after all these years to remember the exact time sequence. When did the Heil Hitlering and singing of Nazi songs start at school? When exactly did the children stop coming to the timber yard? When was the privilege of being part of the group denied to Susi and me? However, I have a distinct feeling that the new regime hit me before it really hit my parents because of my exposure to other children's behaviour.

Chapter Twenty-Two

FATHER'S DELUSION

In the late 1980s, the archives with details of Nazi persecution in Lippe and other parts of Germany were at last opened to the public. I was told that this new openness coincided with the deaths of still powerful former Nazis.

In one of the articles sent to me, I saw an item about a Jewish brush manufacturer from Lippe. In the early days of the regime, he had written a letter that criticized scaremongering about Nazi persecution. There was only one Jewish brush manufacturer in Lippe. I wrote to the archivist in Detmold and was duly sent the following:

> To the State Government of Lippe (*Lippische Landesregierung*)
>
> With reference to the inflammatory propaganda [*Hetzpropaganda*] being conducted against Germany, we have felt it our duty to clarify the real situation to our foreign business friends, as you will see from enclosed copies. Unfortunately we have no other foreign business friends with whom we are still in contact, since, owing to the ever more difficult economic situation, our circle of foreign business friends has been narrowed down to these two firms.
>
> We are convinced that these two firms, which are regarded as prominent concerns, will do everything to combat these horror stories [*Greuelnachrichten*].

We feel it our duty to submit the two copies for your information.

Respectfully
Hermann Katz & Co
[Parts of Father's signature are just visible]

The letterhead is impressive. "Hermann Katz and Co." is in a bold calligraphy font with elaborate flourishes for the capital letters.

The article from which I learned about Father's letter also stated that the brush factory had its own woodworks and dressed its own fibres. Details of two bank accounts and a post-office account were given, as was the stand at the Leipzig Fair, the most important in Germany. From the numbers, it looks as if Father's exhibit occupied three rooms on the second floor of the *Dresdner Hof.*

The identical letter—sent to Messrs. G. van Herrewege, Gent, Belgium; and to Messrs. J. Vanderkerkhove and Lalemann, Iseghem, Belgium—makes one cringe even more than the one to the Lippe Government:

> The unscrupulous agitation pursued abroad against Germany induces us to write you this letter. We request you kindly to note that it is only agitation, meant to harm Germany abroad, and that the [stories of] atrocities [*Greueltaten*] being disseminated are without any foundation. Here in Germany a new revolution (dispensation) [*Umwälzung*] has been taken in all calm and with the best discipline. The government treats everyone who loyally supports it, with fairness, irrespective of his religion. We regard it as our duty to bring this to your notice and, in view of our old and agreeable business connection, we request you to oppose these horror stories [*Greuelnachrichten*] in every form, and to inform your friends that this is a matter of inflammatory propaganda directed against the new government, kindled by unscrupulous elements in an inexcusable manner.

We very much hope that you will help in this matter and will inform your friends in the sense indicated above. We express our very best thanks to you in anticipation, send you our greetings and are

Respectfully Yours

What could have induced Father to write such obsequious and wrong-headed letters? He obviously wanted to curry favour with the authorities. "Here is a Jew," says the subtext, "who is a good German, a true patriot." But Father *was* a patriot. He did not want Germany harmed. He was also genuinely convinced that hostility from abroad could only damage the Jewish cause. His letters were written in April 1933. They show the mood of quite a number of Jews at the time. Also in the spring of that year, letters were sent by a number of Jewish organizations criticizing inflammatory propaganda against Germany. So, Father was not alone.

The euphoria and the delusion evidenced in these letters soon vanished. Still, both my parents and many of their friends were convinced—and remained convinced for a long time—that anti-Jewish sentiment was a passing phase. The Nazis might not be easy to displace, but they would change as they became more secure. And they would realize that they needed the Jews. As always, I kept my ears open. Hjalmar Schacht, the Nazis' economics wizard, often came up in the conversations I overheard. He seemed to have replaced von Papen as our saviour. He would convince the leadership that Jews were necessary to keep the economy going. "The war has passed, the inflation has passed, this too will pass, when they come to their senses," I heard Father say. "We have to keep our head and not panic."

With hindsight, one can see how utterly wrong they were. My parents and others like them were so German that they simply could not believe that their own country did not want them.

I think that, deep down, Father also had a sneaking admiration for the Nazis—before they showed their true colours. The words "best discipline" in the letter to the customers give the game away. Father liked discipline. He also liked poetry, the liberal arts, and French culture. I wonder what would have happened, had he not been born a Jew. Which aspect of him would have won?

My parents continued in their folly for some years. It nearly cost them their lives. There had been a previous warning. My parents chose not to heed it. They saw only what they wanted to see, only heard what they wanted to hear.

Chapter Twenty-Three

DER FÜHRER AND THE KAISER'S TREACHERY

A year has passed since Father's obsequious letter to the government of Lippe.

"*Der Führer* has come," said Mother, bursting with secret knowledge.

"Has he come to see what Jews eat for breakfast? Aryan children perhaps?" said Father. It was Sunday morning, the one leisurely breakfast of the week. "Hush," said Mother, finger to mouth. "Walls have ears."

Father knew perfectly well to what Mother was referring. *Der Führer* was the somewhat unfortunate title of the Illustrated Magazine for the Brush, Comb, and Celluloid Goods Industry.

And I knew why the March 1934 issue of this worthy publication was especially important. I had noticed the whispered consultations between Mother and Fräulein Nagel, the office typist. I smelled a secret and squeezed it out of Fräulein Nagel. I had tried Mother first, but she still did not trust me, even though I was known as someone who kept secrets when I promised. "You'll know soon," Mother said, which made me even more determined not to wait. I used all my wiles on Fräulein Nagel and succeeded.

Mother opened the sky blue covered journal at the centre page. I stood behind Father, pretending innocence. "My God" (*Um Gottes Willen*), he whispered, as he saw his photograph. Mother put her arms around him, and so did I. Father purred and glowed. *Der Führer* had interrupted an important article on "The New National Socialist

Ordinance on Factories and Wages in the Brush and *Pinsel*[31] Industry [Reprint Prohibited]" with a framed centre spread. On the left side was a glossy page size photo of Father, ultra stiff white collar, smart-spotted tie, thick upturned moustache, clear grey-brown eyes, hair cut very short, looking more like a *Junker* warlord than a Jewish businessman. Mother must have sent an old photo. Father still had his hair.

The editor had written, asking for Father's details and the sacred facts had been dictated to Fräulein Nagel. They were found distilled on the right page, facing the photograph:

HERMANN KATZ, SCHÖTMAR
50 YEARS OLD

His Motto: "Only through untiring industry[32] is success achieved!"

Hermann Katz, founder and sole proprietor of brush manufacturers Hermann Katz & Co. in Schötmar, Lippe, was born on 14th April 1884 in Laubach (Hessen), the son of businessman Joseph Katz. He went into the textiles business. Through his perseverance and striving for success, he won the sympathy of his superiors, who advanced him so rapidly that he was able to set up his own business in Metz at only 24 years of age. But only for a short period: On the very first day of mobilization his duty towards the Fatherland called out to him, a duty he fulfilled up to the last day of the war. Now it was necessary to build up again, a doubly difficult task because he had to flee Alsace, leaving all his possessions behind. For the present, he stood before a void.

He turned to the small Lippe town of Schötmar. There, on 19th March 1919, in small, rented rooms, he founded a brush

---

[31]　A *Pinsel* is a sub-species of brush, where the fibres are concentrated, usually in one hole, not scattered over a wider area. Artists' brushes and shaving brushes are examples of *Pinsel*.

[32]　The word is "*Fleiss*," a real favourite with Germans, at least in my day. It means industry, application, diligence, effort, hard work—the opposite of laziness.

factory. He married in 1919 and through their joined efforts husband and wife built up a business that soon gained a good reputation in the industry. In the spring of 1924 the building of the present factory was begun. Later a woodworks and a section for dressing fibres were added, and over the years the factory was equipped with the most modern machinery. Despite the exceptionally difficult economic situation[33] the business, housed in its new-built premises since December 1924, was able to expand and develop from year to year. In 1926 the factory was again extended substantially and a sawing mill was built. Today, as he celebrates his jubilee, the fifty-year-old, together with his wife, can look with pride on a firm, whose construction and expansion required the utmost application[34] and unremitting[35] energy. Cordial good wishes!

Who but I remembers this article today? In 1934, coming as it did fourteen months after the Nazis' accession to power, it was sensational. That a respected trade journal could pay such a tribute to a Jew! Father wrote an obsequious letter to the editor, Dr. Carl Grüb, expressing his astonishment and "a happiness greater than any material goods could provide." He added, rather pointedly, "The fact that *even today* restless striving is still appreciated, has *once more* filled me, as a businessman of the old school, with joy and pride."

That article was a disaster. It confirmed my parents' belief that they had nothing to fear. Father had lost some of the naive confidence expressed in his letter to the Lippe government a year earlier. The words in his letter to the editor indicate as much. Yet, he still believed that Hitler's anti-Semitism was a passing phase.

"Once he has achieved his goals and made Germany strong again, he will come to his senses and realize that Germany still needs its Jews. Schacht will convince him."

---

[33]   Former employees have testified that even in the "bad times" of the early 1930s, their wages were always paid on time, see Wiesekopsieker, op. cit., p. 160.

[34]   "*Fleiss*" again.

[35]   Another possible translation for "*rücksichtslo*" is "ruthless."

Mother had her own analysis of the situation:

> "It's all the fault of the Jews from Eastern Europe [*Ostjuden*]
> with their kaftans, their side curls and their sharp practice.
> They have spoiled things for us. They make the Jews stand out.
> Why can't they conform when they come here? They are the
> ones the Nazis really want to get rid of, and quite right too."

Mother went by hearsay. I don't think she had ever seen an *Ostjude*.
The kaftaned species did not exist in our part of the world, and Mother
was not well travelled. But, had she met them, she would have found
them alien. She had far more in common with the gentile neighbours
who cut her in the street than with some orthodox lady from Krotoshin
who wore a wig (*sheitel*) to protect her hair from the gaze of men.

Mother, in particular, fought hard to preserve her German heritage.
True, some people were talking about emigration, but they did not
have our solid background. She paid out a large sum to have a family
tree prepared. She may have felt herself a von der Schulenburg, but the
aristocratic connection could never be proved. The next best thing was
to find proof that the Silberbachs had deep roots in German soil.

And indeed they had. Research found that Mother's paternal
ancestors—if Grandfather was indeed a Silberbach—had lived in
northwest Germany since the Thirty Years' War (1618-1648). That was
as far back as the records went.

But even if the poor woman had been able to prove that she was
descended from the Jews of Roman Colonia, it would have made not
the slightest difference. For the Nazis, a Jew was a Jew was a Jew. Our
variety was a greater threat to the purity of the German nation than the
Ostjuden, who were easy to recognize.

My parents lived in a fool's paradise. Business was better than ever,
boycotts or no boycotts. Between 1933 and 1935, the factory achieved
its highest number of employees.[36] And then, look at Father's reputation.
A centre spread! A letter from the trade federation congratulating Father
and wishing him well, personally and professionally! No one could touch

---

[36]   Wiesekopsieker, op. cit., p.161.

them. But my parents very soon found out that they had enemies, and from an unexpected quarter.

Our office was presided over from behind a large crowded desk by the formidable Fräulein Kaiser. Around her revolved lesser luminaries like Herr Müller and Fräulein Nagel, with smaller desks and more meagre stipends. The office boys and other small fry were confined to a back addition, out of Fräulein Kaiser's immediate line of sight, but subject to her periodic sorties. She controlled her staff as tightly as she laced her corsets. Anyone who slacked felt the whiplash of her tongue. My parents had great respect for Fräulein Kaiser and interfered little with her work. I was under strict instructions to be very polite to her, something I did not find difficult. Fräulein Kaiser was not the kind of person with whom you took liberties.

She was a short, thickset, hard-faced woman with glaring brown eyes and a swarthy complexion, her swept-back dark hair exposing her merciless features. She sat at her desk like an empress in a round, well-padded chair, encased in severe brown suits. When she rose to inspect her domain, she propelled herself awkwardly, but with determination, towards her victims.

"There you go again. Wrong addition. What I have to put up with! Not capable even of simple arithmetic." She rolled her eyes and pointed to me. "The boy could do better."

When she was away, "the boy" strode up and down the office, chest out, cheeks puffed up, pretending to be the scowling gorgon. "No slacking now," I commanded the grinning staff.

To those outside her jurisdiction, Fräulein Kaiser affected a certain bonhomie of the hail-fellow-well-met, no-nonsense variety, to which her deep booming voice gave credence. The unwary might have mistaken her for a gruff spinster with a heart of gold. Sensitive persons knew better. Her eyes gave her away. They bored holes into you.

Fräulein Kaiser made clumsy and rather half-hearted attempts to humour the bosses' brat who infected her office on the pretext of looking for his Mutti. She heaved her considerable person over me and asked, with a grimace aspiring to a smile but unable to make the transition, what games I was playing and with whom. Tenderness was not her strong point. I was not deceived and kept my distance, politely of course.

When the unthinkable happened, I was hardly surprised, but my parents were dumbfounded. Fräulein Kaiser who had been with the firm for years, who had become a respected, if not well loved, institution, was demanding money with threats. On the pretext that she had been hard done by, she was blackmailing my parents over some irregularity that she threatened to disclose to the authorities. She may have chosen to become aware that Mother sold sawdust to the butchers and pocketed the proceeds without declaring them. My parents were not sharp or brave enough for anything on a much grander scale.

The Kaiser—Fräulein Kaiser had become *die* Kaiser—had chosen her time well. The Nazis had abolished the last vestiges of the Weimar Constitution and were digging in. Jewish businesses were under pressure. My parents could not take chances. They managed to scale down their employee's demands, but they paid up. The Kaiser, who now revealed that she had embraced National Socialism with all her Nordic heart, agreed to forego the service she was about to render the state and departed, her handbag filled with Jewish lucre.

I was only seven at the time but, as usual, well informed. I always made it my business to know what was going on, and my parents had no secrets from me. I was even able to be of some assistance to them in their battle with the Kaiser.

One of my favourite lavatories was the one in the office, much to the ire of staff in need of the facilities. It was a cozy place, warm and comfortable, with a nice brown seat. During one of my undisturbed sessions there, I overheard the Kaiser plotting strategy with an accomplice in the corridor outside. I must have been *in situ* for so long that they thought the place unoccupied. When I realized what was going on, I hardly dared move from my privy position.

When the conversation had stopped, I peeped through the keyhole to make sure the coast was clear and rushed to Mother with the enemy's latest plans. With my good memory, I was able to report more or less verbatim—she said this, he said that. A few days later, there was a terrific confrontation, the Kaiser facing my parents in her brown getup, legs astride, eyes glowering. It heralded her final exit. Even though she left our little stage well heeled, she left full of ill will, a Third Reich Malvolia, still vowing to be avenged on the pack of us. We never heard from her again.

The Kaiser's defection was a warning my parents would have done well to heed.

Chapter Twenty-Four

THE WASHERWOMEN OF LAGE AND THE PRODIGAL'S RETURN

Our life was changing. Frau Schmidt, Frau Mueller, Frau Hagemeier, and their like—I am not giving real names—who had admired me as the spitting image of my famous grandfather, now kept their distance. This is the sort of exchange I often heard:

"Hermann, can you imagine, Hilde Bratwurst crossed the road when she saw me coming, just to avoid greeting me. And to think that I have known her since we were children. She should be ashamed of herself." In those days, Mother still allowed herself to be angry each time she was snubbed.

"Next time you see her, *you* cross the road first," said Father, smiling his puckish smile. He was on his travels most of the time and had contact with liberal-minded businessmen in large cities. He did not greatly care about these slights, but Mother was not to be comforted. She had lived in the same small town practically all of her life. She recognized every nuance of behaviour. To be ignored or regarded an outsider hurt her deeply. Every time someone cut her or, even worse, made an anti-Semitic remark, it went to her soul. She was a great patriot, German first, Jewish a long way after.

Like someone crossed in love, she still found it almost impossible, years later, to forgive her old country. Father, on the other hand, behaved as if nothing had happened when he visited Germany after the war. He took up where he had left off.

Father enjoyed a robust common sense. In the midst of all of this, when Jewish minds should have been on other matters, Mother was focused on something else. She had received a letter from a solicitor acting on behalf of one of the Bad Salzuflen Frau Obermeyers—the richer one, a daughter, or grand-daughter-in-law, of Grandmother's matchmaking relative. It accused Mother of spreading the slander that Frau Obermeyer had not been received when she called on one of the great department store families. These families were the Jewish aristocracy. The solicitor wanted to know from whom Mother had heard this untruth and demanded an apology.

Mother was very upset. Father said, "Don't worry. We'll go to the cemetery and see which female gossip died recently, and then we'll write that she told you." I don't know if they actually employed this ruse, but the matter petered out. Perhaps Frau Obermeyer realized that Jews had more important problems.

Mother sometimes saw anti-Semitism where there may have been none. Take the case of *Frau Doktor* Lux from across the road, delicately nurtured, well educated, the possessor of a fine fur coat and marooned in Schötmar as consort to *Herr Doktor* Lux. She was noted for her snootiness well before the advent of National Socialism, and even though she merely continued to ignore Mother's existence, she was still a *Reschante*.

Reschante is derived from *Risches*, a new word that was on everybody's lips. I asked Father what it meant. "It comes from the Hebrew word *rosho*, which means bad, wicked. It is used a lot to describe Haman. You remember who Haman was?"

"Yes, Vati, of course I do. He is in the Book of Esther and he persecuted the Jews."

"Precisely. *Risches* is what people have who don't like Jews."

Risches (the "sch" is pronounced like the English "sh") then is a Yiddish word for anti-Semitism. For some reason we called a male anti-Semite a *Rischeskopf* (*Kopf* is German for "head"), while the word *Reschante* was applied to the female of the species. *Risches* was used with the auxiliary: to have. A person had *Risches*.

As time went on, more and more of our neighbours and former friends caught the disease. It was not that they became rabid anti-Semites overnight. A few did, but for most, there was a long incubation period. For a time, there was little active hostility. Most people just did not want their reputations sullied and their prospects dimmed by being associated with Jews. People who did were pilloried in the press as *Judenfreunde* (friends of Jews), *Judengenossen* (companions of Jews), and even *Judenknechte* (slaves of Jews). Sometimes they were named.

Before I condemn, I have to ask myself what my fellow Jews and I would have done in similar circumstances. Only those of our neighbours with the highest principles escaped the infection. The rest just did what was prudent—some happily, others reluctantly. Unfortunately, crossing the road and not seeing Jews grew into not seeing the concentration camps and the gas chambers.

The evil increased by small incremental steps—ignoring, disliking, attacking, and ultimately murdering. "Who is responsible for all misfortune?" the cheerleader bellowed at rallies or on the radio. "*Die Juden*," roared the crowd. People had this drummed into them so often that they came to believe it, and they behaved accordingly.

Prosperity was increasing; there was more employment, although it was mainly caused by rearmament. People loved and cheered their *Führer*. The Nazis were doing well, making Germany great, so they must be right about the Jews.

At home, things also changed after a while. My parents and their Jewish friends now glanced around before they talked politics. They opened doors to see if anyone was listening. Only with fellow Jews could they talk freely, and they did. I heard the word "criminals" (*Verbrecher*) more and more often. I do not remember precisely as to whom it was used, but there were plenty of candidates. Men, who under normal conditions, would be subject to police warrants, were ruling a great nation.

I was given strict instructions. "Never repeat anything you hear. Not even to Else and Erna. Not even to your best friends. Is that understood?" They said it over and over again because they knew that I was a gossip. But I realized that the situation was serious. I could see that my parents, my all-powerful parents, were afraid, and it left a deep impression.

My parents had no secrets from me. I was present at all the grown-up conversations, especially after my playmates had abandoned me. I did not speak, but I listened.

It was not only the doors that spelled danger. The downstairs sitting room faced the street. Because of our high ceilings, the room's windows were so high up that a man could stand under them and listen without being noticed from inside. One day, looking out, we caught someone in the act. From then on, people talked in low voices, even when the windows were closed. In later years, Jews often preferred to go without a telephone, because they had heard that engineers were adding bugging devices when installing or repairing telephones.

Again, I do not remember exactly when it all began, when we began to talk in whispers, but I know it happened.

These were times when family rifts were a luxury that could no longer be afforded. Although my parents were still optimistic about our future in Germany, we had to put our own house in order. It was time for the great reconciliation between Uncle Walter and Grandfather.

Uncle Walter had been living in Lage with his wife, Minna, and had been exiled by Grandfather for sixteen years now. His return to the fold was the result of growing pressure from outside and Grandfather's increasing frailty. Grandfather was ready to welcome his son and his son's family, but he was too stubborn to make the first move. It fell to Mother to be the prime mover in this affair.

Her chance came with the decline of Grandfather's brother, Uncle Julius. He was childless, and since the death of Aunt Pauline in 1932, he had been sinking ever deeper into squalor. He was prosperous, like most of the Silberbachs, and still did some cattle trading. He owned a handsome house at the end of our road, more imposing than ours because two grand columns supported the large balcony. The house was far too big for him, even though he had rented out the top floor.

I had to visit Uncle Julius to deliver the *Schlemmerhappen* cigars that I bought for him and, of course, to collect my tip. Whenever I went there, I held my nose. Clothes were strewn about, dishes were unwashed, and there was a pervasive lavatorial smell. I had a delicate nose and could not get out quickly enough.

Mother's scheme had the simplicity of genius. Uncle Walter and family would move in with Uncle Julius, look after him, take over his business, and become his heirs. It would solve the problem of what to do about Uncle Julius, and it would heal a family rift that should have been healed long ago.

Negotiations were delicate. Uncle Walter had to be persuaded, Uncle Julius had to be persuaded, and Grandfather's face had to be saved.

Mother had a knack of drawing others, especially her menfolk, into her own schemes. It was instinctive talent rather than conscious artifice. She first involved and then enveloped her victims in her designs. She derived genuine pleasure from the support or acquiescence into which she had inveigled them.

Certainly, there was no one who had mastered the art of handling Grandfather like Mother. He was given gentle hints of what was afoot and was gradually, and willingly, drawn into the net. In the end, Grandfather believed that he had thought up the brilliant plan himself. And Mother gave him a loophole. He did not have to admit that he had been wrong in the first place. He wanted a reconciliation, and she allowed him to give the impression that he was relenting for the sake of his brother.

Feelers were sent to Uncle Walter. He was willing, if there were guarantees about the inheritance. Uncle Julius proved more difficult. I was present at a Sunday afternoon family meeting when the matter was discussed. Uncle Julius mumbled something into his cigar-stained moustache about losing his independence and no longer being master in his own house. But he could not stand up to the powerful combination of Mother and Grandfather—one cooing sweet reason, the other also speaking reason, but not so sweetly.

"Soon you won't be able to look after yourself," Mother was saying, "and then you'll have to go into a home."

"I can get a housekeeper," Uncle Julius muttered defiantly.

"A stranger," Mother replied, "you'll be bossed about by a stranger. If Walter comes, you'll have a family of your own. You'll keep your house, your business will carry on, and you'll have an interest in life."

Grandfather was more curt. "Don't be a fool, man. You only pay after you're dead. All the rest is profit. Who do you want to leave your money to—the Salvation Army?"

One day a strapping handsome young fellow of twelve or thirteen appeared at our door. I noticed his large leg muscles. He was introduced as my Cousin Walter, and before I could say anything, he was whizzed off to the sitting room, where for once the door was firmly shut against me. Walter gave me a very pleasant smile, which I thought was generous of him, considering I was clearly not in his league.

Cousin Walter was the go-between, taking messages back and forth, before the principals met face to face. The next time I saw Walter, he was not smiling. He was puffing and frowning. When he had caught his breath, he blurted out, "My father has been arrested."

There was consternation as everyone questioned him at once. Walter told his story:

"My father had been to the cattle market at Paderborn, but he did not come home that night or the next day. My mother was desperate. She went to the local police. They said that they could not help her. So she took the train to Detmold. She traipsed from one government office to another until she found an official who thought that he might be able to help."

Cousin Walter continued, "'Is he of Israelite descent?' the official asked her. When she replied that he was, the official left to make some enquiries. When he returned, he said, 'He is in protective custody. You will know why.'

"My mother had no idea why, unless it was because he was a Jew."

We heard later what had happened. As my uncle was passing through Detmold from Lage, he was arrested on the instructions of a local party bigwig, one Herr Wedderwille. He was what was called *ein hohes Tier* (literally, a high animal), perhaps as high as a *Gauleiter*.[37] The Wedderwilles harboured a grudge against Uncle Walter.

In one of Uncle Walter's meadows, a small pier jutted out into the Werre. The local women would bring their washed clothes there and rinse them in the river. One of those making regular use of the pier was the future Frau *Gauleiter*, i.e., Frau Wedderwille. At some point, my uncle, fearing that his cattle might injure themselves on the pier, had it removed. This was his right. It was on his land. The Wedderwilles never forgave him. When the Nazis came to power, they took their revenge.

Uncle Walter was released after ten days. One of those with whom he shared the "protection of the State" was the courageous editor of the Social Democratic People's Press, a Jewish man named Fechenbach. He was beaten up by Nazi thugs in the street and, after being released from hospital, was taken into "protective custody" to "protect" him from the rage of the German people. While being thus protected, he was

---

[37] A party leader of a regional branch of the Nazi Party.

murdered. The official version was that he was shot trying to escape while being transferred from the Detmold jail to a concentration camp.

Fortunately, Uncle Walter was not considered worthy of such special protection. He had his life, Fechenbach, his fame. In Lage today, they celebrate Fechenbach week.

A few weeks later, Uncle Walter was again arrested and put into "protective custody." Perhaps he needed protection against the vengeful washerwomen, ready, like some Westphalian Bacchae, to tear him from limb to limb. No charges were brought against him, and after about a week, he was released. He had been taught a lesson, and so had we all. We were living in a new era of lawlessness.

At this time, we had no thought of trying to escape Germany and the Nazis' clutches. The better-informed Jews in large towns were starting to emigrate, but we were still firmly rooted in German soil. Uncle Walter had enemies, said my parents. They had none now—they had dealt with the Kaiser and her blackmail.

Still, it was clearly necessary to get Uncle Walter out of the immediate orbit of his enemies as quickly as possible. Negotiations for the family's move to Schötmar were hurried up. I could not wait to meet them all.

A ticket to hear Göbbels speak in Bad Salzuflen on 4 January 1932

Hitler speaking in Bad Salzuflen on 14 January 1933

Uncle Walter

Minna

NEW RELATIONS

Chapter Twenty-Five

LONG-LOST RELATIVES

"Let the little ones come to me" (*Lasset die Kindlein zu mir Kommen*), said Grandfather, quoting the New Testament and not knowing it. He could not bring himself to visit the prodigals' lair, at least not yet. So much the better, I thought. There will be more room in the car.

It was the appointed day when Uncle Walter and family would cease to be a postscript and enter the main stream of my family consciousness. We piled into the green Nash—Father and Karl in front; Grandmother, Mother, and me in the back.

"What do they all look like?" I kept asking, fidgety with anticipation. To no purpose—Mother had never seen them, and Grandmother would not admit that she had.

We drove up the uneven cobbles of the Neue Strasse into the Lange Strasse, which really was long by Schötmar standards, past the Town Hall, downhill past the pink palace of the Stietencron family and into open country. Half an hour later, we pulled up in front of an old-fashioned *Fachwerk* farmhouse, a squared framework of black beams. As we approached the front door, I could see traces of a much larger opening.

We knocked and out came a good-looking woman in a silky blue dress with white polka dots and matching jacket. Her eyes were round and friendly, with just a veil of shyness. "I'm glad you have come," she said in a broad country accent.

I started to make my *Diener*, the low bow with optional heel click that well-brought-up German boys produced like a Pavlovian reflex, when suitably stimulated by the right kind of adult. (Grown men often performed a similar "service" for the right kind of lady.) As I bowed, she stopped me, bent down, and gave me a peck on the cheek. The blue dress rustled reassuringly. I noticed the hairnet that kept the greying hair in place.

So, this friendly woman was the cause of the long family rift. Mother had just given Aunt Minna the kiss of peace when, looming behind her, a man in a chef's apron barked, "Come in! Make yourselves at home! Don't treat us like strangers!" Uncle Walter had inherited the paternal larynx and had adopted his consort's country accent. He kissed his mother, gave his sister a bear hug and his nephew a pat on the head. Spreading out his long arms, he herded us into the *Diele*, the large central hall around which the house was built. His feet turned inwards in a kind of waddle that made him look like an oversized mother duck taking her ducklings to safety. The apron added to that impression. You would not have caught Father wearing one of those.

Uncle Walter was built on the grand scale. My parents were not short, but he exceeded them by fully a head, a large head at that. Everything about him was big—his hands, his feet, his arms, his broad chest, and long body; only his legs were not in scale. Like his father's, they were too short for his body and would give him trouble later in life.

He was a handsome man, with a strong Jewish face. Mother could have passed as a German country woman, but there was no mistaking Uncle Walter's ancestry.

If Mother felt embarrassed at facing her brother again, I did not notice. My eyes were stuck to the table at the centre of the hall. Spread out before me on blue and white Copenhagen china was the biggest most mouth-watering high tea I had ever seen. Enticing me was a huge selection of cold meats and practically every sausage you could think of—light grey liver sausage, inflated beer sausage, smelly garlic sausage, soft rust-coloured *Braunschweiger*, brain sausage known as *Cervelatwurst*, and several kinds of salami.

There was potato salad and gherkin salad and *Lachs* (so-called smoked salmon, in Germany it was nearly always some substitute). There were cheeses and varieties of bread—white bread, rye bread with and without caraway seeds, and dense black pumpernickel.

From the kitchen, carrying a plate of sliced tomatoes and tiny gherkins, came a pretty fifteen-year-old girl with large brown eyes, a rosy complexion, full lips and wavy, chestnut-coloured hair. The overall effect was somewhat marred by a large, bumpy nose.

"My little daughter" (*Mein Töchterchen*), said a proud Uncle Walter. Gertrud was Uncle Walter in female form—tall, gawky, angular, and gauche. As she went in and out, carrying dishes of sliced tomatoes, more gherkins, a bowl of butter patted into a shell pattern, she was forever turning her shoulders, as if unsure what angle to present to the world. Uncle Walter gave her a proprietorial look as if to say, "See what I have produced." Then he could contain himself no longer.

"What do you think of my little girl," he asked. "Isn't she beautiful?"

"She'll turn many heads and break many hearts," said Father, always liberal with his compliments. Gertrud's rosy cheeks went a deep red.

Mother admitted that Gertrud was "a nice girl" (*ein nettes Mädchen*). I could tell she was being insincere. Mother liked girls who were open and outgoing, who dressed smartly and without frills, girls who were *sportlich*, like Gisela. She looked her niece up and down. That shrinking manner, that awful bow that covered half her dress. Here was a suitable case for improvement.

Uncle Walter and his treasure went into the kitchen to help Aunt Minna put the finishing touches on the meal. As soon as they were out of hearing, Mother began to pump Cousin Walter, whom I already knew from his Schötmar visits, with leading questions about his family's circumstances. Mother had named him "*der kleine* Walter." He was a well-built, good-looking boy of about twelve or thirteen with dark curly hair, *klein* (little) only when compared to his giant of a father.

Walter was very different from his sister. He was friendly, natural, and self-possessed, showing no undue deference to the newcomers. He sidestepped Mother's questions with practised ease. She was no wiser when Uncle Walter waddled in from the kitchen, bearing a steaming pot of sausages, followed by Aunt Minna with another pot, and Gertrud with a plate of yet another variety of salami.

Grandmother had been looking at the wild and heathenish medley on the table with some distaste, even before this latest batch arrived. She had long given up trying to wean her dear ones from their heathenish ways, but she had learned to protect herself. If a cruel fate had sent her to live among the ungodly, there was no reason why she had to eat with them.

"Do you have a small table?" she asked her son.

"Of course, Mother." Uncle Walter turned to his son.

"Walter, bring your grandmother the side table."

A place setting was prepared at the small table. Uncle Walter came over with one of the pots of sausages and put some squat fat frankfurters on his mother's plate. Grandmother surveyed them with suspicion.

"They're all right, Mother," said Uncle Walter, patting her on the shoulder. "I got them from Hammerschlag, and also this salami." He pointed to the plate Gertrud had carried in. Hammerschlag of Lage was the most renowned kosher butcher in our area.

Grandmother still hesitated. Uncle Walter could see that she was turning over in her mind whether to make an issue of the crockery. He forestalled her.

"We have given you our new white plates and cutlery, Mother," he said. "We will keep them especially as your meat dishes. They have never been used before. I give you my word."

Grandmother looked doubtful, but she ate.

Meanwhile, Aunt Minna was going around with the other pot. I could see that here was the real thing. Aunt Minna stacked several long rose pink frankfurters on my plate. Heaven. I was on my third one when Mother gave me one of her looks. It said, "A well-behaved little boy does not stuff himself in other people's houses." Uncle Walter caught it. He wagged his finger at me.

"Don't look at your mother," he boomed. "You don't have to be shy here. We are your family."

I was not shy. As I was putting mustard on my fifth sausage, Mother's eyes said, "You are eating as if we starved you at home." I wanted to tell her, "We never have real frankfurters at home," but pretended not to notice her look.

I had been too busy with my sausages to give voice to a question that had been troubling me. I knew there was another cousin who was my contemporary, and I wanted to inspect him as a possible playmate.

Father had been sitting with the women of the house, telling slightly risqué jokes in that dry way he had. Gertrud blushed, but he had Aunt Minna in fits of helpless laughter. He was just describing how the policeman caught the countrywoman stealing apples—one of his standbys—when I turned to Uncle Walter.

"Where is Helmut?" I asked.

Uncle Walter jumped up as if a snake had bitten him.

"Helmut! Helmut! Come here this instant!" he roared in a voice that proclaimed him a worthy son of his father. Uncle Walter would not have needed his right hand and his left to bring down the temple of Dagon. His voice alone would have sufficed. However, it failed to produce the missing miscreant.

"Where has that boy got to?" he asked no one in particular, and no one cared to reply. Even though the family was occupied with its guests, the youngest member's absence cannot have gone altogether unnoticed. The others must have thought it best to leave well enough alone. Not so Uncle Walter.

"Go and find your brother and bring him here at once," the angry parent told his older son. *Der kleine* Walter disappeared. A few minutes later, he came back with a straw covered little boy in tow. Helmut had sought refuge in the loft, from where he could watch us.

"Don't be hard on him," pleaded his elder brother. Uncle Walter refrained from making a scene.

"Kiss your grandmother and your Aunt Emmy," he said gruffly.

Helmut did no such thing. He looked about him like a trapped creature of the wild and, seeing no other means of escape, dived under the table. It was some time before he yielded sufficiently to the threats and entreaties of his loved ones to poke out a strangely shaped little head. When all of him finally emerged, he would not kiss, nor would he speak. Not one syllable.

"What sort of a savage is this?" I wondered as I saw his fierce frightened brown eyes. There were only three and a half months between us, but he looked much the younger. I was taller and tubby, he, small and sinewy, though he later grew quickly in all directions. The short pants of my sailor suit bulged with bottom and thigh, his knee-length grey bumpkin shorts hung limp over straight skinny legs. My face was like a full moon, his, rather like an upside down equilateral triangle, broad on top, pointed at the base. His features were sharp, mine cherubic. My hair flowed in broad waves, his brown mop stood up straight, like

Strubbelpeter's.[38] We were opposites, destined to become the closest of friends, the keenest of enemies.

Sometime earlier, while tackling the *Lachs*, I had heard the call of nature, but in the excitement that followed the eruption of Helmut, I had forgotten to heed it. Now it could no longer be denied. Those sausages I had devoured wanted out. I whispered my need to Walter and he took me to the place of relief. He pointed with pride to a brand new water closet.

"This is like the one you have in Schötmar," he said proudly.

"Of course it is," I replied. "What's so strange about that?"

It transpired that in their part of the world, drains were a new phenomenon. Until recently, the sludge had been collected by cart every month. Running water too was a comparative novelty. Before it was installed, they had drawn their water from an outside well by pump. I thought of my smart Cologne cousins. They turned up their snooty noses at Schötmar and its ways. What would they make of these people?

When I returned to the hall, feeling lighter and ready for more, I found Aunt Minna distributing *Topfkuchen*, a Madeira-type fruitcake stuffed with glazed cherries and sultanas. Mother complimented Aunt Minna on her baking. I concurred. "It's very good, Aunt Minna," I said, remembering Erna's dry and shrivelled cakes, and my speech came from the heart. I was promptly rewarded with another slice. Not for the first time the thought crossed my mind that there would be good pickings for me at this table once it transferred to Schötmar.

Uncle Walter did not fail to tell us that Gertrud had helped her mother with the cake. From an early age, I was on the lookout for the quirkier side of human nature and so kept a close eye on Gertrud. Throughout the meal, from behind lowered eyelids, she threw adoring glances at her father and he, proud, looks at her. They were clearly besotted with each other. It was Grandfather and his daughters all over again, perhaps even more so.

"Go and show Aunt Emmy what you have knitted," Uncle Walter told the apple of his eye. After a little show of modesty, Gertrud went out in search of the precious artefact. She came back with something pink that she lay before an unenthusiastic Aunt Emmy.

---

[38]   A character of a German popular tale for children, *Strubbelkopf* means "fuzzy hair."

Her skill in knitting was but one of Gertrud's many virtues and accomplishments. Her father also praised her good nature, her cooking, her sewing, and her cleanliness. At the mention of this last quality, Aunt Emmy pricked up her ears. Under that unpromising exterior, a kindred spirit might be lurking. And so it proved.

The conversation flowed on with no contribution from Helmut and little from Gertrud. Cousin Walter, who did not share his siblings' heavy tongue, gave us the benefit of his expertise on sport and cattle prices. When the grown-ups began discussing the impending move, he took me on a conducted tour. Helmut tagged along, a silent witness. He was becoming more human by the minute. He still would not speak, but at least I managed to establish eye contact.

We stopped in front of a glass cabinet to admire Walter's sporting trophies. He was a very good athlete and footballer. To the Nazis' acute embarrassment, he had won the Tschammer von Osten Landespokal, an important cup named after Hitler's minister of sport. The trophies did not greatly interest me, but next to them stood a Prussian blue crystal vase. Whether by nature or nurture, Mother had passed on to me her passion for things blue. I could not take my eyes off that vase. It gave me a feeling of bliss in the pit of my stomach. Sport is all right for those with no soul.

"Do you have a bank account?" Walter suddenly asked, a propos of nothing. "How much do you save each week?"

I had to admit that I neither had a bank account nor could I save. My pocket money was a pittance; my commissions from rent collecting and cigar fetching were ludicrous. After essential expenses, such as the occasional slice of apple cake, there was little left. What with his sports trophies and his bank account, I realized that I was not in Walter's league. I wondered if Helmut saved.

We climbed up to the loft, Helmut's recent hiding place, well stocked with cattle fodder and bedding. Walter forked some through an opening to the stables below. He pointed to the vestiges of a hole in the roof, now filled in.

"When this house was first built," he informed me, "the straw was winched up from the street through that hole." I was not sure how they got it up now, but clearly there had been a lot of progress since those dark days.

We went down to the garage to inspect the family vehicle, an old Ford. Walter started the engine with some difficulty, using a crankshaft, proudly proclaiming that he could drive the vehicle, another sign of his superior status. There was no time for a demonstration. It was time to feed the cows.

Helmut opened the stable door. At last I had come face to face with the source of the effluvium that I had long sniffed from afar. Here were fifteen fat Friesians, contentedly taking their high tea at the trough. I hoped they enjoyed their feed as much as I had mine that day.

Chapter Twenty-Six

COUSIN HELMUT COMES TO TEA AND COUSIN GERTRUD GETS AN EDUCATION

Some Sundays later our newfound relatives paid us a return visit. I received them at the door in one of my mother's boy outfits. I had recently graduated from dark brown velvet and brown shoes to sky blue linen and white shoes. It was thus arrayed that I now stood before my astonished cousins.

The linen outfit was a fetching two-piece collarless jacket with matching shorts—very short as the fashion demanded. My crêpe shirt had a little Peter Pan collar; and with the white shoes went long white socks. Faced with this apparition, the tongueless Helmut looked sideways, held his hand over his mouth, and sniggered. In the sailor suit I had worn to Lage, I had looked overdressed; now I had gone beyond what any self-respecting boy could tolerate.

I knew I looked ridiculous. Other boys had made this plain to me in the way boys do. Mother summed up the principle that governed her choice of my raiment. "One always wants to have them even more beautiful than they are already." (*Man will sie immer noch schöner haben wie sie schon sind.*) It was a saying she had picked up from some other crazy mother.

Mother pursued her goal with single-mindedness. Her favourite for me was the long silky blouson with ornamental buttons. Around it, held in place by long loops, hung a very loose belt that dropped almost to my groin. Mother also wore this kind of belt. It was very fashionable in those days—for ladies. In school photographs, the other boys appear in sensible pullovers or in shorts with braces, while I shine in my shortie nightshirt with the absurd belt. Even before the late and unlamented Adolf came into my life, I stood apart. He merely gave me an extra shove into the wings.

Mother considered the loose belt very *sportlich*.

"But my blue suit is not *sportlich* and my white shoes are not *sportlich*," I protested.

"Perhaps not, but they are elegant. You must always look nice. Never underestimate good appearance. When you get your birthday presents, which packages do you look at first?" Mother answered her own question. "Those that have a nice wrapping, of course. If you received a present wrapped in dirty brown paper, you would leave it to the last, wouldn't you?"

"Yes, Mutti."

Mother screwed up her nose as if she had detected a bad smell. "It's the same with people. If they look unappetizing, they get left to the end. No one wants to have anything to do with them. You'll remember what I say, won't you?"

"Yes, Mutti."

I remembered. Mother's homilies are engraved on my consciousness like words chiselled in stone. Even today, I do not like being scruffy and tend to avoid scruffy people, however beautiful their souls.

Had I been wrapped in brown paper that day, I would have made a better impression on Helmut. Perhaps it was the shock of my appearance that finally propelled him to speak.

"What's your favourite game?" he asked abruptly in a high-pitched voice.

"*Völkerball*," I replied.

"I don't know that game. Can we play it now?"

"No, stupid. It's a game between nations [*Völker*]. It needs lots of players. Those on the outside throw the ball at those in the middle, who try to dodge it. If you are hit by the ball, you are out. The one who hasn't been hit is the winner."

"Sounds like a silly game to me," said Helmut, to whom the Swiss mentality was foreign.

"It's all right. I like being in the middle and dodging the ball."

"So you don't get your soppy clothes dirty."

"I don't wear these all the time. Mother makes me put them on when we have visitors."

"I wouldn't put on those things, even if my mother told me to."

It was no idle boast. Helmut, as I came to know to my cost, had a will of iron.

He would have made a stand against those clothes, but I could not fight my mother. I have always found it much easier to resist wise guidance than misguided love. When Father tried to wean me from my selfish ways, I put up a very firm stand, but when Mother drew me into her joint ventures, which included the buying of my outfits, I became jelly.

I tried to get away from the subject of my clothes.

"I'll show you our timber yard later," I told Helmut. "And then we can play hide-and-seek. It's a terrific place for hide-and-seek."

Helmut blocked my exit.

"Whoever heard of playing hide-and-seek in baby wear?" And revealing a bellicose streak, he added, "If I catch you, I'll rub your white shoes in the mud." He gnashed his teeth in a rather nasty way as he said this. Clearly the boy meant business.

I was beginning to like Helmut despite, or perhaps because of, his pugnacity. I was willing to risk my shoes changing colour to play with him, only this was not the time for games. In our family, bread came before circuses. First, the ritual of stuffing the visitors had to be gone through. Helmut, however, had other ideas.

We took our places at the dining table. In the way of the Silberbachs, Mother piled food on her guests' plates, mostly herring. If you liked herring, Mother's table was the place for you. They were present at her high teas in most of their numerous modifications: salted, pickled, soused, rolled up, bloated, bismarcked, matjessed, and maidened. With them came their small kinsfolk—the sprats. They stared at you in their dozens with tiny glazed eyes from a dark-gold sea of oily fish skin.

Helmut gazed at the creatures of the deep heaped on his plate but made no move to ingest them.

Mother looked up from the bloater she was tackling, not her first, judging from the skeletons on her plate.

"Don't you like fish?" asked she in the perfumed voice she used for difficult people. Helmut made no reply. Mother put some kosher salami on his plate. Helmut sat there in his grey knee-length bumpkin shorts and studied his hands.

"Stop your nonsense! Eat, boy!" Uncle Walter's voice rose but stopped just short of a shout. He was not on home territory.

Helmut took no notice of the giant leaning over him. His cheeks were red, but otherwise, the little inverted triangle of a face gave nothing away.

"Perhaps he would like something sweet," crooned Mother, pointing to some dry biscuits. She had clearly come to the conclusion that the boy was an imbecile.

"Leave this to me. None of you know how to handle boys." Grandfather spoke with authority. "I'll get him to eat."

"All right, you try," said Uncle Walter wearily, "but don't count on it."

Grandfather grabbed his walking stick with one hand and Helmut's arm with the other and took him into a corner. He jangled the coins in his pockets and counted two shiny marks on the sideboard.

"Here are two marks, my boy," he said in the softest voice he could muster. "No, I'll make it five marks." Three more coins emerged from the capacious pocket. He patted Helmut's head.

"All you have to do," he told his grandson of the downcast eyes, "is to eat a sandwich for the sake of your grandfather, and the coins are yours. That's a fair offer, isn't it?"

Now, five marks constituted a fortune. Fifty times my rent collector's commission! Five marks would buy fifty slices of apple cakes at Kordmöller's. I was never offered that kind of money. How could Helmut refuse?

Refuse Helmut did. He never even looked at the assembled riches. A crestfallen Grandfather collected his coins and hobbled back to his seat, muttering that he had never come across anything like this before. For once, he had met his match.

Still, he made more fuss over my cousins than he ever made over me. Aunt Grete's children were royalty, Uncle Walter's, novelty. Even more than before, I was wallpaper.

Meanwhile, Helmut continued to study his digits. He had made up his mind not to eat, and he did not eat. Neither his father's threats nor his aunt's blandishments, nor even his grandfather's enormous bribe could persuade him to eat a single morsel or utter a single sound. He sat there, lips pursed, firm in his Trappist stance.

Herring, I learned later, was not Helmut's favourite food, and he was none too fond of kosher salami, either. But that was not why he fasted. He would not have eaten even if his favourite dish had been put in front of him. I couldn't see why the grown-ups did not catch on. Helmut simply disliked having to eat in a strange house with strangers who claimed to be his nearest and dearest relatives. When he first met us, he had crawled under the table, and now he was hardly aware of the dishes, but all too aware of his new family. He looked at the food, and at his hands, only to avoid meeting our eyes.

The thought crossed my mind that here was a genuine savage in captivity, like one of Karl May's Indian braves. I had been taught to hide my feelings, but Helmut had not yet benefited from Mother's civilizing influence.

Helmut did not miss much by fasting. Except for Mother, no one seemed to enjoy the meal, though only Grandfather dared voice his feelings. No herring lover either, he had to make do with Aunt Alma's adulterated sausages and was heard to mutter darkly, "If I have to eat flour, then I'll eat bread." (*Wenn ich Mehl essen muss, dann esse ich Brot.*) I shared his sentiments. The flour laden kosher salami, not matured and inflated to twice a salami's normal size, threatened to crumble into its pink and white constituent bits. The frankfurters were pale imitations of pale imitations. With them went Erna's vinegary potato salad.

For Mother, no high tea was complete without *Harzerkäse*, a smoked, rolled-up cheese that does no credit to the Harz mountain region from where it originates. It manages to assault at least three of any sensitive person's senses, possibly four, since it is none too pleasant to the touch, leaving only the sense of hearing unmolested. It looks like Vaseline trying to revert to a more liquid state, it has a putrid odour that makes camembert seem like rose petals, and it tastes like decay with caraway seeds. That day its perfume wafted through our dining room, almost as potent as that of the fifteen fat Friesians attacking the chinks in Uncle Walter's *Diele* (hall). The newcomers politely declined the proffered delicacy, leaving Mother to feast alone.

"Can I play with Helmut in the timber yard?" I asked Mother. She used Helmut's argument.

"What, in your good clothes?"

It was a tactical error. "I can always change," I rejoined quickly.

Mother saw that she had lost the first round, but she always won in the end by virtue of sheer moral superiority.

"No, I don't want you two dirty today. What will Aunt Minna think? You can show Helmut the timber yard, but I rely on you not to do any climbing or running about. And no getting your nice shoes dirty. And not more than ten minutes! You can play with Helmut when he comes to live here, and you have your old clothes on. Today, just show him around and give him something to look forward to."

She added, "Before you go, ask Erna to give you the carpet sweeper."

This was Mother's latest weapon in her fight against dirt and dust, and she wanted to show it off to the backwoodsmen from Lage. Perhaps they had never even seen one. I came back with the gleaming instrument. Mother told me to put it in a corner. She would demonstrate later.

"Can we go now?" I asked.

"Yes, but don't be long. You don't want to miss the cake, do you?"

I preferred not to answer that one, and we made our exit. I led Helmut along the cobbled roadway that ran alongside the factory. Our factory was a long low-slung building that stuck out behind the dignified office building (*Bürohaus*) like the long tail on a dowager. As the road came to an end, the whole area broadened out into our huge timber yard with the sawmill at its centre. I watched Helmut's face and saw his eyes grow wider and wider. All this is mine, I thought, but I tried to look nonchalant. "Those are beech trunks," was all I said.

The smaller trunks were left out in the open, stacked crosswise into squares. They were dark green and smelled dank. Thinking that Helmut was rather dim, I chose to emphasize the obvious:

"If you hide in one of these, no one will find you, provided you keep quiet and don't sneeze."

"I would throw in some stones or even stink bombs if I had them. That would soon flush you out." Helmut did not smile as he said this. So the boy played foul. No one had ever used such methods to flush out prey. As it transpired, Helmut did not use them either. He merely wanted to puncture my smugness.

We looked each other up and down. I looked at his bumpkin shorts, he at my well-filled ultra short ones.

"Race you to the top of that stack," Helmut challenged.

"I can't today. You heard me promise my mother that I would not play."

"Mother's boy," Helmut sneered. "You won't play because you'll lose. You're too fat." I couldn't let that pass. "And you're a runt," I said.

"I'll catch you up," said Helmut, gritting his teeth. "Look at my father."

Helmut was as good as his word. He ended up being taller than I—and fatter.

I wanted to take up Helmut's challenge to race him. I knew these stacks and felt that I could beat him. But I had made a habit of keeping promises, especially when they were made to Mother.

"I can't play now, but I'll show you our horse," I said, hoping to mollify Helmut.

"Oh, all right then," he said grudgingly.

Hektor was munching peacefully and noisily at his trough. He had a small establishment not far from the noisiest part of the factory, where the brushbacks were sculpted, but all was peaceful that Sunday. He welcomed us with friendly neighs. Hektor liked human beings, even when not bearing gifts. We patted him, but the promise to Mother was calling me, and we had to take our leave. I looked down at my shoes. My heart sank.

"My God! I've got something on my shoes," I told an unsympathetic Helmut. It wasn't much, but it was yellow and came from Hektor. Trying to wipe it off only made it worse. I tread very gingerly until we were out of the stable. We returned to the dining room, redolent of horse.

Mother did not pick up the scent. Her examination of my clothes was cursory. She did not even notice the telltale yellow spot on my white shoes. There was no reproof, even though we had been away half an hour. Mother's attention was elsewhere. She was in teaching mode.

Herrings and *Harzerkäse* had demanded Mother's undivided attention. She had launched her education of cousin Gertrud over tea and Erna's dry cake. The girl was at the age when she had to be prepared to fight one of the greatest of life's battles, the battle against the corruption of moth and dust. Mother surveyed the perils that faced the *Hausfrau*.

"The little pests get into everything. Uncle Hermann likes to put a rug over his knees when he reads. I bought him a beautiful new one in Bielefeld last year. While he was away travelling, I left it on his chair. And what do you think, Gertrud? The beasts ate holes into my lovely camel hair blanket. It shows that you can't be too careful. But I have learned my lesson."

After this diatribe against the winged enemy, Mother continued with a paean to the weapon that kept them at bay.

"Mothballs are such a godsend, and so cheap. Don't be afraid to use them. The more the better. I know some people don't like the smell, but they give me a sense of security. I have a very good make that is slightly perfumed. I will give you some to take home. Don't forget to remind me."

Gertrud made one of her funny neck turns and nodded her head.

Adjuring her niece to place mothballs at strategic points in all areas vulnerable to attack, Mother then turned to the other great enemy. She explained her fighting methods, warning her new pupil of the dangers that lurked in corners.

"That's where it likes to settle. Large surfaces are easy. You can use a duster or a brush. But you can't always get in there." Mother pointed to the nearest corner.

"A *Pinsel* [a kind of paint brush] may help. You can also use one for sideboard legs—anything that is carved. But, sometimes you just have to use your fingernails for the corners. There is no other way. The first thing I look at when I enter someone's home is the corners. They tell me whether the *Hausfrau* is clean or dirty. And now, Gertrud, I'll show you around the house."

Confident of the outcome, Mother was about to let Gertrud conduct her own litmus test on Schülerstrasse 17, when I interrupted the tête-a-tête.

"Can I play with Helmut again, Mutti?"

"Definitely not. It's getting dark. You just sit here and talk with Helmut." Mother did not know what a task she had given me. While talkative enough when alone with me, Helmut kept mum in company. I left him to his own devices and followed Mother and Gertrud on their dust safari.

"Look at this sideboard, Gertrud," said Mother to her niece of the downcast eyes. Gertrud looked up from her bow to see Mother point a well-manicured finger at the squat legs of a Wilhelmine monster occupying the corner of the room.

"Do you see any dust in those crevices?" she asked her niece.

Gertrud gawked at the crevices in question, which separated the strands of a crudely carved lion's mane.

"No, Aunt Emmy," she replied dutifully and truthfully, turning her shoulder.

"When I see dust in any place where people don't normally look for it," Mother pontificated, "on the legs of a sideboard, or on the skirting, under the furniture, and of course in corners, I know it's more than a question of dust. You can be sure that in such a home the cups are not clean, the household linen is not clean and, more than likely, the *Hausfrau's* own clothes are not clean. *Oben hui, unten pfui.*"

Let no one say that the German language cannot be crisp and to the point. In four short words, Mother summed up the discrepancy that can exist between a woman's elegant outerwear on the one hand, and dirty underwear and unwashed private parts on the other. For some reason, the saying was never applied to men.

Mother practised what she preached. Not even her worst enemy could have accused her of *unten pfui.*

Mother's house was an extension of herself. She kept it in the same spotless condition as her own person. Her brother said she suffered from *Putzfimmel,* her sister, from *Reinlichkeitsfimme,* an obsession with cleaning and cleanliness. It was, and probably still is, a condition common enough among German women. Mother had the disease, which is deliberately passed on from female to female, in an acute form. She was about to pass it on to a niece who was wide open to the infection.

It was only their second meeting, but Mother quickly sensed that she had found someone who would see things her way. Even though the girl made little contribution to the proceedings beyond saying "Yes, Aunt Emmy" and "No, Aunt Emmy" in the right places, while turning her head and shoulders with each affirmation and denial, Mother's intuition must have told her that she was not handing over the wisdom of a lifetime to an unworthy disciple. Why else spend so much time with her niece on a day when so many important matters had to be discussed? Few can resist the prospect of making a willing disciple, and Mother was Grandfather's daughter. Into the evening twilight, Mother continued to instil her version of domestic virtue into an attentive niece.

The subject of dust had been left behind; not exhausted, for that could never be, but adjourned for their next meeting in daylight hours.

Personal hygiene had not yet been touched upon; that would come when they knew each other better. Mother was on the subject of underlings and how to treat them, an important subject since her staff were the troops in the battle Mother was waging.

Mother put her arm round her niece and wagged her right forefinger:

"Remember, Gertrud, you must always treat those beneath you as you yourself would want to be treated." I had been preached too on that subject many times, but for Gertrud, it must have been a somewhat academic point. She had no one beneath her to treat like herself. Still, she delivered another very convincing "Yes, Aunt Emmy."

Gertrud was an attentive listener. I thought she looked rather strange, staring at Mother with her mouth half open, but it was evidently a pose that could draw from Mother a steady stream of wisdom.

Mother cited the example of a certain *Frau Doktor* who was so rude to her domestics that they never stayed more than a few weeks, forcing the *Frau Doktor* to do her own housework until she found replacements. The lady was at present in one of those in-between periods, doing her cleaning and dusting in silk stockings and high-heeled shoes, and it showed. The house was in a mess. Clearly, so far as the treatment of domestics was concerned, expediency and morality pointed in the same direction.

Mother erred too far the other way; witness her checking the gleaming sideboards for dust at 6:30 a.m. and removing any offending particles herself. If the carpet showed a few flakes of fluff, she went over it with the red carpet sweeper, well pleased to have won another victory over the enemy.

"Why don't you leave the cleaning to the girls?" Father pleaded with her more than once. "You work so hard in the factory all day."

"Oh, it's easier this way, Hermann. It doesn't take long and I know it's done properly."

Mother gave away only half the truth when she said this. She went on her forays when the staff was absent mainly because she did not want to cause offence. Only major shortcomings, such as vast areas of undusted surface, elicited a very gentle reprimand.

"I think it would be good to tidy up the boy's room, Else. He is so untidy."

"And, Erna, please be so kind as to polish the kitchen stove today." She never said, "Erna, please be so kind as to cook us a decent meal today." It was always about cleaning and polishing.

Mother never sacked anyone, and no one ever seemed to want to leave, and no wonder. She showed a genuine concern for the welfare of her employees, whether in the house or in the factory. There was the widowed Frau Profet, a large woman with dark hair, a red face and very bad legs, whom Mother had once employed and whose son she had given a job in the factory. Frau Profet's life was one unending tale of woe, but she never seemed to exhaust Mother's sympathy and support. She never got any gratitude from those she had succoured when she most needed it.

While Mother was unfolding her cautionary tale of the *Frau Doktor* and the missing domestics, a moth had the misfortune of straying into her line of vision. It was a shining creature with tinsel wings, like the tutu of a Degas dancer.

"Stupid insect, why could you not have stayed in the garden. But no, that was not good enough for you. Too dark and dull. It had to be the bright lights for you, and look what happened!"

Mother clapped her hands together and something grey fell to the ground. She picked up the corpse and put it in the wastepaper basket, lest someone tread it into the carpet. Then she rubbed her hands clean. The creature left no stain, no reminder of its glory, just some grey powder on a woman's hand. No Lady Macbeth was she; Mother did not even bother to wash her hands. Her action had been automatic. Anything that fluttered aroused her killer instinct. No nonsense about treating those beneath you as you yourself would want to be treated.[39] Mother was protecting her territory.

---

[39] I said nothing at the time, but when I was older and wiser, at school in England, I took steps:

"Dear Sirs," I wrote to the Royal Society for the Prevention of Cruelty to Animals at 105 Jermyn Street, London, W.1.

I hope that your wholly commendable activities extend to the moth—an animal too, after all. My good mother puts the prevention of cruelty to clothing very high on her scale of values. With a zeal and a thoroughness that would be commendable were it not applied to such a dastardly end, she systematically exterminates all moths and moth-like creatures on which she can lay her hands, and she commands other members of the family to follow her example. A mild woman, unable to stand the sight

"We must close the windows," she said. "The hordes are just waiting to come and do mischief."

Mother instilled her persecuting zeal into her receptive niece. Gertrud soon became expert at clapping her hands and examining her clothes and blankets for signs of moth damage. The heart-to-heart

---

of blood, and the soul of goodness, her predatory instincts seem to be aroused only at the sight of the moth family. She has even been known to exterminate a butterfly which sought shelter in my room.

I do not think that I shall ever be able to persuade her to live and let live—to realize that the life of the clothes moth is more important than the life of the clothes. But the clothes moth is only one among a large variety of moths. The others allow clothing to die of natural old age. If only I could get my mother to understand the difference between the clothes moth and the harmless varieties I might be able to strike a bargain whereby I consented to punishment for the guilty, while she stopped the slaughter of the innocent. I understand that there are pamphlets explaining and illustrating the activities of the clothes moth, while distinguishing it from its pacifist neighbours. I wonder if you could help me obtain them, or direct me to any other literature on the subject.

You may consider that my request does not come within the province of your beneficent activities. My mother is not needlessly cruel to moths, killing them slowly and with relish. She pounces on them as part of the general struggle for the survival of the fittest, and usually secures instantaneous death. But I maintain that killing animals needlessly is a form of cruelty. It also comes under the sin of pride. The right to destroy life which we did not create can only have been given us for self-defence, or, at the most, for sustenance. The innocent moths do not threaten my mother or any of her possessions. Nor does she, so far as I know, relish tasty meals of fried moth prepared in the secret recesses of her kitchen.

I hope that you will not allow my facetious manner to hide the underlying seriousness of my intentions, and that you will help me stop the abuses which I must daily witness in my own home.

I am your Society's grateful admirer.

P.S. Enclosed stamped addressed envelope.

talks continued on subsequent Sundays, when the care of nails, hair, the uses of Mousson Crème, and furniture arrangement were also on the agenda. The lessons proved a great success, precisely because the aunt's precepts coincided so closely with the niece's own inclinations. Gertrud kept Aunt Emmy's sayings in her heart, and Aunt Emmy felt amply rewarded by the spotless home Gertrud kept when she had her own establishment.

Three days later, I received the following reply:

> Dear Sir, Thank you for your letter of the 14th August. I appreciate what you say, but I am afraid that the moth for the purposes of the Protection of Animals Act, 1911, is regarded as an insect and not an animal. It is not protected by law, and this being so, it is impossible for us to take any action in the matter to which you refer and I regret that we have no literature on the subject.
>
> Yours Faithfully, A.W. Moss, Chief Secretary.

Chapter Twenty-Seven

MY ADOPTED FAMILY

"At Uncle Walter's, they have *Kohlrouladen*.[40] At Uncle Walter's, they have real frankfurters. At Uncle Walter's, they have marvellous *Pickert*.[41] At Uncle Walter's, they have the best plum tart, with real egg custard under the plums. They make so much that they have to take it to Kordmöller's[42] to be baked in the oven there."

My reports probably annoyed Mother and Erna, but they produced no change in our monotonous diet. Erna would not compete, so I took my business elsewhere.

As I made my way up the back stairs of Uncle Julius' house, I was met by a clash of odours—mouth-watering scents from Aunt Minna's kitchen on the left and the whiff of *Schlemmerhappen* cigars, often mixed in with something very unpleasant, from Uncle Julius' quarters on the right.

Since the death of Aunt Pauline, I had not been a frequent visitor at grumpy Uncle Julius' imposing square villa. I went once a week, strictly on cigar business. But once the Lage family had taken up residence, those back stairs leading to the kitchen got to know me very well indeed.

---

40 Mince meat wrapped in cabbage leaves and bathed in brown gravy.
41 A potato cake made with flour and yeast, and stuffed with sultanas. After the yeast makes it rise, it is beaten down and fried in a pan with oil. Lippe's national dish.
42 The local baker.

I chose my time carefully: not too early, so as not to overstay my welcome, and not too near the crucial lunch hour, so as not to make it seem that I had only come for a meal.

"Can I play with Helmut?" I wheedled, as I entered the roomy yellow kitchen, the hub around which the household turned. I wanted to play with Helmut, but even more I wanted a meal. Aunt Minna always obliged. In the early days, I made some pretence of declining the invitation. This charade did not last long. Very soon it was taken for granted that I would stay.

Aunt Minna, in her blue and white overall, her head covered with a scarf to protect her hair, rubbed the flour off her hands.

"You can play with Helmut or do anything you like, so long as you keep out of my way. I don't want either of you in the kitchen until lunch is ready. None of your sniffing around and poking your fingers in the saucepans."

My fingers behaved, but my nose was working overtime. I smelled *Pickert*. Aunt Minna, born and bred in Lippe, made a marvellous *Pickert*. It was even juicier than Frau Poppe's. I was waiting for my share.

"And don't wander off to the timber yard," Aunt Minna added. "I don't want you late for lunch."

"We won't be late," I promised, with feeling.

Aunt Minna never made a fuss the way Aunt Grete did. Her speech was short and to the point, but she was generous.

I finally located Helmut. He was not a boy with whom one could discuss Friederich Barbarossa or the quarrels of Frederick the Great with Maria Theresa and Madame de Pompadour. He knew nothing of the heroism of Queen Luise as she faced the upstart Bonaparte. No matter. I adapted to my surroundings, as I have always adapted, an accepter of situations more than an initiator. We ran around the timber yard, he with his socks hanging down to his ankles, mine almost up to my knees. In the winter we skated on Grandfather's meadows. At least once a week, often twice, we went to the cigar shop for Uncle Julius.

Now we settled down in a corner of the living room to play *Doppelkopf*, a complicated card game. Helmut threw down every card with great force, as though it were a trump. He had picked up this habit from the adults, who played *Skat*, the other popular card game. That was strictly for men and some mature adolescents, like Walter. Money changed hands.

My playing was more subdued and cunning than Helmut's, but we made a lot of noise as we tasted triumph and disaster. More than once, Uncle Julius, red-faced and bleary-eyed, scooted us out of the room. We kept our hands and continued our game when and where we could, hurling insults in turn at each other and at the absent Uncle Julius.

Uncle Julius also had the nasty habit of interrupting an exciting game because he had run out of cigars. Until Helmut came on the scene, I had been the sole purveyor of cigars to Uncle Julius. Now we shared the commission, which was pitifully small, considering the hazards involved. The *Schlemmerhappen*, a mild brand with very light-coloured leaves, favoured by Uncle Julius, were only found in a shop almost overhanging the dreaded Bega.

When I saw the Bega again in 1987, it was just another piddling stream, but as a child it was for me an object of terror. It ran dark, green, mysterious, far, far below the road. Luckily, the shop was on the nearside. Had I needed to cross the bridge, I would have insisted on hazard pay. Even so, I ran back, clutching the long fat cigars, eyes averted from the stream, but pursued by the sound of rushing water.

On rare occasions, in a sudden burst of courage, I ventured onto the bridge. Clutching the railings, I looked into the depths and felt them beckoning to me. I saw myself dismembered, as in a Greek story I had read, my bones scattered among the green stones that broke up the stream, my weeping mother crying to my distraught father.

"If only we had given him more pocket money, he would not have had to risk his life for the sake of Uncle Julius' cigars."

I was glad when Helmut came to join me on these occasions, even though my pittance was now halved. His presence gave me strength. Sometimes we crossed the bridge to look at another watery grave. The Werre, of Wedderwille fame, ran parallel to the Bega, a little further down the road. It was terrifying, not because it flowed too far down, like its tributary, the Bega, but because it flowed too high up. The Werre was a violent stream. Especially after heavy rain, it ran perilously close to the road bridge and then made a steep descent into the distance.

Helmut and I were inseparable, except when we were not on speaking terms, which alas, was much of the time. Try as I may, I cannot remember what our quarrels were about, only that they were frequent. Perhaps

Doppelkopf provided the *casus belli*. We both took our cards seriously. We became known as *die feindlichen Kousins*, the inimical cousins, though really we were only quarrelsome. We did not hate each other; we just could not get along.

The rejecting world outside, which threw us too closely together, must have played its part, but there were also differences of temperament. Helmut was quick to anger; I was quick to take offence; and both of us were stubborn. Neither wanted to be seen making the first move towards the reconciliation that we both desired after the first few days of hostilities.

When fate, in the form of family gatherings brought us face to face, Helmut glared at me with dark reproachful eyes and then looked quickly away. I did my *beleidigte Schönheit* act, lips pursed, nose in the air, pretending not to see him. "The offended beauty" was what my parents called me because I was so ready to take umbrage when I felt there had been an affront to my dignity and status.

With my parents, I took time to nurse my wrongs. I waited for some kind of apology in words, or in the form of a hug or a kiss, or even, where Father was concerned, a joke. Then I forgave them. But with Helmut, time was not on my side. My interest in a reconciliation was greater than his. So long as hostilities lasted, I suffered the pangs of separation, not only from my friend, but also from the delights of his mother's cooking. That really hurt.

I waited impatiently for Uncle Walter to notice that we were not on speaking terms and bang our heads together. He always obliged.

"Why are you two not speaking to each other?" he asked, towering over us.

Neither of us dared go into the trivial issues involved. We stood there, looking sheepish.

"You should be ashamed of yourselves. Shake hands now, and don't let me catch you quarrelling again."

We did as we were told and started playing together, self-consciously at first. In no time, the quarrel was forgotten, and we became inseparable once more.

When there were no family meetings, my position was more difficult. Probably I could have done without Helmut's company for a little longer, but when I thought of all the lunches I was missing, I grew desperate.

I got even more sick than usual of Erna's food, now that I was used to the real thing. Something had to be done.

"I am going down to Uncle Walter's. Do you want me to take any message?" With feigned nonchalance, I accosted Grandmother, Grandfather, Mother, or whoever might have business with Uncle Walter. They knew something was up because I did not normally offer my services in this way. When they had no message, they made one up—all except Grandfather, who was not sensitive to my feelings. Half an hour before lunch, I ran down the road and presented myself at the house. Panting, I passed on my urgent message, adding, with a look of despair, "I must go now."

"Aren't you staying for lunch?" Aunt Minna had uttered the magic words.

"No, I'd better not."

Aunt Minna raised her eyebrows. Now it was her turn to reconcile us.

"You and Helmut haven't been squabbling again? Come to think of it, I haven't seen you for some time."

I hung my head.

"Yes, you two have fallen out," said Aunt Minna with just the fraction of a smile. She called, "Helmut, come here."

Helmut appeared, the anger gone from his eyes. The handshaking ceremony took place, both of us feigning reluctance. I had regained my friend, my home away from home—and my lunches.

The advent of my new relatives was a godsend. It was not just the food, though, heaven knows, that was important. Here was a real family. Sometimes they laughed, sometimes they quarrelled, but they were together. By comparison, mine was an apology for a family, with a mother home only early mornings and evenings, a father sailing in at weekends if I was lucky, and no brothers or sisters. No sooner had my relatives settled down in Schötmar than I adopted them as my own. I did not actually sleep at their house, but when there was no school, and I was not quarrelling with Helmut, I foisted myself on them for much of the day.

One Friday evening, after the Lage family had been settled in our street for some time, I blurted out, "At Uncle Walter's they have chicken more often than we do. Sometimes they make chicken soup." Father was home, and I was in the midst of slurping our monotonous Friday evening soup with its mushy carrots, leeks and celery, and lumps of disintegrating beef.

"Would you like to live at Uncle Walter's then?" asked Father, his eyes twinkling.

That made me think. I would never have admitted to yes, but in the first flush of enthusiasm for the new arrivals, I might have thought yes. Now I was not so sure. Our Erna's food was a heavy burden, and I still had to bear it most of the time, but the family down the road also had their cross. Its name was Uncle Julius. I had no great desire to live close to him.

Uncle Julius had been a grumpy mumbler as long as I could remember, but sometime after Uncle Walter's family had moved in, he started to mumble terrible things into his drooping red and grey moustache, things like *Mörder* (murderers). He was referring, not to our friends in the Nazi Party, but to the relatives who shared his home. He was convinced that his food was being poisoned, and what he mumbled at home he said aloud elsewhere.

Also, he now made little effort to control his disability. It got to the stage where, as with Hektor, our horse, one knew exactly where Uncle Julius had been. Aunt Minna was convinced that it was deliberate. She and Gertrud had to clean up the mess. Uncle Julius showed no gratitude. On the contrary, he took the attitude that in coming to live with him, Uncle Walter and family had won the lottery.

"They have said *A*, now they must say *B*," was Mother's harsh comment when the complaints came streaming in. I am sure that when the family had said *A*, they did not suspect just how malodorous *B* would be.

They had Uncle Julius on their hands until Uncle Walter decided to emigrate. Uncle Julius bought himself into a very good old-age home in Emden. He had the misfortune to survive into the 1940s and was deported. "Destination Unknown" state the records. The Final Solution had no built-in age limits. Again, I have to ask forgiveness of the dead.

As I got to know my relatives better, I found out that their family life was not as warm as their food was good. The children seemed to get along with each other, but I was not so sure about the parents. When Uncle Walter barked at Aunt Minna, he sounded uncomfortably

like his father, even though he did not goad Aunt Minna the way
Grandfather goaded Grandmother. Aunt Minna answered back in
her slow country way, but only to defend herself. She had none of
Grandmother's bite.

Father's nervous rages at Mother died down as quickly as they blew
up. They were always followed by remorse and Father's smile of deep
contentment as he received his kiss of forgiveness. There was no such
kissing when my uncle and aunt made up. They seemed too far apart
for that. Things went on as if he had not shouted.

When Uncle Walter flew into one of his rages with Aunt Minna or
the boys—he never shouted at Gertrud—his speech became even more
ungrammatical than usual. He was too angry to be aware of his lapses, but
at other times, he knew well enough that his command of the German
language left something to be desired. He looked very sheepish when
he quoted—against himself—a verse that summed up one of his most
frequent grammatical sins:

> *"'Mir' und 'mich' verwechsl' ich nich',*
> *Das kommt bei mich nich' vor."*

The verse is untranslatable. It illustrates a mix-up of accusative and
dative, common in our part of the world. In denying the mix-up, it
commits the sin it denies.

My cousins' speech, too, was subject to lapses from correct German
usage, and Mother, anxious that her boy should speak only the highest
of high German, was not altogether happy about our growing intimacy.
It was not just my cousins' speech. She considered Uncle Walter's boys
too rough and uncultured to be fit companions for the likes of me. From
the time that I was tiny, she had drummed into me the adage:

"*Sage mir mit wem du umgehst, so will ich dir sagen wer du bist.*" (Tell
me what company you keep, and I will tell you who you are.)

Mother would have liked to see me surrounded by doctors' sons, a
frequent guest at their homes, with the *Frau Doktors* telling her, as she
met them in the street, what a wonderful well-bred little boy I was. But
this was 1934, and Aryan doctors' sons were not exactly queuing up to
keep the company of me and my kind. There were no Jewish doctors'
or professionals' sons around.

"Hermann, I wish the boy could play with some boys from better homes," she told Father, but she did not prevent me from playing with my cousins.

Mother's worst fears were to be realized all too soon. There was no point in asking my cousins to do penance at Erna's table. All I could offer them in return for their parents' hospitality was the use of our timber yard.

For me, they could not have come at a better time. Having long ago lost my parents to the demands of their factory, I was losing my remaining playmates as well. The Wortmann sisters, like their parents, remained friendly, but they were older than I, and so were most of the Jewish children. True, Ursula Eichmann and Rolf Hamlet, who had held their tryst among the logs and had shattered my stork-dominated universe, still paid the occasional state visit, but since they had found each other, they were no longer very interested in hide-and-seek.

My timber yard, my kingdom, was empty. Walter and Helmut helped to populate it again. Walter sometimes brought older Jewish boys, like Egon Hamlet (Ingelore's admirer) and Günter Wallhausen.

On one occasion I was playing hide-and-seek with Walter, Helmut, and Egon Hamlet. They were seeking, I was hiding. I had chosen the roof of the oil drum shed. Our oil supplier, Herr Bacharach, a great friend of Father's, had done his work well. There were so many oil drums that a whole line of them protruded beyond the cover provided by the shed into the open space in front of it.

The shed was set against the sawmill. If you crouched on the roof, by the sawmill wall at the back, only a giant could see you from the ground. Alas, if you were clumsy like me, you could be heard. My pursuers suspected my presence on the roof, but since it was laborious to climb up, Walter got hold of a large pole. Standing on an oil drum, he poked it all over the roof, trying to flush me out. I could not resist the temptation. "I'll show them what I'm made of," I thought, and grabbed the pole. Walter pulled; I hung on for dear life and fell, face down, onto one of the oil drums.

Howling and bleeding, I was carried home and placed in front of my distraught Mother. My nose bleed would not stop; my face was growing larger and bluer by the minute. Mother feared her babe's last moment had come.

"What have you done to him?" she screamed at the boys. There were frantic phone calls to the doctor, backed up by messengers. "Please come before something terrible happens." When the doctor arrived, he tried to calm Mother. "The boy has no injuries that time will not heal."

Still, I looked terrible. My eyes were bloodshot, my nose was cut and bruised, I had acquired protruding blue lips, and the lower part of my face was swollen black and blue. Unkind contemporaries, who came to see the damage, assured me that I looked like a pig. The fleeting glances in the mirror that I allowed myself told me that the description was apt.

To protect me from the ribald comments of the ruffians who had brought me to this sorry state, and from others of their kind, Mother kept me indoors for three weeks. I sat behind the curtained window, like Bertha Wallhausen's unmarried sister, watching the world, envious that others were playing. A specialist was called. He discovered a small breakage in the nose, but said it was not worth operating on at this stage of my growth. I have lived with it ever since.

Walter was summoned to appear before Mother and was given the scolding of his life. And all because he did not know with what a clumsy oaf he was dealing. It was some time before he could show his face in our house again.

From left to right: Helmut, Minna, Gertrud, and Cousin Walter

Vernon in white shoes

From left to right: Bertha, Emmy, Vernon, Cousin Walter,
Gertrud, Frau Birkholz, Helmut, and Siegfried

From left to right: Vernon, Emmy, Ingelore, and Helmut

Uncle Julius' House in Schötmar

FOLLY

Chapter Twenty-Eight

THE BLUE SALON

When my mother was determined to do something, she usually did it. In the early years of Nazi misrule, she did some quite incredible things.

Mother had long nursed plans to zone off part of Grandfather's meadow behind the factory to plant an orchard and more vegetables. Father was not enthusiastic.

"We have more fruit and vegetables than we know what to do with," he said, and even that great bottler, Grandmother, objected.

"We don't use up all the fruit we have bottled. We already give a lot away. Why do you want more?"

Grandmother hated waste. She and Father often agreed. Both were religious and on the stingy side.

Opposition was useless. Mother had made up her mind. She did not really want more fruit. Like her father, she loved new projects; she loved to watch things develop on foundations she had built. I also suspect that, without being fully aware of it, she wanted to lay down more roots in German soil. Then they would not be able to drive us away.

The ground was dug, a wire fence put up, and seventy fruit trees were planted. I remember the number because Mother often repeated it, first with pride and later as an example of her own folly. There were apples, cherries, plums, and pears, and, Mother's pride and joy, apricots and peaches. The trees looked wispy and exposed in that meadow, flanked on one side by the timber yard.

But Mother was in her element. In her blue overall with headscarf to match, and old shoes, well worn at the promontories, she tramped back and forth between factory and infant orchard, supervising and encouraging. She tried to entice everyone to watch and admire the new life blossoming in unpropitious soil. She tried to tempt me.

"Come and look. We'll even have peaches, and you love peaches. You can help me water the trees."

I was not interested in peaches for the future. I wanted them here and now. My ideal was *Schlaraffenland*, that magic land where the goodies fly into your mouth. Not for me the laborious process of growing things; and I could not imagine how peaches would ever grow on those silly little trees.

I went to the orchard with Mother. It was her project. No one else favoured it. I wanted to give her my support. She took determined steps, swaying slightly on her stocky heels. Time was precious. I trundled after her, kicking stones.

From behind, Mother looked just like one of her workpeople, an ample, rounded countrywoman, covered in a thin layer of sawdust. Even face on, she could have been mistaken for a machinist. Only her hands gave her away, not because she feared to get them dirty, but because she gave them a lot of time and Mousson Crème. *Frau Doktor* Lerner's lessons had stuck. Even so, they had clear work lines, scrubbed clean of dirt with one of our arched nail brushes. They were not the hands of a lady of leisure.

Mother shored up the soil around the trees, and I watered them. Uncle Walter saw us from the meadow, where he was tending his cows.

"Agriculture and stock farming, little sister" (*Ackerbau und Viehzucht, Schwesterchen*), he shouted, waving his long arms.

I picked up the phrase and bandied it about. From then on, the family teased Mother about her passion for agriculture and stock farming, though the latter was of course Uncle Walter's province. Mother detested anything to do with cattle.

She did not mind being teased. She had got what she wanted. In between the trees, she planted strawberries to add to our glut. There were also vegetables and asparagus beds. The asparagus and strawberries did well in our sandy soil, but the fruit trees did not seem to prosper. Still, by the time of Auschwitz, they must have borne some fruit for the greedy neighbours who took over the orchard.

Mother was also in favour of extending the factory. Plans were drawn up for a new machine house extension (*Kessel-und Maschinenhaus*).

"Drexhage says, and I agree with him, that once the extension is built we can become one of the major employers in Lippe Detmold. It will give us a chance to expand all around." Mother trusted Meister Drexhage, the factory manager. Together they ran the factory, Mother in her dark blue overall, Drexhage in his dark grey one, she the real manager, he the technician. Drexhage was a man of few words, but he knew his machines.

"It's all very well for Drexhage," said Uncle Walter. "He doesn't have our problems. It might be better to wait and see how things develop before you spend all that money."

"Better to build in France," said Grandfather.

"You must be mad," said a visiting relative from Kassel.

Father, elated by the positive article about him in *Der Führer*, agreed with Mother.

"I can sell anything this factory can produce. Business is better than ever. A few Nazis may stop buying, but there are others out there waiting to buy our goods. They know that there are no better brushes made in Germany. Pfingst of Minden [owner of a large department store] will take anything we can make."

Father also reported, "In Hamburg, they were telling me that Hitler is secretly building cruisers. If he rearms any further, France and England will give him a kick where it hurts. That will bring him to his senses."

Father was an inveterate optimist, a man of great charm, very popular with his customers. Hamburg, where he did much of his business, was one of the most liberal cities in Germany. Had Father not been such an inspired salesman and had our business suffered more in the early days, my parents might have come to their senses sooner.

The ventilation system at the back of the factory was built because it had to be built. However, the machine house extension was put on hold and never got beyond the planning stage.

The orchard and the factory plans did not mark the end of Mother's follies. There was worse to come.

"This room has the best proportions in the house and it is wasted. Look at it!" Mother's hand sweep took in the dingy wallpaper, the faded curtains and the country furniture of my grandparents' large upstairs room.

"Those long windows and the balcony door give the room space. What I could make of this room!"

Make something of it, she did. All her life Mother was obsessed with interior decoration. It was her artistic outlet. She longed to transform the commonplace into the beautiful. In England, once we could afford a home of our own, she turned every house we lived in upside down. When she had got it the way she wanted it, she moved us on to new pastures. That was her karma. It is so easy to see these patterns in others' lives, so difficult to do anything about them in one's own.

"Life is so short and death so long" (*Man lebt so kurz und ist so lange tod*), she mused, quoting one of her own mother's sayings to justify her extravagances.

Before my parents moved from their apartment to our family home, Mother's imagination had had plenty of time to roam over the spacious rooms, ruminate on their potential, and spin schemes. Unfortunately, it was not until well after the Nazi takeover that she had sufficient funds to put her grandiose plans into effect.

While the Reichstag was burning and the knives were out for Röhm and his gang, while German freedoms were being eroded by the *Gleichschaltung* (the Coordination Law) and Hindenburg became a puppet in Hitler's hands, while the Jews were being hounded out of public and professional life and Hitler was preparing to march into the Rhineland, Mother proceeded, step by step, to turn the first floor into a shrine to good taste. The rest of the family, who all loved her, looked on, helplessly, as life ebbed from one room after another. My grandparents ended up in the two front rooms on the ground floor, where they glowered at each other across the hallway like two heraldic animals guarding the homestead.

Mother's finest achievement was to turn the shabby upstairs sitting room into the Blue Salon (*Blaue Salon*). Mother pronounced it "salong," like "sarong."

"I am just as particular as Frau Elsbach. I don't want any gaps. And don't save on the underlay." Mother had taken time off from the factory to give instructions to the specialists from Bielefeld, who had come to lay the carpet. She was well aware of her role as a trailblazer. No one in her circle had a fitted carpet. Hers may have been the first in Schötmar. It had to be perfect.

"Isn't it a wonderful colour? It looks so beautiful, even without any furniture!" Mother needed admiration and reassurance, and I was there to provide them.

"Yes, it's very beautiful, Mutti." I wasn't faking. I shared Mother's passion for blue. That gorgeous expanse of sapphire carpet gave me a glowing feeling. Even today, as I stand before a Claude landscape bathed in blue light, or come upon an ornament of lapis lazuli, visit the Bluebell Wood at Kew, or see delphiniums in full boom, I feel that all is well with the world.

As the room took shape, we both admired the blue velvet curtains and the chairs. Mother had the chairs upholstered in the same colour blue as the carpet. She liked to call them Chippendale, but they were Chippendale's hefty German cousins.

Mother chose ebony furniture; it went well with her blue colour scheme. It was heavy Wilhelmine stuff with short plump paws and lions' heads and manes popping out here and there. Every year, on Father's birthday, some new monster made its appearance: *Kredenz* (sideboard) Number One, *Kredenz* Number Two (twice as long as Number One), *Vitrine* (display cabinet)—all marked by the same heavy elegance. Even though each piece was swathed in corrugated cardboard, Mother left nothing to chance. She supervised every stage of its progress from delivery van to salon.

"Be careful! I don't want the furniture chipped or scratched. Mind the rail! The wood has just been repolished. Your firm knows that I am very particular."

She squeezed herself between furniture and rail, preferring to face injury rather than have any harm come to her precious chattels.

When Mother and I had decided where to put the dinosaur, and it had been unwrapped, dusted and put in place, she sent me to call Father.

"How do you like your birthday present, Hermann?"

"Very nice, very nice."

"Don't you like the long, clean lines? So simple, yet so elegant."

"Very simple, very elegant." He pinched her chin and gave her a peck on the cheek.

"And how much did this elegant simplicity cost me?"

Father's eyes narrowed as he smiled his mischievous smile. "My birthdays are always expensive." He was happiest when his wife was happy, and he had played some part in that happiness.

The Blue Salon was opened three or four times for what Jane Austen calls "company of consequence," but it was never lived in. It was a sanctuary where the devout could come and worship at the altar of elegance. As with a temple or a mosque, you left your shoes outside.

Cousin Walter, a boy of spirit, rebelled.

"I don't take my shoes off when I go into our sitting room at home and I'm not going to take them off here. No, not me." He shook his head vigorously to show that his mind was made up.

Walter was not allowed to enter the Promised Land though, like Moses on Mount Pisgah; he managed to catch some glimpses from afar through an open door.

"You are a mother's boy. You do everything your mother says," he told me when she was out of hearing. "I wouldn't lower myself like that. Why don't you put up a fight?"

He said it, not to tease or hurt me, but in a fatherly sort of way. His words made no impression. I did not feel that I was lowering myself.

Mother and I remained the chief worshippers. She tried to involve Father but "I like what you like" was all she could get out of him.

"Vati is a very good man, but he has no taste." Mother did not mind discussing Father with me, or anything else for that matter, always excepting the reproductive process.

Sometimes she liked to open the door of the salon and poke her head in without entering the sacred precincts.

"Isn't it beautiful to see everything in order?" she whispered, her face lit up with joy.

At six each morning she inspected the sanctuary for dust; and when she came home for lunch, she made little rearrangements to please the god of beauty. Mother was always striving for perfection. I was her acolyte. We rarely disagreed.

"I will move the chair a little to the left and you tell me if it looks better that way. I think the white lady is dwarfed by the vases on the sideboard. Shall I try her on the table? What do you think?" I was flattered that my opinion was sought and valued. I learned to notice fine detail.

The lady under discussion was a white porcelain Leda, confined with her swan in a type of basin. She must have been Rosenthal, for that was Mother's great passion. Mother detested multicoloured figurines. There was no Dresden or Meissen in her display cabinet. She liked white Rosenthal, bronze statuettes, modern silver—clean lines, no knick-knacks, and nothing with gold. Mother did not care for gold, except in jewellery. She thought it vulgar. Years later, in England, when fitted furniture came into vogue, all her friends chose gilded mouldings. Mother's were off-white and matt, the same colour as the cupboards. Elegant simplicity again.

She made some compromises. A portrait hung in the Blue Salon. It was of me, naked white chest, chubby cheeks and thick wavy brown hair. That was allowed a gold frame. Also, the lampshade was of dark gold silk. Mother had first wanted blue silk. Then she changed her mind. "One can have too much blue."

Finding the right lamp was her greatest problem. She scoured the stores of Bielefeld for the largest available fitting and shade, but could find nothing that came up to her vision of the room.

"Go back to your suppliers," she implored. It took some time before the store came up with something large and simple enough for her requirements.

The same drama was repeated in London when we moved to a larger house. Mother had firm opinions about the glass chandeliers, so popular in England.

"I can't stand all those bits and pieces. They are like something out of a curiosity shop, and a nightmare to keep clean." She sighed. "Why am I so unlucky? Why can't I find the right lamp?" But not one of London's major department stores could get her what she wanted. In despair, she imported a twelve-armed brass octopus from Germany.

It was in a London department store, looking for furniture, that Mother had the heart attack that was to prove fatal.

Chapter Twenty-Nine

THE COFFEE CIRCLE

We were sitting down to our Friday evening meal. Father had just come home from one of his sales trips. He had told Mother about a new boycott of Jewish shops. Now it was her turn to impart the latest news. She could hardly bear to wait until Father had finished saying the blessings. She was about to burst:

"Hermann, the Elsbachs have just installed the most wonderful *Herrenzimmer.*"[43]

A *Herrenzimmer* was not a "men's room," as the literally minded might suppose. The Elsbachs already had more than adequate facilities.

"Herr Elsbach and his friends can relax there after dinner in comfortable leather armchairs and smoke their cigars." Mother's cheeks were flushed with excitement. "Frau Elsbach bought him a large desk where he can write his personal letters. The room has everything a man can ask for."

Mother came to the point. "I think you should have a *Herrenzimmer* too, Hermann. You work so hard. You deserve some comfort. Paul has a *Herrenzimmer*. If he deserves one, you certainly do. We will break through from the Blue Salon to the boy's bedroom. That will become your special room. When we have guests, you can take the men straight from the Blue Salon to your smoking room, and I won't have cigar ash all over my blue carpet."

---

[43] It is possible that it may not have been the Elsbachs, who were department store barons, but it was a grand family of that kind.

Mother's eyes took on that visionary look, Grandfather's look when he was laying plans. Father's look said, "God give me patience." A new sideboard was one thing, but another new room . . . His frugal nature was often at war with his love for his wife.

"But I don't need a smoking room, Emmy. My old desk is perfectly adequate, and you know we never have guests in the Blue Salon. We always eat downstairs."

By his next birthday, Father had his smoking room. He also had a monumental mahogany desk, a heavy brown leather writing case with a perforated ornamental border, and a scantily dressed bronze dancer who had Father's initials inscribed under her feet. She was to be his seal. She had a larger sister, who graced a round mahogany table.

Again Mother tried hard to draw Father into her latest project.

"Do you like this material, Hermann?" She was showing him samples for the thick brocade curtain that was to divide the smoking room from the Blue Salon.

"Yes, it's very nice, Emmy."

"And this one?"

"That's nice too."

"Which do you like better?"

"I leave it to you, Emmy. You have such good taste."

"I like this one best," said Mother, showing him a third sample.

"You are right, of course. That is by far the best."

"I wish you would take an interest, Hermann. This is going to be your room."

"But I am happy if you are happy. I only supply the cash."

And so it continued until the end of their lives. Father had worked his way up from a poor background. His first impulse was to resist extravagance, but he could not begrudge his wife anything. His greatest joy in life was to see her happy, with him supplying the wherewithal for her contentment.

Years later, as soon as he came home from one of his sales trips in England, a man in his sixties and early seventies still representing dozens of firms, he brought out the order sheets for her to see and calculate what he had earned. She patted him, kissed him on the forehead, and told him what a wonderful man he was. His face glowed as if he had been vouchsafed the beatific vision while still in the body. And when, during his attacks of angina, she smoothed his brow, the pain seemed to ease for a time.

She had that effect on her menfolk. Her approval meant everything. We were well aware of her foibles and teased her constantly, but we loved her for the quality of her being.

Father never used his smoking room. He was not meant to use it, and he did not want to. He had no taste for magnificence. In every house we occupied, he commandeered the smallest room for his den. He liked a place where he could relax and not be afraid of scratching a chair or spilling ink.

The *Herrenzimmer*, like its companions on the transformed first floor, was for show, to be admired by visitors and, above all, by Mother herself. After she had drunk her fill of perfection in the Blue Salon, she would draw aside the brocade curtains and gaze upon perfection in a different, brown and red guise. Perfection, like my looks, could always be improved upon. As she admired her handiwork, Mother's mind ranged over possible new acquisitions and new ways of displaying the things she had.

Once the public rooms were ready, Mother began work on the private apartments. There was no new bedroom for me. I may have slept downstairs, but I also recall being relegated to one of the guest rooms in the office building, where I had nightmares. My parents' new bedroom had the same colour scheme as the Blue Salon, ebony beds, curtains of blue damask, and bulging silky eiderdowns of an incredibly deep royal blue. I sometimes went into the bedroom just to look at the eiderdowns.

On the rare occasion when the house was completely full with guests and they had to sleep in their new bedroom, my parents used the old red featherbeds with their starched white covers. The new eiderdowns were purely for show.

Like all our other household effects, the beds and eiderdowns were inherited by the S.S., who stole the large containers with all Mother's precious chattels that we had stored in Bremen for transport to the United States. They were ready to be shipped when war broke out.

The eiderdowns may have faded and frayed, but Mother's furniture was of lasting quality. For all I know, sideboards (*Kredenzen*) Numbers

One and Two may still be gracing a home in Bremen, or perhaps in Hamburg, not far from the Chief Rabbi's house where Mother first imbibed her notions of good taste. It's a nice thought.

The new bedroom had a dressing room (*Ankleidezimmer*) en suite. Mother was once again a pioneer. A dressing room was something unheard of among our friends. The long row of fitted cupboards was the only part of the upstairs museum in use.

The new bathroom—blue tiles, of course—did not get much use either. We had to take our bath in the cellar. One unlikely user was our young neighbour, Egon Hamlet. It was there that he deloused himself when he came back from Buchenwald concentration camp. But Mother was elsewhere at that time.

When all the work was completed, the first floor apartments were thrown open to the public. This happened only once.

The Jewish community was turning in on itself. Some well-to-do women had organized a Saturday evening coffee circle (*Kaffeekränzchen*). It began as a coffee and cakes women-only affair, but soon men and children, smoked salmon and sausages made their appearance. Each woman tried to outdo her predecessors; and Mother, not to be outdone, outdid them all. No *Harzerkäse* this time. It was smoked salmon and cream cheese, fish in aspic, Hammerschlag salami, the lot.

Food, however, was not Mother's main concern. She had asked to be the last hostess, first time around the circle, so that the new rooms would be ready for viewing. Her friends would come to gape in awe, marvelling at how such elegance was possible in Schötmar.

Mother knew she was taking a risk. She was especially worried about the blue carpet. She could not very well treat her guests like the family and ask them to leave their shoes in the hall. So what was to be done? I was the only one to whom she could open her heart. I understood her concerns, even if I did not share them. She wanted her work to be admired and, at the same time, wanted to protect the rooms for which she had laboured so hard.

"I think the best thing we can do is to put the men in the *Herrenzimmer*, where they can do less damage. The youngsters will squeeze onto the balcony. You can look after your friends there. I will be with the ladies in the Blue Salon, but who will keep an eye on the men? Vati won't have finished his prayers, so he'll be late. In any case, I can't trust him in these matters. He has no respect for beautiful things. If I ask my brother, he'll only laugh at me."

Mother, her brow furrowed, closed her eyes in thought and found the solution. "Alfred Hamlet is a responsible sort of man. I'll ask him."

Alfred Hamlet had come to visit his clan across the road. He was in textiles, in Essen or some other city in the Ruhr, a smart, good-looking man, who had risen above his cattle-dealer background.

Mother explained why she had decided to entrust the women with the blue carpet: "Women are more careful than men. They know what it means to keep a house clean and tidy. When the men come home, they find everything in order, and they think the *Heinzelmännchen*[44] did it."

Mother did not trust her ladies so completely that she failed to take reasonable precautions. There was a rug under the table and runners had been placed at strategic points.

"Go down and remind Erna to be sure to make them wipe their shoes," Mother told me as she made nervous last-minute adjustments, waiting for the guests to be brought upstairs.

First to be received in the Blue Salon was Mother's best friend, Rosa Silberbach, thickset husband Salomon, and daughter Hilde in tow, the former ominously puffing at a long cigar. Aunt Rosa was a stately grey-haired woman with sad grey eyes. As she bent down to kiss me, I watched the hairy pimples on her chin and cheeks come ever closer. Mother could have written her own version of "In Praise of Older Women." Our house was always full of them. Mother was not too proud to learn from their greater experience.

Aunt Rosa, in severe black satin with black toque, complimented Mother on her rather daring dress, a button-through, navy *Bleylekleid*,[45] with shiny mother-of-pearl buttons. But this was nothing compared to the admiration she expressed for the miracle Mother had created.

"I find it incredible what you have made of this room, Emmy." (*Ich kann es gar nicht fassen, was Du aus diesem Zimmer gemacht hast, Emmy.*) Hilde, a girl in her twenties, who was all Mother thought a young lady

---

44 Benevolent gnomes who secretly perform household tasks.
45 *Bleyle* was a well-known jersey wool brand.

should be, concurred. Mother glowed, but I could see that she was also wondering how best to shunt cigar-puffing Salomon to the smoking room. Help came in the form of the Hamlet and Eichmann clans, which arrived together.

"I think you gentlemen will be more comfortable in the *Herrenzimmer*," said Mother, separating the rams from the ewes. "You look after them for me, Alfred, until Hermann comes. See that they have all that they need. Hermann just loves his *Herrenzimmer*."

Making sure that men and children had been hived off to their respective stations, Mother turned to receive the compliments of her peers. They came thick and fast.

"You have such good taste, Emmy." (*Du hast solch'nen guten Geschmack, Emmy.*)

"Where did you buy the lamp?" (*Wo hast Du die Lampe gekauft?*)

"I like the carpet. A wonderful shade of blue and so well fitted." (*Oh, der Teppich gefällt mir. Ein wunderschönes Blau und perfekt gelegt.*)

"Yes, such a sideboard would look very good in my dining room too." (*Ja, solch'ne Kredenz passte auch in mein Esszimmer.*)

Mother, like me, needed constant reassurance. She drank in the compliments like champagne, but she did not get drunk on them. She kept her eyes open for crumbs that had strayed further than the festive Rosenthal china or the linen tablecloth. She stooped down discreetly to pick up the offenders and her friend Anna Hamlet, who knew Mother's ways, helped with the good work. Aunt Anna had a dark ravaged face that must once have been beautiful. The signs of the cancer that was to take her life were already apparent. She was very very thin.

I watched the pair bobbing up and down. I had left my post on the balcony and moved among the guests, handing around plates of sandwiches and petit fours, hunting for any crumbs of information I could pick up. Mother was all eyes, I, all ears.

Everything went as it should—for a time. The men played cards and talked cattle in the *Herrenzimmer*. The women gossiped and paid compliments in the Blue Salon. The youngsters were crowded onto the balcony. The boys played cards and stuffed themselves; the girls talked about boys.

The rot set in while Mother was taking a small delegation of women around the private apartments. As ill luck would have it, Father chose this time to join the company after his prayers. He had no interest in cards or cattle talk and, forgetting or disregarding his instructions, joined those ladies who had remained in the Blue Salon.

As usual, Father told jokes and made the ladies laugh. That was too much for Secko Silberbach, a celluloid goods manufacturer with a roving eye swivelling behind thick lenses. Mother called him a *Schürzenjäger*, an "apron-chaser." Secko, who could see what was going on through the drawn-back curtain between the two rooms, joined Father in entertaining the ladies in the Blue Salon. More men broke rank and some of the youngsters, hearing the laughter, followed. Soon the sexes and generations were hopelessly mixed and all, except for a few hard-core card players, crowded into the Blue Salon.

This was the scene that met Mother's eyes as she returned with her ladies from a no-doubt-triumphant tour of inspection. She looked about with horror, and then upwards as if to implore aid from a higher power. Then she got busy trying to save what she could. Crumbs were not the only problem. I saw her shunt an ashtray under Julius Silberbach's cigar (this Julius Silberbach was brother to Salomon, not Great-Uncle Julius) just as several centimetres of grey ash were about to yield to the pull of gravity.

"I put out so many ashtrays just in case," Mother whispered to me. "Fetch some more from the *Herrenzimmer* and put them near the smokers. I have to have eyes everywhere. Look, there are even bits of sandwich on the floor. If someone treads them into the carpet, what shall I do?" Mother quickly picked them up to avoid that danger.

Disasters never come singly or, as Mother sometimes said, "*Alles Schlamazel*[46] *kommt auf einmal.*" Just as she was getting the ash and crumb crisis under control, a second front was opened by, of all people, Alfred Hamlet.

"It's all very beautiful, Emmy, but do you think you were wise to make all these improvements under the present conditions? Things are not getting any better for us. We never know how long we shall all be in Germany."

Living as he did in a city, Alfred was more in touch with the wider world.

---

[46]   A Yiddish word meaning misfortune.

"That's just what I told my sister," chimed in a disloyal Uncle Walter. Mother flushed. "We work hard all week. We have no other enjoyments. At least we can enjoy our home."

"The Nazis won't last forever, and even if they do, they'll have to change their ways. They will need the Jews." This was Father, gallantly supporting his wife.

That was the moment *die rote* Erna chose to make her announcement. Erna Eichmann was the most spectacular thing in the room. She was known as "red Erna," not for any leftist political leanings, but for her mane of violent red hair, which she wore like an offensive weapon. A bright green dress added to her lustre, but clashed with the room's colour scheme. She already had the eyes of the men upon her. Those of the women now followed as she declared: "We are making plans to leave for South Africa. There is no future for us here."

Mother's face turned from red to white. Her eyes went dead, as they always did when she was very upset.

"Can I pass you the strawberry tart?" she said loudly to her neighbour, Aunt Rosa, adding more quietly, "That's all right for people with nothing to lose."

The strawberry tart tactic had no effect. The dream had been shattered. They were all talking at once now.

"It will pass. We just have to stick it out," said Salomon Silberbach. I did not call him "uncle."

"We are staying," added Aunt Rosa. "There is too much at stake." They were very wealthy.

"What about my cousin, Fredi?" asked Secko, addressing the whole room. "He is making arrangements to move his family to England." Fredi Silberbach was a prosperous textile converter who lived in Cologne. He too had something to lose.

"That's all right for him," rejoined Julius Silberbach, he of the cigar ash. "He has business connections in England. He can do as well there as here. But I can't take my cattle to England and Emmy can't take her brush factory."

"If we were younger, we could start in the Wild West," joked Paul Hamlet, husband of Anna and father to Egon. "As it is, we'll just have to stay." No one laughed.

"What else can we do?" asked the Wallhausens, who had no connections abroad. They were not well-off and had been asked to the coffee circle, even though they were not expected to reciprocate.

Secko Silberbach looked serious. "We may not have much longer."

Hilde Damer backed up her sister. "Erna is right, Secko is right. It can only get worse. Erna and Father will go first, and I will follow with Willibald."

Some women had just been gossiping about Hilde's tottering marriage to the gentile and very handsome Herr Damer, of which Willibald, one of the hard-core card players, was the offspring. All that was now forgotten. Mother's miracles were forgotten. She sat there, tense and forlorn, as they attacked her dreams. But she fought back. She had nursed her fantasies of the first floor transfiguration for so long; they had fed her imagination so often as she was getting her hands dirty in the factory that she was unwilling to surrender them to changing circumstances. The massive furniture was a kind of breakwater against the tide raging outside. Behind it, she could create her own ideal world of elegance and beauty.

Like many of us, Mother could not bear to look truth in the face. She clung to her dreams.

"So long as we have a single brick left, we are staying home." (*So lange wir noch einen Backstein haben, bleiben wir zu Haus.*)

*   *   *

Salomon and Rosa Silberbach joined their daughter Hilde, who had married in Holland. After the German invasion, all were deported to the East and perished.

Julius Silberbach was luckier than his brother. He went with his family to Uruguay, but returned to Germany after the war.

Red Erna wowed them in Cape Town.

Hilde Damer ended up in Bulawayo, then Rhodesia, where Willibald became a transport millionaire.

Some other members of the Eichmann clan, which was closely intertwined with the Silberbachs, were also saved.

Susi, my classmate, and Ursula, who had told me about the facts of life, went first to England and later joined their grandfather and aunts in South Africa.

Susi's parents and Ursula's father were deported. Her mother, the beautiful Ilse, sister of my Aunt Erna, had died earlier of cancer.

Alfred Hamlet, his wife, and one of his sisters went to the United States, to be joined there by Egon via England. Another sister went with her family to Palestine. I visited them in 1949. Anna Hamlet died of cancer.

The Wallhausens also perished. During the war, their son Günter managed to get to Sweden and ended up in Australia. He was the only Jew from our town who escaped during the war. The rest were murdered.

Secko Silberbach and his family settled in England and continued in the same line of business. Secko was the great survivor of my parents' generation. He was alive, well, and living in Birmingham at the age of ninety-four. He died aged ninety-five.

*   *   *

When my parents and I went back to Schötmar in 1951, we found that our home had been converted by the local government council into four apartments for the families of policemen. The house looked shabbier, but otherwise much the same, though the balcony had disappeared. We passed the front door, but Mother did not ring the bell.

Our house in Schötmar; the Blue Salon spanned the
three windows on the right on the second floor

BONDAGE AND DELIVERANCE

Chapter Thirty

THE IRON MAIDEN

While my mother was busy planting her orchard and transforming her home and my father was waiting for Hitler to come to his senses, the rulers of the new Germany were busy drafting some interesting new legislation.

On 15 September 1935, the Law for the Protection of German Blood and Honour (*Gesetz zum Schutz des deutschen Blutes und der deutschen Ehre*) was promulgated, to be followed two months later by the Reich Citizen Law (*Reichsbürgergesetz*). These pretty sisters, adorned with various elaborating decrees, became known as the Nuremberg Race Laws. We were told that "from a race-biological point of view, they had to be regarded as a single unit."

In a preamble to the first law, the good lawmakers of Nuremberg revealed what had moved them to pass, unanimously of course, this precious addition to the corpus of German law:

"Imbued with the realization that the purity of German blood is the precondition for the survival of the German people and inspired by the most unshakeable determination to secure the German nation for all time, the Reichstag has unanimously resolved . . ."

It turned out that the way to fulfil the Reichstag's noble aim was to prohibit sexual congress between Jews and nationals of "German or allied blood." Only the exclusion of people of alien blood could ensure the health of the German people, "that eternal spring and eternal fountain which gives new life," which had indeed given life to such masterpieces of the human form as Adolf Hitler, Hermann Göring, and Dr. Paul Josef Göbbels.

"Just look at that rogues gallery," said Father, holding up a photograph of Nazi leaders. "That lot would fit any police warrant." Much had changed since his early grudging admiration of the new orderliness. "They have faces like rear ends." Father used the German-Yiddish compound *Tochesgesichter*.

"If that is what Aryan ancestry produces, you can keep your small Aryan Proof Card and your large Aryan Proof Card, and even your Ancestor Passport." The *kleine Arier Nachweiss*, the *grosse Arier Nachweiss*, and the *Ahnenpass* were among the delights dreamed up in the new laws.

Mother put her hands over her lips. "Walls have ears." It was the time when she started opening doors to see if anyone was listening. One day, we had caught a man standing under the downstairs sitting room windows.

Father had a point about the top Nazis. There were many Germans who conformed to the Nordic ideal, but very few of them were to be found among the Nazi leadership—the gross loutish Göring; the crippled Alberich of a Göbbels; Himmler with his naked civil servant's face; Ley, the labour leader, a fat and exceptionally ugly little man; and then the *Führer* himself, who was not exactly Nordic beauty contest material. Julius Streicher, who ran the virulently anti-Semitic broadsheet, *Der Stürmer*, looked like one of his own paper's caricatures of a Jewish bloodsucker. These people had projected their own ugliness of body and soul onto the Jewish stereotype.

With the benefit of hindsight, we can see that the Nuremberg Laws pointed straight to the gas chambers, but when they first came out, many Jews, Father included, thought them a bit of a joke. There was all this business about racial dishonour (*Rassenschande*) and its consequences—the half-breeds (*Mischlinge*). With an awareness of the finer points of their subject that was positively Talmudic, the Nazis created half-breeds of the first degree (two Jewish grandparents) and half-breeds of the second degree (one Jewish grandparent). The former could not marry the latter and the latter could not marry each other. Three-eighths Jews were generously counted as quarter-Jews and five-eighths Jews, as half-Jews. Such generosity did not extend to three-quarter and seven-eighths varieties. These unfortunates had such a preponderance of Jewish blood that they were for all practical purposes Jews. So even if Mother had been able to prove the truth of her aristocratic grandfather, it would have done her no good.

"You are not even a half-breed of the first degree," Father teased. "If you divorced me, you could not marry an Aryan, even with special permission. You are stuck with us Jews." Mother gave a thin smile. A sense of humour was not one of her strong points.

All this was good for a joke and hardly seemed to concern us. But sandwiched between the extramarital relations clause and another one withdrawing from Jews the privilege of flying the national flag, there was a clause that would directly affect our lives. It forbade Jews to employ women of German or allied blood under the age of forty-five in their households. A Jewish household was defined as one that contained one or more Jewish males over the age of sixteen. The aim was to protect the vulnerable Aryan female from the libidinous urges of the Semitic male (*vor rassischen Gefährdungen zu schützen*). The Nuremberg Laws allowed Aryan women already in Jewish employ to continue, provided they had reached the age of thirty-five by 31 December 1935.[47]

Else certainly did not qualify, but my Else was half lost to me even before the Nuremberg Laws. She had accepted the hand of my rival, August Beckmann, head of our dispatch department. August was tall and dark, but not handsome like his younger brother, Fritz, and certainly not good enough for my beautiful Else.[48] He had a closed face; one never knew what he was thinking. There was not much love lost between us. I did not like that he was going out with Else; I think he resented the attention she paid me, and considered me a general nuisance.

"Did you get any stamps for me today, August? Have you seen my Mutti, August? Where is Else going with you on Sunday, August?"

They married early in 1935. I do not remember attending the wedding, but Else's daughter recently sent me their wedding photograph.

---

[47]   The Bad Salzuflen town archive contains a poignant letter from Grandfather, written one month before his death, in which he pleaded to retain the services of a young nurse. The authorities curtly dismissed his plea, additionally noting his relations with non-Jewish women in years gone by and his "unworthy" treatment of the factory workers.

[48]   Despite my early judgement, August proved to be an exemplary husband, and the marriage, blessed with several children, was a happy one.

Else looked more beautiful than ever in her white gown and veil with August by her side, upstanding and proud. There are two children sitting on either side of the photo, their legs dangling from high chairs—a girl in bridesmaid's finery on the left, and a boy, immaculate in a velvet suit, on the right. A more miserable-looking child than that little boy you have never seen. That boy was I.

I do not recall if Else stayed with us until her new home was ready or only came in occasionally to help out. But after she moved to her new home, she visited us only once more. She had put on weight. I ran to hug her, but she kept me at arm's length.

"You have to come and see my new apartment," she said. "It's really very modern."

I went the next day, alone. She had not asked Mother. Else lived on the first floor of a pleasant house overlooking the *Krumme Weide*, a kind of village green.

"I miss you so much, Else," I said, tears in my eyes.

"Come and look at the kitchen," she said. "It's more up-to-date than your kitchen at home."

It was a sunny room with a view of the green. The centrepiece was a kitchen cupboard with mottled yellow celluloid doors. The flecks glinted in the sun. The colour changed, depending on where you stood.

"You must come again soon," said Else.

She lived within easy walking distance, but I do not remember ever seeing her again.

Else's behaviour fuelled Grandmother's gloomy view of the world and its ways. Had we not treated her as one of the family? Had we not practically brought her up? Had she not found a husband and happiness through us?

Grandmother used every opportunity to remind the world of the closing sentence of the official letters she had received each time one of her sons had given his life for Germany: "You may rest assured of the Fatherland's gratitude." (*Der Dank des Vaterland's ist euch gewiss.*) Now Else had joined the Fatherland on Grandmother's list of ingrates.

One could make out a better case for Else than for the Fatherland. Here was an ordinary young woman, just starting married life. She did not want her neighbours pointing at her for associating with Jews. Bad enough her husband still worked for them. Most of us are like Else. We do what is most conducive to our comfort.

Mother often warned me about the company I kept. "If you touch pitch, you get tarred" (*Wer Pech anfasst besudelt sich*), she said. One could understand Else. In the Third Reich, we were pitch.

I don't know whether the Nuremburg Laws permitted Erna to stay with us, but she also left. She moved to another town and made a good marriage. Her husband was quite a few years older and well situated. I think he owned a shoe shop. One hopes he was not fussy about his food.

Erna came to visit us once with her husband, very happy and looking extremely smart. Her happiness was short-lived. She died of cancer before we left Germany. Grandmother, never slow to draw a moral, said it was God's punishment. And she did not mean that God was angry with Erna for the way she treated the fruits of his earth in her cooking pots.

Some weeks or months before Erna left us, Mother's beautiful diamond engagement ring went missing—the ring that had caused her sister Grete so much heartache. Erna was the chief suspect. She had been cleaning the bathroom where Mother thought she had left the ring. The evidence was, at best, circumstantial. A few weeks later, the missing jewel seems to have resurfaced, metamorphosed into a fur jacket, an elegant leather handbag, and patent leather pumps. These additions to Erna's wardrobe clinched the matter for Grandmother.

"How could she have afforded all this in such a short time if she had not stolen your ring, Emmy? And after all we have done for her."

"I think you are right, Mother," replied my mother. "I would not have expected this of her. But what can we do? When I confronted her, she denied ever having seen the ring."

It was no use calling in the police. Who would take a Jew's word over that of an Aryan!

Maybe Mother made a mistake. If Erna had taken the ring, she might not have wanted to visit us again. Who knows?

The spiteful little clause in the Nuremburg Laws that forbade Jews from employing in their households women of German or allied blood under the age of forty-five brought Luise Strate into our lives, replacing my Else.

Fräulein Strate was well above the statutory age, probably in her mid to late fifties. Considerations of age apart, the good lawmakers of Nuremberg could rest easy that this particular Aryan rose would be quite safe. Fräulein Strate had long ago made her decision: once a virgin, always a virgin. No man, be he Jew or gentile, would ever penetrate that armour, even had he felt the daunting task worth pursuing. That was Karl's (the chauffeur's) opinion, and he knew about these things.

Luise Strate was a straight-backed, plump, iron-grey battleaxe. Her eyes were grey, her complexion was grey, her dresses were grey, and she had iron-grey hair, piled into a bun. My immediate impulse was to keep a safe distance.

Mother introduced her as Fräulein Strate, and Fräulein Strate she remained. Not even Mother dared call her Luise.

"Fräulein Strate has come to look after us. She hails from Lage, where Uncle Walter used to live. Show her how well you can behave." Always the same story—good behaviour, good behaviour. Fräulein Strate's pale parchment face folded into a grimace. She made some throaty noises about our becoming good friends. If they were meant to reassure, I was not reassured. Her looks belied her words. And those rasping sounds—like Tallulah Bankhead on an off day—did nothing to instil confidence. Where was my golden Else?

First impressions can be misleading, but they often contain an element of truth. Fräulein Strate was not really an aggressive person. She had a way of advancing upon you, squarely and full front, which made her seem so, but it was a defensive stance. She was forever on the lookout for something that might give offence—and plenty did—so that her defences were always mobilized. The long grey skirt that was her shield pushed forward as she advanced.

Fräulein Strate had recently returned to her hometown after twelve years in America, where she had taken care of the houses and offspring of rich New Englanders. Why couldn't she have stayed there, I thought, unaware that mature women were not exactly queuing up to work for Jews.

I do not know why she came to us in the first place. She was no philo-Semite. I caught one or two murmured remarks about Jews, especially when I misbehaved. On the other hand, she was no Nazi

either, though after a year and a half of coping with me, she must have
been tempted to join the Party.

After I had recovered from the initial shock of having her in the
house, we had a brief honeymoon. I lapped up her tales of life in the
good old U.S.A., the grand houses and the grand parties for hundreds
of grand people, with Luise Strate right in there, masterminding it all.

"And then Mrs. Diefenbaker said to me, 'I leave it all to you, Luise.
You are so good at getting things done. I'll go and make myself beautiful
before the guests arrive.'"

Mrs. Diefenbaker evidently looked stunning, though Fräulein Strate
pulled a face when she spoke of the tons of rouge, with which the woman
plastered her face. "They all do it, these American women."

I longed to go to America to see these painted women. Americans
evidently loved painting themselves. Winnetou and his redskins did it
before they went to war. Like most German boys, I lapped up Karl May's
novels. But Mrs. Diefenbaker was not going to war!

Then there were the children's parties that the invaluable Luise had
organized. I had never heard of Christmas crackers.

"Two children pull, one at each end. There is a great bang and out
comes the secret present. I made sure that each pair of children had at
least two crackers so that there would be no squabbling about who got
the present. The older one got the first, the younger, the second."

I could see Fräulein Strate herding the children into neat two-
by-twos, but who cared when they enjoyed such marvels as musical
chairs—another new concept—with a live band, and twelve different
varieties of cake to follow. This America really was *Schlaraffenland* (a
magic land where all wishes are fulfilled).

Fräulein Strate's thin, straight lips, which barely moved as she spoke,
moved neither more nor less when she sang, though her habitual look
of dissatisfaction disappeared for a moment. I imitated her heavily
accented American with unfortunate accuracy. It took some time to
unlearn later on.

Our new help had more to recommend her than her knowledge
of English. She was an excellent cook, much superior to our Erna. In
particular, she taught us how to deal with our strawberry glut. We had
more strawberries than we, and all our friends and neighbours, could
eat. There were no refrigerators. For some reason, only plums and

gooseberries were used for jam, not strawberries. Grandmother's bottling mania ensured that we always had eighty to one hundred bottles of strawberries. Strawberries do not take kindly to bottling. There they were, in their serried ranks on the wooden cellar shelves, dark brown and waterlogged, shadows of their former selves.

Erna could think of nothing better than to serve them for dessert straight out of the bottle. Fräulein Strate, with her New England experience, had other ideas. She boiled up the tired old things with gelatine, placed them on a delicious eggy sponge cake, and topped them with whipped cream. They were reborn. We remembered Fräulein Strate when Mother herself made "Strate Tart" for us in England—with fresh strawberries.

Mother was only too happy to leave our sustenance in Fräulein Strate's capable hands. Her priorities were very different when it came to cleaning and room arrangement. Here, Mother was like a lioness. There were awkward moments when Fräulein Strate felt thwarted. Her normally grey complexion took on a threatening shade of red. She never lost an opportunity to remind us of her superior experience, with twelve years in America to her credit. Mother always managed to calm her down with kind words and compliments about the latest meal. Throughout her stay, Fräulein Strate conveyed the feeling that, having done us the honour of lending her presence to our non-Aryan household, the least we could do was to let her have her own way.

I was full of admiration for Fräulein Strate as a pastry chef of genius and a purveyor of new words. What then compelled her to chase me with a carpet beater one Monday morning? She was giving some poor carpet a merciless whipping with all the strength of her powerful arms. Her instrument of torture was a bamboo beater shaped like a flat lotus on a stalk, all curves and curlicues, bursting with inner tension unresolved. While she was thus engaged, some chance remark of mine produced in her a sudden desire to change, not her mode of activity but its object. Her patience with me, evidently worn thin, snapped just when the means of retribution was conveniently at hand.

I did not fancy having a mandala imprinted on my seat and ran into the house as fast as my little legs would carry me. It was a tactical error. I should have stayed out in the open. Up three flights of stairs I ran, into the loft, she after me, panting. There she caught up with me, lunging out with her beater. She nearly had me cornered, but I managed to escape around the central chimney. I ran down the stairs and out into the street, followed by the enraged Strate brandishing her weapon and shouting imprecations. Fear gave me wings. In the end, puffing and blowing, she gave up the chase and limped back to the house, vowing retribution.

Fräulein Strate bore me no permanent grudge. Underneath that grey carapace, there was a good woman who enjoyed pleasing, if she was allowed to do so in her own way. I had reason to be grateful for her skill and kindness when, some months later, I came down with jaundice.

It was a hard time. I looked yellow and felt blue. The local doctors seemed to be getting nowhere. Mother, again fearing that her boy was on his way out, turned to desperate remedies. Someone had told her that sheep lice were a remedy for jaundice. I was forced to ingest thousands of the little creatures, baked for me by the Strate in a pleasant enough dough. Heaven knows how Mother obtained the wretched things. Ours was not sheep country. The lice did no good.

When she had exhausted the possibilities of fringe medicine, Mother submitted me to the more orthodox remedies of Dr. Richzenheim, a new discovery called in from Bad Salzuflen. Dr. Richzenheim looked the typical Jewish savant, an older fatter version of Gustav Mahler, with a goatee. He was not Jewish.

"That man must have some Jewish blood in him," said Mother. But no, he could not produce even a Jewish grandmother. This was just as well, because at a later time of great trouble, this pure-blooded Aryan was to prove very helpful to us.

Under Dr. Richzenheim's regimen, I progressed from baked lice to a revolting dark tea that had to be drunk three times a day. Sheep lice come back, all is forgiven, I thought. This horrid beverage was given credit for my eventual recovery, but I prefer to think that Fräulein Strate's American-style sandwiches did the trick.

During her time in New England, Fräulein Strate had become a mistress of sandwich making, and she put her skills to good use in my time of need. Dr. Richzenheim had forbidden any butter or fats. Only the leanest of meats were allowed. Fräulein Strate, ever happy to please, made me huge rye bread sandwiches with boiled ham and lean white chicken, a great delicacy in those days, when poultry was festival food.

They were garnished with lettuce leaves, herbs, and much else. They were delicious—the one ray of light during those dreary days at home. I was allowed to eat the sandwiches immediately after taking the foul tea. I gobbled them up, grateful to my erstwhile pursuer.

Even so, I never really liked Fräulein Strate. I always compared her unfavourably to my Else. Whenever I think of Else, the colour that comes to mind is gold; for Erna it is rust; for Fräulein Kaiser, dark brown; and for Fräulein Strate, it is grey. Else and Erna had been there when I first woke up to the world. They were part of my family, like the aunts and my favourite factory workers. Fräulein Strate remained an outsider. She stayed with us less than two years. Then her cup was full, and she left. I was not sorry.

Chapter Thirty-One

THE TRUTH DAWNS

My parents, like so many of their kind, considered themselves German citizens of Jewish faith (*deutsche Staatsbuerger jüdischen Glaubens*). The Nazis did their best to persuade them that they were nothing of the kind. They neither were Germans, nor were they citizens. As for their faith, had they worshipped Hitler as god, it would have made no difference. They were *Juden*. It was a matter of blood. "Only people of the same blood can be fellow citizens." (*Volksgenossen sind alle, die gleichen Blutes sind.*) It took my parents some time to get the message.

Had they read *Mein Kampf*, they would have learned that they and their kind were using their faith as a smokescreen to persuade the Aryans that Jews were not a nation but a religious community. The housepainter from Braunau had their number. He saw through their pretences and recognized them for what they were, a nation of parasites, a foreign organism battening on its host.

"It was my intention," he told his confidant, Otto Wagener, "merely to strip the mask from the satanic faces of these Jews, this nation of parasites. The German people must learn not to be deceived by this mask any longer. To recognize the Jew is half the battle."[49]

---

[49] "And, of course, that is why the Jew always tries to avoid being recognized . . . It is not for nothing that they introduce conformity in hats, eyeglasses, even suits! Because a Jew-cranium is stuck so deep down between the raised Jewish shoulders, they've seen to it that others, too, must have the same ugly high shoulders. In every jacket and coat, and especially in women's dresses and blouses, the shoulders are

And Father believed that Hitler would see reason!

The learned commentators on the Nuremberg Laws were more polite than Hitler. They did not actually call us parasites; they used the word *Gastvolk*, a guest people. But they made it quite clear that the aim of the laws was Hitler's aim: to spot the Jew and keep him apart.

"The Jewish guest people will from now on be divorced politically, culturally and above all biologically from the German people." (*Das jüdische Gastvolk wird vortan politisch, kulturell and vor allem biologisch vom deutschen Volk geschieden.*)

My parents did not realize that they had all along been guests in their own home, had indeed been members of a tribe of cuckoos. The lesson still took some time to sink in, even though the Reich Citizen Law spelled it out very clearly: "a Jew cannot be a citizen of the Reich" (*Ein Jude kann nicht Reichsbürger sein*).

My parents' German roots ran so deep that they did not believe what they were told. They were German, and they were staying put. Mother's phrase about remaining in our home as long as we had a single brick left became a shibboleth to be trotted out whenever more sensible people advised us to get out.

Our forefathers had lived much longer in Germany than most British Jews had lived in England. My parents were more like the descendants of the Sephardic Jews to whom Cromwell had opened the doors. They were German through and through.

Mother, especially, was a great patriot. I often teased her about this later. "If, God forbid, you had not been born a Jew, you would have been one of the first to join the *Frauenschaft* [Hitler's League of German Women]. You might even have been an anti-Semite." Mother did not deny it.

---

systematically raised with cotton and other padding. And the Jewish outfitters persuade their customers that this is the fashion, that this is beautiful! And the stupid people . . . dutifully believe them, and in time they actually come to find it beautiful. And they never have an inkling that they have to allow their God-given noble Aryan figures to be so pathologically disfigured, merely to make it harder to recognize the Jew's back on sight."

Hitler, *Memoirs of a Confidant*, ed. Henry Ashby Turner Jun., Yale University Press, New Haven and London 1985, p.93.

"Perhaps you are right, but what were we to do, shut up in that small insignificant town [*Kaff*]? We had no idea how the rest of the world lived." And she added, "I know it's sinful to say this because so many people suffered and died, but in one sense we can only thank Hitler for hounding us out of Germany and letting us enjoy the English way of life."

She became a fervent admirer of that way of life. She loved the freedom of a society where everyone could do his or her own thing, so unlike the one in which she had been brought up. But in the midthirties, her thoughts were very different, very German. She and Father tried to mould me in their image.

One day, I was called up to the Blue Salon, always a sign that an important visitor had arrived. I was introduced to a tall young man dressed up rather like a Hitler Youth *Oberbannführer* in black shorts with buckled belt and other accoutrements. He was the regional leader of the *Bund Deutscher Jüdischer Jugend*, the League of German Jewish Youth. This was a contradiction in terms, so far as the Nazis were concerned, the words "German" and "Jewish" being mutually exclusive.

My parents had summoned the young man to see if he was the sort of person to whom they could entrust the heir to an important brush factory. He was cross-examined about the backgrounds of his boys and passed with flying colours. He even had some scions of the department store barons on his books. He told my parents about the group's ethos and promised to make a man of me. The words "marching" and "tents" and "comradeship" and "hard work" and "self-sufficiency" sent shivers down my soft spine.

"Do I really have to join?" I pleaded, when this model of German-Jewish youth had left.

"Yes, it will do you good," said Mother. Even she thought that I could do with some toughening up, so that I could protect myself.

"And you will meet boys from very good homes. That will stand you in good stead all your life." She again trotted out her all-time favourite: "Tell me with whom you consort and I will tell you who you are." (*Sage mir mit wem Du umgehst, so will ich Dir sagen wer Du bist.*)

My parents knew little about Zionism, except that they were against it. Anything that could dilute our German identity was suspect. So, while more far-sighted Jews sent their children to groups like the Zionist Maccabi that would give them a sense of Jewish identity to replace their vanishing German heritage, I was made to join what seemed like a sister organization of the Hitler Youth.

We met in Herford and went on hikes, singing our marching song:

"Wir lassen alles in der Tiefe liegen,
Bringen nur uns selbst hinauf zum Licht.
Wir wollen in der klaren Höhe siegen,
Einen Weg nach unten gibt es nicht.
Komm, komm, lockt der Schritt,
Komm, Kamerad, wir ziehen mit,
Komm, komm, lockt der Schritt,
Komm, wir marschieren mit."

(We leave everything behind in the depths,
Only bring ourselves into the light.
We want to conquer in the clear heights.
For us there is no way downwards.
Come, come, the march calls us.
Come, comrade, we are on the move.
Come, come, the march calls us,
Come, we are joining the march.)

We were made to sing this nonsense so often that words and tune still remain with me. I was never the marching type and did not feel at home in the BDJJ any more than I would have felt at home in the Hitler Youth in different circumstances. As far as I recall, we had no shoulder boards, lanyards, or daggers, but in other respects, we came as close to our sister organization as it was possible without the benefit of a Hitler. There was the same emphasis on marching, on the hard life, and even on the flag. Ours was black, like our shorts.

In the Wiener Library, I came across some publications of the German Jewish Youth that express remarkable sentiments. Here is a paean to the flag:

"Wenn ihr Blick zur Fahne herüberwandert, geht ein stolzes Leuchten in ihren Augen auf-ein Gedanke durchzuckt sie: unsere Fahne! . . . Unser ganzes Sehnen, unser ganzes Wollen, alles was uns erfüllt sollte sie verkoerpern: unsere Fahne." (When their gaze wanders towards the flag, a proud light

rises in their eyes—a single thought flashes through them: our flag! . . .
Our beautiful black flag . . . . All our longing, all our desires, everything
that fulfils us—all that our flag should embody.)

Hitler wanted to produce a hard cruel youth, and here we have the
Deutsch-jüdische Jugend singing "a hard new song" and wishing for "a
hard difficult life." Just the right outfit for someone who has gone for
the soft option all his life.

I felt much better with the boy scouts. I even rose to be deputy patrol
leader. But that was England.

Perhaps it is not so remarkable that the ideals of German Jews
resembled those of our gentile peers. Our forebears had lived in Germany
for hundreds of years. However much the Nazis tried to deny it, we were
German. In the Wiener Library, I found the remarkable credo of one
Senta Meyer. It was in the *Denkschrift der deutsch-jüdischen Jugend*, the
Journal of German-Jewish Youth, printed in Hamburg in 1930, three
years before the Nazis seized power.

"We are youth, German, Jewish, German-Jewish youth," she writes,
and then goes on to present her credo for each member of the compound
"German-Jewish youth." This is how she feels about being German:

> We are German; the German landscape gave us the first
> experience of the feeling of home; the German language made
> cultural experiences [*Bildungserlebnisse*] possible for us.

> We are Germans! Here is our home, where our forebears
> have lived and suffered for centuries, and shared the fate of
> our German fellow men of other creeds; German soil is our
> home soil, the ground in which our dead have been buried
> for many centuries. The German language is our mother
> tongue, in which we not only speak to each other but which
> we have helped to form and culture. And is community of
> language not also community of thought? German culture is
> our culture; we are conscious of being its proud bearers; we
> are not just its outward witnesses; this culture is our deepest,
> most inward, most innate experience. We belong to our
> German people and land, inseparably bound, because we
> want to belong to them . . .

And so she goes on . . .

> We fight for our German nature, not despite the fact that we are
> Jews but just because we are Jews, proud upright people who,
> without overestimating themselves, know their own worth.

Methinks the lady doth protest too much. The subtext hints at the precarious situation of Jews in Germany, even before the Nazi seizure of power.

Though they could not have expressed them as eloquently as Senta Meyer, hers were also my parents' deepest sentiments, especially my mother's. When the terrible truth finally dawned, it was as if a lifelong companion had turned around and said, "It's all over."

"*Wir stehen vor einem Nichts*," was how Mother put it. We stand before a nothing, a void. Father at least had his religion and his innate optimism; Mother had tied up everything in her house, her factory, her town, her country.

"So many years we have worked to build up the factory and to have a nice home—and all for nothing. I never thought Germans could behave like that. I do not recognize my country anymore, my own country."

Father said, "We'll build something up again. After I was expelled from Metz, I also found my feet again."

"But you are not so young anymore. Then you were in your thirties; now you are in your fifties. Who could have thought that Germans would sink so low?"

I do not remember exactly when the change began, when emigration ceased to be only for those with nothing to lose. There must have been some straw that broke the camel's back. Perhaps the Nuremberg Laws had begun to bite. Perhaps it was the brown-shirted yobbos marching past our house, singing:

> "*Wenn das Judenblut vom Messer spritzt*
> *Dann geht's nochmal so gut.*"

If you are told, even in song, that when Jews' blood spurts from the knife, things will go twice as well; it will make even a patriotic Jew think twice about his position.

Another song, a gem called *Heil Hitler Dir* left Jews in no doubt where they stood. I translate:

> "Germany awake from your bad dream
> Don't give any room in your land to the Jewish stranger.
> We want to fight for a new beginning,
> Aryan blood must not perish . . . .
> All these deceivers—we throw them out,
> Jewry, get out of our German home.
> Only when the threshold is cleansed and clean,
> Will we be united and happy."

My parents finally took the hint.

The first sign that they were considering emigration came when Pfingst of Minden and his wife paid a state visit. Minden is a beautiful town situated on a bend of the River Weser. Herr Pfingst was the owner of its largest department store. When my parents spoke of him, they always gave him the territorial title, Pfingst of Minden.

Herr Pfingst was one of our most important customers, but he and his wife had not come to talk business. They had come to discuss the hitherto unthinkable. The Pfingsts were wealthy people who had something to lose. They would know whether it was time to leave Germany.

They were ushered into the Blue Salon, a sign of their high status. He was enormous, with a bald bullet head. The wife was equally large. They looked like something out of *Der Stürmer*, but then so did the Birkholzes who, in the good times, used to invade our house—and they weren't Jewish.

The Pfingsts were a kindly couple. They complimented me on my linen suit and my parents on having such a nice boy. The nice nine-year-old was present throughout the discussions. My parents entrusted me with all their troubles. I knew more than what was good for me. I grew from a boy who liked hide-and-seek and *Völkerball*, into a little old man, and old I have remained ever since.

The talk went something like this:

Father said, "We don't know what to do anymore. We have put everything into our business. So many years of hard but joyful work. You know yourselves that our products are second to none. Are we to give it all up? I was always against emigration. I thought that these people are criminals, but they are not stupid. They will see that the German economy will suffer if they drive out the Jews. But now I am no longer sure. Those mad new laws. Everything is getting more difficult. My brother in Giessen is making plans to leave, so is my sister-in-law in Cologne. People in the larger cities know more of what goes on."

Mother chimed in, "We have no trouble selling our goods. The business is going as well as ever. My husband is popular with his customers. But the DAF is making trouble. We had a contented workforce but they have put in an *Obmann* who obstructs me at every level."

The DAF, the *Deutsche Arbeitsfront*, was the giant Nazi labour organisation that replaced the trade unions. It was run by the *Gauleiter* of Cologne, the ugly little drunkard, Robert Ley. The *Obmann* was the man they had put in charge of the factory workforce.

"I never thought Germans could behave like this," Mother continued. "They march in front of our house singing dreadful songs about Jews. We have been good citizens, good Germans, and now they treat us like this."

I sat there, looking from face to face, saying nothing, but drinking it all in. I do not remember exactly what the Pfingsts said, but the gist of it was: Don't do anything rash; wait and see. They were people with a lot to lose. They waited and, I think, paid for their mistake with their lives.

Fortunately, we took a different course. Our first journey to Holland was in 1936. My grandmother was liberally endowed with female cousins, two of whom had married Dutchmen. One lived in out-of-the-way Groningen, in the very north of Holland. The other, Henriette Zeckel, had retired to Scheveningen, the seaside resort just outside The Hague. Henriette had two sons: Alex, who had pursued Aunt Grete long ago; and Adolf, a well-known Rotterdam neurologist. We sent Adolf a message to ask if he would be willing to store some suitcases for us. He agreed. By that time, it was too late to send out money, at least for people like us, who did not know any shortcuts.

The three of us set out from Schötmar station, accompanied by a large number of suitcases covered in crinkly black leather, the kind that resembles Persian lamb. There was a top layer of brushes to give the appearance of a business trip. Below that were the clothes and the household linen, embroidered *ES* (Emmy Silberbach, Mother's maiden initials). Below that were the shoes, crammed with table silver, also engraved *ES*. Fortunately, both my parents wore large sizes. Everything was surrounded with paper to give the appearance that the paper kept the shoes in shape. The smaller of the bronze dancers, the one with Father's initials engraved at the base, was also fitted into one of his shoes. The other dancer was too big, even for Father's shoes, and was eventually stolen by the S.S. in Bremen, where our things were stored to go to America.

On this and other trips, we took out practically Mother's entire dowry. We were helped by kind friends, who also took out some cases. Thus it was that my parents arrived in England with only ten shillings in cash but with about thirty suitcases full of clothes, shoes, underwear, table silver, and enough household linen and brushes for several generations of users. Much of the silver was later stolen from our house in London. As for the linen, fine white covers for the enormous featherbeds under which we sweated in Germany, discarded once we got used to English blankets; huge, square, hand-embroidered pillow cases, far too large to fit any British pillow; linen table cloths, too large to fit our British tables; enormous linen napkins, today all stacked away in cupboards, brown-spotted and unused. But the brushes—they are still as good as new, bristles strong, lacquer intact, still in use after more than sixty years. Hermann Katz and Co. went in for quality.

Not long ago I came across some of Father's nightshirts. He had insisted on taking those that had escaped Mother's *razzia*, when she imposed the pyjama regime. They were very long, very wide, with a large neck opening—perfect dress wear for fat middle-Easterners. The Nazis could have had those.

We went to Holland two, or perhaps three, years running. Every year we breathed a bigger sigh of relief as we crossed the frontier. It felt so good to travel in a country where being Jewish was not a crime. Father got fidgety as we approached Bentheim, the frontier station, but Mother stayed very calm, smiling sweetly at the customs men. "Just clothes, personal belongings and some samples. My husband is going to visit customers to get export orders." The letter *J* was not yet stamped on our passports and my parents had not yet become Hermann Israel and Emmy Sara. But the customs people, and the S.S. guards, who also patrolled the train, must have suspected that we were Jews from the name "Katz." Still, we never had any trouble.

"Look at the houses," said Mother, "how neat everything is. Like dolls' houses, each with its own little garden and those lovely big windows with potted plants in them. The rooms look so clean; you could eat off the floor."

It was the highest accolade Mother could bestow. No curtains were visible, so you could look into the little front rooms.

"All the houses look the same," I butt in.

"That doesn't matter," replies Mother. "The main thing is that these people are house-proud. However small the house, it is well kept and looks beautiful."

"Look, Vati, Hengelo." I was more interested in the names of the stations than in Dutch interiors. "What station comes next?"

"Ask Mutti," says Father. "She will know."

Father and I exchanged knowing smiles about Mother's well-known ignorance of geography and many things besides. Mother did not know, and she did not care whether it was Almelo or Amersfoort. She smiled indulgently.

"Play your little games," she seemed to be saying. "I am happy the way I am."

The Dutch were a very friendly people, very helpful when we asked the way or had any problems. Their country was very flat, all green meadows and red brick.

Our first stop was Rotterdam, where we disgorged our cases. I had the best breakfast ever in the hotel—lots of cheeses and cooked meats and fish and eggs. The Zeckels and their children were very kind to us. They worried about our staying in Germany and advised us to get out as soon as possible. They took us to Scheveningen to see Aunt Henriette. I don't remember her, but I remember my first glimpse of the sea from the safety of her window—that huge grey expanse of moving water, those towering waves, much more powerful even than the mighty Rhine. On that stormy day, I had no desire to explore it more closely.

Sometime in 1940, a letter arrived from the United States. "Look," said Mother, "it's from the Zeckels, postmarked New York. I wonder if they are on holiday or if Adolf has gone to a conference there?"

When we opened the letter, we found that the family had left Holland. Adolf was convinced that Hitler would invade. "I am a student again. I have to take medical exams so that I can practise here."

The Zeckels were wiser than poor Aunt Rosa and her family. They got out just in time.

After one of our trips to Rotterdam, freed of excess luggage, we went on to Belgium for a seaside holiday. Father thought it best for us not to return home via Bentheim, just in case some customs officer with a good memory noticed that we came back much lighter than we went out. In any case, he had long wanted to take us to La Panne, where he had spent some happy days as a young man.

"It's dull and flat like Holland," I complained. "I haven't seen a single castle."

"Wait till we go back," said Father. "There will be mountains and tunnels and castles galore." He was in his element. His French was still in good form, and he was overjoyed when a bearded professor we met on the train took him for a Frenchman.

"It's wonderful to talk in a civilized language again," he said.

"*Nous sommes tres heureux,*" Mother chipped in, to show that the *Höhere Töchterschule* had not laboured in vain. Still, it was felt that she stood in urgent need of French assistance for her shopping expeditions, lest she asked again for *une blouse pour la vache,* or something of that sort.

"Repeat after me," said Father. "*Donnez moi le fromage pour quatre francs.*" Mother enjoyed a healthy appetite and had to supplement the meagre hotel diet. She and I went to the cheese shop. When the word *frommasch* fell from Mother's lips, a wave of shame came over me and I slunk away into a corner. When we went shopping again, I stood nonchalantly in another part of the emporium, hoping to convey the impression that I was in no way connected with the large woman making those appalling sounds. Even though I could not speak much French, I had a good ear. Father had accustomed me to the sounds of French from an early age.

This time the sea was calm and not at all frightening with many people bathing or sitting on deckchairs. Father pointed to the Promised Land in the distance across the dunes.

"That is Duenkirchen. The French call it 'Dunquerque.'" He pronounced the word impeccably. "We'll go over to France and see the harbour there, once we have settled down."

We never made it to Dunkirk. I was not sorry. France looked just as dull as Belgium, with those ugly dunes and their wisps of vegetation. I liked lush scenery and mountains.

I splashed about in the sea with the other children. It was so easy to make friends where no one knew I was a Jew. I was decked out in a plain white singlet and some rather inelegant black pants. Mother noticed that some of the other boys wore smart striped jerseys, and we went shopping to fit me out with one.

Mother herself went into the water wearing a plain dark blue bathing costume with the inevitable loose white belt drawing attention to her not inconsiderable waistline. Father and water were not on good terms. He never even got his feet wet. He sat in a deckchair reading his French newspaper or passing the time of day with mature women, whom he soon had in fits of laughter.

He looked incongruous in his smart double-breasted suit, spotted tie, grey homburg, and spats. On one of those embarrassing shopping expeditions, Mother bought us all berets so that we should look like the locals. She also persuaded Father to discard his spats and don white tennis shoes, but that was as far as he would go. The three of us strolled along the promenade trying to look Gallic. For a time, the burden did not exactly lift, but it moved sideways.

At the hotel, we made friends with a couple somewhat older than my parents. They came from Courtrai or, as they preferred it, Kortryk, since they were Flemish. They told us that the Walloons staying in the hotel would not speak to them. (The two nations occupying this small country are still at loggerheads.) The Walloons' loss was our gain. Our two families became close friends, especially Mother and Madame de Bruyn. Mother again showed her willingness to learn from an older woman, always seeking the wise mother she never had and which she herself wanted to be.

Madame de Bruyn had a jersey blouse with vertical stripes. Mother bought an open-necked dress in almost the same material. The two women were about the same size. There is a photo of them in their bathing costumes, standing in shallow water with me between them—a hillock between two mountains. There is also a photo of the five of us—they had no children—on the sand in front of the Hotel Terminus, surrounded by a crowd of friendly Belgians.

Mother always called Madame de Bruyn "Madame." Madame was an exemplary housewife and a great knitter of speckled-wool slipovers for young boys. They arrived regularly in the post and were on the tight side. I took one of them with me to England. Madame gave Mother a brooch of golden leaves with a red stone in the centre. Mother wore it to the end of her life.

Although we were in a free country, my parents did not tell the de Bruyns that we were Jews. We had been told so often that we were an inferior race, that we had half come to believe it. We had become ashamed of being Jewish. When the pressure was really on, after the *Kristallnacht*, we stopped writing to them. They must have wondered what happened to us.

After the war, Mother traced them through the Belgian embassy in London. She wrote and told our story, and how we had withheld the vital information. "It would have made no difference," Madame replied. "We liked you as people. Your faith is immaterial." The families corresponded again for a while, and my parents met them on one of their trips to Europe.

On the way back home from La Panne, we stayed in Brussels. It was my first capital city—we had not stopped to look at The Hague.

"What is that big building on the hill?" I asked Father as we stood on the hotel balcony.

"That is the Palais de Justice. They still have justice in this country."

Later we wandered around the imposing government buildings and up to the Palais de Justice. I thought it the grandest building I had ever seen, with all those Greek columns—and was duly disappointed, when I made the pilgrimage up the hill on a more recent visit to Brussels.

Soon after we arrived at the hotel we saw a woman weeping and screaming, "*Mon Dieu, mon Dieu, mon enfant, mon enfant.*" She had misplaced her child. It was found soon after. Typical Gallic hysteria, Mother thought.

During our stay, I developed my twice-yearly rash of boils. A doctor was called. I was so uncomfortable that I was put to bed in the hotel room with a sedative, while my parents went shopping. Mother told me to lock the door from the inside. When they got back, they knocked and shouted in vain. I was so fast asleep that I heard nothing. Mother, the screaming woman still fresh in her mind, did her own version of *Mon Dieu*. She was convinced that I had been abducted. For some reason, there was no pass key, and Mother got the staff to put up ladders. When they climbed onto the wrought iron balcony, they saw me in bed, fast asleep. "*Mon Dieu, mon Dieu, mon enfant, mon enfant*" became a family saying.

Father's promise of excitement on the way home was fulfilled as the train passed the Ardennes. I could not contain myself. "Vati, another tunnel, and another." In the end, I counted at least twenty-eight. We passed through Charlemagne country and Father told me about his coronation, and about Pippin the Small who was Charles the Great's (Charlemagne's) father. In German, the word *gross* means both "great" and "tall." Pippin, though small, was wild and courageous as a lion in battle, but mild as a lamb towards the defeated foe.

We felt so gloomy as we passed customs and saw the uniformed men with their swastikas. It was like being back in a cage. Those days in La Panne were the last really carefree moments before I saw my parents in Cardiff on 30 August 1939. It was back now to the hated nightmare of my new school.

Chapter Thirty-Two

HUMILIATION

I asked a relative, a prominent scientist, to help me with his memories of the *Städtische Realschule*[50] of Bad Salzuflen, the local grammar school that, for our sins, we both attended. He recalled the natty hats, with different coloured rims to indicate the level of seniority. He recalled a long and tedious afternoon compulsorily watching Leni Riefenstahl's film, *The Triumph of the Will*. He recalled the occasional races in the playground. "And that's all," he wrote. The teachers were a total blank. *Oberlehrer* Felten rang no bells. Not a word about the persecution of Jewish boys.

I too remember the hats. Not your floppy English school cap. These hats had body and hard shields. I was proud to show off my pale lilac-blue model, even if the braid gave away that I was only in the lowly *Sexta*, the first form. Our numbers ran in reverse from *Sexta* to *Prima*.

I had forgotten about Leni Riefenstahl's Olympic marathon, but how could he have forgotten our form master, *Oberlehrer* Felten, strutting into the classroom arrayed in various shades of diarrhoea, with jackboots the colour of firmer specimens.

"*Heil Hitler!*"

"*Heil Hitler!*" The class, with several years of heil hitlering behind them, responded as one man. I kept my arm down and my mouth shut. *Oberlehrer* Felten shot me a dark glance. With a name like Katz . . . it

---

[50] The school was also known as the *Städtische Oberlschule*.

registered. During my twenty months at the school, I never heard a kind word from him.

The S.A. man surveyed his charges. "I am *Oberlehrer* Felten," he rasped. "When you address me, you will address me as *Herr Oberlehrer.* Is that understood?"

"*Ja, Herr Oberlehrer.*" The class again replied in unison. There were no laggards. This time I joined in.

The other teachers did not make as much fuss about their titles, but right from the start each wanted his due: *Herr Studienrat, Herr Studienassessor, Herr Studiendirektor, Herr Doktor.* In the beginning was the title. It took us a few days to get them all sorted out.

At my primary school, *Lehrer* (teacher) Sasse had been plain Herr Sasse. The *Realschule* had only one *Lehrer,* the gym teacher, but even this lowly creature insisted on being called *Herr Lehrer.* He was called Horn, or some such name, but we were not to call him Herr Horn.

The correct title had to be used on every occasion. No "may I leave the room, sir?" It was always "May I leave the room, *Herr Studienrat?*" And woe betide if you addressed him as *Herr Studienassessor* by mistake. A *Studienassessor* was a *Studienrat* in waiting. At the bottom of the ladder was the *Studienreferendar* waiting to become a *Studienassessor,* and very near the top was the *Oberstudienrat* waiting to become perhaps a *Studiendirektor* who, in turn, might move to an important school and become a *Herr Oberstudiendirektor.*

The more exalted ranks did not descend to the lowly *Sexta,* but we saw a lot of *Oberlehrer* Felten. I have a feeling that he was not a university graduate. He did not have the easy authority of the *Studien* types. They just assumed they would be obeyed. He gave the impression of an insecure man with a chip on his shoulder. He ranted on about authority and wore his party uniform on every possible occasion. But even an *Oberlehrer* in charge of the *Sexta* could lord it over the hated Jews.

He had a great time when it was his turn to teach us *Rassenkunde.* This could be translated as "race theory," but "raceology" is perhaps a better word, since the subject was taught with the same sense of certainty as the neighbouring geology lesson. Pleistocene and Pliocene, Aryan, and non-Aryan—these were scientific facts. *Oberlehrer* Felten dwelt lovingly on hooked Semitic noses, protruding Semitic lips, and crinkly Semitic hair, fixing me with mean, dark eyes as he drove home his points. No matter that I did not really conform to type.

Rassenkunde was a weird mixture of guesswork and fantasy, with a few facts thrown in. Thankfully, we were not taught the related disciplines of *Rassenseelenkunde, Rassenpsychologie,* and *Rassen Psycho-Anthropologie.* At the top of the race table were six white European races: *nordisch, faelisch, ostisch, westisch, ostbaltisch,* and *dinarisch.* All these were "kosher," if *Oberlehrer* Felten will forgive the word, but most kosher of all was the Nordic race—light haired, light eyed, light skinned, firm chinned, long limbed, with a long, narrow cranium, and, most important, a small, well-projected nose, its root very high.

Oberlehrer Felten was dark haired, sallow skinned, dark eyed, with a receding chin, and, if I remember well, a rounded cranium. I forget the nose. His chin and cheeks were black with frustrated stubble. He did not explain to which of the kosher races he belonged, but he felt he owed it to his beloved *Führer* to fit him into an Aryan slot. Since not even his best friends could have described Adolf Hitler as a Nordic Adonis, or indeed an Adonis of any sort, he was assigned to one of the races occupying the Southeastern corner of the Fatherland; I think it was the dinarian. I do not recall any discussion of the *reichspropagandaministerial* cranium.

At the bottom of the pile were the Jews and the Negroes, as they were then called, different in race but equally dangerous to the goal of racial purity, hence the words *Verjudung* (judaization) and *Vernegerung* (negroization). It was a blessing that Hitler never got his hands on black people.

Mixed in with the lore about craniums was rudimentary teaching about language groups, since the distinction between Aryan and non-Aryan was originally one of language. It was never explained to us how our Indian-language cousins acquired dark skins, or why blond Hungarians, Finns, and Estonians nevertheless spoke in barbarous non-Aryan tongues. Miscegenation, no doubt. We have to thank an Englishman, Houston Stewart Chamberlain, Wagner's son-in-law, for some of this wisdom. Hitler and his race theorist, Alfred Rosenberg, were much influenced by his speculations.

Sometimes I think *Oberlehrer* Felten could not have been all bad since he taught music at the school. But then, Wagner was a nasty piece of work, although a great composer. We tend to forget how compartmentalized human beings are. Like many of his Nazi Party friends, like some of the worst butchers, *Oberlehrer* Felten may have been a good family man, an animal lover, as well as a lover of music.

I remember another master, a young *Studienassessor*. He sometimes exchanged his black gown for the Party uniform, but was never unkind. He was handsome and did conform to the Nordic stereotype.

And then there was the master we had to call *Herr Doktor*. Dr. Behrens taught us English, the language of my friend Shakespeare. I quickly took to English, and to Dr. Behrens, until one day he came through the classroom door dressed in full S.S. officer's rig. I could hardly breathe. So, this cultured man, who spoke English (of sorts), who had always been studiously polite to me, was also my enemy.

Dr. Behrens was plump and unathletic looking. The uniform did not flatter him. He somehow reminded me of his chief, whom I had seen on the cinema news. Dr. Behrens was a different shape, but he had the same small eyes, the same bald face, and wore the same rimless glasses. How did I ever think of him as my friend?

Dr. Behrens had a son in our class, blond, plump, and far from friendly, but perhaps, under instructions from his father, not among my persecutors. He too had to call his father *Herr Doktor*.

One day, it must have been well into 1938 when I was in *Quinta*, Dr. Behrens asked the class a question. I jumped up with the answer.

"Sit down, Jewish pig," shouted a boy at the back of the class. Others took up the call. Dr. Behrens spoke, "Quiet please. Stop this unseemly behaviour. So long as Jews are still allowed in the school, we have to treat them as fellow pupils. I want no repetition of this scene."

Not long after came the *Kristallnacht*, the night of broken crystal, after which Jewish children were forbidden to attend school. It was said that Aryan children could not be expected to sit on the same benches with them. The S.S. man may have known what was to come. Give him credit though, I do not remember any other master curbing the boys' anti-Semitic fervour.[51]

---

[51] I have tried to verify the correctness of my memory of Dr. Behrens as an S.S. man, because he was so kind to me, but no one would give me any information.

Boys can be the cruellest form of God's creation, especially when they hunt in packs. My fellow students at the *Städtische Realschule* of Bad Salzuflen taught me that hell exists, and it is other boys.

At primary school in Schötmar, the children knew who I was—some had known me since our toddler days. They had played in our timber yard. Their parents knew my parents. I was never a particularly popular child—the way my mother dressed me precluded that—but I was tolerated. The teacher, Herr Sasse, though a convinced Nazi, was never unkind to me. As the Nazi period wore on, the children became more distant. There were a few active anti-Semites. The blond close-cropped Goeke twins, sons, I seem to recall, of the infant school caretaker, more than once invited me to go to Palestine. But the boys did not gang up on me. It was a mixed school, and the girls were a softening influence.

All that changed when I got to Bad Salzuflen, where I was unknown. I sat next to a boy named Kiso, scion of a land-owning family. We became friends for a little while, but he soon distanced himself when he saw how the other boys treated me, though he never joined in the baiting.

The boys began to waylay me on the way to school. It was a good half-hour walk. The first part was peaceful. I walked along the tree-lined avenue linking the two towns, satchel on my back, sometimes gathering conkers on the way. I passed the place where I first saw the swastikas back in 1932 and walked down to Bad Salzuflen. As I turned left along the road leading up the hill towards the school, I began to collect followers, like the pied piper of Hamelin. By the time I reached the Catholic church, I had collected a full gang—fellow pupils joined by other riff-raff. I have a vague recollection that the son of the church caretaker was one of the ringleaders. What is it about caretakers' sons?

They used all the weapons in their armoury. Every day I had to run a gauntlet of stones, kicks, trip-ups, and football tackles. They changed tactics so that I never knew from where the attack would come. Someone behind me opened up my satchel and threw out my books, while another tripped me up as I tried to retrieve them. And there was abuse, endless abuse.

"Doesn't it stink here?" The boy holds his nose.

"What can you expect?" says another. "There's a lousy Jewish pig here. I could smell him at a distance."

Most popular of all was the evergreen ditty:

"Jude Itzig,
Nasen spitzig,
Augen eckig,
Aschloch dreckig."

(Jew Isaac,
Nose pointed,
Eyes square,
Arsehole dirty.)

I heard that refrain practically every day of the school year. There were others like *"Judah verrecke"* (perish Judah), which the boys had learned from their elders. By the time I had reached the awesome neo-Gothic pile in the Hermannsstrasse, at the top of the hill, I was a wreck. Bowed and broken, trousers dirty where I fell, I trundled along the cold corridors towards the comparative safety of the classroom.

This is not what my mother's pampered upbringing had prepared me for. Mother, who had not wanted me to consort with rough boys, had no cure for the tortures these ruffians put me through, and the BDJJ had not hardened me enough. I suffered more because, by nature or nurture, I was a coward. My pursuers, like dogs, sniffed my fear, and that made them all the more keen to hunt their prey.

I recall a Jewish boy, Hans Obermeyer, younger and smaller than I. A group of ruffians set about him in the playground. He fought back vigorously with his little fists and got a bloody nose for his pains. I am sure he suffered less long-term injury than I did. He hit out rather than took in. I took it all to heart, every word, every blow.

My distant cousin, the one with the short memory, told another relative that he did not remember anything of our school because he had deliberately blotted out that period of his life. *Beato lui.* I must have blotted out something too, but it was not deliberate. It still festers as fear and insecurity. How do you handle almost two years of daily humiliation? What could not be faced has gone underground.

Try as I may, I cannot recall the names, or even the faces, of my tormentors. The only names and faces I remember are those of Kiso, who did not join in the persecution, and Behrens Junior, who was too high and mighty to bother. There was also a "half-breed of the first degree" in my class, a languid pretty boy with large light eyes and wavy blondish hair. He did not look Jewish and tried not to be Jewish, giving me a wide berth whenever he decently could. Who could blame him when he saw what they did to me?

My worst time came in *Lehrer* Horn's gymnastics classes. The boys could bait me more freely, and I gave them plenty of scope. I fitted the Jewish stereotype so snugly. I was flabby, cowardly, not fond of physical exercise, and my mind worked overtime. There was no plucky, pugnacious little Obermeyer to correct the impression. He was in the class below mine.

We always began with a hymn of praise to Altvater (ancestor) Jahn (1778-1852), the father of German gymnastics. This nobleman and reformer was an enthusiast for physical exercise at a time when it was not yet fashionable. I shuddered when the hymn began: *O, Altvater Jahn, we follow the path that you have shown us with your flaming spirit. We guard your heritage so that the holy faith called Germany will never die.*

> *"Du Altvater Jahn,*
> *Wir folgen der Bahn*
> *Die Du uns gewiesen*
> *Mit flammenden Geist.*
> *Wir hüten Dein Erbe*
> *Das niemals ersterbe*
> *Heiliger Glaube*
> *Der Deutschland heist."*

I hated Altvater Jahn and all his works.

Central to our exertions in his honour was a series of wooden horses with smelly leather rumps, wooden legs, spread-eagled. We were supposed to jump over these beasts, our hands on the rump for support but preferably no other part of our bodies touching it.

"Come on, boys! That's more like it! Make Turnvater [gymnastics father] Jahn proud of you! Jump like true Germans!" Herr *Lehrer* Horn, big, paunched, and slow moving—if ever a gymnast, now definitely an "ex"—urged us on.

Most of the boys took his advice. They sailed over the rumps in the way old Jahn would have approved. When my turn came, thirty odd mocking pairs of eyes were on me. I jumped, landed on the rear of the horse, wriggled forward, and angled myself down, not daring to look around me, cheeks glowing with shame. The boys roared with laughter. Some sneered, "Fat Jews can cheat, fat Jews can't jump, fat Jews should go to Palestine," and other such endearments. They gave physical expression to their thoughts when they could, buffeting me and tripping me up.

"Quiet boys," said *Lehrer* Horn, but the laughter and the sneers continued and ate into my heart. Surely, hell is other boys.

Lehrer Horn made me try again and again, but I never succeeded in getting over even the smallest horse. The Jew will fail, thought the boys, and the Jew did.

In England I found to my surprise that I was not totally unathletic. I did quite well in the long jump and took to cross-country running. My legs were better than my arms. I still walk a lot, swim, and play a little badminton.

I turned to my parents for help.

"You have to be brave, and continue. If you don't learn, you'll never be anybody. There are no Jewish schools near us and you don't want to be sent away, do you?"

"No, Mutti. I want to stay with you and Vati. If only those boys would leave me in peace. They are beasts."

"Concentrate on your lessons," Father told me, "especially on English. You'll need English. We will not stay here forever. Meanwhile, *denk an Goldschmidt's Junge.*" That was the family's polite version of "you can lick my behind." I cannot recall why thinking of Goldschmidt's boy came to be associated with this unhygienic conduct. All I know is that he went back some way—he was Mother's mother's mother's brother.

When my parents could not help, I turned elsewhere—to God and to a little girl. Every night I asked God to protect me from my tormentors. My demands were not exorbitant. I did not ask him to let the torment cease—that would have been asking for the impossible. I just asked, "Please, dear God, don't let it be so bad tomorrow." The Deity rarely obliged. Every day seemed worse than the one before. I woke up with a feeling of fear in my stomach, a sense that things would be bad—and they usually were. Perhaps I asked too little from God. Because I did not expect much and did not really believe in his power, I did not get much.

I really learned to pray later on, in England, when Mother was still in Germany and in great danger. It was so bad that God just had to help—and he did.

The little girl lived in a beautiful white villa with green shutters in the leafy avenue leading to Bad Salzuflen. I passed it every day on my way to school. Once or twice, I saw her come out of the house. She was like a princess, a chauffeur by her side carrying her school satchel. I looked at her and she at me, and they drove off.

She may have been a year younger than I, petite, with long dark hair and lovely deep dark eyes. Soon I took to hanging around the house, waiting for her to come out. We looked at each other, she drove off, and I went on my way to another day of torture. One morning she appeared without her chauffeur, and we started walking towards Bad Salzuflen together as if it were the most natural thing in the world, she going to her school and I to mine. I don't remember what we talked about, only that I was happy in her company.

When I got home, I told Mother. She said the girl belonged to the wealthy Hoffman's Starch family.

"There's some Jewish blood in that family. I don't know how much, but I am sure they are not pure Aryans."

That gave me courage. The next time we walked together, I poured out my troubles. She said those boys were beasts and that I was much too good for them. That pleased me no end. I looked forward to our walks. Fortunately, she had to turn off before my oppressors caught up with me. She never saw me humiliated.

I think I was equally fascinated by the girl and her background. She seemed to belong to another world, that world of gracious living to which Mother aspired but could never quite reach. She never asked me into the house. Then one day, she was gone. I hung around for a few days. Once I saw a woman go into the house and plucked up the courage to ask about the girl. "She has gone away," the woman said. I never saw her again.

Whenever I think of that girl, the colours that come to mind are white and bottle green. I see her in a white dress with a green blazer. Perhaps I superimposed some English schoolgirl on the vague image I have of her. Perhaps it was that white villa with its green shutters.

Once she had gone, I was again left to face my fate alone.

Chapter Thirty-Three

KING FOR A DAY

"Meinen Reichtum kennt ihr jetzt,
Doch das Beste kommt zuletzt.
Bin ich auch sehr reich an Barem,
Ist das Schönste doch mein Harem.
He da, Sklaven bringt mir rasch die
Wunderschöne Königin Vashti."

(All my riches now you know,
But the best I'll last you show.
Though my wealth is quite untold,
My harem quite outshines my gold.
Hey there, slaves, go fetch the queen
For Vashti's beauty must be seen.)

No one would have called my erstwhile classmate, Susi Eichmann, *wunderschön* (most beautiful), but she wore a permanent expression of melancholy, not unsuited to a luckless queen. Her cousin Ursula—smaller, older, and much prettier, with bewitching almond eyes—looked suitably alluring as Esther, the Jewish orphan who replaced the prudish Vashti in my affections. For I was Ahasuerus, King of the Medes and the Persians, rich in gold and still richer in odalisques. I reigned "from India even unto Ethiopia, over a hundred and twenty provinces." Quite a change from the cowed boy hounded at school.

We were in my palace of Shushan, or rather, in the synagogue of Detmold, capital of our small state, where the Schötmar/Bad Salzuflen Jewish thespians were performing a Purim play on bare floorboards, with green hangings for a backdrop. The year was 1938, the month, either February or March, the period when the festival of Purim is celebrated. It is a festival of liberation. The Book of Esther tells how the modest Vashti's very proper reluctance to exhibit herself in front of her husband's rowdy and gluttonous friends led to the orphaned Esther marrying out of the faith and delivering the Jewish people. God works in mysterious ways. The new queen, aided and abetted by her adopted father, Mordechai, undid the evil designs of Haman, son of Hammedatha, the Aggagite. Pharaoh merely enslaved the Jews; this man was intent on genocide.

I forget who acted the part of Haman in our play, but we all knew who was the Haman in our lives. He shared his predecessor's initial, and there was no prospect of an Esther or Mordechai delivering us from him. In the end, he got his comeuppance, like Haman before him. Haman got his on the gallows, fifty cubits high. Our *H* got his in an underground bunker, but not before he had caused untold harm. God was very slow this time.

The doggerel that I quoted above and then freely translated in the spirit of the original was my opening speech. A narrator had just given a lurid description of the feast during which the king made the demand that so offended the queen's modesty. Her message was short and to the point: "I send my greetings to the king, but even in the presence of my sweet one, no other man, be he of high or low estate, will see even so much as my nose ring."

> *"Sagen Sie, ich lass ihn grüssen,*
> *doch vor Angesicht des Süssen*
> *Siehet hoch nicht noch gering*
> *Osser*[52] *'mal den Nasenring."*

I will not pretend that the drooping Susi gave an electrifying performance. Not even decked out in royal purple could she manage to

---

[52]   *Osser* is a Yiddish negative. A free translation would be "not on your life."

look regal. Her long nun's face quivered on cue, but she was not gutsy enough to portray a woman who would defy an all-powerful monarch. Also, it was hard to believe that the beautiful queen would have sported such exceptionally long pigtails.

Her cousin Ursula, my new consort, was more convincing. I don't think shocking pink had been invented in those days, but Ursula's gown was the nearest shade to it then available. With so many women competing to fill Vashti's place, she had to attract the king's attention.

> "*Ahasver beschaut sie kritisch:*
> *Sie sieht aus etwas semitisch.*
> *Doch, a la bonne heure,*
> *Sonst gefällt mir Esther sehr.*"

> (Ahasver becomes a critic:
> She does look somewhat Semitic
> In good time I'll make my claim.
> I like Esther just the same.)

At least we could still laugh at ourselves.

Ursula's beauty *was* somewhat Semitic. It evidently appealed to the boys, who were always hanging round her. At ten, I was not mature enough to appreciate her thirteen-year-old charms. Still, she was petite, and I was tallish for my age, and I think our love scenes carried conviction.

The royal dress at the real Court of Shushan happened to be blue and white, so my navy blue *Traininghose* and white shirt were quite appropriate. The jogging pants that had so often seen its owner humiliated, now bore witness to his triumph. I might not be able to jump wooden horses, but I could hold an audience. Fitted out with tinsel crown, a golden sceptre that had started life as a broomstick, and other royal accoutrements, I exuded majesty. No matter if my navy blue sweater, made from Hitler's *ersatz* wool, had the texture of a saucepan cleaner and the feel of a hair shirt; no matter if the jogging pants hung loose on me—care, if not exercise had thinned me down—they had the bagginess proper for an oriental potentate. No matter if Susi's red coat, which I wore over my suit for the wedding, was too small and short for me. No matter if my protruding beard, abundant and well curled, was glued on in a way that made me look Assyrian rather than Persian. No matter. I had the audience eating out of my hand. At school I was the persecuted misfit. Here, among my friends and admirers, I *was* Ahasvuerus.

No talent spotter signed me on—Ahasvuerus was to remain my only theatrical role. I did not muff my lines like some of my fellow players. After all, I had been reciting birthday poems from the time I could talk. But, it must have been the conviction of my acting that won over the audience. My manner of speaking verse was lamentable. I paused at the end of each line, sometimes leaving the definite article dangling, severed from its life—giving noun or adjective—*bringt mir rasch die . . . wunderschöne Königin Vashti.* Not that the cause of dramatic poetry lost much.

The versifier and director was our Hebrew teacher, a fat youngish man named Alexander. He had followed the charismatic *Lehrer* Rülf, who bettered himself. Bad Salzuflen, where our lessons took place, was not an important centre of Jewish learning. Herr Alexander took some liberties with scripture. He failed to distinguish two different events. There was the king's first feast, where he put his power and his riches on display—a modern equivalent would be a six months' special exhibition of the crown jewels, the royal art collection and the royal share certificates, combined with military parades and march-pasts. This long period of ostentation was followed by a seven-day binge in the Court of the Garden of the king's palace. Also, according to the Book of Esther, the king sent, not slaves, but his seven chamberlains, to bring Vashti before him.

Few of the audience would have cared about such minor deviations. They knew the subtext. The play's theme of persecution and liberation was painfully relevant in 1938. Perhaps that was why we received such a great ovation. The fur-coated women clapped and clapped, unaware of the cries of pain they were wearing on their backs. Before too long, the skins of their own kind would be turned into lampshades and other articles of use.

After the applause had died down, Purim sweets were distributed— *Hamantaschen* (pastries with poppy seed filling), and for some reason, Easter eggs. Then the cast was invited to lunch by leading Detmold families. I ended up with a very grand couple, who were friendly with

Mussolini, of all people. One of their offspring, who lived in Italy, had made the connection. Over an excellent poultry lunch—off blue china that would have made Mother green with envy—the husband portrayed Mussolini as almost a philo-Semite. He would curb Hitler's excesses and remind him of the error of his ways. The couple showed confidence about the future and, I think, paid for it with their lives.

A year, or perhaps even a few months, earlier, I would have had to report to Mother on every detail of the grand house that I had visited: the layout of the rooms, the furniture, the colour and texture of the curtains, the carpets, the china, and so on. Now she only wanted to know what these knowledgeable and well-connected people had said about the present situation. When I came up with the story of Mussolini as the saviour of the Jewish people, Mother laughed a bitter laugh. "I only wish I could believe that."

Our play was perhaps the last happy memory I had of life in Germany. It must also have been one of the last happy celebrations in the Detmold synagogue. It was one of the seven hundred odd synagogues burned down later that year.

Chapter Thirty-Four

"I IMPLORE YOU"

"I implore you, grant us an affidavit."

The office staff had gone home. I was sitting at Fräulein Nagel's tall tiered typewriter, typing with two fingers as I still do today on my flat laptop, only I no longer write life and death letters.

Under Dr. Behrens' expert tutelage, my knowledge of English was proceeding apace. In my capacity as the family's English scribe, I needed certain words that the worthy *Herr Doktor* had not taught us. There was the English for *anflehen*, for example. Strong, hard, cruel, National Socialist youngsters had no need for such a word. I looked it up in Father's *Langenscheidt's*, the pocket dictionary he used for his English studies: *anflehen* . . ."implore."

I sent the same kind of letter to Mr. Emil Buschoff, a New York philanthropist, who had provided an affidavit for Uncle Moritz and Aunt Erna, to the Warburg banking family, our distant relatives, to Herr Bacharach, our erstwhile oil supplier, now resident in New York, and to others I do not recall. It went something like this:

"I am ten years old. I write to you because my parents and I need an affidavit so that we can emigrate. Only you can help us. We cannot stay here any longer. We are in desperation. I implore you, grant us an affidavit."

My begging letters always ended with the same refrain. It sounded pathetic, coming from a child, and was meant to.

Father tried to help me with English composition. In his orderly way, he was going through *Langenscheidt's* from *A* to *Z*. He had a little red notebook in which he jotted down useful words that he freely misapplied and horribly mispronounced. He suggested, "Necessitate an affidavit," a longer more important sounding word.

"But that's wrong, Papi. 'Necessitate' means *erfordern*. We want the English for *brauchen*, which is 'need.'"

"Yes, seeer," said Father, clicking his heels and giving a military salute. He pronounced it like the French "sire."

"It's not 'seeer,' Papi, its 'sir,' as in 'her' and 'thirst.'" The tongue twister "thirst" was beyond him, but he could say "her" and therefore "sir." However, "seeer" it remained to the end of his life. In the heyday of the department store magnates, it was always "Seeer Fraaazer" for Sir Hugh Frazer and "Seeer Clore" for Sir Charles Clore.

Fortunately, Father did not experiment with English in letters that accompanied mine. He realized German was a safer option.

"Learn as much English as you can at school," he told me. "You will need it soon. We have to get out. It's only a question of time."

"I will do my duty, wherever it may be" (*Ich stelle meinen Mann, wo es auch sein möge*), he said to Mother during the Friday evening meal.

"I know that, Hermann. But to start again from scratch after the twenty years' hard work building up the factory."

"I have done it before and I will do it again," said Father. He was referring to his expulsion from Metz when the French took over after World War I. He had built up a flourishing business there.

They were a very different pair from the "if we have only a single brick left" stalwarts. Even Mother had switched sides. She was now firmly behind Red Erna in her conviction that there was no future for us in Germany. Too many things were happening to keep up the old pretences. The Nazis were putting on the screws, especially in the economic field, where they hurt.

When he came home on Friday evenings, Father had to report failures as well as successes. The boycotts were biting.

"We can't buy any more from you, Herr Katz. We would like to, but we can't. You understand." Dresbach, our traveling salesman, reported similar comments.

Uncle Walter and other Jewish cattle dealers were also experiencing difficulties. Their greatest scourge was a former pig dealer named Reibke, a wealthy man who also owned a hostelry. He wanted to take over the cattle business from the Jews and went around telling farmers, "We have heard that you still deal with Jews. Where is your German honour? If you continue, we can make life very difficult for you."

Some farmers remained loyal. They began delivering cattle to Uncle Walter early in the morning or late at night. Cattle were also exchanged at a tavern halfway between Schötmar and Extern, where many of the farmers lived. In this way, no one would see them delivered. Snoopers would be put off the scent. But it was an uphill struggle. Uncle Walter knew it could not last and sent young Walter to the ORT school in Berlin, where he would learn various skills so that he could look after himself in America.

One of Walter's companions there was Willibald Damer, Hilde's son, later to make his fortune in what was then Southern Rhodesia. Hilde's father, Herr Eichmann, had been thrown out of his firm, Damer, Quest and Co., by one of the partners, Quest, a rabid Nazi. His case was not unique.

In our factory, Robert Ley's DAF, or *Deutsche Arbeitsfront*, the official Nazi trade union, was making trouble. It had installed as factory *Obmann*, or chairman, a man called Hamann. I am almost certain this name is not a trick of memory. Later on, this man was to prove worthy of his namesake. Meanwhile, he crossed Mother wherever he could.

"I can no longer run my own factory in the way I want," I heard Mother complain more than once. "When I say something, the *Obmann* tells the workers to do the opposite. And I have to keep my mouth shut."

Most of the factory people were loyal. My parents were good employers. But when someone sets out to make trouble, he can usually find grievances to exploit. Hamann was expert at this.

Our remaining Aryan friends were making themselves scarce. Frau Birkholz, who used to spend months in our house, now found the journey from Potsdam too long. I remember only two Aryan families in Schötmar who kept up contact with us.

The Wortmanns and the Schmidtpotts shared the same large half-timbered house—not always without friction—and the same *Plumpskloo*. The Wortmanns lived on the left side of the *Diele* (hall), the Schmidtpotts on the right. The Wortmanns were very devout Protestants; the Schmidtpotts were left wing. Only those with firm principles—religious, moral, political—could hope to withstand the pressures around them.

Fritz Schmidtpott, the former office boy, was now our confidant. He was a lanky youth with a spotted face, a very long nose and a tendency to stoop. He proved a sterling friend. I kept on hearing "Fritz will do it." Whenever there were jobs that only Aryans could do, be it purchasing or dealing with the authorities, Fritz did it. Herr Adam, the office manager, also remained loyal, but my parents did not dare speak openly to him the way they did to Fritz. After all, Herr Adam remained a member of the Party.

"These s#&*s should be hanged," said Fritz. The Wortmanns would not have talked this way, but they made it clear that they were with us and that what the Nazis were doing was wrong. Frau Wortmann, who had a severe hairstyle but a kindly face, still came over to see us. Her daughters, Magdalene and Erna, did not shun me like the other children. Herr Wortmann, I was to learn later, listened regularly to the BBC during the war, a very dangerous thing to do.

Frau Wortmann did us a great service. She got her sister, *Schwester* Anna Witte, a school friend of Mother's and a *Diakonisse* (a member of the order of deaconesses), to persuade her colleagues to take Grandmother into the *Diakonissenhaus*, their home for old people in Detmold. It was a place of safety for Grandmother, who was quite senile now. We would not be able to take her with us if we left; no country would take her in. Mother would not have left her alone, so my parents might well have finished like the Gruenewalds, Uncle Walter's tenants. They sacrificed their chance to emigrate because South Africa would not accept their crippled son. They were deported and murdered like the other Jews who stayed behind.

After the war, Mother sent *Schwester* Anna a Christmas parcel every year until we heard from the Wortmanns that she had died.

If only there had been more people like the Wortmanns and the Schmidtpotts. Most *Schötmaraner* did not wish us ill: they kept their distance and their noses clean. They did not want to sacrifice the chance of profit and advancement. That was all they might have lost. We had not yet come to the stage where helping or harbouring Jews had become a capital offence.

There was a minority, which grew in size as time went on, that wished us very ill. Many were riff-raff; some were prominent citizens. Decked out in their nauseous uniforms, they marched up and down the

Schülerstrasse (now Schlageterstrasse) singing their sweet songs about Jewish blood spurting from the knife, some the worse for drink after a bout in the Wevelsburg. Sometimes they marched at night, carrying burning torches. You could see the lights going out in Jewish houses as their songs preceded their arrival. We put the lights out too and moved to the back rooms. I stood behind the curtains to watch, and be terrified. Was I secretly wishing that I could be one of them?

The S.A. potbellies did the marching; the S.S., more intelligent and of better physique, did the planning. And the Gestapo took to raiding Jewish houses. We were spared at that time, but Jews became very frightened. The elderly Gruenewalds had got hold of some dollars for a rainy day. They were terrified that the dollars would be found. Uncle Walter told them to bury the precious currency in the garden. They would not listen and burned the dollars in the stove.

And at home, until the *Schwesters* took her in, Grandmother was screaming the house down. Not a happy time.

Chapter Thirty-Five

FAREWELLS

Every day we waited for those letters from America. There was great excitement when the first reply arrived. Mr. Emil Buschoff said that he would do his best for us and would set the legalities for an affidavit in motion. The Warburgs replied that they were fully committed, but they would try to help us when we came to America. Father's old friend, Bacharach, also said that he would do his best. In the end, we received affidavits from both Emil Buschoff and Bacharach.

Even if you were lucky enough to have an affidavit, or two, as in our case, it did not mean you could take the next boat to New York. You only got your quota number, which meant that your name was on a waiting list. Your number was all-important. Only when it was called could you get your entry visa to the States.

Our city relatives, blessed with more foresight and more contacts than we possessed, had their affidavits sewn up relatively early, and therefore had earlier quota numbers.

We drove to Giessen to pay a farewell visit to Father's brother, Uncle Moritz, and his wife, Aunt Erna, who were off to New York.

Mother was still in her house-proud mode.

"How sad for you to leave behind this elegant apartment," she told Aunt Erna. "You have made it so beautiful."

"We are happy to leave while we still can," replied Uncle Moritz, looking spruce as ever. "I advise you to do the same."

Aunt Erna took a photo of me on that visit. I am wearing unfashionably long pants. Was Mother losing her grip? On one side of me is a heap of manure, symbolic perhaps of the country our relatives were leaving and in which we were still confined; on the other side, a cherry tree, as yet without leaves, perhaps representing hope.

That photo may have been taken in Laubach, Father's birthplace, where, as in the rest of rural Hesse, you were never far away from heaps of manure. We all went there from nearby Giessen for a family reunion. Grandfather Joseph was dead by that time, so there was only Father's sister, Aunt Helene, and her husband, Uncle Josef. It was the last time we would see them.

Another photo, taken on a Sabbath afternoon walk, shows Aunt Helene standing between her two brothers. She looks the typical blonde Hesse country woman. She is in her best cape collar dress, dark blue, enlivened by white flowers. In view of what happened to her and Uncle Josef, the photo is unbelievably moving. The large round sad eyes of that saintly woman still haunt me.

Next, we travelled to Cologne to discuss possible emigration with our well-informed relatives there.

Before taking a taxi to Marienburg, we went to the station restaurant to have lunch, so as not to arrive hungry at Aunt Grete's. My apple pancake had just arrived, nicely browned, with juicy-looking apple rings. I had coated it with plenty of sugar from a silver shaker and was taking my first bites when three men sat down at the table next to us. One was in his fifties perhaps, the other two in their late twenties or early thirties. They were not completely drunk, just slightly tipsy. The older man—florid, with a round head—leaned over to us.

"It's a great thing," he spluttered," to see a German family together, united as one. Look," he told his younger companions, "here we have a real German mother, with her strapping German son and the German father who provides for them. *Heil Hitler!*"

The pancake lost its flavour. We made affirmative noises as the food stuck in our throats. The man went on in this vein for some time and then showed us his card. Our hearts sank. He was what we called *ein hohes Tier*, a high-up (literally, an elevated beast) in the Nazi Party. The men were not in uniform, but the card was real enough. We gobbled down some food and prepared to make our exits, saying we had a train to catch.

"Stay," said the man, "we'll show you Cologne." They could tell by our accents that we were not locals.

It could be that they were baiting us, but I doubt it. We did not look stereotypically Jewish. Mother, though dark haired, could certainly have passed for an Aryan woman. We had made sure before we went into the restaurant that it did not have a "Jews not welcome" sign.

"It was a real privilege to meet you," said Father. "I am only sorry that we have to catch our train."

We escaped to shouts of "*Heil Hitler*," much of my pancake left uneaten. They were wishing us a good journey; we were wishing never to see them again. My knees were wobbly.

That Nazi was not so wrong. We were the ideal German family. My parents embodied all the German virtues: *Fleiss* (application, hard work), *Ordnung* (orderliness), and in Mother's case, all the *Hausfrau* virtues.

We noticed that anti-Semitism was more open and more advertised in Cologne than in our small town. Everywhere we saw signs or scrawls: *Jüdisches Geschaeft* (Jewish business), *Hier wohnen Juden* (Jews live here), *Juden unerwünscht* (Jews not welcome), or, more severely, *Juden Zutritt verboten* (Jews forbidden to enter). Cousin Gisela recalls seeing Jewish men herded into dustcarts quite early on in the Nazi era.

Uncle Paul's plans were well advanced by that time. He was adept at discovering information. Sometime back, he had located some distant relatives of his in the United States and persuaded them to send his family an affidavit. He then bribed an American consular official in Stuttgart to advance his quota number so that they could leave sooner. In a big city, one could make good contacts. Aunt Grete was always talking about their Mr. Lowe, a British official at Cologne airport, and their Mr. Stephenson who taught them English at the Berlitz School in Cologne. But they were still in Germany in November 1938.

Gisela had enrolled in a boarding school in England in 1934, which a friend of Uncle Paul's from a Jewish World War I veterans' organization had located. It was called Hamilton House in Tunbridge Wells. Ingelore followed Gisela to the school one year later. Gisela was so happy at Hamilton House that we tried to find it again on one of her visits to England after the war. The buildings still stood, but it was no longer a school.

When Aunt Grete came to Schötmar to make her good-byes before they emigrated to Chicago, she was not well received. Grete was her usual effusive self. She hugged and kissed her half-demented mother, knowing that she would never see her again. Grandmother half understood, but refused to let the message sink in. Mother, always jealous of her sister, claimed to understand only too well. She told us that Grete and Paul had made their own arrangements for leaving Germany without consulting us; that they had sprung them on us only at the last minute; that they had sent their girls to England without telling us; and that they had never suggested finding a place for her boy in England, even though they had "all those connections in England." And then she would say, "This after all she had done for them."

When, years later, I spoke to my cousins about this, they painted a very different picture.

Gisela explained that her mother told Mother many times that it was time for them and everyone else in the family to leave Germany, but Mother always replied that they could not leave because of Grandmother.

Cousin Walter added that if Grete had told my parents that they were making their plans to leave and that my parents should also emigrate, they would never have listened. He remembered that they were still at that time going on about staying put until they had not one brick left.

Grete and Paul redeemed themselves later in Mother's eyes. They got the two Walters an affidavit when their original sponsors withdrew their support. They offered us an affidavit too, though we no longer needed it. Their Mr. Stephenson was also of help to us in our early days in England. Above all, they put pressure on Paul's sister to send us the life-saving guarantee of support, which got my parents an English visa, when our American quota number had not yet come up. Not a bad record.

By the time our relatives left, my parents were very willing to listen. In the old days, it had been, "Schacht won't let them do anything foolish. Schacht knows he needs the Jews. So long as Schacht is at the helm, we are safe."

But Schacht had departed the economics ministry in late 1937. He had been a moderating influence because he feared too much anti-Jewish activity would damage the economy.

Now Göring was in charge, and his task was to squeeze the Jews out of German economic life. We now found difficulty in getting raw materials; allocations to Jewish firms were cut down. Göring also made sure that Jewish firms received no further government contracts. Then there was the bother about registering all Jewish property valued above fifty thousand marks. I knew about that because my parents were in constant conference with Herr Adam, their business advisor, about what they should declare. Under the new law, they could not sell property without permission.

In October 1938, my parents, like other Jews, had to submit their passports to have the letter *J* stamped on them.

The Nazis had a thing about names. They said that Jews changed their names to hide their identity. Certain changes of name were no longer recognized. Jewish children were only allowed to use Jewish names. Had I been born after 16 August 1938, my parents would have had to choose from a list ranging from Abel, Abieser, and Abimelech to Zephanaia, Zeruja, and Zervi. The choice for girls was similarly limited—the list began with Abigail, Bascheva, and Beile and ended with Zipora, Zirel, and Zorthel.

These absurdities were signs that the pace was heating up. They were mere pinpricks compared with what was to come. My begging letters to America had been written none too soon.

Chapter Thirty-Six

KRISTALLNACHT

The crash woke me up. Mother, an early riser, was already in the bathroom, finishing her toilet.

"Mutti, Mutti, what's happened?" I shouted as I ran to her.

"*Jotte, Jott.*" Mother reverted to dialect, as she called on the Deity. Her face was white. I was terrified.

"Stay where you are," Father commanded as he emerged from the bedroom in his new-fangled pyjamas.

"It's safer at the back of the house. If they come in, I'll go down and talk to them."

There was the sound of more crashing glass. There were shouts of "Jews out," "Perish Judah," and something about the sins of international Jewry. The shouting was somewhat muffled. They did not roar the way they did when they marched through the streets. That made it more frightening, like gathering thunder. Now they were at the front door. It sounded from upstairs as if they were smashing it down. I was sure they would come and get us, beat us up, or worse. Then quite quickly, the commotion died down. They had similar visits to make.

I crept to an upstairs front window. It was very dark, but I could make out some figures in S.A. hats and others who were not in uniform. They were giving the same treatment to the Hamlets' house, opposite us, and to the Wallhausens, and to Aunt Alma's house. There was something lacklustre about their performance, as if not all of them were enjoying what they were doing. There wasn't that Party Rally enthusiasm.

Gingerly, we crept down to inspect the damage. It had sounded worse than it was. They had merely broken the glass in the front door and all the lower windows. In the days that followed, the glaziers had a field day.

It was November 10, 1938, the tail end of the infamous *Kristallnacht*, the night of the crystal, so called after the Jewish plate glass[53] smashed that night throughout the land. It was the night the cat stopped playing with the mice and started to pounce.

"Trust a Pole to make a bad situation worse," Father commented when he heard the news that a young and desperate Polish Jew had murdered a German diplomat in Paris. "As if things were not bad enough already. And then Herr Gruenspan[54] comes along and puts the boot in."

I laughed out loud. "What a funny name, Vati. Whoever heard of someone called Gruenspan?"

"Yes, it is funny," said Father. "The Nazis will laugh. They consider us the *Gruenspan* [verdigris] of the nation." He turned to Mother. "They will laugh for another reason. Mark my words, Emmy. We have not heard the last of this. That stupid ass has given them the excuse they wanted."

Father was right. If it had not been Gruenspan, it would have been something else. Prisoners from Dachau had been brought in as early as September to start building five extra barracks in Buchenwald. The rulers of Germany were just waiting for an excuse to bring the Jews to their knees. Now it had been handed to them. Göbbels was put in charge of hate propaganda. Heydrich, the Gestapo chief, looked after the action. The *Völkischer Beobachter* newspaper wrote ominously:

"The shots fired in Paris will not go unpunished. Of that, Jewry can be certain."[55] The broken glass was just the prelude.

As day dawned, Walter came running in.

---

[53]   Another version has it named after chandeliers smashed in shops.

[54]   The proper Polish spelling was "Grynszpan."

[55]   Lionel Kochan, *Pogrom: November 10, 1938.* London: Andre Deutsch, 1957, p. 42.

"The synagogue is burning," he panted. "I tried to save our ping-pong table and the equipment, but those swine would not let me in." We used to play ping-pong in the synagogue hall. "It doesn't look as if it will burn down completely, but a good part has been gutted. Those swine!"

At home, it was cold, even with the central heating on. Between nine and ten, there was a knock on what remained of the front door. The local police were there, in their funny, high helmets. They were decent men, by and large. They had known us all their lives, and some, at least, were not happy about the events of the day. They could have taken Father right away, but they gave him an hour in which to report to the Town Hall with a small overnight case.

There were some vile Nazis in Schötmar, but if you had the misfortune of being a Jew in small-town Germany, Schötmar was not one of the worst places. We heard later that in nearby Lage, they had burned down a house next to the synagogue inhabited by a mixed marriage family. In Schötmar, no Jewish houses were destroyed.

I do not remember the police searching our house. They may have done so. They certainly searched Uncle Walter's, after they had taken him away. They found a regimental cap and ceremonial belt that had belonged to Erwin, one of the two brothers of Uncle Walter and Mother, who died in World War I. Aunt Minna gave the intruders a piece of her mind:

"These objects are keepsakes in honour of a man who gave his life for Germany" (*Der Dank des Vaterlands ist Euch gewiss*), she said bitterly, quoting, as Grandmother had so often done, the standard mode of thanking the Fatherland employed to comfort the bereaved. Is this the thanks of the Fatherland?

The police said nothing and took away the mementoes. They had a job to do.

Mother concentrated all her energies on the suitcase. She ran around the house, rummaging in drawers, trying to contain her fears by fussing over Father's pyjamas and socks. Father had the luxury of being driven to the Town Hall by his faithful chauffeur, Karl. His next journey was to be less comfortable.

As the Jewish women began to venture out, rumour followed rumour. The men would stay in Lippe; they would be sent further a field. They were all going to concentration camps. In the afternoon, an elderly policeman, a very decent man—I think his name was Steinkampf—came by on his motorcycle. He told us that Father and Uncle Walter had asked for some extra things. Steinkampf allowed Cousin Walter to deliver them. In her confusion, Mother had forgotten to pack some eau de cologne. She now made good the omission and sent two bottles of her favourite 4711 brand. They proved to be lifesavers, and not for the obvious reason.

Over the next few days, the news filtered through. The men had been taken to concentration camps. Synagogues had been burnt throughout Germany. Acres of plate glass had been smashed. Karl, our chauffeur, who lived in Vlotho, in the Weser valley, reported that in nearby Minden, the Pfingst's department store was a shambles. In Hamburg, S.S. men had urinated on Torah scrolls as they lay smouldering in the streets. Their silver shields, jewelled crowns, and bells had been stripped off.

According to Professor Meier Schwarz of Jerusalem,[56] the number of synagogues burned or destroyed was not 191, as reported by Heydrich and Göbbels, a number still mentioned in history books. It was 1,118, not counting 288 prayer rooms. Professor Schwarz also says that some historians speak of thirty-six Jews killed, whereas more than three hundred were murdered that night. And then there were the suicides. As for the number of businesses affected, I have seen the figure of 7,500 quoted.

Ministerpräsident Göring was not pleased. We know that from the evidence produced at the Nuremberg trials.

"It's senseless to ransack a Jewish warehouse, burn the goods and then a German insurance company has to bear the loss . . . . It's as though I were to set fire to our imported raw materials."[57] (The plate glass was made in Belgium.)

Göring did not want broken glass; he wanted money. Nothing must interfere with the process of spoliation. He proposed a punishment fine of one thousand million marks on the Jews.

"That will do the trick. The pigs won't commit a second murder so quickly. Incidentally, I wouldn't like to be a Jew in Germany."[58]

---

[56]   *Kristallnacht Memorial.* Circular letter, dated June 1989.
[57]   Kochan, op. cit. pp.110-11.
[58]   Ibid, p.116.

Heydrich found a neat solution to the problem of insurance claims. Yes, German insurance companies must not default. They will pay out the money to the Jews and then the State will confiscate it. "Then appearances are formally kept up."[59]

"We were wrong," said Father in later years, "the way we blamed the Polish Jews. They were Jews like us, often better Jews because they knew the Torah and kept the Law. We were so narrow-minded. Hitler would have taken action against us, Gruenspan or no Gruenspan. The boy was distraught about the way his parents had been treated. And he got the wrong man. Vom Rath [the murdered diplomat] was not even a real Nazi!"

Göring imposed his one thousand million fine. It was to be paid for by a levy of twenty-one percent of Jewish wealth. How was Mother to pay our fine, when most of our fortune was tied up in fixed assets, stock, and raw materials?

"If only Vati were here. He would find a way." Mother always discussed important problems with him on the weekends. But where was Father now? Mother was sick with worry over him.

I remember her slumped in a purple armchair in the *Privatkontor*, the private factory office. She had just had a long session about the wealth levy with Herr Adam and Meister Drexhage, who were her only business confidants at that time. She looked pale and exhausted. It was very unusual for Mother to give way to exhaustion, but these days she did. Either she was hyperactive, jumping up to find something or other, even during meals, or she was very tired. Worrying about Father during the night did not help.

She was fighting on so many fronts. She had to fight for raw materials. Even loyal old suppliers like Delbanco, Meyer and Co. had to restrict allocations to Jewish firms.

She had to fight the Nazi union boss, Hamann, who opposed her every move. Drexhage advised caution. "Don't upset him," he told Mother. "He can cause trouble." How right he was.

She had to fight to keep the house clean. On the home front, our Jewish helper, Alice, who, despite her extramural activities, was a good worker, had left us to seek her fortune elsewhere.

---

[59] Ibid.

And Mother worried about me. I was at home because I had been forbidden to attend school. An edict had gone out soon after the *Kristallnacht*, expelling Jews from Aryan schools. Aryan children could not be expected to sit on the same benches with them. I still have the Headmaster's letter, dated 28 November 1938, in which Herr Dietze, now a *Herr Oberstudiendirektor*, reported to the *Herr Reichsstatthalter* (lieutenant governor) of Lippe and Schaumburg-Lippe, that on November 15, he had dutifully expelled the three Jewish boys at the school. My name came first, either because of the alphabetical order or because I was in the *Quinta* (Class 2) whereas the other two were in the *Sexta* (Class 1).

"What will become of you?" Mother sighed, putting her arms around me. "Without education, you cannot get anywhere. We'll have to send you to England, like Gisela and Ingelore."

"I don't want to go to England, not without you, Mutti. And I can't leave you. Now Vati is away. You need me," I protested.

"You are right. I need you now. We'll discuss it with Vati when he comes back." She looked towards the window as if searching for him.

Of all her problems, that was the worst. What could she do to get Father back? Endlessly, the Jewish women of Schötmar discussed the fate of their men. The rumour went around that a valid exit permit from Germany would ensure an exit permit from the concentration camp. Mother and Aunt Minna decided to send young Walter to Cologne. Uncle Paul might help through his friend, the U.S. consular official in Stuttgart. On his way to there, Walter saw the coffin of Gruenspan's victim, Ernst vom Rath, at one of the stations—he thinks it was Essen. It was being guarded by S.S. men.

When Walter got to Cologne, there was no Uncle Paul. He had escaped the *razzia*. He had gone into hiding from the Nazis. The local police had given him advance warning.

Walter sent him a message, and Uncle Paul sent a message back, promising to see what he could do through his friend in Stuttgart. The consul's list of patrons was later discovered, and Uncle Paul was in deep trouble. For several months after the *Kristallnacht*, he and Grete would meet secretly each night at midnight until Uncle Paul and Aunt

Grete managed to get out of Germany to Chicago. Gisela and Ingelore remained in school in England.

Meanwhile, we heard that Father was definitely in Buchenwald concentration camp. Mother tried every way she could think of to get Father released. One of them almost proved fatal.

Chapter Thirty-Seven

CONFINED IN BETHEL

"Frau Katz, a very serious charge has been brought against you. Party Member Hamann has declared that he heard you say in your factory that *Herr Ministerpräsident* Göring should be shot and the whole government with him. We want to know from you if you made that statement."

"Of course I made no such statement," Mother told them. "It is absurd of Herr Hamann to make such a charge."

"We will be conducting further investigations, Frau Katz," said one of the men. "Remember that it is the word of a respected Party Member against your word. It is a matter of the utmost seriousness. You will be hearing from us, Frau Katz."

Mother was telling Aunt Minna what had happened.

"Outwardly I was very calm, but inside I felt as if I had been shot." The two men had left not long ago. They wore *Lodenmäntel*, those green tentlike overcoats that still make me shudder when I see German tourists in them on the streets of London.

We were in the downstairs sitting room. Mother was sitting in the red armchair that had been Grandfather's.

She was no longer calm, even outwardly. She stroked her forehead from left to right, and upwards, into her hair. Her freckled arms were full of goose pimples. The colour had gone out of her face. There was fear in her eyes. I knew what fear looked like.

Her enemy had struck, and he had chosen his time carefully. Mother was alone. Father and Uncle Walter were guests of *Herr Ministerpräsident*

Göring at one of his Saxon estates. This was the *Obmann's* chance to vanquish his employer once and for all.

Mother always denied that she had voiced those admirable sentiments about Göring and his colleagues. It stood to reason. You did not say those things, even in the privacy of your own home, without first making sure no one was listening. You certainly did not say them within earshot of a Nazi trade union boss who was your particular enemy. Wasn't it Mother who kept telling everyone that "walls have ears" (*Wände haben Ohren*)?

And yet, and yet . . . as I am writing this chapter, a small doubt creeps in. Why Göring? If Hamann had fabricated this story, would he not have gone all the way and named the *Führer* himself as the object of Mother's vain hopes? But it was Göring who had imposed the one thousand million marks fine on Jewish businesses. It was Göring, the man in charge of the economy, who was making life impossible for Jewish businesses. And it was Göring, the jovial fatty, who had instituted the first concentration camps. Could it be that an exasperated Mother, desperately worried about Father's imprisonment in one of those camps, and struggling to pay Göring's levy and keep the factory running, could it be that Mother had for a moment forgotten herself? Perhaps she had inadvertently whispered some remarks about Göring's greed that the *Obmann* overheard and had exaggerated into a demand for his execution. Or was the *Obmann* being Machiavellian in choosing Göring, the levy raiser, rather than the Olympian *Führer*, to make his story more plausible? I shall never know the answer.

Mother began to cry. "What have we done to deserve this?" she sobbed. "We always prided ourselves on treating our workers so well, and now they do this to us."

Aunt Minna bent over her, patting her gently and murmuring something in her slow country accent. "It will be all right," said young Walter. "I will help to look after things. I look after the business for Father now."

Only I said nothing. I was paralysed. Mother breaking down was a natural disaster. The solid earth was giving way under my feet. I wanted to run away but couldn't. The last time this kind of breakdown had happened was at Grandfather's funeral. This was worse, much worse. There was danger, and there was no Father to protect us.

A counsel of family and friends was held. It was decided to call in Dr. Richzenheim, he of the jaundice tea. "We must get her into Bethel at once," the good doctor advised, "before the Gestapo can hold her for preliminary investigations."

Bethel, which in Hebrew means "House of God," was, and remains, a small town of hospitals and psychiatric clinics, situated in the hills above Bielefeld. It was founded by the Lutheran Pastor Friedrich von Bodelschwingh at the end of the nineteenth century and was run by the Protestant community. The Gestapo would be less likely to follow her there. We would gain time.

Dr. Richzenheim stroked his goatee as he explained the urgency of Mother's case on the telephone. He had to make several calls before the Bethel authorities would agree to take her in. He signed a document certifying that Mother had suffered a *Nervenzusammenbruch*, a nervous breakdown.

Karl made ready to drive Mother to her new home. Aunt Minna accompanied her. She was the only close relative still around. I stood by the car.

"How can I leave you, how can I leave you?" said Mother, tears streaming down her face. Again, I was paralysed. It was the first time Mother had left home without me. Mother, who ran the factory single-handed, who had planted the orchard and designed the Blue Salon, who bought my clothes and heard my confessions. This was much worse than Father being taken away. He was always away, travelling for the factory. But Mother! I blanked out. I went into the kitchen, sat down on a low wooden chair, spread out my legs, and looked at my feet, perhaps to convince myself that I still existed.

I was now alone in the big house. Else and Erna had long gone, and their songs had gone with them. Stern Luise Strate and free and easy Alice had also gone their ways. *Die Kölner* (the Cologne lot) had emigrated; Gisela and Ingelore were in England, and their parents had recently arrived in Chicago. Frau Birkholz kept her distance in Potsdam. Grandfather, who had made the walls reverberate, lay silent under black granite. Grandmother was in Detmold in the care of the deaconesses. Father was in the concentration camp and Mother in the asylum.

The place was creepy, especially at night. In the day, I could blank out or forget the present, reading about the past. At night, I had bad dreams and woke up fearful, listening for noises.

I should have said that I was as good as alone. There was Hannah, a waiflike creature, no longer young, who had seen better days. She did not make a strong impression. I even forget what she looked like, except that she had black hair and vague dark eyes. Hannah could not cook. We ate mostly cold food, bread and cheese, sausage and eggs. I was glad when Aunt Minna sent Helmut, as she often did, to bring food or call me over. Hannah did little cleaning. She knitted, sewed my trousers, and darned my socks, and occasionally she talked. She talked of the days, sometime in the distant past, when she had been handmaid to a certain princess, the incarnation of all the virtues of aristocratic womanhood.

The princess had a majestic name. Once I got my tongue around it, I began to use it like a mantra, repeating it over and over:

"Prinzessin Friederike Juliane Zu Salmhorstmar . . .
Prinzessin Friederike Juliane Zu Salmhorstmar . . ."

Paradoxically, Hannah was also the first to explain to me the true aims of Zionism, the creed my parents and the League of German Jewish Youth had taught me to despise. Hannah foresaw that the Jews would one day return to their ancient homeland, though I doubt she ever saw that day. Shut up in a large house in a small town in the middle of nowhere, with a screaming grandmother, anxious parents and a spoiled child, all waiting for the axe to fall, and, once it had fallen, alone with a spoiled child, her only consolation was to look back to the palace and forward to Zion. She had no connections abroad, no immediate plans to emigrate. She must have perished in the Holocaust.

I now had the run of the place. I could have lived in the Blue Salon. I knew where the key was in Mother's dressing room. But it would have been a betrayal of Mother to sit there without her. I opened the door to the Blue Salon and, looking neither right nor left, went straight through to the *Herrenzimmer*, the smoking room Father never used. There I found my escape route from the present—those shiny collected works that no one ever read, imprisoned there in Mother's posh bookcases.

I had plenty of time. "So long as Jews are still allowed in the school . . ." Dr. Behrens had said. Now they no longer were. That was the only good thing to come out of the *Kristallnacht* for me.

There was some sort of Jewish school in Detmold. Ursula Eichmann went there, and my parents might have sent me too, had they been home. I am glad they didn't. Ursula, cycling to the station, was waylaid by some youngsters, girls as well as boys, and thrown to the ground and beaten.

I hardly went out. I sat for hours on Oma Billa's rug in the *Herrenzimmer*, reading, reading. I read widely, mostly plays. They fitted my mood. There was drama in my life. I soon gave up on Goethe—I found even his plays dull. I read a lot of Shakespeare in translation. The histories were my favourites. They told a story you could get your teeth into. I liked Conrad Ferdinand Meyer's stories, Joerg Jenatsch best of all. But in the end, I always came back to Schiller's plays. I adored his noble sentiments, expressed in majestic cadences, his heroes and heroines, ennobled by their stand against the tyranny of power and cruel fate. Only the highest of high tragedy could do justice to my feelings.

I remember the thrill when I first read that scene in Maria Stuart where the two queens meet—a meeting invented by Schiller for dramatic effect. Mary kneels before her captor and asks Elizabeth to stretch out her hand and raise her up. Elizabeth says coldly, "You are in your proper place, Lady Mary, and I thank and praise the mercy of God, who did not ordain that I should lie at your feet as you now lie at mine." Mary replies with the unforgettable lines:

"Denkt an den Wechsel alles Menschlichen!
Es leben Götter die den Hochmut rächen!
Verehret, fürchtet sie, die schrecklichen,
Die mich zu Euren Füssen niederstürzen-
Um dieser fremde Zeugen Willen, ehrt
In mir Euch selbst, entweihet, schändet nicht
Das Blut der Tudor, das in meinen Adern
Wie in den Euren fliesst!"

She reminds Elizabeth that everything human is subject to change. There are gods who punish pride. Let Elizabeth fear them, the terrible ones, who have cast Mary at her feet. For the sake of the strangers present, let Elizabeth honour herself in (showing mercy to) Mary. Let her not desecrate the blood of the Tudors that flows in both their veins.

I took on Mary's fiery nature as she hurled these defiant words at the all-powerful bastard, Elizabeth. I seized the flag with the Maid of Orleans as, fatally wounded, she sees heaven open its gates. Above all, I identified with Wallenstein's descent from triumph to disaster.

I loved the Wallenstein plays, perhaps because, like Shakespeare's histories, they told a long story. For two or three days, I could lose myself in them. When thoughts of Father and Mother came up, I dispersed them in reveries about Wallenstein's fluctuating fortunes. Sweep unpleasant thoughts under a brightly coloured carpet! Rather the Thirty Years' War than the Third Reich!

But my all-time favourite was Don Carlos, just as the opera was later to become my favourite Verdi. So many great themes in one story—the hero fighting for freedom, confronting his father and the church, eternally bound in friendship to the noble Posa, the hero hopelessly in love with his stepmother and betrayed by the fascinating Princess Eboli.

As I read the play, I made an interesting discovery. When good times, such as holidays, were coming to an end, Father or Mother used to sigh, "*Die schönen Tage von Aranjuez sind nun vorueber*," pronouncing *Aranjuez* like a combination of the French *orange* and *jouer*. But the actual line in the play is, "*Die schönen Tage von Aranjuez sind nun zu Ende.*"

The sense is the same: the happy days in Aranjuez have come to an end. I was thrilled to have spotted the small mistake. I will tell Father, I thought. He has been misquoting his beloved Schiller.

Then I remembered where Father was. The good days were definitely over.

I could hardly bear to leave my books, but reality was knocking at my defences. I could not shut my ears to the rumours about beatings in Buchenwald. And I could not escape the visit to Bethel.

Aunt Minna took me by the hand as we went to the waiting car. The faithful Karl drove us the forty minutes or so it took to reach our destination. We passed the hillside café where Mother and I had stuffed ourselves with *Sahnehörnchen* and *Bienenstich*. We saw the high observation tower of Sparrenburg castle with the exciting underground fortifications that Father and I had explored. But thoughts of cream cakes and mediaeval castles could not make me forget where we were heading.

We reached the citadel of the mentally ill and were taken to a large high-ceilinged room where inmates met their visitors. It was very bare, with just a few chairs and a table. We waited for some time. At last Mother came in. She was dressed in a loose grey institutional smock, looking paler and thinner than I had ever seen her. Mother never wore grey. It was not her colour. She looked terrible. When she saw us, she started to weep hysterically and continued weeping.

"My child, my child," she kept on crying, as she put her arms around me. I felt even more discomfort than I felt pity. Towards the end of our short visit, she grew a little calmer. She talked business with Aunt Minna, but when the nurse came to take her away, she broke down again.

It was in those dark days that Aunt Minna really showed her mettle. She never wavered in her loyalty to her husband and his family. She went to the authorities to plead for Uncle Walter's release. She met with Herr Adam and Meister Drexhage, who ran the factory for Mother, to see if there was anything Mother needed to know. She sent Helmut with food. She came to the house herself to make sure that I was all right and that everything was in order.

There were no effusive huggings and tears, à la Aunt Grete, just a pat and a few comforting words: "Don't worry. Your parents will soon be home and everything will be back to normal. And now, let's get some food into you." A great lady.

We lived with rumours. The men were being sent home from the concentration camps. They were not being sent home; they had been moved from Buchenwald to somewhere even worse. Those who had served as frontline soldiers in the war were being released. One day, without warning, Father appeared, haggard but unbowed. He still held himself like a Prussian officer. No great water lover, he jumped into his bath and lay there some time in the hot water before he scrubbed himself. But there was no joy in his freedom, no sense of relief. He had come back to an empty house, a house empty of Mother. I asked about Buchenwald, but he would not talk about it, not yet.

My memories of those days are like an empty house. The walls, the outlines of the story, are there, but the house has no furniture in it—no life. Everything is grey, like Mother's institutional frock. I usually manage to see the funny side, but there is nothing to laugh about in this part of my story.

The day after his return, Father went to Bethel. As usual, he got into the front seat of the Minerva, next to his friend, Karl. There were five empty seats in the back. I was glad not to be filling one of them and grateful to Father for not asking me to come. Bethel terrified me.

"We must get Emmy home at once," Father told Uncle Walter and Aunt Minna after his return. "The Gestapo may come here to interview her, but we have to take that risk. If she stays in Bethel, she will really go mad. What began as a charade, will become the reality."

When she came home, Mother was no longer crying.

"Let me look at you," she said to me. "You have become so thin. We must get you to eat."

It was she who was thin. Her dresses hung loose on her, and she looked grey, but her greatest worry was over. Father was back at her side.

"Now I can breathe again" (*Jetzt kann ich wieder atmen*), she said.

Her troubles were far from over. The Gestapo did come again, and their visit was followed by a pre-trial examination. Mother described what happened.

First she was interviewed alone. "I denied the charge. I was quite calm," she said.

"Do you then accuse Party Member Hamann of lying?" asked one of the assessors.

"I accuse no one of anything," Mother replied. "I only know that I did not make that statement."

Mother was then brought face to face with her accuser.

"The charge you have made against Frau Katz is a very serious one," the chairman told him. "So serious that, if you confirm it under oath, Frau Katz could go to prison for a long time." I remember the phrase Mother used very well: "*auf lange Zeit ins Gefängnis.*"

"I appeal to your conscience, Herr Hamann," Mother put in. She was reprimanded for interrupting, but her appeal was successful.

For what seemed like a lifetime, the *Obmann* was silent. The still small voice was very still and very small, but he listened to it. Perhaps he had just wanted to harass Mother with the Göring story and had not meant it to go further.

He prevaricated. He *thought* that he had heard Mother say those words. He was almost certain. The machines were going at the time. He may have misheard, but he did not think so.

The courts still dispensed some vestiges of justice at that time. Mother was let off with a warning. The *Obmann* was told to be more careful in the future before he brought charges.

Mother had missed her first appointment with death. It was the beginning of 1939. Had she been sentenced, she would never have come out alive. But the grim reaper was keeping an eye on her. He would approach her again in the not-too-distant future.

Chapter Thirty-Eight

GUESTS OF THE STATE

Before they were allowed to leave Buchenwald, Father and Uncle Walter had to sign a document stating that they had neither received nor witnessed any ill treatment. The facts of their lives as guests of the German state were somewhat different. At first they avoided questions to protect Mother. As her physical and mental health improved, the truth gradually came out.

"Your 4711 saved our lives, Emmy." Father kissed Mother's full dark hair just above her forehead. He did that when he felt tender, and I caught the habit. "We were so parched, we thought we would pass out. Then I remembered your eau de cologne. I also gave some to Walter. We used it to moisten our tongues every so often. It was too precious to drink. Mind you, it didn't taste as good as it smelled but it took the edge off that terrible dryness."

I had slunk into a corner, pretending to read in case I would be sent out of the room. That would have been disastrous. I had to know everything. The precaution was unnecessary. My parents never had many secrets from me, and nowadays there seemed to be none, even for something as terrible as this.

"We were herded onto cattle trucks. At various gathering points, more men were squeezed in. During that long slow journey, we were without food or water. But, at least we had your eau de cologne."

When the hungry and severely dehydrated men finally arrived at Buchenwald in beautiful Saxony—the word "Buchenwald" means beech wood—they were met by a reception committee.

"We had to pass through a long narrow corridor, not much more than this wide"—Father stretched out his arms in parallel. "It was lined with armed S.S. men. They laid into us with their rifle butts to get us acclimatized. They weren't choosy. I saw sick elderly men who could hardly stand up after that terrible journey, being beaten by those louts. The corridor was the ideal place for what they had in mind. There was no escaping their blows. We were caught."

I had meant to keep quiet, so as not to draw attention to myself, but I could not contain myself.

"Is that where Uncle Walter got his swollen face, Vati?"

"So, Monsieur le Curieux has been taking it all in. *Monsieur fourre son nez partout*"—he who pokes his nose in everywhere.

"But I want to know what happened to you and Uncle Walter," I protested. "You are my father."

Father put his hand on my head as if in blessing.

"Yes, my boy. You have a right to know. When we get out of this benighted country, we will have to tell the world what went on in and to Germany. Yes, they got Uncle Walter in the face and in the legs, and what blows! As you know, there is a lot of Uncle Walter to hit. They went for me too, but I was in the war. I knew how to move. I pretended to be hit where I was not. I got away with just a few bruises."

"Terrible. Terrible that these things should be done to innocent people," said Mother, shaking her head. "What has Germany come to?"

"I really thought our end had come." Father smiled with relief that it hadn't. "Walter was moaning with pain. I said to him, 'Walter, we will sell our lives dear' [*wir verkaufen unser Leben teuer*]. I said it to him again later. It just came out. I had no idea what resistance we could put up."

Father was not wrong about the danger they were in. Two hundred and twenty-four of those taken to Buchenwald after the *Kristallnacht* did not return.

I had asked Uncle Walter about his swollen face when he first came back. He had put me off with a "we'll talk about it later." Now I knew. He was to suffer with his legs for the rest of his life. This was partly hereditary, but Buchenwald did not help.

"Our hair was cropped short," Father continued. "I didn't give them much work there." He touched his close cropped sides. He had nothing on top.

"They noted down our particulars and issued us prison pyjamas. Then they put us on parade. Our names were called out. It took a very long time. I could take it. I had been a soldier. But it was very hard on the old and sick to stand for so long. They did not give us our first meal until evening. It was hardly worth eating, but we were ravenous."

Father had not told the half of it. I heard more at Uncle Walter's, when Mother was not present.

"They crammed us into wooden barracks. We slept on the floor, packed so close we could not stretch ourselves. It wasn't easy for me. I take up a lot of room." Uncle Walter pointed to his own massive frame. "Even with so many in the room, it was bitterly cold."

"They tried to wear us down with endless roll calls and knee bends. Those knee bends hurt after the beating I had."

Uncle Walter rolled up his trousers and showed us a knee, still very red and swollen. "Then they made us run at the double. Some of the older men collapsed. A few died."

"The S.S. carried riding whips and they liked to use them." Uncle Walter gave a good imitation of an S.S. man at work. "We often heard the screams of people being punished because they had fallen afoul of some stupid regulation. I kept to the rules. I had had enough the first time round."

I was listening with increasing horror. It wasn't so much pity as a feeling in my stomach that this could be happening to me. I had read about the horrors of war when following Frederick the Great's battles with my friend, Werner Böthel, but that was glory. The boys at school had been cruel, but theirs was mostly mental cruelty. They did not beat me, at least not severely. Now, I heard for the first time about people being tortured on the grand scale. What Uncle Walter said next made the deepest impression, because I could see and feel it in my imagination. Young Walter brought up the subject.

"Tell us again about the latrines, Father," he said.

Uncle Walter shook his long head.

"That was unbelievable. At first there was only one latrine for thousands of men. You had to wait your turn in the rain and the cold. Remember, it was November. Some men could not wait. After a few days most of us had diarrhoea. The stench in the huts was terrible."

Uncle Walter looked at me and smiled. "That latrine was not your mother's blue-tiled throne room, just a pole suspended over a cesspit.

You had to be careful not to lose your balance. It was bad enough in the daytime. At least sick people who fell in could be helped to safety.

"The night was a different story. They had made a regulation forbidding us to leave our quarters at night, even to go to the latrines. That was the cruellest regulation of all, especially with so many cases of severe dysentery. Some men were so desperate that they defied the regulations and ventured out in the dark. If the guards caught them, they knocked them over with their truncheons into the cesspool. When the unfortunates tried to climb out, the guards pushed them back. They drowned in the muck."

Father had let Uncle Walter tell his tale. Now he said, "And not far away in Weimar, Goethe and Schiller lay buried in the Fürstengruft." I don't think these authors were on Uncle Walter's reading list, but I knew what Father meant.

The story of the latrines gave me nightmares. I was sitting on a long pole, narrow as a broomstick, gazing at the brown mess below. It was a very vivid shade of brown, almost auburn. I saw no guards, but suddenly I was teetering on the edge. Before I could fall in, I woke up. Later, I ruminated about my nightmare and about the stories I had heard. Cesspit and pole, I can still see them today.

"This cries to heaven" (*Es schreit zu Got*), said Mother, whenever the subject of Buchenwald came up. "How could such things happen in a civilized country?" Many people all over the world asked the same question, but nothing was done to stop the Nazis in their tracks. Perhaps it was too late by that time. Mother, of course, had asked the wrong question. She should have said, "In a country that once was civilized."

Father and his companions had only been given a taste of what was to come. Their journey in the cattle trucks did not prove to be their last. They went home, except for the 244 who lost their lives, some of them in the cesspool. Buchenwald, Dachau, Sachsenhausen should have been a warning to the world. It should have known that terror would not end there.

Terrorism is normally the work of a lunatic or fanatical fringe. When the State itself becomes the terrorist, when all the power and resources of the State are used to terrorize and violently oppress helpless minorities, it is imperative that those who have the power to do something about it, not cross the road and look the other way. Violence is no respecter of frontiers. It seeks an ever broader stage on which to display itself.[60]

The Nuremberg Laws had been a clear signal that there was no future for Jews in Germany. The *Kristallnacht* marked the beginning of the end. Jews were now excluded not only from schools and universities but from cinemas, theatres, circuses, sports facilities, and even from parks. Göbbels had proposed special park benches for Jews. That did not seem enough. I saw a notice somewhere, "Jews enter this park at their own risk" (*Juden betreten diese Parkanlange auf eigene Gefahr*). We had come some way from "Jews not wanted" (*Juden unerwuenscht*).

I went with Mother on her boring "shopping for emigration" expeditions, hoping they would be crowned by a shared gastronomic experience. It was not just the quality of the *Sahnehörnchen* and *Bienenstich*; it was sitting down with Mother, enjoying and appreciating these delicacies together. Nowadays, it was rarer to find a tearoom without a "Jews not wanted" sign or worse. When we did find one, we felt uncomfortable eating in public.

---

[60]   How is it possible that a government not only permitted the horrors of Buchenwald and Auschwitz, but actually initiated them? In recent years, other governments, such as Cambodia, the Congo and Rwanda, have also initiated and committed atrocities (though without German efficiency). Maharishi Mahesh Yogi has taught us that on the ultimate level, every government is the product of the collective consciousness of its people. I saw the truth of that when looking at the almost uniformly violent images displayed in an exhibition of German pre-Hitler graphics at the British Museum. Hitler and his gang were the incarnation of the German collective consciousness of that time. Wise men who care for their country should ensure that the collective consciousness does not reach a dangerous level of turbulence. The use of techniques that calm and elevate the consciousness of the individual is the only answer. Many studies have shown that Maharishi's Transcendental Meditation is an effective method to achieve this goal. Even a small percentage of the population practising the technique can have a disproportionate effect. See *Scientific Research on the Transcendental Meditation Program: Collected Papers, Volumes 1-6,* Rheinweiler, West Germany: MERU Press, 1976, specifically the *International Peace Project in the Middle East: The Effects of the Maharishi Technology of the Unified Field,* David W. Orme-Johnson, Charles N. Alexander, John L. Davies, Howard M. Chandler, and Wallace E. Larimore, Journal of Conflict Resolution, Dec 1988; vol. 32: pp. 776-812.

"Soon we'll have coffee and cake in a nice English restaurant," said Mother, still blessedly ignorant of the quality of the English coffee and cake of those days.

I normally went to the cinema with my cousins, but on rare occasions Mother and I saw a film together. Mother loved Beniamino Gigli. We had seen a film in Bad Salzuflen, where we were not well known, with the little man singing his heart out to a lady twice his height, who wore an enormous white hat. Mother had cried. All that was over now. We did not dare even go to Bad Salzuflen.

These were pinpricks. The main thrust of the measures taken against Jews after the *Kristallnacht* was economic. In the end, the Nazis got much more than the thousand million marks Göring had demanded. They simply made the Jews sell to Aryans and confiscated the proceeds. Decrees went out forbidding Jews to own or manage any shops or businesses, and ordering them to deposit their securities with the State.

Among the businesses compulsorily "Aryanized" was the proud firm of Hermann Katz and Co. It has been in existence for twenty years, created *ex nihilo* by my parents' untiring diligence. The new owner was a farmer named Karl Kuenne. He had no previous connection with the brush trade, unless it was by way of pigs' bristles. I seem to remember that Herr Kuenne paid seventy thousand marks for our complex, of which we saw not a pfennig.

Not only were we doing our bit to keep *Reichsmarschall* Göring in fodder; we were also making our contribution towards the armaments shortly to be used against those who refused to heed the danger signalled by our fate.

The Nazis had robbed my parents of their livelihood and their capital, but they gave them handouts for their immediate needs. An allowance of one thousand marks arrived with German punctuality on the first of every month. (It was money that, as it turned out, nearly cost my parents their lives.) We would not be allowed to take any money out of Germany, so Mother used whatever was left over after living expenses had been covered, to buy things we might need in England, belted raincoats and the like. My parents' sense of belonging to our land, to Germany, had been completely hammered out of them. Their one thought was to get out of "this terrible country."

I was reflective enough to find it strange that my parents did not mourn the factory into which they had put so much of themselves, which had been the centre of their lives for so many years. Mother found it strange too.

"We worked so hard for so many years, but now it is gone and I feel only relief." When the papers had been signed, Mother expanded her cheeks, compressed her lips and through a small cavity breathed out the hopes and dreams of twenty years.

In one sense the *Kristallnacht* proved a blessing. It destroyed any lingering hopes that things might change and that there was still a future for us in Germany. It gave the Jews nine month's notice to get out while they still could.

Chapter Thirty-Nine

BAYSWATER COMES
TO SCHÖTMAR

Aunt Grete's Mr. Stephenson arrived in Schötmar in a long grey overcoat, accompanied by Mrs. Stephenson, flounces showing under a voluminous brown cloak. They had come to pick up the money required to guarantee us a temporary visa for England and deliver it in London to the Sterns, Uncle Paul's sister and her husband. The sum needed, I seem to remember, was two hundred pounds. The visa would enable us to stay in England until our U.S. quota number came up.

Mr. Stephenson was medium height and thin. He had a long thin face, thin lips, a thin, very hairy nose and bushy reddish upwardly striving eyebrows. He looked like a slightly seedy version of the typical Englishman of stage and screen, and he came armed with the typical Englishman's accoutrements, the bowler hat and the rolled umbrella. Mrs. Stephenson was shorter, fatter, and considerably older. She had dyed red hair, and her face was completely covered in peach makeup, thickly applied over the wrinkles. She wore a loose-fitting frilly two-piece outfit. A long necklace dangled over an overexposed bosom. When I was introduced, my manners completely left me. I just stared.

In their native habitat, the Bayswater region of London, no one would have given the pair a second glance. In Schötmar they were a sensation, he for his textbook Englishness, she because she looked like a woman who had fallen and was still falling. What hold, our family and friends asked themselves, could she have over that good-looking husband of hers? It must be money. On one point, all had agreed. Father voiced their sentiments, "*Die Stephenson* [pronounced Steffensen] *hat die Hosen an*" (she wears the trousers).

If there was one person Father liked less than a lazy woman, it was a bossy one. Like it or not, Father would have to get used to the breed. In the country that produced Elizabeth I and Margaret Thatcher, the female of the species was more often than not the dominant partner. Mrs. Stephenson was only the first of a long line of strong-willed Englishwomen we met or lodged with in the 1940s, who held their husbands in a grip of iron. It happened too often for mere coincidence. The man might brag loudmouthed in the local pub, or, in the case of one of our landlords, preach bloody revolution, but at home it was "yes, dear," "no, dear," and a cup of tea for the wife first thing in the morning. The woman would remain supine, caressing some malodorous dog or uncaring cat, who, likely as not, had shared the conjugal bed, and wait for the husband to serve her tea and biscuits. The man would make the purring noises of the underling, trying to ingratiate himself with the all-powerful one, who would continue her stately lie-in as he went to work for the gas board. He would come home at night, only to be directed to do various jobs that needed doing around the house, and after supper he would deal with the washing up.

How unlike the home-life of my own dear parents! Father never touched a washing-up cloth in his life. He was to stand up to the English gorgons who were to give him shelter like a man, so much so that one of them accused him of trying to gas her. But that was in the future. For the moment, there was Mrs. Stephenson, the pants wearer, giving him a foretaste of what was to come.

As well as the money, the Stephensons also took with them various bits of silver and jewellery, not all of which found their way back to us. No matter. They were doing us a great service—against payment, of course. My parents discussed plans for sending me to England with them. Good Jewish parents that they were, their main concern was that I continue my education. What else would have persuaded Mother to send her darling out into the world alone?

"You cannot go on sitting in the *Herrenzimmer* all day reading those books. That's not the same as getting an education that will take you through life." Mother shook her head sadly. "No, it's not the same thing."

"But I am learning a lot about life from my reading," I pleaded. "And I am reading Shakespeare. That will be useful in England. I don't want to go to England alone. I want to wait and go with you." Tears started to come. I almost got Mother to cry too.

"It will only be another two or three months," she said, hugging me," and we shall all be together again." She knew what a fearful little soul I was.

"We would have liked our son to go to a private school like my sister's children," Mother confided to the Stephensons. "But it is too late for that now. If only my sister had taken me more into her confidence. We will be lucky if he gets a place on one of the *Kindertransports.*"

My parents had heard about the World Movement for the Care of Children from Germany, recently founded in London to give temporary refuge to young victims of Nazi persecution. After the *Kristallnacht*, the British government decided to allow five thousand young people to enter the country, with the World Movement guaranteeing that they would not become a public charge. By the outbreak of war, 9,354 children had been saved. I was to be one of the 9,354.

"We would be grateful if you could keep an eye on him when he comes to England," said Father. "Of course the Sterns will be there, but it will be good for him to have some English people to whom he can turn." The Stephensons promised, but I remember visiting their dingy Bayswater *ménage* only once.

On 15 February 1939, the factory was sold. On March 2, I was to join my *Kindertransport*. It was a very strange time. For the first time, my parents were unemployed. Their main concern now was to get our chattels into the containers that were to take them to the United States. Herr Bona, the Italian forwarding agent, was a frequent visitor. If Mother could no longer enjoy her Blue Salon in Schötmar, she was determined to enjoy it in New York or Chicago.

I remember very little about my last days in Germany. Only the visit to Grandmother stands out. She received us in bed, propped up by pillows, wearing her pale lilac robe. She was well into her eighties, but the features were still beautiful. The sisters had swept up her hair into a bun, supporting it with those brown combs I had known from early childhood. They had also calmed her down. She talked quite sanely about her life in the home and freely voiced her complaints—the Oma Bertha of old. When she kissed me good-bye, there were tears in her eyes and in mine. She knew, and I knew, that we would not meet again.

Mother was desperate about having to leave Grandmother behind, once she and Father would join me in England.

"No country will take her in. We cannot take her with us, and we cannot stay here," she told the sister in charge.

"We will do our best to protect her," the deaconess assured Mother. She added, "I do not think she has very long to live. *Altersschwäche* [senile decay], you know."

Mother took some comfort from that prognosis. The sister was right. Grandmother died not long after I left Germany.

As the day of my departure approached, my fears grew. I had never been away from home without my parents, except to visit our relatives in Cologne. What would I do, alone in a strange country? How would those strangers treat me? Would my English be good enough?

"I was not that much older than you when my parents sent me to Alsace-Lorraine. It was far away, like a foreign country. I stood my ground [*Ich stellte meinen Mann*], and you will do likewise." Father raised his lower arm and clenched his fist. Cold comfort. I was not the manly type. Mother's words were more soothing:

"So long as your parents live you have nothing to fear." It was true that Mother had no grounds for her confident assertion, but this was a message designed to soothe a fearful heart, and it got through.

My parents came to Herford or Buende with me on the train, but I do not remember the farewells. I only recall the black beret that I wore and the group of people waving at me near the railway line, where it passed our timber yard. Uncle Walter towered above them all.

The *Kindertransport* arrived at Bentheim, the dreaded frontier station. The people in charge of us went into conference with the authorities, but we were let go without much ado—another lot of young undesirables unworthy of the honour of living in the Third Reich. I felt relief as the train set off, but also fear of the unknown.

Still, I had my moments of glory. "You watch," I told an audience of the not-so-well-travelled, "the next station will be Hengelo, and then Almelo, and then Deventer . . . I have done this journey many times."

I did less well on the boat from Hoek van Holland to Harwich. It was my first sea journey, and I was miserably sick. I looked at England through a queasy stomach. No castles, no windmills, no pretty Dutch houses—just identical rows of red-brick ugliness. When we reached London; the red brick was covered with grime. No sign of the Tower, or the Thames, or the Houses of Parliament.

We arrived at the flawed cathedral, known as Liverpool Street Station. Broken glass, grimy pillars, floor none too clean. What a contrast to the *Hauptbahnhof,* the main railway station, at Cologne!

On the outer fringes of the station, where it faces Liverpool Street, we were divided into groups and assembled with our number tags. As we waited for our names to be called, I caught sight of my first red double-decker. I stood there disconsolate, in my overcoat, with my short pants and long sagging socks, as, one by one, my companions left with their sponsors. No one seemed to want me. I was growing desperate, when at last I heard my name. The Sterns had been caught in a traffic jam.

It was a great relief to see a familiar face. Although I knew her as Aunt Hede, Uncle Paul's sister and I were not on kissing terms. As we shook hands, I made my customary low German bow, the *Diener.* Aunt Hede looked horrified.

"You must never do that again," she instructed me. "People here do not like it. Remember, you are in England now!"

Chapter Forty

BUCKINGHAMSHIRE PARADISE

Mrs. Alice Elizabeth Redwood Bolton, Auntie Dot to her chosen ones, came running into the garden.

"Where have you been? I've been hunting for you everywhere." She shot me a sharp glance with her ultra light blue no-nonsense eyes. Her ruddy face looked young, though she must have been in her fifties. She had snow-white hair of a kind I had never seen in Germany. It gave her a kind of albino look.

"A very nice lady has just called from Great Missenden. She wants to invite one of the boys in the hostel to spend the Easter holidays with her family. She has a beautiful home and the boy will play with her grandchildren. She told me to choose any boy I thought suitable and"—Auntie Dot gave me another searching look—"I have chosen you. 'I know just the boy for you,' I told her. 'He is very well behaved and I think you will like him.'"

"Thank you, Auntie Dot," I said gratefully. "Thank you very much for choosing me."

Auntie Dot had a soft spot for me, even though I was a lazy gardener. I had one great quality: I was a good listener and Auntie Dot had much to talk about. Her life was haunted by a tragedy. She had borne a son, Paul, late in life and lost him at the age of eight. He was a boarder at Gayhurst School in nearby Gerrards Cross. Auntie Dot never tired of singing his virtues and lamenting her loss.

I was doing time at Woodside Hostel for Refugee Boys in Loudwater, near High Wycombe, which Mrs. Bolton ran together with her husband. The regime was a little harsh, but I was not unhappy there.

We gardened, cleaned, learned to repair shoes, and worked at our English so that we would be able to attend the local school. Speaking German was strictly forbidden. Mrs. Friedman, our Viennese cook, gave us the same meals every week—roast beef on Sunday, cottage pie on Monday, macaroni and cheese on Tuesday, roast lamb with bread and mint sauce on Wednesday, cold lamb Thursday, fish on Friday, and I forget what on Saturday. The food was good, thanks to Mrs. Friedman and our sponsors. Discipline was fairly strict. If we made noise late at night, Mr. Bolton would go on the prowl and pronounce those terrible words: "See you in the morning." The punishment was usually a reprimand, but Mr. Bolton was not a man to be taken lightly. He spoke little—she did all the talking—but he exuded authority.

The prospect of spending a holiday elsewhere was not unwelcome. Auntie Dot took me to the office to meet my new benefactress, who was talking to Mr. Bolton. She was a tall elderly lady with a large hat and kind eyes.

"Would you like to come to my house in Great Missenden for the Easter holidays?" she asked with a reassuring smile. "My grandchildren will be there. Rodney is about your age. Angela is a little younger. I am sure you will get on well with them."

"Yes, madam. I would like that very much," I replied. I avoided her eyes and looked shyly at the long costume jacket, speckled with white spots, and the long necklace she wore over her jumper.

"No need to call me madam. I am Mrs. Boston." Her voice was soft, her smile friendly. I felt that she liked me. It can't have been my looks. At nearly twelve, I was going through a very ungainly phase.

I had just met one of the sweetest, kindest people I was ever to encounter. For me, Laura Annie Boston came to embody the best of England, that country of soft green hills and kind gentle people, so different from the hard harsh country I had left. England has become a harder coarser country over the years, but there are still outposts of Boston gentleness.

A few days later, a low-slung sporty-looking car drew up in front of the hostel. Sybil Boston, the youngest daughter, had come to collect me.

She was a beautiful woman, thirtyish, with an open face, an English rose complexion, and the air of a sportswoman. I was sure Mother would have liked her. As it turned out later, she did. One of the photos Mother kept by her bedside was of Sybil and me sitting together on the grass.

As we drove through lovely Chiltern countryside, Sybil asked me about Germany. She was so free and direct—no German formality. She treated me as if she had known me all her life. My English was quite fluent, and I talked without restraint about my family and background, and about the persecution we suffered.

On the outskirts of Great Missenden, just as the road turned towards Little Kingshill, we drew up in front of Lansdown, a large Edwardian country house. The upper part was half timbered, the lower, brick, almost hidden by creepers. There were several large chimneys.

Sybil's older sister, Peg, welcomed us at the door. She was greying, less pretty than Sybil, and more reserved. I was taken upstairs.

"Where shall we put him? In the pink room or the blue room?" Sybil asked Peg. She turned to me. "Which would you prefer?"

So these were now to be my concerns: which part of heaven to choose. At the hostel, I slept in a dormitory with little furniture except for the iron bedsteads. At Lansdown, the high well-sprung beds were piled with cushions. There were bedside tables and lamps, armchairs, sideboards, a dressing table. The curtains, bedcovers, and armchairs were of the same flowered pink material, for I had landed in the pink room.

"Perhaps you would like to take a bath now and then rest and change for dinner," they told me. "Mother is looking forward to seeing you. She has had to go out."

At the hostel we were lucky if we could take a bath twice a week. These people bathed twice a day. And they changed for dinner. Mother had morning and afternoon dresses, but to change for dinner, in your own home, on a weekday, was unheard of.

When the gong sounded for dinner, I went down, a little afraid of what I would find. I found a sea of colours. The ladies were all in long evening gowns. The colours were much stronger than those worn by the sober German women I was used to. During my stay, I saw kingfisher blue, eau de nil, magenta, royal blue, bright pink, shades of gold, worn by the three daughters, Sybil, Peg and Mrs. Walsh, the mother of

Rodney and Angela, tall, very thin and divorced, or maybe widowed. Mrs. Boston herself preferred claret or grey. They rarely wore the same dress two nights running.

I had just managed to catch the tail end of gracious living in pre-war England, when the prosperous could live as only the super rich can today. Perhaps it was a lifestyle underpinned by the spoils of empire, but what civilized living has not been supported by underprivilege elsewhere? Today, we, in the first world, live on the cheap raw materials produced by the third.

The parlour maid wore a starched white apron and frilly white cap. She walked around each person, so that she could serve from the left. She held the silver dishes gracefully, bending lower for the children. It took me some time to help myself with reasonable grace. At first I was shy and took too little. Later I plucked up courage and took as much as the others.

It was all very different from what I was used to. At home, Erna, and later the Strate, had just plonked the dishes on the table. At the hostel we had no choice. Mr. Bolton meted out the portions, fifteen pairs of eager eyes making sure that he dealt fairly.

I noticed that they did not use tablecloths in the dining room. Mother would have been horrified. Instead, there were mats and place settings on the highly polished wooden table. I was to learn later that tablecloths for main meals were lower middle class.

I acquitted myself well at the table. Auntie Dot was very keen on teaching the young barbarians English table manners. In the short time I had been in England, I had mastered the trick of holding my fork upside down. Valiantly, I pushed my peas up the fork—like walking up a down escalator. I tipped my soup away from me, another absurd habit, and drank it sideways from the spoon. And I remembered Auntie Dot's litany: don't talk with food or drink in your mouth, don't eat or drink when you still have food in your mouth—something that Mother, with all her attention to manners, had not taught me.

Only my clothes made me feel uncomfortable. While Rodney, my contemporary, wore a smart grey suit with long pants—and later, on occasion, a dinner jacket—I appeared in a greenish suit of coarse Hitlerian cloth with a short square jacket and short pants, well filled at the top but baggy, almost flaring outwards above the knees. I still wore very short socks in place of the knee-length ones favoured by English schoolboys. The days of my brown velvet and blue linen splendour were definitely over.

Yet these marvellous people treated the plump shy, badly dressed refugee boy as one of them. No condescension, no fuss, just simple human kindness. Soon I felt thoroughly at home. I was expected to conform to their habits, which included going to Little Missenden Church on Sunday mornings. Mrs. Boston did ask if I would mind joining them, and I had neither the heart nor the courage to refuse. I had already been church-trained by Auntie Dot, who came from a Plymouth Brethren background.

Going to church was no hardship. I loved joining in those tuneful English hymns. My favourite was Eternal Father, strong to save, with its refrain:

"O hear us when we cry to Thee
For those in peril on the sea."

Everyone sang and prayed together, very different from our fairly orthodox synagogue where people did their own thing and rattled off prayers as fast as they could. In church there was what Germans call *Andacht*, a kind of respectful attentive devotion. Reform Judaism has adopted this approach. When I first went to one of its services not so many years ago, I was strongly reminded of the Church of England.

Little Missenden Church was more beautiful than the modern church near the hostel, where Auntie Dot took her "little heathen." It was of Saxon origin and the timbers of the fifteenth-century porch were made from a single block, I was told. It had fine wall paintings. There was one of fish swimming around St. Christopher's feet.

The stone floors were very cold and the sermons, very boring. Normally, we children were excused from them, but I sat through one or two. Had he not been preaching to the converted, old Reverend Davies' congregation would have been small indeed. As it was, the small church was full. The ladies again were very elegant in their flowered dresses and dark wide-brimmed hats, their silk stockings and pumps.

The custom of the house that I liked best was late breakfast. You came down when you liked and helped yourself from the covered silver dishes on the sideboard. Scrambled eggs, delicious lean bacon, sausages, tomatoes, kippers, or smoked halibut, and even fried potatoes. Imagine, fish and potatoes for breakfast! Afterwards, toast and marmalade. The German word for jam is *Marmelade*, and that's what I thought I had taken. I nearly spat out the brusque orange peel. But I soon caught the marmalade habit, like so much else that was English—*homo naturaliter angliae.*

After lunch, we retired to the drawing room for coffee. This long sunny beautiful room faced the garden. There were sofas and armchairs of all sizes, covered in light flower patterns with lots of cushions; there were little antique tables, arranged in no perceptible order. I was experiencing the casual lived-in comfort of the English country home, so unlike the home life of my own dear Mother. Peg was a keen gardener. She had vases of fresh flowers all over the house. Her biggest display was in the drawing room.

The garden was large with formal gravel paths, box hedges, mysterious bowers, and hidden vegetable patches. It was at Lansdown that I first encountered the English lawn. The Bostons had two large lawns, separated by a slope. They were cut, rolled, weeded, and staked by Peg and the gardener.

"The grass is so bouncy, Miss Peg," I said as I watched her. "It's like stepping on my mother's carpet with its underlay. In Germany the grass is much longer."

"It's hard work," said Peg. Thank God, she did not ask me to help her. I had come to hate gardening at the hostel, especially the weeding.

It seemed a shame to push the croquet hoops into this fine carpet of a lawn, but I found they did no harm. I loved this new gentlemanly game. At least, that was the way we played it. I found in later years that it could rouse passions.

I enjoyed taking tea in the summer house, but the picnics were an even greater treat. We went in the large car and, somewhere in a clearing by the Chiltern Woods, set down our hampers and spread out the blankets. Angela played mother and handed out cakes, scones, biscuits, and, above all, those wonderful English sandwiches—very thinly sliced white and brown bread with the crusts cut off, divided into little triangles. By rights you could stuff two into your mouth and still have room for more. The trick was to eat them slowly, with the relish they deserved. They were filled with tomatoes, cucumbers, fish paste, egg, soft cheese, and chocolate spread—yes, chocolate! I did not approve of chocolate sandwiches. It was one of those mix-ups of categories, like Erna's sweet vegetables.

Rodney was tall and thin, like his mother, with a closed face. Angela was a head shorter, with a pleasant open face, and very lively. I played croquet and tennis with them, but never really got close to either. (Later, I came across Rodney at Oxford, where he was studying medicine, but again no friendship developed.) I still have a postcard showing Lansdown, which I sent to my parents in Germany. "I hope to have some post from you soon," I write, adding, "keep your nerve" (*Behaltet Eure Nerven*). A boy who could write this to his parents did not have that much in common with untroubled English children from prosperous homes.

My real friend was Mrs. Boston. She was more my age. We went for long walks, the tall old lady and the little old man. I told her how worried I was about my parents, even though their plans to join me in England were well advanced. She looked at me with her kind mild eyes and told me to trust in God and in Jesus Christ. I expressed my doubts about Jesus as the Messiah, and she did not press me. We talked a lot about religion.

One day, on our walk, she slipped me half a crown, twelve and a half pence by today's reckoning, but in those days a small fortune. It could buy you five visits to the cinema on a Saturday afternoon and enough farthings (one quarter of a penny) to put in the church collection bag for 120 Sundays. She gave me another half crown when I went back to the hostel. "You must come back to us for the summer holidays," she told me. "We all like you."

I also went for walks with Sybil, the daughter I liked best. It was Sybil who helped me most with my English. I wanted so desperately to speak good English and had asked them all to correct me when I made mistakes. Only Sybil took up my offer.

"You can't say: 'I like being *in* Lansdown.' It has to be: 'I like being *at* Lansdown.' You can say: 'I like being in England, I like being in Great Missenden,' but it has to be: 'I like being at Lansdown.'"

She also took me to play tennis at the house of some neighbouring Warburgs, who were intrigued when I claimed a distant relationship. This Warburg was married to a beautiful Swedish countess. Sybil's elderly admirer, one Captain Bouquet, often came on these expeditions. He was white haired, had a military bearing, and sported a fine moustache. It was all above board. I think there was a Mrs. Bouquet, though I never saw her.

We gathered young nettles in the woods. When cooked, they made a wonderful vegetable that tasted like spinach. We picked mushrooms, played tennis and croquet, went for picnics. After experiencing hell in Bad Salzuflen and purgatory in High Wycombe, I had tasted paradise in Great Missenden.

Chapter Forty-One

THE FALL

I fell from heaven with a bang. My holiday idyll was drawing to a close, and I was thinking without much relish of the life to which I would be returning: dormitories, communal food, hostel boys, gardening, and being preached at. These were to be the least of my worries.

There was a phone call. Mrs. Boston came back into the drawing room and took my hand. She looked grave, her eyes full of kindness and pity.

"You must be brave, Vernon. Your father has sent a message from Germany."

My stomach felt hollow.

"Your mother has been arrested. Your father thinks there has been a mistake and that she will be released soon. He wants us to do what we can from here to get her free. We will try to contact the Foreign Office. I will pray for her and you must pray too."

I did not cry. Life these last years had been too serious for silly tears. There was just that awful feeling in the pit of my stomach; there was fear, great fear. Of course, it was serious. What would happen to Mother? She had been saved once, and now she was in trouble again. Had the *Obmann* business resurfaced or was it something else? But what?

"Please God, save my Mutti. Please God, save my Mutti." I did not move my tongue, but my thoughts were so loud that God must hear them. God was a safer bet than the Foreign Office, though he had not done much to save Jews. Still, I begged Mrs. Boston to do what she could. It would have been easier if she had known why Mother had been arrested. Mrs. Boston had not spoken directly to Father. He had got word through to the Sterns, who had phoned the Boltons, who had phoned the Bostons.

My hosts were even kinder to me than before, if that were possible, and I continued to enjoy the remaining days of my stay with them. It must be like that with the relatives of hostages. You cannot think of your loved ones all the time; your immediate environment takes over. But just below the surface, there flows a river of fear, of foreboding, that can bubble up any time of day or night, especially night.

We went on another picnic. Did she get enough to eat? Mother was a big eater. She liked her food. They took me to Whipsnade Zoo. I had been promised a visit to Hagenbeck's Zoo in Hamburg, but that never materialized. The only wild animals I had seen were those that performed in the circus that occasionally came to our part of Lippe.

Peg explained that Whipsnade was not like other zoos. It tried to reproduce the animals' natural habitat. They actually had room to move about and play. I loved the animals, especially the brown bears, walking upright like huge teddies, or running about in their spacious quarters. What sort of cell did she have? Was there a lavatory inside? Were there others with her in the cell? Could she wash properly?

There was no more news from Germany. I felt more and more certain that it was the old *Obmann*-Göring affair, otherwise, why Mother? I told Mrs. Boston the story on one of our walks.

She put her hand on my shoulder. "Pray to God," she told me. "Pray to Jesus Christ too. He answers prayers. I know it from experience. I have prayed to him for your mother."

Mrs. Boston would have liked me to become a Christian, but she never pressed the point in the crude manner of Auntie Dot. On my next holiday visit, which took place while Mother was still in prison, one of my fellow guests was a Polish Jew who had converted to Christianity. The Reverend Lodz, as he was called, was a sympathetic and deeply religious man. I am sure Mrs. Boston had asked him to speak to me, for he gave me a lot of his time. He quoted extensively from "our" prophets. Had not the prophet Micah said?

"Thou Bethlehem, Ephratah, though thou be little among the thousands of Judah, yet out of thee shall come forth unto me that is to be ruler in Israel; whose goings forth have been of old, from everlasting."

The reference to Bethlehem seemed very clear. That could not be coincidence. Isaiah's prophecy quite clearly confirmed Matthew, chapter 1.

"And there shall come forth a rod out of the stem of Jesse, and a branch shall grow out of his roots. And the spirit of the Lord shall rest upon him."

And had not Isaiah even prophesied the virgin birth?

"Behold a virgin shall conceive and bear a son."

And the crucifixion: "Because he hath poured out his soul unto death: and he was numbered with the transgressors."

The Reverend Lodz built up an impressive body of evidence.

There were references to Jesus bearing our sins, to God's son, to the resurrection. The Psalmist and the prophet Habakkuk were brought in as foretelling the advent of Jesus. I had been taught by my father to revere the psalms and the prophets. It all seemed very convincing. I was too naive to reason that the authors of the Gospels might have tailored their accounts to fit in with the old prophecies. And yet I was not fully convinced.

"But, Reverend Lodz, if the Messiah has already come, how could he allow my mother to be in prison? If the 'light of the gentiles' is really Jesus, as you say, he is supposed to bring out the prisoners from prison. It says so here in Isaiah 42."

I too knew how to quote from scripture. Mrs. Boston had lent me a Bible, and I had made a special study of Isaiah because of all his prophecies foretelling the advent of Jesus.

"If you pray to him with all your heart, he will release her from prison. He will release us all from the prison house of our own sins. He has *already* released us. We have only to accept his gift. That is the deeper meaning of the passage you quoted just now. Besides, we can never know why the Lord has placed us in a certain situation. Look at Job. He was good, just like your mother. Look at Jesus Christ himself. He was without sin and yet he died on the cross. But his mission was a special one. I am sure your mother will be all right."

The Reverend Lodz—darkly handsome, learned, convinced—was a persuasive advocate. I was teetering on the brink. It was my natural conservatism, combined with Auntie Dot's crude proselytizing that saved me, or damned me, depending on your point of view. On my return to

Woodside, Auntie Dot undid much of Reverend Lodz's careful work. How I hated that passage from John 3:16, which she quoted to us, *ad nauseum*:

"For God so loved the world that He gave His only begotten Son, that whosoever believeth in Him should not perish, but have everlasting life." And then, two verses later, the sting in the tail: "He that believeth not is condemned already."

Mrs. Bolton put me off Jesus Christ. It seemed so absurd that just by believing, one would be saved, whatever one's bad deeds. It *was* absurd. Mrs. Bolton did not explain that there is a difference between subscribing to a tenet and a complete inner surrender that transforms your heart and penetrates your bones, whether it be directed to Jesus Christ, Amida Buddha, or Lord Krishna.

The Jewish organizations, who contributed to the hostel's upkeep, had come to hear about the band of "little heathens" trooping off to church every Sunday morning. They did not know that we stood in no real danger. Our enthusiasm was so lukewarm that we always made sure that we had a farthing to make a tinkle in the collection bag; we thought a halfpenny too high a price to pay for an hour of boredom.

I think I was the only one who did not mind going to church. It was not just that I wanted to keep on the right side of Auntie Dot. I liked some of the service. The sermons were a pain, but the prayers gave me some comfort. To this day, I know most of the Church of England Sunday morning service by heart, and can repeat it with all the right clerical inflexions: "Dearly beloved, I pray and beseech thee, as many as are here present . . ."

There were certain refuseniks in the hostel, who, holding firm to the faith of their fathers, declined to set foot in the temple of the non-Messiah. *They* would not be recommended as suitable guest material to charitable ladies from the home counties.

It was the refuseniks who complained to the Jewish authorities. A Jewish teacher was sent to save us from St. John's promise. Auntie Dot stood in the door, barring access. Miss Pearlman, bulky and determined, pushed her aside. She gave her lesson, her mission being to bring us back to our roots. The next time she appeared, Auntie Dot stayed out of the way. She told me that the sight of Miss Pearlman's oily skin and bosomy Jewishness made her physically sick.

The battle for my soul was joined. Mrs. Bolton had given me the New Testament, authorized version. Now Miss Pearlman gave me the Authorized Daily Prayer Book in Hebrew and English.

I liked the parables and the Sermon on the Mount, but I could not get myself to pray to Jesus Christ. In church, on Sundays, I joined in the psalms and the prayers addressed to God, but kept silent and made my mind a blank whenever Jesus was mentioned. It seemed a kind of betrayal to go over to him. We would not be in all this trouble if it were not for Jesus. It was he who made us different.

I turned instead to the God of Abraham, Isaac, and Jacob. He had not been much help to me at the *Städtische Realschule* of Bad Salzuflen, but in my heart of hearts, I had never expected him to help. This was different. It was a matter of life and death. Mother had to be saved. She had to. I said the morning and night prayers for young children and also some longer prayers—in English. I had to know what I was saying to God. Though I could read Hebrew—rather slowly—I understood the meaning of only some of the words. During the day, I prayed inwardly whenever Mother came into my thoughts.

Auntie Dot prayed too. She was a good, if often misguided, woman. Miss Pearlman did not offer to pray. No sentimentality there. She had given me the means, and it was up to me to do my thing. Mrs. Boston prayed, I am sure. Father prayed fervently, and Mother prayed too. She always turned to God as a last resort and on the High Holidays when she could not get on with her housework. In the only letter of hers I can find, written at the Raven Hotel, Droitwich Spa, not long before she died, she reminds me not to forget to say *Kaddish* for my father on the anniversary of his death. She regarded religion as a private affair between herself and God.

I don't know who had the Lord's ear, but he listened.

I was back in Great Missenden for the summer holidays. This time we were a large party. There were other grandchildren from the North of England; there was Mademoiselle, a very charming, pretty French governess with dark hair and smiling eyes. Mrs. Walsh took us all to London Zoo where the animals had less room, but where you could see them close at hand, and where the ice cream was superb.

I continued to go to the Bostons during the early part of the war, when life at Lansdown became less sumptuous. The parlour maid had disappeared into war work as had the cook. We served ourselves at the table to food cooked by the Boston daughters. They still changed for dinner. We collected nettles, mushrooms, and berries. These holidays were the high point of my life. I continued to correspond with Mrs. Boston until one day Sybil replied to my letter, telling me that her mother had died. I was very sad to lose my friend.

It was during that first summer holiday that the telegram arrived. It was addressed to Mrs. Boston, Lansdown, Great Missenden, Bucks. It read:

"*MUTTI HEUTE ZURÜCKGEKEHRT—VATI*"
(MOTHER CAME BACK TODAY—FATHER)

It was the best news I ever received in my life.

Mother had missed her second appointment with death, but it was a close call. The telegram was dated 4 August 1939.

The full story came out later.

Chapter Forty-Two

IMPRISONED IN FULSBÜTTEL

Sometime in 1937 or 1938, Julius Silberbach, Aunt Rosa's brother-in-law, brought home with him from one of his journeys, a large blousy lady and installed her as his housekeeper-companion. He was a widower, and she was either widowed, divorced, or *mal maritata*, I forget which. They later married in South America.

Frau Schneider had curled jet-black hair that may have been dyed, and very red cheeks that may have been rouged, and she dripped with diamonds. I was fascinated by a huge diamond that scattered a bluish light in all directions, as she moved her pudgy hand. The question of whether the diamonds pre-dated Julius Silberbach, who was rich, was much discussed, but never resolved.

Despite her suspicions about the hair and the cheeks, Mother took to Frau Schneider the moment they met. Reflected in those jewels, Mother saw the lights of the big city, the sophistication and knowledge of the world that Mother lacked and longed for. Frau Schneider joined the long line of older women at whose feet Mother was pleased to sit.

When Father was resident in Buchenwald, Frau Schneider told her about a Uruguayan consul, who, against a large consideration, issued visas to concentration camp inmates. Valid visas were passports to release, and all Mother wanted was to get Father out. Walter's mission to Cologne had failed to produce immediate results. So Mother jumped at the Uruguay option and paid up. I have a vague memory of the pair of them, Mother and Frau Schneider, phoning the consul, in the *Herrenzimmer* of all places. It was dangerous, since Jewish phones were being tapped—some people even ripped out their phones—but Mother was desperate.

The consul was later caught, and his list of subscribers found. It included Mother's name. She was arrested and imprisoned in Fulsbüttel, a suburb of Hamburg, the city where the consul had his base.

Mother did not speak much about her experiences in prison, but I gathered that she was not ill-treated the way the men had been in Buchenwald. She struck up a friendship with an aristocratic chief wardress, a Frau von Something or Other, a woman who recognized an ideal *Hausfrau* when she saw one. She gave Mother work in the ironing room, which was the best thing that could have happened to Mother under the circumstances.

Mother's experience in prison seems to have been far less traumatic than her stay in the Bethel institution, when she was so worried about Father's fate in the camp, as well as her own trouble with the Gestapo. Now it was Father's turn to be desperate. Anything—anything to get his wife out and leave Germany behind.

I think it was Uncle Walter who heard about Heinrich Skapowker. It was he who went to Hamburg to meet this gentleman. The rendezvous was at a nightclub, called, I think, the Alcazar. It was on the Reeperbahn, the red-light district by the port, which has been called the world's most wicked mile. We used to sing a song, "*In Hamburg auf der Reeperbahn.*"

Herr Skapowker was a small man, ugly as sin, according to Uncle Walter. He called himself a *Wirtschaftsberater*, an economic adviser, or accountant. He was in fact a go-between: he moved between the S.S. leadership and their victims. One thinks of the S.S. as fanatics, motivated solely by a crazy ideology. In fact, some of their leaders were extremely corrupt. At their second meeting, Herr Skapowker, in Uncle Walter's presence, telephoned—yes, telephoned—the Prince of Darkness himself. Whether it really was Heinrich Himmler who answered, we shall never know, but that was how Herr Skapowker addressed the party at the other end of the line, using his correct title.

Whether it was Himmler or not, it was someone who could produce results. The price for Mother's release was upped several times as more people had to be taken care of. Luckily, my parents still had resources on which Göring had not yet laid his hands. I do not remember the sum that finally changed hands, but it was large. Father had to trust Skapowker. He had no other choice.

The date of the trial was put forward. Mother could not be told about the bribe, since there were always guards about. Skapowker acted as her unofficial lawyer, advising her at every step. She put up a very brave show, as she had done in the Göring case.

"I only did what any wife would have done," she told the presiding judge. "Would you not have done the same if your wife had been taken away to a camp? I have a clear conscience. I meant no harm to anyone. All I wanted was to get my husband free."

Mother stood up well under pressure. It was she, not Father, who dealt with the authorities in Germany. During the early years in England, when things were very difficult, it was she who kept the family together. Father had a lower breaking point. The only time Mother succumbed was in Bethel, where, surrounded by the mentally disturbed, she brooded over Father's fate and her own.

Mother was acquitted. Herr Skapowker sent her flowers with a note, which she kept. It shows him as a man of good sentiments and casts a light on Mother's faith. The note is rather difficult to decipher. Herr Skapowker uses the old-fashioned *Suetterlin* script, which we learned at school before the Latin script. I think this is what it says:

"My dear Mrs. Katz, Flowers often bear silent witness, and these are meant to tell you that the spokes of your wheel of fate were as strong as your trust in God. May the future bring you only what is good and beneficent. Your H. Skapowker." (*Meine liebe Frau Katz, Blumen sind oft Stumme Zeugen, und diese hier sollen Ihnen sagen, dass die Speichen Ihres Schicksalsrades so stark wie das Vertrauen zu Gott waren. Möge Ihnen daher die Zukunft auch nur Gutes und Gütiges bringen. Ihr H. Skapowker.*)

The incredible part of the story is this: Heinrich Skapowker, intimate of S.S. leaders, was a Jew!

"He looked like three Jews," said Uncle Walter.

"He was not good-looking," said Mother, "but he had great charm. He knew what was due to a lady."

The money Father handed over could never have settled the debt we owe Skapowker. He saved Mother. I wonder if he managed to save himself. I so much hope that he did, but I fear he did not.

Chapter Forty-Three

GOOD-BYE, EGYPT

I still have the telegram the Sterns sent from Cardiff: "Visa Ba/23210 through Berlin Consulate Herman Mimy [sic] granted." The year was 1939, the hour 14:30, but time has worn off the day and the month. A surety of two hundred pounds sterling had to be placed before the visa could be granted. The money had been given to Aunt Grete's Mr. Stephenson when he visited us in Schötmar.

Other documents were needed before my parents could exit their Egypt. A release had to be obtained from Herr Künne, the new owner of the factory, now renamed *Westdeutsche Bürstenfabrik* (West German Brush Factory):

"I hereby attest to Herr Hermann Katz, owner of the former firm, Hermann Katz and Co., Brush Factory, Schötmar, which I have taken over, that he conducted the business in accordance with the regulations and that I have so far had no grounds for complaint."

Herr Künne was a decent man. He could have made trouble.

Father also had to prepare a short curriculum vitae for the German authorities. In it, he confirmed that his factory, after being in existence for twenty years, was duly "Aryanized" on 15 February 1939.

Then there was the affidavit Father had to swear before the United States Vice Consul in Bremen, stating that the household goods he was sending to his brother in New York had been in his possession for more than one year:

"Before me, Francis A. Lane, Vice Consul of the United States of America at Bremen, Germany, duly commissioned and qualified, personally appeared Mr. Hermann Israel Katz, of Schötmar, Lippe, Germany, who being duly sworn according to law, deposes and says . . . ."

Father had signed his curriculum vitae "Hermann Katz." For the affidavit, Mr. Lane had to use the additional name a kindly government had bestowed on him and all other male Jews. I left Germany before I could be similarly blessed. Mother, like other women of her kind, was presented with the name Sara.

Father did not mind Israel, but Mother hated her new Jewish-sounding name. It was another humiliation. German gentiles did not use names like Sara, David, Rebecca, and the like.

It is surprising that the Nazis, with their passion for neatness, did not give their Jewish ex-citizens names that were cognate. Sara was Israel's (Jacob's) grandmother. Why not Abraham and Sara, or Israel and Leah or Rachel? But then, nothing is perfect in this world.

Mother did not want to go into exile without making sure that her chattels would follow. They had been squeezed into two containers—we called them "lifts"—five metres by four each. These were destined for the United States. Mother would have to do without in England, which we considered a temporary sojourn, until the U.S. quota number came through. Then a more settled life would begin in the Land of the Free, complete with *Kredenzen* (sideboards) Numbers One and Two.

A last-minute meeting was arranged in far-off Dresden between Father and the forwarding agent, the Italian Bona. Father sent a telegram to Bona's bosses, Hoelzer and Co., Bremen, saying that he could not keep the rendezvous, and suggested Leipzig instead. Bona wrote back from Prague on August 16 that he could not travel via Leipzig because there were no adequate connections. It was urgent that Father meet him in Dresden on August 24, immediately after the arrival of his train at 12:36 p.m. There are no documents to confirm whether the meeting took place.

The two containers never made it to America. Restitution enquiries after the war found that they had been looted by the S.S. This must have been either in Bremen or Rotterdam. There is correspondence dated April 1940 to show that they were ready to be shipped to Rotterdam, after our relative and good friend, Dr. Zeckel, had paid the storage fees.

Something was saved. Eleven trunks, one parcel, one hat case, and a bicycle arrived in Cardiff via E.C. Downing, Agent, on 27 December 1939. They had been sent by Aunt Minna from Germany, via Dr. Zeckel, and contained the belongings of my parents and the two Walters. The bicycle was for the younger Walter.

There was no real joy, however. Four pieces of luggage were missing, as Father wrote bitterly to the Rotterdam agents on 8 January 1940—perhaps at Mother's invitation. There were men's suit jackets without the trousers and women's skirts without the matching jackets, thus proving conclusively, wrote Father, that something had gone very wrong. There is no record that the missing luggage was ever found.

When great worries are over, smaller ones fill the vacant spot. But those trunks and the suitcases they personally brought over were all that my parents had. They were allowed to take out only the equivalent of ten shillings (half a pound sterling) in cash. There were a few pounds leftover from the money Mr. Stephenson took out, but that was it. They had escaped with their lives, but they were broke.

It was the thought of future penury that almost cost my parents their lives. My parents were saddled with enormous taxes. They had to find their share of the *Sühneleistung*, the expiation payment imposed on all Jews, and they had to pay the *Reichsfluchtsteuer*, the Reich flight tax, for the privilege of fleeing the country that did not want them. The whole thing came to about sixty-nine thousand marks. Herr Künne eventually paid seventy thousand marks for the factory, its contents and Hektor, the carthorse, but there was a gap between the time the taxes were due and the Künne sale. So my parents had to endure the humiliation of a *Pfändungsverfügung*, a decree of forfeiture. They were in effect bankrupted. This was the reward for all their hard work and for giving employment to so many people, sometimes in very hard times.[61]

My parents never saw a pfennig of Herr Künne's money. The Nazis confiscated everything, but on the first of each month, they paid my parents a thousand marks for living expenses. Father wanted to wait until September 1 for the next instalment to come through, whether

---

[61] For details of the whole sorry business, see Wiesekopsieker's excellent research, op. cit, especially p.168.

to buy more things to take to England or somehow to smuggle out the money, I cannot tell.

Uncle Walter would have none of it. His house was near the railway line, and he had seen a lot of troop movements in August 1939. Something was up. There was no time to lose. He said to Father, "Hermann, if you and Emmy want to stay, you can stay, but I am leaving."

My uncle told this story a number of times after my parents' death. There was pride in his voice. He wanted to make it quite clear that but for him my parents would have perished.

Cousin Walter had left for England in May, via Ostend. He remembers that the S.S. boarded the train in Aachen to inspect the passengers. They asked him to show his Hitler Youth pass. He managed to spin some story about where he had left his pass, but it was a tense moment. He had a valid transit visa for England, but did not have to use it because he travelled on a special program organized by the Quakers.

Uncle Walter got out by a scam. He had no visa, but he was able to use his son's. They had the same name, and no one bothered to check closely.

My parents and Uncle Walter travelled by train to Rotterdam, where my parents collected some suitcases stored with the Zeckels. From Rotterdam they took a boat to Tilbury on 29 August 1939. It was the last boat to sail that route before Hitler invaded Poland. The next day I saw them in Cardiff.

I had been there for a week, having made my way from High Wycombe by bus. Uncle Alfred Stern kept me on meagre rations, and I remember hankering after the relative plenty of the hostel. But as to the moment of reunion with my parents, the moment I had longed for so much, I remember nothing at all about it. Perhaps it was an anticlimax. What I remember is the joy of that telegram, "Mother came home today." Then I knew I would see them again, that everything would be all right. It was, but only just.

On September 3, I travelled back to the hostel. At Gloucester, we changed drivers. Some of the passengers got out to stretch their legs. They came back with the news. Prime Minister Chamberlain had announced that my new country was at war with my old. Now Hitler would get his comeuppance. I did not realize then what a narrow escape my parents had made. The war would close the doors on the Jews still in pharaoh's domain.

The early days were hard for my parents. Father had known some poverty and hardship in his youth. For Mother, it was a new experience, but she adapted better than he did. She was lucky. She was able to get work as a supervisor in the wire-drawing and wire-twisting department of a Cardiff brush factory, at the princely salary of three pounds, one shilling, and three pence per week. She was in her element again.

Then came the edict that "enemy aliens" had to move from sensitive areas. Cardiff is on the sea, so Mother lost her job. They had to move inland. There were desperate calls to the Boltons and the Bostons to see if they could find a place for my parents. In the end, they landed in a hamlet called East Challow, near Wantage, where young Walter was working on a farm. Mother spent much of her time on her knees, scrubbing monastery floors, still fighting the good fight against dirt and dust, and being paid for it. She left with a glowing testimony from the nuns. I am sure that monastery had never been so clean before she came on the scene and was never so clean again after she left it.

Father and Uncle Walter could not get work in Cardiff. They sat at home and moped. Father crammed his notebooks with nonidiomatic English, preparing for the day when he would make good. Meanwhile, they were all paying guests of the Sterns. Mother paid over her wages to them and some of the little Stephenson money they had left.

Alfred Stern may have helped save my parents' lives, but he was a petty tyrant. Small, dark, pudgy, balding, rosy-cheeked—he strutted about in his domain terrorizing those in his power. My first week in England, spent at his home in Barnes, was a nightmare. I was without my parents for the first time in my life, in a strange country, and he could see that I was timid, so he set out to frighten me. He bawled at me for no particular reason, flashing his dark eyes and pink-faced fury. He monitored my every bite and told me that my greed was bankrupting him. I think he enjoyed my fear and discomfort. The hostel in High Wycombe came as a welcome relief.

Now it was my parents' and Uncle Walter's turn. He treated them like naughty children. They had to be in bed by nine o'clock; otherwise, he would do his blazing eyes act and scream at them. And 27 Neville

Street was not the place to satisfy healthy country appetites. They all knew what was expected of them.

"Emmy, do you want a second helping?"

"No thank you, Alfred."

"Hermann, do you want a second helping?"

"No thank you, Alfred."

"Walter, do you want a second helping?"

"No thank you, Alfred."

"Very good. Then there's enough for me to eat." Alfred Stern piled up his plate and kept eating away. The new immigrants sat, watching hungrily.

Father and Uncle Walter were furious. How dare the little upstart treat them like this. Mother advised calm.

"It's not important. We won't be at his mercy forever. What matters is that we have left that terrible country. We are free now. How wonderful it is to be free!"

From left to right: three bathing beauties—
Emmy, Vernon, and Madame de Bruyn

From left to right: Emmy, Vernon, and Hermann in La Panne, Belgium

Vernon's class at the *Städtische Realschule* of Bad Salzuflen; Vernon is in the middle of the second row wearing a white shirt; *Oberlehrer* Felten is on the left in the second row

Vernon, the cherry tree and manure in Laubach

From left to right: Hermann, Helene, and Moritz

The burned synagogue in Schötmar after *Kristallnacht*

From left to right: Hans Stern, Hedwig Stern, Frau Stern, and Alfred Stern

The Boltons (second row on the right) and the hostel boys;
Vernon is the fourth from the left in the second row

Lansdown

The Bostons at Lansdown; from left to right: Vernon, Mrs. Boston, Peg (sitting), Mrs. Walsh (mother of Angela and Rodney), Captain Bouquet, Angela, Rodney, the nanny, and two of Mrs. Boston's grandchildren

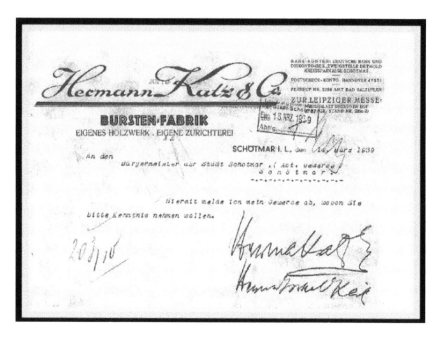

Father's letter confirming the end of his ownership of the business that is
signed both as "Hermann Katz" and as "Hermann Israel Katz"

Mother

Father

Uncle Walter

From left to right: Cousin Walter and Gertrud
soon after they came to England

From left to right: Mother and Father

The family and friends in England in 1962; this was
the last photograph of Mother before she died

From left to right: Vernon, Ingelore, Cousin Walter,
and Gisela in England in 1992.

Vernon

THE RETURN

Chapter Forty-Four

THE RETURN

October 1988

I did not mean to go back—ever, but here I am at Bad Salzuflen station. I do not recognize a thing—no landmarks of any kind. It would have been different had I arrived in Schötmar, but its tiny train station disappeared long ago. So has Schötmar itself, absorbed along with even lesser townlets by greater Bad Salzuflen.

It is thirty-seven years after a brief post-war visit with my dear parents. The salt spring spa is celebrating its five hundredth anniversary. It has much to celebrate. Some years it attracts more visitors than any other spa in Germany. Jewish visitors' week was part of the celebrations. That was in August. I was invited, but the invitation did not reach me.

So why go now? I need to check some facts for this book. I hope to lay some ghosts to rest. I want to see the Wortmann-Flieder family with whom I have kept in touch. Maybe I'll see Fritz Schmidtpott, our former office boy and confidant, if he is still alive.

I am quite scared. What will be released from the dungeons of the mind? What will I learn that I would rather not know? The crimes that were committed will cry out until the end of time, and here I am among those who committed them. But, as Mother used to say, "I have said *A*, now I must say *B*." I have started these memoirs, and I must see them through. What a brave old boy!

I alight at the best hotel in town. No pension for me—none of those fat white mansions bulging with bow windows and crowned with little alcoves—with names like Haus Eden, Haus Berlin, Haus Schönemeier. At the Maritim, I'll suffer in comfort. Friendly young people receive me. Nothing to fear there. I go down to dinner, and there they are, ample bottoms pressed into opulent armchairs, the old people with their evil-looking faces. They watch sullenly as I take my place. In that huge dining room, I see but a single kind mild face, an elderly woman sitting alone beside the square wooden pillars.

I explain to the headwaiter that I prefer vegetarian food, though I will eat fish, but no meat of any sort.

He bows. "*Natürlich, Herr Katz.* [Of course, Mr. Katz.] *Kein Problem.*" "No problem" has caught on in Germany too.

Had I signed in as Dr. Katz, the bow would no doubt have been deeper, but I did not want to be Herr Doktored throughout my visit.

My fellow diners fix unfriendly eyes on me. Does the name "Katz" bring back any memories?

Some days later in Bielefeld, I look at the huge black-bound memorial volumes that contain the names of those who were murdered. The books are almost too big to handle. In the volume that contains the letter "K," I do a rough count of the Katz's there. Just under seven hundred names.

The day after my arrival, I walk in the Kurpark, the spa park, autumn foliage gleaming on the trees, as well as under the trees, where they look like offerings. I walk past the dahlias and come to a perfect little circular temple, its domed roof supported by Greek columns. In its middle, walled in and out of sight, the holy of holies, the spring of life—the water. This is the Leopoldssprudel, said to be the oldest spring in Bad Salzuflen. How often I walked past it on those longed for outings with Mother and my cousins.

I could not have chosen a worse place than Bad Salzuflen. Nearly everyone is my generation or older. Those involved in the Final Solution were not just a few. There were many thousands. While post-war German governments did their best to make amends for the crimes of their predecessor, the judiciary were notoriously lenient towards former Nazis. Many of the judges served under the Third Reich—no others were available. They looked after their own. There must be some very nasty customers still at large.

People stare at me aggressively as I walk in the park. When I return their gaze, they look away. Sometimes I look at them first, and they also look away. Do they really have such evil eyes or am I imagining it?

Some of the women's eyes seem worse than the men's. They wear these pudding basin hats or the tall, almost conical hats we used to call *Rischeshüte* (anti-Semite) hats. I see one particularly dangerous-looking black velvet specimen, topped by a white feather. The face beneath it does nothing to reassure me. This woman is dressed in a check hunting costume. She carries a stick and has thick sturdy legs with well-developed calves, the kind that are a common sight from the Rhine to the Urals, but rare in the Home Counties, the sort that don't look good in court shoes. Diana the Huntress is wearing sensible low heels.

She stares at me aggressively, and when I return the stare, she looks away. That happens again and again, whether it is the square woman in the square-cut raincoat or the sharp-nosed man in the *Lodenmäntel* (a green overcoat common in Germany). They stare and look away—aggression and guilt. If I look at them first, they also look away. These old people have something to hide. When you have lived twelve years under a brutal dictatorship, it is hard to come out unscathed. And most of them loved their housepainter until he led them to defeat.

There is something about those eyes. The eyes were the first thing that struck me in 1951, when the eyes were younger. They are hard, with a suppressed violence. Or is it all my imagination? The dark smiling eyes of the Yugoslav maid at the hotel come as something of a relief.

Some weeks later, back in England, I see a play on television, based on the life in Germany of Christabel Bielenberg, an English girl married to a German. A posse of female air raid wardens on patrol, shouting "*Heil Hitler*" catch the heroine bending over the radio listening to the BBC. It's a tense moment, but I could only laugh. The English girls playing the gorgons had such mild humorous English eyes. No one could mistake them for Nazis, despite their uniforms and their peaked caps with Nazi insignia.

I walk through the forest to the salt-water springs. The woman at the ticket counter is speaking on the telephone. Her forehead creases, her voice rises, she hits the air, and she is laying down the law. Broadly built, middle aged, hard faced, wearing leather bands on her wrists, she looks like the type who wipes the floor with her husband, should there be a man unfortunate and foolish enough to occupy that position. At last, she stops shouting at her unseen adversary, puts down the phone, and turns to me.

"One ticket for the baths, please."

"Do you have your *Kurkarte*," she growls. The grainy voice fits her perfectly.

The *Kurkarte*, or spa card, is the passport to the baths, the pump room, the orchestra and much else.

"I am sorry. I left it at my hotel. I can give you the name of the hotel."

The square chin juts out in my direction.

"Spa cards are there to be shown; otherwise what is the point of issuing them?" she snaps. "I'll have to charge you extra."

She has chosen the wrong customer. I bite back.

"Ticket ladies are there to issue tickets, not to jabber on the phone and keep customers waiting."

There is a chorus of approval from the queue that has formed behind me. Her linear eyes arch into a look of surprised dislike. She issues the ticket and says nothing. I notice that it is at the lower price, the price for the privileged spa cardholders.

My policy has worked.

My father disliked lazy women. I dislike bossy ones, not the women who wrap you round their little finger—I rather like those—but the bullies who try to impose their will on you. You must not give them an inch.

As I savour my victory and pocket my change, I notice the woman's feet. She is wearing lace-up boots. As she gets up from her chair to answer the phone again, I notice that she limps.

The Italian proverb goes something like:

> *"Se a ciascun l'interno affanno*
> *Si vedesse in fronte scritto,*
> *Quanti mai che invidia fanno,*
> *Ci farebbero pietà."*

(If only one could read
People's distress on their foreheads,
No one would envy another,
Rather one would have pity.)

I had to see her feet to feel sorry—sorry for her disability and sorry about my hostile thoughts. Yes, she did keep us waiting while she fought her battles; yes, she is probably not all sweetness and light, but in charging me extra, she would only have done her duty. Thoughts are things. They are returned to you. She probably picked up my signals and returned my dislike before I even opened my mouth.

I have to be careful. My reactions show a nasty vindictive streak. Worse is to come.

I go to bathe in the salt springs. There are four large basins: hot, warm, warmish, and cool. The owner of a potbelly tells me that it's good for the circulation to change from one to the other. I go into the warm one, which is outside. The eight or so watering holes, founts where the fresh salt water bubbles up, are all occupied by large women. Some let the bubbles massage their backs, some, their behinds. One woman, with pumpkin breasts and thighs like temple columns, lets the water bubble up her cleavage, smiling with contentment.

There they all are Holbein's burgesses and their wives—in bathing caps. Yes, bathing caps are compulsory, the notice says so, and I am not wearing one. The outsider again. They look at me reproachfully, but no one says anything. I look at them. It is a long time since I have seen such a collection of nasty faces in one spot—gross bodies, hard eyes, fighting noses. I notice the fighting noses of the men. They jut out from under the bridge and come to a point—the point of attack.

Look at that man with the broad head, elongated narrow eyes, and high cheekbones. Now there's a Nazi type. I could do a *Stürmer* feature on him. But he looks like Adenauer, who was no Nazi. And that fatty with his fat face and hard eyes, a typical Nazi. But he looks like the recently deceased Josef Strauss, and he was no Nazi either.

I am not being fair to my German friends. Yes, some of my best friends are Germans, and that's the truth. I have some really good German friends.

It has to stop. What am I doing? These bathers are real people, not stereotypes, not collections of humours. I am dehumanizing them. That is how Final Solutions start. And here I am, doing just what the Nazis did to the Jews. I am not seeing people as human beings—as fathers, mothers, brothers, children. Of course, there are such things as group traits, but scratch them away, and you have an individual, melancholy or happy, thoughtful or active, straight or gay, unique, irreproducible. Scratch away the individual qualities and quirks, and you have a soul. Scratch away the limitations of the individual soul, and you have just one universal reality.

That is my belief, but my guts are shouting something else. They say, "You people are not pleasant to look at. I don't like you." And for the older people, there is that most nagging of questions: Where were you and what were you doing in those twelve years from 1933 to 1945? Did you just stand around shouting "*Sieg Heil*" and waving flowers, or did you do more and switch on the gas? Those years have marked me as they have marked them. I cannot fully transcend my history.

At least the youngsters look much like youngsters elsewhere in Europe. I don't have to play the eye game with them. And they matter more than a few old Nazi has-beens. To those old Nazis I say, "Enjoy the evenings of your lives as best you can. I don't want revenge, only that what was done should not be forgotten, explained away or swept under the carpet. The more squarely it is faced, the less its burden."

If it were up to me, I'd leave those old people to their consciences. But it's not up to me.

Schoolchildren in Bad Salzuflen were sent out to ask what people knew about the Jews. The replies were mostly: "We do not know; we do not want to talk about it." The teacher who published the research received hate mail.

Whenever you talk of the Holocaust to a German who lived through the Third Reich, the reaction is nearly always the same. It is as if you pressed a button and out comes:

"We did not know" and "We suffered too." If only people of the older generation could bring themselves to accept some responsibility for the actions of a regime most of them supported with enthusiasm, if only they could say "we are sorry" and shed a few tears, they would feel so liberated. But no. That is too much to take on board. Better to shove it under the carpet and let it fester.

Quite a few Germans of younger generations—I met some of them on this visit—face the Holocaust head on, but not many of their predecessors' generations can bring themselves to do so. They always feel that they have to defend themselves.

I have also met some younger people, who, while not denying the Holocaust, are a little fed up with having it rammed down their throats. After all, it was before their time. They have a point, but those who do talk about it and face it are the finer people.

Next day, Magdalene Wortmann collects me at the hotel. Her parents and aunt showed us kindness in hard times, and we met the family on our 1951 visit. Thirty-seven years is a long time.

"Would you have recognized me without Margriet?" I ask. Magdalene has brought along her niece who visited me in London a few years ago.

"Well, I don't know. You used to have that lovely wavy brown hair."

Everyone who knew me long ago remembers that hair—long gone. It must have been my best feature. She sends me a kindly smile. I would not have recognized her. I only remember those golden pigtails of long ago. She now has short grey hair curled by a good hairdresser. She is tall and thin like her father. I expected her to be pious and dowdy. Pious she is, but dowdy she is not. Under a grey fashionably cut raincoat, I see an elegant blue crew-neck sweater with shiny self-colour spots.

"You have good eyes, Magdalene."

She looks embarrassed, but I had to say it. I have seen few good eyes these past two days. Hers are true and deep blue.

We talk of Margriet's London visit. Last things first. It helps to bridge the gap.

Magdalene is deeply religious, but she does not push her religion; it is so much part of her.

Margriet drives us to their house. I don't recognize anything on the way. Where is the Allee, the avenue of trees where we used to walk on Sunday afternoons? Where are those chestnut trees that marked the early stations of my cross—the walk to Bad Salzuflen and high school? Where is the grand Hoffman house where my little girl friend lived?

Where is the *Hoffmansstift?* All gone, swallowed up by a road-widening programme.

Magdalene explains, "That modern building on the left is the new town hall. That's where the *Hoffmansstift* used to be." That was the local hospital, funded by the Hoffman starch family.

Where is Schötmar? We go into a huge supermarket. Supermarkets don't belong to the Schötmar of my imagination.

"You must remember the Wevelsburg." Magdalene points to a corner hostelry painted a particularly loud come-hither shade of green.

I remember the name more than the place. That was where Fritz Schmidtpott used to take Grandfather to get away from Grandmother and see a bit of life. Wasn't it owned by that Nazi pig dealer who made things difficult for Uncle Walter? I must ask Walter when I get back to England, when I get back home. This place certainly does not feel like home.

When we get to the Neue Strasse, where the Wortmanns live, there are reminders of the past. The cobblestones are still there, but without the horse dung. Grandmother's rental house, where the Dreiers kept their pigs and the Schlichts their piano, was bombed and is no more. It jutted out into the road, which is now wider. The Wortmann house is not to be seen. We stop in front of a modern two-story house. "Why did you pull down your beautiful old house?" I ask Magdalene. "We could not save it. The beams were rotting. And the new house is much easier to run."

I am welcomed by Magdalene's younger sister, Erna, and her husband, Hans Flieder. Erna is very *hausfräulich*, the typical Schötmar *Hausfrau*. She wears a sensible warm-looking violet cardigan, the kind they used to make in Clackmannanshire. She has a great sense of humour. Hans is smallish, red-faced with faithful blue-grey eyes. I am among the good Germans.

We speak of our parents. "Erna, you look like your mother. I can see her now in the kitchen with a rolling pin and flour on her hands." Erna brings a photo. Frau Wortmann is dressed entirely in black with a wide-brimmed black hat. Her long face has a sad expression.

"Mother always looked so serious. I have never been able to find a photo of her smiling. She was a serious woman."

"But a good woman," I add. "She knew that what was happening in Germany was wrong."

"So did my father." Magdalene brings a photograph of him. He is tall and thin.

"Yes, Magdalene looks more like our father," says Erna.

"He was just a simple cigar maker working for Wetzler and Co., rolling cigars. He rolled cigars all his life."

I had not realized that we had a cigar factory in Schötmar although in my day, most people there smoked cigars. One saw fewer cigarettes.

"But he knew what was right and what was wrong," Magdalene continues. "He thought for himself. He would not join the party and he would not let me join the BDM.[62] And, to tell you the truth, I was sorry at the time. I resented it a little." She speaks softly and with feeling. "All my friends were in it. I wanted to be with them, go for outings, and dress up—the white blouse and blue skirt, the knotted handkerchief. And they had those lovely multicolour wool jackets at the time, 'Berchtesgadener' I think they called them, after Hitler's home. I felt left out."

I like her honesty. I like it very much. Most Germans of her generation would not admit such thoughts, but she has nothing to hide.

"I understand that very well, Magdalene," I reassured her. "As a child you want to be like other children. You don't want to be an outsider. So no one in your family joined?"

"Yes, I did in the end," said Erna. "Someone had to bale out the family. Someone had to join. It was known that we were against the regime. Also, I needed to do it to get a job. So I had to sacrifice myself." She smiled, a little shamefacedly. "We had to be careful too. One of my mother's sisters was a great Nazi. She used to go to Berchtesgaden regularly, just to catch a glimpse of Hitler.

"And then, Hitler did offer employment—the motorways and so on. He knew it was all for war, but how were we to know that? People were better off. My mother did not approve on religious grounds."

And then she said the thing that I have heard many Germans say, even decent ones like this family.

"You know, we too suffered in the war."

---

[62] Bund Deutscher Mädchen, the Nazi League for German Girls, which was the female branch of the Hitler Youth.

I wanted to say, "Of course you suffered hardship, bombing, occupation, all the horrors of the war that your government inflicted on the world. But your relatives and friends, the people who worshipped at your beloved church and others like it—they were not snatched from their homes, herded into cattle trucks, subjected to unspeakable indignities and finally crammed naked into airtight chambers and gassed. How can you possibly speak of the two things in the same breath?" But these were good people, people who helped us when others turned away from us. I did not want to spoil our get-together. But perhaps I should have said something.

Erna remembers the war. "I can see my father crouching over the old radio in the front room—listening to the BBC—we called the radio the 'Göbbelsblaster.' He sent me walking up and down the street to warn him if someone could look in. Listening to the BBC was a really serious offence. My father always said that the war would end badly for us."

"I'll always be grateful to your mother's sister for what she did for my grandmother," I tell them. "Yes, our 'Nisse' [Deaconess].[63] She wished she could have progressed further in her order. We saw it from her diaries. She had a strong will and found it difficult to bend."

"Perhaps she saved my parents' lives. Who knows whether my mother would have planned to emigrate had she not known Grandmother would be safe with the deaconesses?"

We then spoke of my mother. They had a photograph of her standing with some of the workpeople at the back of the factory.

"Your mother always wore that blue overall with kerchief to match. She looked just like her factory hands. And isn't that Hans Profet on the far right?" Erna points to a figure in plus fours and overall. "He became a great Nazi."

"My mother used to help his mother a lot," I said. "In the end, she got small thanks."

"Your mother was always helping people," Erna replied. "We had an old stove and your mother always made sure that we got some wood shavings and small logs to burn. I remember she asked me to leave a sack outside the house so that she could fill it with really good firewood.

---

[63]   She arranged for Grandmother to live in the home run by the sisters.

That was towards the end, because it wasn't good for me to be seen in the factory."

"You were always such a well-spoken boy," Erna recalls *a propos* of nothing in particular. "Your mother always took great care that you spoke only the best German. Not like us."

It reminds me that I have been chatting easily in German for two hours, my accent remarkably like that of the sisters (Hans came from East Germany). How effortlessly one slips back into the mother tongue. It makes no difference that the mother country behaved like a wicked stepmother.

Magdalene takes me back to the hotel. I catch a glimpse of our old house.

"I did not want to take you that way while it was light on the first day. It would have been too much of a shock. It's in such a bad state."

In the dark, it did not look all that different, but something was missing.

"What's happened to the balcony?"

"They had to pull that down. It was becoming dangerous."

The next day I see why they did not want to shock me. The house is in an awful state. It can't have had a coat of paint since I last saw it thirty-seven years ago. It used to be a lovely dark gold; it is now a dirty dove grey. The paint is crumbling. The window surrounds, painted white a very long time ago, are crumbling. A pane is missing above the once grand entrance door. I am completely unmoved by the sight of my old home. Or perhaps I refuse to let it move me.

Our house looks like a decrepit old woman when compared with the blousy *nouvelle riche* that rises up behind it. The former *Bürohaus*, where the Kaiser once ruled in tightly corseted splendour, now shines in bright pink glory, with new picture windows. It has been made into a family house by the daughter-in-law of Herr Künne (who "bought" our factory from my father) and is in a good state of repair.

"Your house is used to house immigrant workers and the owners have neglected it. I think it will be difficult to go in and see it," says Hans. "I could take you around but no one ever answers the door." These kind friends don't realize that after fifty odd years, I don't really care. I don't care one little bit.

We walk into the garden by the side of the house. It is a wilderness with overgrown grass and a young pine tree where the fountain used to be. No fountain, no grotto, no big lime tree. The south side of the house is bare, the paint is crumbling, and there is no clematis. The three false windows are bare.

"Why did they build false windows, and on the south side too?" I ask.

"It was so that they would have space to put the furniture there on the walls," someone replies. "They had big furniture in those days."

The space between the two houses where I played with Grandmother's defective wagon on my fourth birthday is so tiny. I remember it as huge. Our house looks smaller too, and I say something about how small it now seems to me.

"Oh no," says Erna. "It was one of the finest houses on the road. You were important people [*Ihr ward Leute*]. You had central heating. You even had sunblinds." That was my mother again. "No one else on the road had sunblinds. Old-fashioned shutters, yes, but not sunblinds."

We walk down the former vegetable garden by the side of the factory—just overgrown grass. A single plum tree remains, but no beds of strawberries or asparagus. There does not seem to be much activity in the factory. It makes ballpoint pens now. It seems smaller than I remember it. I was a boy, and everything seemed larger.

And then we walk behind the factory. The space there has grown bigger. It's enormous. No sawmill, no sheds, no piles of wood. There are now nine garages where Hektor's pad used to be. Next to them, in a field, the beginnings of a bus cemetery with one grave—the remains of a pink and green bus turning to rust. We walk to the right where the big shed with the cut wood used to be—another ten garages there. "The whole space must be twenty thousand square metres," says Hans. "They can only build in the surroundings. Not in the centre."

There are some of Mother's fruit trees, quite tall now, loaded with red apples. But most of the trees have been fenced off.

"They are in the Kordmöllers' garden. They must have bought some of that space."

It seems that my contemporary, Robert, the hare-lipped one, has been a master baker for forty years. He has just had a heart attack. Did I want to see them? Not particularly. I don't think they were rabid Nazis, but when things got bad, they turned their faces from us—and they were our next-door neighbours.

There is now a road where the path between the meadows used to be. It starts at Uncle Julius' house. We walk to his house at the end of the road. The stables are now a beer and soft drinks depository. There is a line of red and yellow plastic containers. A Mercedes standing in the courtyard with an open boot seems ready to be loaded with bottles. A yellow automat on the side of the house carries the legend *Zigaretten*. Smoke on one side, drink on the other—more business for the funeral parlour up the road.

The house is in good condition, even without its balcony. The four white columns, now relieved of their burden, stand guard over a veranda. Two columns stand free, and two half-columns are attached to the house. By the side entrance, where I went up to get my lunch in Aunt Minna's kitchen, there are now those large modern windows.

On what was our land, they have built a large block of very modern-looking flats with curved ship-like balconies. Next to it lies a long low-slung white building. Hans explains that this is the church of the Jehovah's Witnesses—all on our former property.

Erna remembers the time when this area was the *Holzplatz*, the log depository, where we played hide-and-seek. The woodpiles were so thick that no one could find us. Mother's orchard folly now feeds little Kordmöllers. Good luck to them. In other circumstances, I would now be master of it all, but I have absolutely no regrets.

Feelings are quite different when we leave the factory grounds, and I see the houses opposite ours. It is hard to recognize any of them. They are all tarted up. The Hamlets' house has been transformed into a fine family house. It seems that the new owners were not allowed to destroy the *Fachwerk*. They just covered it with a layer of modern material—a washed effect in camel brown. There are those large modern windows again. The house belongs to an undertaker. The stables behind the house, where Paul Hamlet kept his cattle, are now an undertaker's parlour. It reminds me too much of the giant undertaker that was the Third Reich.

The Wallhausen's place, with its square modern windows, is also unrecognizable. So is Aunt Alma's house. It has two shop windows in place of one. The window behind which the *unglückliches Kind* (unfortunate disabled child) sat among grey meat and flour-filled sausages, now displays reproduction furniture. The old inhabitants would not recognize the graceful white building.

It feels wrong somehow that there is nothing that reminds us of the old inhabitants. How can anyone bear to live in those houses? Our house, where no one died an unnatural death, could have been modernized. But the houses of those murdered should have been left as they were, as memorials. But how could they? Then Germany would have thousands upon thousands of museums. My friends comment how tastefully everything has been converted. I keep my thoughts to myself.

Sander's *Konditorei* (pastry shop) is still there. The present incumbent, third generation I am told, is as fat as his predecessors. What can you expect when you work among such delights? Herr Rosenwald's shop, where they doled out the sweets for us children, is gone. It must have been where Alberto's, the Italian menswear shop, is now. We walk up the Aechternstrasse and stop in front of a house much like any other. That was the synagogue, Erna tells me. I can't believe it. But then I notice the ornamental railings at the top of the house and signs of old windows on the side, outlined in lighter colour cement. The woman who bought the house was not allowed to pull down anything that remained of the old synagogue; she could only build over it. The house of God that had been put to the torch was not to suffer final elimination by the bulldozer.

The house looks so much smaller than the synagogue. Pastor Höhner, friend of the Wortmann-Flieder family, is to remind me the next day that they played football with the Torah scrolls. I feel the desolation of this place. How can people live in such a house? Well, they do.

I have had enough for one day. I want to go home.

Erna prepares coffee and cakes to help turn us to other thoughts. I get a tour of their house. Everything is so well built and finished, much better than in English houses.

Erna points to the living room wall. "There are some photos of our old house."

"It's very much like the house I saw next door. You had the same square front addition window."

"Next door belongs to the Güses," says Erna. "You remember old Pitzeritz, who had the little grocer's shop? Güse was his son-in-law and our neighbour is his son."

The name "Güse" reminds me of the French "Guise," but there was little that was aristocratic about the thickset Pitzeritz son-in-law. "He became a Nazi, didn't he?" I ask. Erna confirms my suspicions. "I think you are right."

The next day, Hans accompanies me to Fritz Schmidtpott's house. It is not far from the Town Hall, near the Valhalla Strasse, a nice part of town. Yes, Fritz is still with us. I had phoned him the night before. He lives in a very nice modern house with a frontage of bricks or stones that look like tiles. I see a lot of them in Germany. A well-dressed blonde woman, perhaps in her fifties, ushers me in—Frau Schmidtpott. Fritz has done well for himself. His living room is elegant, like his wife, and bigger than many a London flat. He has let another part of the house.

Fritz is amazing. I have not seen him for fifty years and find little change. He is the same fast-talking, quick-thinking, lanky, long-nosed fixer, know-all with a heart of gold—the same twenty-year-old inhabiting a seventy-year-old body. He does not look his age, despite overcoming severe liver trouble. He married the woman who nursed him back to health. Now it's his heart—cardiac arrhythmia. His wife, considerably younger, is as quiet as he is lively. I like her very much. I feel they make a good pair.

We talk continuously for two and a half hours, pausing merely between sips of coffee and mouthfuls of cake.

I feel completely at home with Fritz. He was my parents' confidant, the one they trusted most completely. The Wortmanns said that they kept contact with my parents through Fritz, who lived in their house.

"The last time I saw your parents was when I came home from *Arbeitsdienst* [the period of compulsory work that the Nazis imposed]. I had to do that, I couldn't help it. On my return, I did some errands for your parents. Yes, I can see your mother now in her blue overall and kerchief. She always carried a pencil on her right ear. Your mother was quite a woman. She ran the factory by herself. Your father was away selling. Sometimes he stayed away as long as five weeks. Karl Weinhorst always drove him. He was no friend of the Nazis either. A thin man, completely bald."

"My father was bald too," I rejoin.

"Your father had a little hair at the back, but Karl had nothing. They got on very well.

"You had Fräulein Holländer [Else] working for you. She married the curly-haired Beckmann. And Fräulein Schröder."

"Erna," say I. "Yes, Erna was her name."

"And something I have thought about for a long time. You had a girl from Berlin, a very nice Jewish girl, about twenty-one to twenty-two, called Alice. Yes, I have often thought about her. I remember we went separately on our bicycles to Lage and there we met. And they caught us. What happened to her? Your mother said she had gone back to Berlin."

Another one infatuated with Alice.

I reply that I think that she must have died in the Holocaust. She had no plans to emigrate.

"Am I tiring Fritz?" I ask his wife, who looks worried.

"He'll be all right, but it'll be better if he sits comfortably."

We move back from the coffee table to the armchairs. Fritz tells of his war and how he made his way back from Russia. Quite dramatic, but I have forgotten the details. I am so happy that I met Fritz again. He died not that long after my visit.

The next day is a day of comparative rest. No walkabouts. The Flieders have invited Pastor Höhner and his wife from Bielefeld, to meet me.

"You must remember Herbert Höhner," says Magdalene. "The family lived opposite, just behind the Hamlets. The father was a carter and handyman. Herbert has retired from his ministry now."

Frankly, I don't remember a thing about him or his family. But he remembers me.

"You wore these fine velvet trousers and you had such beautiful wavy hair." Velvet trousers and wavy hair—my hallmarks. He uses the formal Sie, and I do likewise. With the Wortmann sisters and even with Hans, whom I did not know as a child, I fell at once into the familiar Du. Herbert Höhner was too old to be my playmate. He was friends with Egon Hamlet and Günter Wallhausen. He describes Egon as thin, pale, tallish, Günter as shorter, more muscular. For a time he was also very friendly with Cousin Walter.

"Walter and I were standing about as the veterans' S.A. brigade marched by. You are supposed to salute the flag. Walter and I looked at the marchers and laughed. When I came home, I got such a telling off from my uncle, who was also my godfather. He had been one of the marchers. My uncle said, 'If it hadn't been for me, you'd have been beaten up. Why were you with that Jew?' Later my father told me not to mind what my uncle said."

The pastor and I talked philosophy, but the more mundane things that all of us spoke about later are more interesting.

Erna: "Your mother wore a blue dress with large white spots. Everything fitted 100 percent. Quite the lady [*Ganz die Dame*]."

Vernon: "Yes, she liked to play the lady."

Erna: "She didn't have to play the lady; she *was* a lady. And your father was smart too. He wore light-coloured spats."

Vernon: "And later he bought his hats from the best hat shop in London."

Erna: "As soon as it gets colder, I have to wear a hat."

Herbert: "But you don't buy them in London." (He uses the familiar *Du* with Erna.)

Vernon: "The women here wear a kind of pudding-shaped hat."

Herbert: "Plum pudding."

Vernon: "The women used to wear triangular hats with a feather. We used to call them anti-Semites' hats."

Frau Höhner: "Did your grandparents live here too [as if we were immigrants]?"

Vernon: "My mother had the family's *Stammbaum* [genealogical tree] done. It went back to the Thirty Years' War (1618-1648). She thought it would help them if the Nazis knew how long we had lived in Germany. You can't imagine how German my parents were. They couldn't get it into their heads that they were not wanted in their own country."

Herbert: "One Jewish woman who came for the Jewish week told me that in the early days of the Nazis, her father flew the flag on Hitler's birthday. So *Deutsch National* [German Nationalist] was he."

Erna: "If things had not turned out as they did, would you have stayed in Schötmar?"

Vernon: "I would have become a brush manufacturer."

Herbert: "You had an enormous property."

Hans: "I reckon twenty thousand square metres at one hundred marks per square metre."

Herbert: "At the exhibition, the sum of 144,000 marks was mentioned."

Vernon: "We got only about seventy thousand marks and those were confiscated. After the war, it would have been better if my parents had taken a lump sum in restitution, rather than the pension. They did not live long enough."

Erna: "How old were your parents when they died?"

Vernon: "Father was seventy-five, Mother seventy-two."

Erna: "At least they had some good years."

Vernon: "On the whole, happy years in England, although it was difficult for them at first."

Hans: "I was a prisoner in Siberia for four years. We had a political officer, a Jew by the name of Feuerstein. He came to Russia in the 1920s. He spoke Yiddish, which, as a German, one can understand. People asked us if we saw Russians kill Jews in the German-occupied territories. We could not confirm or deny. But in the Baltic states . . ."

The conversation tails off.

Next day at my hotel, I am to meet Lotte Frass, who was at elementary school with me. She is Frau Bruns now. It must be more than fifty years since I have seen her. I left that school early in 1937. We came across her mother and stepfather in 1951. They ran the "Ratskeller" then, a posh restaurant by the ancient *Rathaus* (the old Town Hall) in Bad Salzuflen. My parents and I had lunch there, but Lotte was away, about to be married.

"How will we recognize each other," I ask her on the phone.

"I am still small," she says. "I have not grown much."

"You are small and I am bald," I tell her.

"Oh, that nice wavy hair is gone?"

"About three hairs remain."

I stand outside the hotel. She is unmistakable, petite, and very smart in a check costume. Grey hair, quite a lady.

She is very vivacious. We talk for nearly three hours. Amazing how one picks up the threads. She met her husband before the war. He came from a family of social democrats and her father-in-law was always in trouble with the Nazis. Her husband was captured in Russia and not released until 1949. His experiences left their mark, and he died young. She has two children, one a doctor. She was a schoolteacher and is now retired. I like her very much—the same lively intelligence she had as a child.

"Do you remember when the class went to the Hermannsdenkmal [the huge statue to the German chieftain in the Teutoburg forest]? Did we go by bus?"

"No," she replies, "we went by train to Detmold."

"And from there?"

"We walked, of course. It's only a few kilometres."

Yes, I remember now, but some of the kilometres were uphill. Quite a climb. I show her a photo of our class with *Lehrer* Sasse, in civvies, but with a Nazi Party badge in his lapel.

"Yes, that was on the school steps in Schötmar," I say.

"Maybe you would like to see a photo of my class in the *Realschule*"—the High School in Bad Salzuflen, also called *Oberschule*.

"Yes, my husband attended that. Oh, that's my husband there."

I do not remember the boy Bruns. I suppose he was not one of my persecutors if his father was such an anti-Nazi. I promise to have a copy made for her.

We talk of the Holocaust, of Indian philosophy. Can it explain those things?

I am happy we met. We have kept in touch.

I have met so many decent Germans, so why do I still have that gnawing feeling about them *en masse*?

There are four of us on our third and final walkabout into the past. Little Anne, wearing a fetching two-piece in her favourite colour, with matching pink windcheater to keep her warm, has joined us in her pushchair. Proud grandfather Hans is doing the pushing. At the corner where Schülerstrasse meets Begastrasse, I get them to pose for photographs in front of a lovely little *Fachwerk* house—Erna in her pudding-basin hat, Hans in his deerstalker, Anne in her finery. Upstairs in that house lived the Hamann sisters, little seamstresses, friends of Mother, who did her tailoring. For her grand square-looking costumes, Mother went to Potts on the opposite side of the Begastrasse. It is still there, still owned by the same family, still the best store in town. I wonder what Mother would have made of the chic scarlet separates designed for broomsticks that beckoned to us from the window across the road.

A little further down the road stood the *Stürmer* display cabinet, where passersby stopped to gape and smirk at thick-lipped hook-nosed monsters. As we pass the large window of a modern shop showing watches and jewellery, I get a funny feeling in my stomach. I am sure that where the shop now stands, there was once a cobbled courtyard leading to the house and stables of bow-legged Salomon Silberbach, whom they called Herz Salomon after his father, to distinguish him from all the other Silberbachs. The house stood at an angle to the street, the same angle as the fruiterer's place next to the watch shop. In the house of long ago, with a faint smell of cow dung wafting through her elegant interiors, Salomon's wife and Mother's bosom friend, Aunt Rosa, fed me chocolates and sweets. They went to Holland to join their daughter and thought they were safe.

We walk on. Erna goes up to a tall thickset woman with lank dark untidy hair. She is wearing a light brown overcoat that has seen better days. She is walking arm in arm with an older grey-haired woman. Erna turns to me.

"Do you remember Helga Deppe? She was in *Lehrer* Sasse's class with you in Schötmar."

"Oh, yes, I remember her. Her father had a grocers' shop on the far side of the Werre." Even as a child, Helga was on the big side. I can see her as she then was, wearing a dress with a check pattern top and plain skirt.

It transpires that Helga remembers me too and my "beautiful wavy-brown hair." The hair again. Shame—I started losing my best feature while still in my early twenties.

Helga turns towards me, but she is off by some thirty degrees. Only now do I notice the yellow armband with the black spots. Helga is blind. She does not seem very interested in my fate and me. She probably has other things on her mind. Slowly she walks away with her guide.

The little train station where Grandfather exacted obedience from his cattle, where Uncle Hugo and Oma Billa dazzled the citizenry on their mission to wed Aunt Grete with their son, where we started our journeys to Cologne, was closed down long ago. But the level crossing is still in operation, and we have to wait for the train to pass. Little Anne waves, but there is no response; it is only a goods train.

The tobacconist Greve, purveyor of cigars to Uncle Julius, is now Janski's, the travel agent, still close to the Bega, but I can see no rocks on which to break my bones and the modern light green iron railings look very secure.

The Werre, which flows higher, nearer to the road than the Bega, has two waterfalls. The one at right angles to the road used to feed the old mill by the side of the river. Erna tells me that she too was frightened by the Werre as a child.

"We grew corn on our allotment. Herbert Höhner's father brought it on his wagon to the mill to be made into flour. We took the flour to the baker who weighed it and gave us credit for so many loaves. Every time we collected a loaf, he ticked it off on our credit sheet."

We reach the Oerlinghauser Strasse. On the corner is the same old Tivoli, pub of the rowdies, not painted in shocking green like the Wevelsburg, but a demure white. We cross the road.

"We have to go through our cemetery," Erna explains. "Yours no longer has a separate entrance." I ask about the large new raw-looking church that hovers in the background. I am told that it is a new Catholic church. The new ecumenism—Protestants, Catholics, Jews, all in the same cemetery.

The first grave I see, just by the entrance, reads: "August und Friederike Dreier." Grandmother's old tenants are here to greet their one-time rent collector. August Dreier, pickled in alcohol, reached a ripe old age.

All the graves are beautifully kept, better than in any cemetery I have seen in England. There is a feeling of openness, flowers, gravel, small evergreens—not much shade.

At the very end of the cemetery, we come upon a shady enclave—no flowers, no shiny gravel, just tall trees and a carpet of ivy and fallen yellow leaves. We are in a different world, quiet and secret. In front, I notice a small grave. It stands out because its little black granite stone is tilted at about thirty degrees from the ground—a child's grave, the grave of the sister I never knew, Margot Katz, who lived for nine days in 1925. She seems to be the only Katz among a plethora of Hamlets, Eichmanns, and Silberbachs.

The oldest graves, arched, ornamented, weather beaten, have only Hebrew lettering, the outline of each grave buried under the leaves and the ivy. Around the newer graves, the ivy has been neatly trimmed. The fashion in the thirties was for severe rectangular black granite stones. Under the largest of these, on the far left, rest my grandparents. The grave is in good condition, but the stone can do with a cleaning.

Erna fetches a can of water and starts pouring it over the stone. I forgot to bring a cloth and take out my handkerchief.

"You keep your handkerchief," Erna commands. "I have an old one here." She starts wiping down the grave. I am touched by this gesture of friendship and care.

We clean my sister's grave, then Great Aunt Pauline's. I see she died in 1930. I was born in 1927, and I remember reciting a birthday poem for her, so my memories go back well before that disastrous fourth birthday when Grandmother's cart broke up into its constituent parts.

Erna brings another can. We get to work on more of the granite graves. The older ones—mossy, time patinated—don't seem to ask for a wash.

Hermann Rosenwald is here. His granite slab tells me he died in 1939, June I think, at any rate before war broke out. He lived to see his beloved synagogue put to the torch and the holy Torah scrolls used as footballs, but at least he was not put to the torch himself. He has a grave with his name on it. Three other Rosenwalds—Hermann's wife, brother, and sister—all well into their seventies, were not so fortunate. They are not here. The shadow of all those who might have rested here, who have no grave to their names, haunts this place, haunts me.

And the Jewish community of Schötmar as a whole? There were no great scholars, no brilliant doctors or lawyers; there was little Jewish learning, little secular learning. This was no Vienna or Granada. Civilization lost little when this community was dispersed, but humanity lost everything—lost itself.

There are two post-war graves. Julius Silberbach, brother of Salomon, could not wait to get back to his beloved Schötmar in spite of all that happened. He had to travel from Uruguay to Canada to get his German visa. He ended his life in his hometown in 1954 and joined his first wife in the graveyard. His daughter attended Jewish week. There are flowerpots on his grave—not very orthodox but neither was he.

The most recent grave is Willy Eichmann's. He was the only full-blooded Jew to have survived the war in Schötmar—thanks to the help of his Aryan in-laws. His daughter, Irmgard, is still living in Bad

Salzuflen, the sole survivor of Schötmar Jewry still *in situ*, and she is only half Jewish, "a half-breed of the first degree," as the Nuremberg laws so elegantly put it.

How is it that this cemetery was saved while the one in neighbouring Bad Salzuflen was razed to the ground and had a factory built over one part and an orchard planted over the other? During the worst period of terror, when even the dead were not allowed to rest, the little Jewish cemetery in the Oerlinghauser Strasse was left in peace because it was Aryan property. Irmgard told me that her father had persuaded a wealthy friend to buy the cemetery and made him promise not to build on it. The canaille could not trespass.

This cemetery dates only from the 1870s; before that, Schötmar Jews were buried in Bad Salzuflen. The graveyard has retained its simple Jewish character—no pomp, no flowers, just greenery and stone. It is well looked after. Erna heaps praise on the authorities. I think that was the least they could do and am not particularly grateful. I am grateful to Willy Eichmann for his brilliant strategy.

Hans has waited with little Anne in the Christian cemetery. Now Erna takes over the childcare. Hans and I have other business. Hans has told the mayor and the *Stadtdirektor*, the town director, that I am visiting and they have asked to meet me. We make our way home for a clean up and then to the new *Rathaus*, the Town Hall, modern, functional and large for a population of fifty thousand people.

We glance at an exhibition of local artists in the foyer, then make our way upstairs to the office of the mayor's secretary. She shows us into a conference room where we settle down on green-upholstered chairs. I am nervous. That old fear of authority. It is deaf to reason. The mayor should be nervous, not I. He comes in, tall, well dressed, wearing a brown jacket in a small check pattern of closely related colours that is the fashion just now. The smile behind the large gold-rimmed glasses is a little embarrassed. He is happy to welcome me back to my hometown. The finely cut features are topped by a fine head of blow-dried hair, worn quite long. He is prematurely grey. He is at least fifteen years my junior, so he is clean. He made some good speeches during Jewish week. The Flieders kept the newspaper cuttings.

The courtesies have just ended when the *Stadtdirektor* enters, and they start all over again. The mayor, or *Bürgermeister*, is a political appointee; the *Stadtdirektor* is the head of the town's civil service. He too is tall, slightly younger than the mayor, a trim athletic, good-looking man with dark wavy hair and dramatic eyebrows arching over clear grey-blue eyes that do not flinch. He is not embarrassed. I feel more at ease with him than with the mayor, whom I judge to be an introvert like me. He offers to take me on a tour of Schötmar the next day. I have already been that way and plead other engagements.

The *Stadtdirektor* hands me a leather-bound volume. They have the signatures of all those who attended Jewish week. Could I sign too? I try to think quickly. Would the dead approve? Clearly it would be churlish to refuse. These are well-meaning people doing what they can to make amends for the sins of their fathers.

They have me down as "Dr. Dr. Sir Katz." At the cost of disappointing expectations, I have to confess that I have neither a double doctorate nor a knighthood. Perhaps they are confusing me with Sir Hans Kornberg, a distant relative, who enjoys these distinctions. Or perhaps they think that in England we are all "Sirs." A thousand to one that neither Queen Elizabeth nor a future King Charles will dub me.

If I am not Dr. Dr., then what are my degrees, if any? "*Heisse Magister, heisse Doktor gar,*" says Goethe's Faust. I have the same degrees, an M.A. and a D.Phil, but from Oxford, not from Wittenberg. I am plain Dr. Katz. And I am in total agreement with my mediaeval predecessor about the value of book learning:

> "*Da steh ich nun, ich armer Thor*
> *Und bin so klug als wie zuvor.*"

> (Here now I stand, poor fool,
> What's more, I know as much as heretofore.)

I do not share my thoughts on higher education with the two gentlemen. The *Stadtdirektor* is also a *Herr Doktor.*

I inform them that I am happy about the way the Jewish cemetery is being kept. The stones could do with some cleaning and the ivy around the older stones should be trimmed, but otherwise, no complaints. Next day, I have second thoughts about the old stones. They look just right in their sea of ivy. I ask Hans, who knows the mayor, to tell him to leave well enough alone.

The two men tell me about the success of Jewish week in August and express their regret that their invitation did not reach me. The mayor shows me the address to which it was sent. Even the astute London postal service—I sometimes think it employs detectives—could not have found me with that address.

The town is making good its promise, made during Jewish week, to transform the desecrated Bad Salzuflen cemetery into a memorial park. It has bought the property and the buildings on it are being pulled down. About time too, I think. After all, it is more than forty-three years since we said good-bye to Adolf and his friends. Again I do not share my thoughts. It probably needed one, or more, generations to face the terrible past. The present mayor is clearly a high-minded man.

"We owe it not only to the dead and the survivors, but to the dignity of our town."

When I was searching for books on Jewish life in Lippe, a kind and helpful Bad Salzuflen bookseller told me how secretive the previous town archivist had been. No doubt he wanted to protect names. She said his successor was opening up the archives. A lot of research into the persecution of the Jews was being done, notably by a young schoolteacher named Höhn, who was getting his students to take an interest into a dark and hidden chapter of their country's history.

I felt that I wanted to meet this young man. He later contacted me and we talked for several hours. He told me, among other things, that a few gravestones were reerected in Bad Salzuflen after the war but not, as research in the archives revealed, on the site of the original cemetery. He showed me a plan of the gravestones and their dates. They had been put up higgledy piggledy—1931 next to 1902 and 1928 next to 1809.

I am glad that the spirit of *glasnost* has hit Bad Salzuflen. I tell the town's leaders that I had heard the archives were at last being opened. They do not seem happy to pursue this line of thought.

"Would you like to see the design of the memorial stone to be erected on the former site of the Bad Salzuflen cemetery?" The director looks at me with his clear blue eyes and asks if I would like a photocopy. He goes out to speak to the secretary.

The secretary brings in the plan for the stone. It is a good design with a menorah, the seven-headed Jewish candlestick, rising from the base. The mayor asks me if the Hebrew lettering is right. It seems all right to me, but I am no expert. The legend on the front of the stone will read:

"In remembrance of the 50 Jewish citizens of Bad Salzuflen and Schötmar who fell victim to the National Socialist dictatorship in the years from 1933 to 1945. The suffering and injustice inflicted on them must not be forgotten." (*Zur Erinnerung and die 50 jüdischen Bürger aus Bad Salzuflen und Schötmar, die Opfer der nazionalsozialistischen Diktatur in den Jahren 1933 bis 1945 wurden. Das ihnen zugefügte Leid und Unrecht darf nicht vergessen werden.*)

Admirable sentiments. If my parents and Uncle Walter had waited three days longer to make their exits, there would have been fifty-three names.

The mayor tells me that eighteen of those murdered came from Bad Salzuflen and thirty-two from Schötmar. They have a list of their names. Would I like a photocopy of that too? I would.

The list is brought in. I read:

Victims of the persecution of the Jews under National Socialist tyranny in Bad Salzuflen and Schötmar 1933-1945.

Bad Salzuflen:

Andermann, Kurt. [Yes, he had a men's outfitter shop in the main road.
We bought clothes there.]
Born 10.12.1919
Bad Salzuflen, Augustastr.4
Moved to Bodenbach/Elbe on 11.7.1938,
Declared as dead, Kz [concentration camp] Bergen-Belsen.
Sources: St. AD 72 Nachlass Staercke No.18
Bundesarchiv [Federal archive] Koblenz, Memorial book, p.28.

I write later to Herr Höhn to find out about the sources. He writes back that St. AD is Staatsarchiv Detmold (State Archive of Detmold); Nachlass Staerke refers to the private documents that *Landrat* (Councillor) Staercke bequeathed to the State Archive for further research.

Berg, Regina; née Adler
Born 16.4.1861
Bad Salzuflen, Adolf-Hitler Str. 33 (Osterstrasse 33)

She must have been over eighty when they herded her from her home. What she must have lived through before she disappeared in Minsk, in icy Russia!

If I read any further I'll make an exhibition of myself. I get up and thank the two men for their courtesy. They are good men. I am glad that such people preside over my hometown. But that terrible list . . .

Might they present me with a framed print of old Bad Salzuflen? It has been done by a very good artist. Very kind of them. Hans takes the print for me. I intend to leave it with the Flieders, but I will take the list.

I dare not look at the list. I fear the list. I know more or less who is on it, but I still fear this list. The list is the most terrible thing that has happened to me since my arrival—worse than the renovated houses of the victims, worse than the synagogue walls in a private house. I had not meant for things to go that far. I was only going to write about the years up to 1939, when my parents and I left.

What's in a list? It only gives the barest of facts—date of birth, address, place of murder, sources of the information. That almost makes it worse. None of the people on it was as close to me as my immediate family, as Else, even as Erna, but the effect it has on me is terrible. It is two days before I allow myself to look at the whole of it. I take it with me on the bus to Bielefeld so that I won't be by myself in the hotel bedroom when I read it. I go through the eighteen Bad Salzuflen names. I did not know them that well, but I start shaking. Obermeyer. Was that the father of brave little Obermeyer at school? I think not. It was probably the husband of the woman who threatened Mother with an action for slander. I think he owned those marvellous old houses in the Lange Strasse that I saw the other day, one of them housing a museum.

And who was Vorreuter, Frieda, Modistin? Was she a milliner? Anyway, I think she had something to do with fashion. I turn to Schötmar. It is getting dangerous.

Max Adler, born 1.1.1864.

I think that he was Moppi, the *Schnorrer* (scrounger), whose smelly person Father felt it his duty to invite sometimes for Friday evening meals. He was seventy-eight when he was murdered.

There are the Grünewalds with their crippled son who looked a bit like Göbbels. They sacrificed their opportunity to emigrate, sacrificed lives for him.

Then come the Hamlets. So far I have suppressed the tears. Now I sob aloud. Fortunately there are few people on the bus.

Hamlet, Hedwig, born 24.6.1891 in Schötmar.

She was two years older than Mother, and she was Mother's friend. Hedwig Hamlet, grey haired, leading her bicycle packed on both sides with saddle bags containing various soaps, which she sells to make ends meet. A typical Jewish plutocrat. She was there, living across the road, when I opened my eyes. From September 1, 1941 until September 12, 1941, she lived at Schlageterstrasse 18. That must have been the time when all the Jews were gathered together in two or three houses.

Declared as dead, Kz [concentration camp] Riga.

Then follow all the sources for this information, ending with the National Archive, Koblenz, Memorial book, p.505.

Hamlet, Paul, born 8.6.1892 in Schötmar.

If I go on, I'll break down completely. These bare facts are incredibly moving. They leave room for the imagination, but I cannot allow my imagination to follow the stations of their cross. And I cannot face the Silberbachs just now.

I arrive in Bielefeld with the list safely stowed away in my briefcase, but with thoughts of our former neighbours that will not go away. Still weepy, I go into one of those omnipresent pastry places for coffee and cakes, to marvel at the contrast between delicious German pastries and dreadful German deeds.

I am heading for the exhibition on "Jewish Life in Bielefeld Down the Ages." When I finally find the building housing the town archive, where the exhibition is being held, I see that ordinary Bielefelders are not exactly flocking to confront their town's Jewish past. During my hour and a half there, I see an elderly couple, obviously knowledgeable, obviously Jewish, a younger non-Jewish German couple, a middle-aged man, and two professional researchers with whom I fall into conversation.

The chief archivist of Lippe, in charge of the Detmold archives, is also there with his young son, who is forever pulling his tall lanky father towards the door. Does he sense the doom and gloom or is it that there are no bright colours to arouse his interest? All the exhibits are in black and white.

While the boy is still pulling, I talk to his father, a friendly open man who will be glad to show me the Detmold archives anytime. It won't be this time. My two remaining days are fully booked.

I ask him about a prominent Jewish family in Detmold that had connections with Italy, with Mussolini himself. I am trying to remember the name of my luncheon hosts after the Purim play. As I question him, my eyes fall on the name "Wertheimer" in one of the exhibits. At once I remember the name of the people I saw forty years ago. Their name was not Wertheimer, but Wertheim.

Yes, he certainly knows about them. Did they survive? No, they were killed. They had two children. It is possible that the daughter survived.

Then it is his turn to question me. I had mentioned the Purim Play and *Lehrer* Rülf, our Hebrew teacher. He is doing some research on *Lehrer* Rülf. Did I remember anything about him, what he looked like? I shrug: small, rather Jewish looking, a shuffler, always busy.

The town of Bielefeld was founded in 1214. Already in 1345, the Jews are mentioned, or to be more precise, it is the *Judensteuer*, the taxes the Jews had to pay, that is mentioned. Göring was not the first. The Jews' tax features as item nineteen among the twenty-one sources of income of one Bernhard, Count of Ravensberg, income that he pledged to redeem a debt. It seems that Count Bernhard was a philo-Semite and the catalogue thinks it likely that he brought the Jews to Bielefeld. We see the document, beautifully written in a rounded script, so unlike the later Gothic squiggles. We see the Jews, wearing their special hats, looking exactly like the tops we used to play with as children, but inverted, with the sharp point at the top. One man is reading; another spreads out his hands in blessing. There is a woman covered in cloths, rather like some Indian women today.

No sooner have the Jews been admitted than they are expelled. The date is 1350. We see pictures of Jews, this time in floppy hats, being burned in a pit. Again, Göring was not the first. We see a picture of a man bringing faggots for the fire. Producing pestilence and poisoning wells are added to the Jews' old habits of child killing, host desecration, and ritual murder. By 1370, they are back, and then gone again. So it goes on until the advent of Napoleon, the great lawgiver and liberator.

Why is it that Jews elicit such hate? We know now about the mechanism of projection, the habit of superimposing the shadowy unacknowledged side of ourselves onto others. Some people must have very big shadows. But why project them on us? Perhaps because we are a little different. We are a peculiar people. God himself has said so.

An old name crops up in one of the signatures: Adolf Wedderwille, *Kreisleiter* (district leader), the very same who put Uncle Walter into "protective custody." I did not realize that a kind providence had given him the same first name as his beloved *Führer*.

There are posters, like one from March 10, 1935 with the legend: "Jews are not human beings" (*Juden sind keine Menschen*).

A kindly young researcher from the old Lippe town of Lemgo, goes out to make me some photocopies. It can't be easy for these younger people to come face to face with their country's history. Another younger man whom I met elsewhere told me, "Our ancestors, our fathers and mothers, made terrible mistakes and were involved in a terrible deed. We are truly, truly sorry." Better than the reaction of many older people: "We did not know, we suffered too." As I am writing this in March 2008, Angela Merkel, the German chancellor, addresses the Israeli Knesset and makes a beautiful heartfelt speech about the Holocaust.

The facts have followed me. When I met Fritz Schmidtpott, he told me how the Göke twins, who gave me a bad time at school, shamefully abused Great-Uncle Julius, an old man in his seventies, before he was deported. He was last heard of in Emden, where he had bought himself into an old-age home.

I heard of Bruno Eichmann's courage as he faced deportation. His cousin Willy, the survivor, had bought him a stout pair of boots for the journey. Bruno could not get into them. "Give me a poke on the behind and I'll jump into them," he joked. Willy's daughter, Ingrid, told me this story. Both Bruno and his sick wife Ilse, sister of my Aunt Erna, died in the Riga concentration camp.

Something terrible came out in one of my conversations with Magdalene and Erna.

"This happened in July 1942," Erna recalls. "One morning there was a knock on the door and there stood Paul Hamlet in his smock with the yellow star. Mother made him come in quickly. I can tell you it was dangerous at the time. My mother sweated blood. She thought that he might have come about the things they gave us to bury in the garden for them, but no. They had collected most of those earlier and there were only a few sheets and table cloths left. That embroidered table cloth you see on the table is one of theirs. We keep it in their honour. The sheets have all got brown spots but we still keep them.

"Paul stood there—white as the bundle he was carrying. They [Paul and Hedwig] were allowed to take a few things and had used their best linen to sew them into a kind of sack. '*Luise, wir müssen fort,*' Paul told my mother. '*Wir kommen nie wieder zurück.*'" (Luise, we have to leave. We will never come back.) He must have guessed what awaited them.

Luise in German has three syllables, "Loo-ee-ze." Erna's voice rose on the *ee* with a kind of scream. It was terrible.

"Paul was the only one of those deported who was seen later on. I heard that one of the *Schötmaraner* [Schötmar people] was stationed in Lodz [at the time, Lodz had been Germanized to Litzmannstadt]. He saw some Jewish prisoners doing roadwork and then he noticed Paul Hamlet. He was sure it was Paul. He went up to him. 'Aren't you Paul Hamlet from Schötmar, old man?' [*Mensch,*[64] *bist Du nicht Paul Hamlet*

---

[64] It is difficult to translate *Mensch*, literally "man." It is used a lot in conversation. In England, we would say "old boy" or "old man," which does not mean that he was old.

aus Schötmar?] he asked. Paul continued with his work and did not look at him. 'Yes, I am, but move on. I can't talk to you.' [*Ja, aber geh weiter. Ich kann nicht mit Dir sprechen.*] That was the last anyone saw of him."

I did not look at the list again until the last night, when Irmgard Eichmann came to the hotel. There is safety in numbers. We went through it in more detail. We went through the Eichmanns. That is when she told me the story of Bruno. Then we went through the Silberbachs. Yes, Uncle Julius had been taken from his old-age home in Emden. He was *verschollen*—disappeared. It is not known where he died. If it was in 1942, he would have been seventy-four. Age was no barrier. They had taken Johanna Eichmann from an old-age home in Bielefeld. She was murdered in Theresienstadt in 1943, also aged seventy-four. They had taken Aunt Alma who was in her seventies, and in Regina Berg, they had taken a woman over eighty years old.

How could they do it? Orders—orders carried out with cool efficiency. That is what the deepest circle of hell must be like, where evil is done, not randomly, but with a calculator.

I found Aunt Rosa and her husband Salomon, but what happened to their daughter, Hilde? She was not there. Could she have saved herself? "Not possible," said Irmgard. "Perhaps she died early."

We come to the last page. There are only two names.

> Weinberg, Adolf, born 10.6.1985, verschollen, wo unbekannt [disappeared, where unknown]

And then the last name.

> Van der Wijk, Hildegard, née Silberbach, born 17.8.1912, Schötmar, Adolf-Hitler Str. 22 (Begastr. 22), Daughter of Rosa and Salomon Silberbach (see above). Emigrated to Holland 10.6.1938. deported from there 4.6.1943. Murdered in Kz [concentration camp] Sobibor. Source: St. AD D72, Nachlass Stärke No.18, Federal Archive Koblenz, Memorial book, p.1525.

She was on the list under her married name.

I went back to my hotel room, and I cried and cried and cried.

This book should have ended in 1939, with Hedwig Stern saying to me at Liverpool Station, "You must never do that [ridiculous bow] again . . . Remember, you are in England now!" That would have made a splendid ending. Full stop. *Finis*. Or perhaps in Cardiff with Alfred Stern monitoring every bite my parents and Uncle Walter took. But I found that I could not rid myself of Germany that easily. Germany, unacknowledged but potent, is still with me, not so much in my memories as in the exaggerated fear that sometimes grips me in everyday life, even in the safety of England. The book was easy; it practically wrote itself. But if I had hoped to exorcise the past with it, I was mistaken. After that visit, I often dreamt of Germany and most of the dreams were not pleasant.

Perhaps I should not have brought up the dark past. My spiritual teacher, the late esteemed Maharishi Mahesh Yogi, used to say, "Don't grope in darkness in order to remove the darkness. Bring in the light."

That is the higher wisdom. But again as my mother used to point out, "When you have said *A*, you have to say say *B*." I started this journey, the story of my childhood, and this is where it led: to Paul Hamlet at the Wortmanns' door in his smock with the yellow star.

Yellow Star

APPENDICES

PEOPLE IN THE BOOK

Alfred Stern—Husband of *Hedwig*, father of *Hans* and *Werner*

Alma Silberbach—A neighbour in Schötmar and a distant relative

Arthur—My uncle who died in WWI; son of *Bertha* and *Siegfried*

Billa—Wife of *Hugo*; mother of *Hedwig* and *Paul*

Count von der Schulenburg—Possibly my great-grandfather, *Emilie's* lover and *Siegfried's* father

Cousin Walter—My cousin; son of *Minna* and *Uncle Walter*; brother of *Gertrud* and *Helmut*

Else Holländer—My beloved *Kindermädchen*

Emilie—My great-grandmother; mother of *Julius*, *Mella*, and *Siegfried*; possible mistress of *Count von der Schulenburg*

Emilie Engel—My great-aunt; sister of *Bertha*

Erna Katz—My aunt; wife of *Moritz*

Erna Schröder—The family cook

Erwin—My uncle who died in WWI; son of *Bertha* and *Siegfried*

Father (Hermann, Vati, Papi)—My father; son of *Henriette* and *Joseph*; husband of *Emmy*; brother of *Helene* and *Moritz*

Fritz Schmidtpott—Brush factory office boy and confidant

Gertrud—My cousin; daughter of *Minna* and *Uncle Walter*; sister of *Cousin Walter* and *Helmut*

Gisela—My cousin; daughter of *Grete* and *Paul*; sister of *Ingelore*

Grandfather (Siegfried)—My grandfather; son of *Emilie* and possibly *Count von der Schulenburg*; husband of *Bertha*; father of *Uncle Walter, Emmy, Arthur, Erwin,* and *Grete*; brother of *Julius* and *Mella*

Grandmother (Bertha)—My grandmother; wife of *Siegfried*; mother of *Uncle Walter, Emmy, Arthur, Erwin,* and *Grete*; sister of *Emilie*

Grete—My aunt; daughter of *Bertha* and *Siegfried*; wife of *Paul*; mother of *Ingelore* and *Gisela*; sister of *Uncle Walter, Emmy, Arthur,* and *Erwin*

Greve—The family carter

Hans Stern—Son of *Hedwig* and *Alfred*; brother of *Werner*

Hedwig (Hede) Stern—Daughter of *Billa* and *Hugo*; wife of *Alfred*; mother of *Hans* and *Werner*; sister of *Paul*

Helene Strauss—My aunt; daughter of *Henriette* and *Joseph*; wife of *Josef* Strauss; sister of *Moritz* and *Hermann*

Helmut—My cousin; son of *Minna* and *Uncle Walter*; brother of *Gertrud* and *Cousin Walter*

Henriette Katz—My grandmother; wife of *Joseph* Katz; mother of *Helene, Moritz,* and *Hermann*

Hermann Weinberg—Husband of *Mella*

Herta Silberbach—Daughter of *Alma*

Hilde Silberbach—Daughter of *Rosa* and *Salomon*

Hugo—Husband of *Billa*; father of *Hedwig* and *Paul*

Ingelore—My cousin; daughter of *Grete* and *Paul*; sister of *Gisela*

Josef Strauss—My uncle; husband of *Helene*

Joseph Katz—My grandfather; husband of *Henriette*; father of *Helene, Moritz,* and *Hermann*

Julius (Jüller)—My great-uncle; husband of *Pauline*; brother of *Mella* and *Siegfried*

Karl Weinhorst—Father's chauffer

Mella—My great-aunt; daughter of *Emilie*; wife of *Hermann*; sister of *Julius* and *Siegfried*

Minna—My aunt; wife of *Uncle Walter*; mother of *Gertrud, Cousin Walter* and *Helmut*

Moritz Katz—My uncle; son of *Henriette* and *Joseph* Katz; husband of *Erna*; brother of *Helene* and *Hermann*

Mother (Emmy, Mutti)—My mother; daughter of *Bertha* and *Siegfried*; wife of *Hermann*; sister of *Uncle Walter, Arthur, Erwin,* and *Grete*

Paul—My uncle; son of *Billa* and *Hugo*; husband of *Grete*; father of *Ingelore* and *Gisela*; brother of *Hedwig*

Pauline—My great-aunt; wife of *Julius*

Rosa Silberbach—A close friend of Mother's; wife of *Salomon*

Salomon Silberbach—Husband of *Rosa*

Uncle Walter—My uncle; son of *Bertha* and *Siegfried*; husband of *Minna*; father of *Gertrud, Cousin Walter* and *Helmut*; brother of *Emmy, Arthur, Erwin,* and *Grete*

Werner Stern—Son of *Hedwig* and *Alfred*; brother of *Hans*

ACKNOWLEDGEMENTS

Great thanks go to my late cousin, Walter Silver (née Silberbach), who shared many vivid memories of our childhood with me. Without his help, this book would have been much less complete.

My cousin, Gisela Mendel Booth, was very generous with her memories and provided wonderful vignettes of life in Cologne. In addition, she corrected some misconceptions. Her sister, the late Ingelore Bonner, also shared her recollections. I am grateful to them both.

Thanks to my cousin, Terry Mandel, for her early help in organizing a portion of the book's manuscript on my computer.

I appreciate the contributions to this book made by my German friends—Magdalene Wortmann, her sister, Erna Flieder, and the late Fritz Schmidtpott. Many points of interest emerged from my conversations with them.

Thanks also to my school friend, Lotte Bruns, for providing memories of our school days.

Stefan Wiesekopsieker wrote a detailed article about my parents' brush factory from which I have drawn. I am obliged to him for his work of commemoration.

I attended classes on autobiographical writing at London's City Literary Institute given by an inspiring teacher, Carol Burns. She taught me many valuable lessons. I hope that when she reads this book, she will realize that at least some of them have been learned.

My friend, Linda Egenes, gave me good advice about writing, and I would like to express my appreciation for her help.

My thanks also to Jörg Höhn for making some archive material available to me.

Finally, I am truly most grateful to my cousins Stephen and Emily Mendel for editing this book and arranging for its publication. I think it was a labour of love for them, but it also relieved me of a great burden. I greatly enjoyed working with them. Without their enthusiasm and help, this book might never have seen the light of day.

Lightning Source UK Ltd.
Milton Keynes UK
UKHW011939121220
375075UK00002B/391